THE
unofficial GUIDE®
ᵀᴼ Universal
Orlando®

1ST EDITION

COME CHECK US OUT!

Supplement your valuable guidebook with tips, news, and deals by visiting our website:

theunofficialguides.com

Also, while there, sign up for The Unofficial Guide newsletter for even more travel tips and special offers.

Join the conversation on social media:

 **@theUGSeries**

 **theUnofficialGuides**

 theUGSeries

 **theUGSeries**

#theUGseries

Other *Unofficial Guides*

Beyond Disney: The Unofficial Guide to Universal Orlando, SeaWorld, & the Best of Central Florida

The Disneyland Story: The Unofficial Guide to the Evolution of Walt Disney's Dream

Mini Mickey: The Pocket-Sized Unofficial Guide to Walt Disney World

Universal vs. Disney: The Unofficial Guide to American Theme Parks' Greatest Rivalry

The Unofficial Guide Color Companion to Walt Disney World

The Unofficial Guide to Disney Cruise Line

The Unofficial Guide to Disneyland

The Unofficial Guide to Las Vegas

The Unofficial Guide to Walt Disney World

The Unofficial Guide to Walt Disney World with Kids

The Unofficial Guide to Washington, D.C.

THE *unofficial* GUIDE®

TO Universal Orlando®

1ST EDITION

SETH KUBERSKY *with*
BOB SEHLINGER & LEN TESTA

k
keen
communications

Please note that prices fluctuate in the course of time and that travel information changes under the impact of many factors that influence the travel industry. We therefore suggest that you write or call ahead for confirmation when making your travel plans. Every effort has been made to ensure the accuracy of information throughout this book, and the contents of this publication are believed to be correct at the time of printing. Nevertheless, the publishers cannot accept responsibility for errors or omissions, for changes in details given in this guide, or for the consequences of any reliance on the information provided by the same. Assessments of attractions and so forth are based upon the authors' own experiences; therefore, descriptions given in this guide necessarily contain an element of subjective opinion, which may not reflect the publisher's opinion or dictate a reader's own experience on another occasion. Readers are invited to write the publisher with ideas, comments, and suggestions for future editions.

Published by:
Keen Communications, LLC
2204 First Avenue South, Suite 102
Birmingham, AL 35233

Unofficial Guide is a registered trademark of Google Inc. in the United States and other countries and may not be used without written permission. Used under license. All other trademarks are the property of their respective owners. Google Inc. is not associated with any product or vendor mentioned in this book.

Cover design by Scott McGrew

Text design by Vertigo Design and Annie Long

For information on our other products and services or to obtain technical support, please contact us from within the United States at 888-604-4537 or by fax at 205-326-1012.

Keen Communications, LLC, also publishes its books in a variety of electronic formats. Some content that appears in print may not be available in electronic formats.

ISBN 978-1-62809-030-7; eISBN: 978-1-62809-031-4

Distributed by Publishers Group West

Manufactured in the United States of America

5 4 3 2 1

CONTENTS

LIST *of* MAPS

ABOUT *the* AUTHORS

Seth Kubersky is the coauthor of *The Unofficial Guide to Disneyland* and a contributor to *The Unofficial Guide to Walt Disney World* and *The Unofficial Guide to Las Vegas*. A resident of Orlando since 1996, Seth is a former employee of Universal Orlando's entertainment department. He covers arts and attractions for the *Orlando Weekly* newspaper, *Orlando Attractions Magazine,* and other publications. You can find Seth online at **sethkubersky.com** or on Twitter @skubersky.

Bob Sehlinger is the author of *The Unofficial Guide to Walt Disney World* and *The Unofficial Guide to Las Vegas* and is also the publisher of The Unofficial Guide series.

Len Testa is the coauthor of *The Unofficial Guide to Walt Disney World* and has contributed to *The Unofficial Guide to Disneyland* and *The Unofficial Guide to Las Vegas*. He is also the webmaster of **touringplans.com,** the official website of The Unofficial Guides.

INTRODUCTION

WHY "UNOFFICIAL"?

DECLARATION OF INDEPENDENCE

THE AUTHORS AND RESEARCHERS OF this guide specifically and categorically declare that they are and always have been totally independent. The material in this guide originated with the authors and has not been reviewed, edited, or in any way approved by Universal Orlando or any other companies whose travel products are discussed.

The purpose of this guide is to provide you with the information necessary to tour with the greatest efficiency and economy and with the least hassle and stress. In this guide we represent and serve you, the consumer. If a restaurant serves bad food, or a gift item is overpriced, or a certain ride isn't worth the wait, we can say so, and in the process we hope to make your visit more fun, efficient, and economical.

DANCE TO THE MUSIC

A DANCE HAS A BEGINNING and an end. But when you're dancing, you're not concerned about getting to the end or where on the dance floor you might wind up. In other words, you're totally in the moment. That's the way you should be on your Universal Orlando vacation.

You may feel a bit of pressure concerning your vacation. Vacations, after all, are very special events—and expensive ones to boot. So you work hard to make your vacation the best that it can be. Planning and organizing are essential to a successful Universal Orlando vacation, but if they become your focus, you won't be able to hear the music and enjoy the dance.

So think of us as your dancing coaches. We'll teach you the steps to the dance in advance so that when you're on vacation and the music plays, you'll dance with effortless grace and ease.

A BETTER MOUSETRAP?

DIE-HARD DISNEY DEVOTEES may want to cover their mouse ears because we are about to utter the ultimate blasphemy: It is possible to enjoy an awesome Orlando vacation without spending a single minute in Mickey's world. For much of the past four decades, the notion of spending a holiday in central Florida without seeing Walt Disney's sprawling wonderland seemed silly. While visitors might take a day or two out of their trip to explore independent attractions such as Sea-World, Busch Gardens, or Kennedy Space Center, the Magic Kingdom and its sister parks were seen by most as the area's main draw.

Much to the Mouse House's dismay, that situation is swiftly shifting. While Walt Disney World is in no danger of closing for lack of interest—attendance at Disney's theme parks hit an all-time high in 2014—its share of Orlando's lucrative tourism market has been steadily and significantly swinging in favor of an energetic upstart located a few miles up I-4: the Universal Orlando Resort.

Originally opened in 1990 as a single theme park packed with advanced but unreliable attractions, Universal Orlando has matured into a full-service, fully immersive vacation destination with enough world-class activities to keep a family occupied for four days or more. Universal Studios Florida, a longtime rival of Disney's Hollywood Studios that draws its inspiration from movies and television, has been almost entirely overhauled since its debut, and it now houses one of the world's top collections of cutting-edge attractions. Universal's Islands of Adventure debuted in 1999 as the most modern, high-tech theme park in the United States, featuring an all-star lineup of thrill rides that makes it the best park in town for older kids and young-at-heart adults.

Together, the two parks are home to the game-changing Wizarding World of Harry Potter, a meticulously imagined multilayered experience that's drawing millions of Muggle fans from around the world to the hallowed halls of Hogwarts Castle and Gringotts Bank. Surrounding the two parks are four (soon to be five) immaculately appointed on-site resort hotels, and a CityWalk nightlife complex full of restaurants, nightclubs, and entertainment options appealing to families and adults.

Universal Orlando's ascendance is not about to bankrupt Walt Disney World, and likely never will—Disney's nearly unlimited dominion over its vast 43-square-mile kingdom practically ensures its dominance. But those who approach Universal with open eyes will find that the resort can provide just as much magic and fantasy in its own fashion. Universal Orlando has an energy, pace, and attitude all its own that might appeal to the most adamant anti–amusement park person, and could even convert confirmed Disney customers. Instead of opting for the same old rat race, consider spending your next vacation playing Quidditch with Harry, saving New York with Spidey, and drinking a Duff with the Simpsons. You may just find yourself asking, "Mickey who?"

IT TAKES MORE THAN ONE BOOK
TO DO THE JOB RIGHT

WE'VE BEEN COVERING CENTRAL FLORIDA tourism for more than 30 years. We began by lumping everything into one guidebook, but that was when the Magic Kingdom and Epcot were the only theme parks at Walt Disney World, at the very beginning of the boom that has made central Florida one of the most visited tourist destinations on Earth. As central Florida grew, so did our guide, until eventually we needed to split the tome into smaller, more in-depth (and more portable) volumes. The result is a small library of titles, designed to work both individually and together. All provide specialized information tailored to very specific central Florida visitors. Though some tips (such as arriving at the theme parks early) are echoed or elaborated in all the guides, most of the information in each book is unique.

The Unofficial Guide to Walt Disney World is the centerpiece of our central Florida coverage because, well, Walt Disney World is the centerpiece of most central Florida vacations. *The Unofficial Guide to Walt Disney World* is evaluative, comprehensive, and instructive—the ultimate planning tool for a successful Walt Disney World vacation, including a condensed version of this book's Universal Orlando information.

The Unofficial Guide to Walt Disney World is supplemented by these additional titles:

- *Mini Mickey: The Pocket-Sized Unofficial Guide to Walt Disney World,* by Bob Sehlinger, Ritchey Halphen, and Len Testa
- *The Unofficial Guide Color Companion to Walt Disney World,* by Bob Sehlinger and Len Testa
- *The Unofficial Guide to Walt Disney World with Kids,* by Bob Sehlinger and Liliane J. Opsomer with Len Testa
- *Beyond Disney: The Unofficial Guide to Universal Orlando, SeaWorld, & the Best of Central Florida,* by Bob Sehlinger and Seth Kubersky

Mini Mickey is a nifty, portable, *CliffsNotes* version of *The Unofficial Guide to Walt Disney World.* Updated semiannually, it distills information from this comprehensive guide to help short-stay or last-minute visitors decide quickly how to plan their limited hours at Disney World.

The Unofficial Guide Color Companion to Walt Disney World is a visual feast that proves a picture is worth 1,000 words.

The Unofficial Guide to Walt Disney World with Kids presents a wealth of planning and touring tips for a successful Disney family vacation.

Beyond Disney is a complete consumer guide to the non-Disney attractions, hotels, restaurants, and nightlife in Orlando and central Florida.

Finally, you hold our newest tome in your hands: our first in-depth guide dedicated to the attractions and amenities of the Universal

Orlando Resort. All of the guides are available at most bookstores and in digital e-book editions.

THE DEATH OF SPONTANEITY

ONE OF OUR ALL-TIME favorite letters came from a man in Chapel Hill, North Carolina:

> *Your book reads like the operations plan for an amphibious landing: Go here, do this, proceed to Step 15. You must think that everyone is a hyperactive, type-A theme park commando. What happened to the satisfaction of self-discovery or the joy of spontaneity? Next you'll be telling us when to empty our bladders.*

As it happens, Unofficial Guide researchers are a pretty existential crew who are big on self-discovery. But Universal Orlando—especially

for first-time travelers—probably isn't the place you want to "discover" the spontaneity of needless waits in line or mediocre meals when you could be doing better.

In many ways, central Florida's theme parks are the quintessential system, the ultimate in mass-produced entertainment, the most planned and programmed environment anywhere. Lines for rides form in predictable ways at predictable times, for example, and you can either learn here how to avoid them or "discover" them on your own.

We aren't saying that you can't have a great time at Universal Orlando, and enjoying the resort requires much less advance planning than the equivalent vacation at Walt Disney World. What we *are* saying is that you should think about what you want to do before you go. The time and money you save by planning will help your family have more fun.

THE SUM OF ALL FEARS

EVERY WRITER WHO EXPRESSES an opinion is accustomed to readers who strongly agree or disagree: It comes with the territory. Extremely troubling, however, is the possibility that our efforts to be objective have frightened some readers away from Universal Orlando or made others apprehensive.

For the record, if you love theme parks, Universal Orlando is as good as it gets—absolute nirvana. If you arrive without knowing a thing about the place and make every possible mistake, chances are about 90% that you'll have a wonderful vacation anyway. The job of a guidebook is to give you a heads-up regarding opportunities and potential problems. We're certain we can help you turn a great vacation into an absolutely *superb* one.

THE UNOFFICIAL TEAM

THIS BOOK WAS AUTHORED BY Seth Kubersky, building on decades of research from The Unofficial Guides by Bob Sehlinger, Len Testa, and the rest of the Unofficial team. Derek Burgan is our Universal food consigliere and contributed vital research to this guide's dining chapter. Jim Hill contributes his signature dish on the stories behind the scenes. Our prologue is excerpted from Sam Gennawey's *Universal vs. Disney: An Unofficial Guide to American Theme Parks' Greatest Rivalry.* Special thanks to Genevieve Bernard for research assistance, proofreading, and patience. Amber Kaye Henderson edited the book, Lisa Bailey proofread it, Chris Eliopoulos and Tami Knight drew the cartoons, Steve Jones created the maps, and Maria Sullivan indexed the book; thanks go to each of them.

CORRECTIONS, UPDATES, AND BREAKING NEWS

LOOK FOR THESE AT THE Unofficial Guide website, **touringplans .com.** See page 25 for a complete description of the site.

LETTERS AND COMMENTS FROM READERS

MANY OF THOSE WHO USE The Unofficial Guides write us to make comments or share their own strategies for visiting central Florida. We appreciate all such input, both positive and critical, and encourage our readers to continue writing. Readers' comments and observations are frequently incorporated into revised editions of The Unofficial Guides and have contributed immeasurably to their improvement. If you write us, you can rest assured that we won't release your name and address to any mailing lists, direct-mail advertisers, or other third party.

How to Write the Authors

Seth Kubersky and Bob Sehlinger
The Unofficial Guides
2204 First Avenue South, Suite 102
Birmingham, AL 35233; **unofficialguides@menasharidge.com**

Or visit us online at **theunofficialguides.com.**

When you write by mail, put your address on both your letter and envelope, as sometimes the two get separated. It is also a good idea to include your phone number. If you e-mail us, let us know where you're from. And remember, as travel writers, we're often out of the office for long periods of time, so forgive us if our response is slow.

UNIVERSAL ORLANDO:
An Overview

PROLOGUE: AMERICAN THEME PARKS' GREATEST RIVALRY

UNIVERSAL STUDIOS DID NOT SET out to challenge The Walt Disney Company in the theme park business. The men who ran the Music Corporation of America (MCA) were quite happy with the industrial tour they created in 1964 at Universal City. The Universal Studio Tour took visitors behind the scenes of the largest and busiest back lot in Hollywood to show how motion pictures and television programs were manufactured. People came from around the world with the hope of catching a glimpse of their favorite star. Unlike Disneyland, Walt Disney's fantasy theme park in nearby Anaheim, the Universal Studio Tour provided an authentic experience not found anywhere else. It was something entirely new, entertaining, and very profitable.

In 1979 MCA bought land in Orlando 10 miles north of Walt Disney World and later announced that they were going to build a motion picture and television production studio. The new studio would have also featured a tour just like the one in California. Lew Wasserman, MCA's legendary chief executive, knew better than to compete with Disney and its dominance with fantasy landscapes. He enjoyed the fact that the two Southern California tourist attractions complemented each other, and he was making money with minimal investment.

Everything changed just a few years later. In 1984 Disney hired Michael Eisner as the new chief executive officer and Frank Wells as president. Before Disney, Eisner had been president of Paramount Pictures Corp., and Wells had been a well-respected executive at Warner Bros. Within two weeks of the Disney leadership change, MCA president and Wasserman's protégé, Sidney Sheinberg, sent a letter to his old friends proposing a meeting to discuss ideas that would be in the mutual interest of both companies.

It made sense to turn to Michael Eisner. While he was at Paramount, Sheinberg had shown him MCA's Florida plans with the hopes of forming a partnership. Eisner liked what he saw. When nothing came of the talks, Eisner blamed the impasse on powers higher up the corporate food chain at Paramount's parent company, Gulf and Western. Now that Eisner was in charge of Disney, Sheinberg thought Eisner would be excited to become MCA's partner in Florida.

During the call, a confident Sheinberg suggested to Eisner, "Let's get together on a studio tour in Orlando. We tried with your predecessors, but they were unresponsive. We think we can help you."[1] Much to the surprise of the MCA executives, Eisner told his old friend, "We're already working on something of our own."[2]

That was not the reaction Wasserman and Sheinberg was expecting. "Ultimately, we were informed that they might want to do one of these tours themselves and they did not want to be accused of somehow, whatever the word was, stealing or acting improperly, if we had a meeting and they later decided to go on their own," Sheinberg later explained. "That signal really surprised us, to put it mildly. It was our first indication that they were off on a plan to do this."[3]

Then, on February 7, 1985, Michael Eisner made headlines at his first meeting with Walt Disney Productions shareholders. Before a packed house at the Anaheim Convention Center, he announced that Disney would soon start construction of a third theme park at Walt Disney World. The heart of Disney's park would be a real working production studio with two sound stages and a working animation studio. Eisner said this "was a way to make the experience more authentic, but these decisions would also serve our production needs as they grew." Regarding the plans, Eisner said they were "the most exciting to come out of Walt Disney Imagineering (WDI) in a long time." He also told the gathering, "We're definitely doing it within a year."[4]

The men at MCA were livid. After reviewing Disney's plans, Sidney Sheinberg claimed that Michael Eisner stole the idea he heard at the 1981 pitch at Paramount. For his part, Eisner claimed the presentation occurred "many, many years" ago and added "when I arrived at [Disney], the studio tour was already on the drawing boards and had been for many years."[5] Eisner ordered his team to work fast. For him, beating Sidney Sheinberg and MCA was critical. "They invaded our home turf," he told *Business Week*. "We will not be intimidated."[6]

A bitter Sheinberg replied, "You're going to have to work awfully hard to convince me that [Eisner] didn't know about [MCA's plans]. That's ridiculous. He was a member of the inner circle at Paramount." He added, "Disney obviously felt they were in trouble and felt they had to do something about it. Disney announced it would do the theme park and would have you believe it's been in the works since 1926—if you believe in mice, you probably believe in the Easter Bunny also."[7]

1   Ellen Farly, "Behind the MCA-Disney War in Fla.," *The Los Angeles Times,* 23 April 1989.

2   Michael D. Eisner with Tony Schwartz, *Work in Progress: Risking Failure, Surviving Success* (New York: Hyperion, 1998).

3   Farly, "Behind the MCA-Disney War in Fla."

4   Walt Disney Productions (minutes of annual meeting, Anaheim, CA, 6 Feb. 1985), Anaheim History Room, Anaheim Public Library, Anaheim, CA.

5   Kathryn Harris, "Florida Fund may Invest in MCA Park," *The Los Angeles Times,* 20 May 1985.

6   Ron Grover, *The Disney Touch: How a Daring Management Team Revived an Entertainment Empire* (Homewood, IL: Business One Irwin, 1991).

7   Farly, "Behind the MCA-Disney War in Fla."

At MCA, you do not get mad. You get even. This is how the greatest rivalry in the theme park industry began.

A UNIVERSAL PRIMER

THE UNIVERSAL ORLANDO RESORT IS located on 840 acres inside the city of Orlando, about 8 miles northeast of Walt Disney World (which is actually in Lake Buena Vista). The resort consists of two theme parks—**Universal Studios Florida** and **Universal's Islands of Adventure**— along with four Loews-operated Universal hotels, and the **CityWalk** dining, nightlife, and shopping complex. **Wet 'n Wild,** a nearby water park, is also marketed under the Universal Orlando banner.

Universal Studios Florida (USF) opened in June 1990. At the time, it was almost four times the size of Disney's Hollywood Studios (originally known as Disney/MGM Studios), and much more of its facility was accessible to visitors. Like Disney's parks, USF is spacious, beautifully landscaped, meticulously clean, and delightfully varied in its entertainment. Its rides are exciting and innovative and, like many Disney attractions, focused on familiar and/or beloved movie characters or situations. Unfortunately, while the opening-day rides incorporated state-of-the-art technology and lived up to their billing in terms of creativity and uniqueness, several lacked the capacity or reliability to handle the number of guests who frequent major Florida tourist destinations.

With only one theme park, Universal played second fiddle to Disney's juggernaut for almost a decade. Things began to change when Universal opened Islands of Adventure (IOA) in 1999. Adding a second park, along with the CityWalk nightlife complex and three on-site resort hotels, made Universal a legitimate two-day destination, and provided Universal with enough critical mass to begin serious competition with Disney for tourists' time and money.

IOA opened to good reviews and sizable crowds, and it did steady business for the first few years. Ongoing competition with Disney, however, and a lack of money to invest in new rides eventually caught up with IOA. Attendance dropped from a high of 6.3 million visitors in 2004 to a low of 4.6 million in 2009, less than half of Animal Kingdom, Disney's least-visited park in Orlando that year.

In the middle of this slide, Universal's management made one bold bet: securing the rights in 2007 to build a Harry Potter–themed area within IOA. Harry, it was thought, was possibly the only fictional character extant capable of trumping Mickey Mouse, and Universal went all out, under author J. K. Rowling's watchful and exacting eye, to create a setting and attractions designed to be the envy of the industry.

The first phase of **The Wizarding World of Harry Potter,** as the new land was called, opened at IOA in 2010 and was an immediate hit. Its headliner attraction, **Harry Potter and the Forbidden Journey,** broke new ground in its ride system and immersive storytelling. Families raced to ride the attraction, and IOA's attendance grew 22% in 2010 and another 28% in 2011.

Universal Orlando

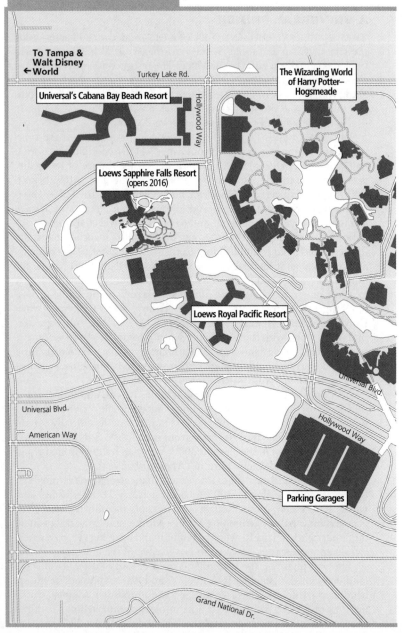

To Tampa &
Walt Disney
← World

Turkey Lake Rd.

Hollywood Way

The Wizarding World
of Harry Potter–
Hogsmeade

Universal's Cabana Bay Beach Resort

Loews Sapphire Falls Resort
(opens 2016)

Loews Royal Pacific Resort

Universal Blvd.

Universal Blvd.

American Way

Hollywood Way

Parking Garages

Grand National Dr.

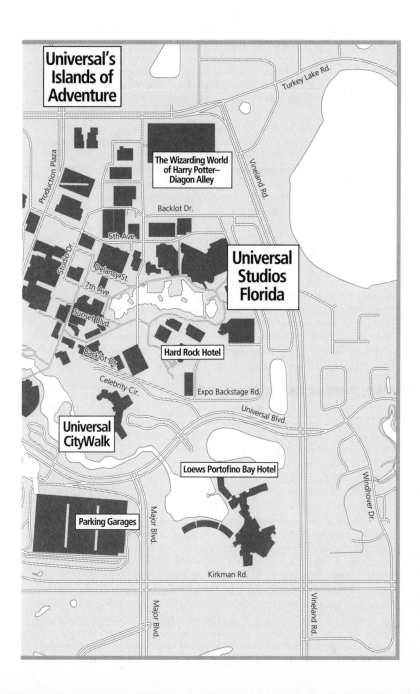

Harry Potter single-handedly upended the power structure in Florida's theme parks. Emboldened by its success, Universal's new owners Comcast—which acquired a majority stake in the NBCUniversal conglomerate in 2011 and purchased full ownership from GE in 2013—embarked on an unprecedented wave of expansions, rapidly adding new attractions and extensions, including **The Wizarding World of Harry Potter–Diagon Alley** at Universal Studios Florida and a fourth on-site hotel.

Now, Universal Studios Florida and Islands of Adventure are state-of-the-art parks vying with Disney parks, whose attractions are decades older on average. Though Disney has expanded the Magic Kingdom's Fantasyland area with new rides and restaurants, that effort is primarily to increase the Magic Kingdom's capacity; none of Disney's latest attractions are the kind of cutting-edge, super-headliner attractions that Universal has built recently and continues to build.

The gamble appears to be paying off for Universal. Universal Orlando's parks posted an impressive 33.7% increase in revenue for the first quarter of 2015, and the Themed Entertainment Association estimated a 17% increase in Universal Studios Florida's attendance for 2014.

Disney and Universal officially downplay their fierce competition, pointing out that any new theme park or attraction makes central Florida a more marketable destination. Behind closed doors, however, the two companies share a Pepsi-versus-Coke rivalry that keeps both working hard to gain a competitive edge. The good news is that all this translates into better and better attractions for you to enjoy.

THE UNIVERSAL DIFFERENCE

EVERY YEAR SINCE WE BEGAN covering the Universal theme parks in *The Unofficial Guide to Walt Disney World,* readers have asked us "why?" Simply stated, Universal is a high-quality direct competitor of Walt Disney World, and we think you should have detailed information on both the Disney and Universal parks so you can make an informed decision about where to spend your time. We also get comments from readers who are under the impression that Universal's offerings are inferior to Disney's. By any objective measure, they are not. In fact, the resorts have become evenly matched in so many aspects that we felt compelled to finally give our Universal Orlando content the breathing room it deserves in this stand-alone guide.

In many ways, Universal Orlando will never achieve parity with Walt Disney World. It's minuscule compared with the 27,000-odd acres of Walt Disney World. The Universal property can't accommodate golf courses, marinas, or campgrounds. And while guest service at Universal is generally exceptional by industry standards, there's something special about the "Disney Way" that some visitors will inevitably prefer. But in the areas where it *can* compete with Disney—namely, in theme park design and attraction quality—Universal has pulled even, if not ahead.

Even hard-core Disney fans, such as this Moncton, Nebraska, reader, are beginning to pay attention:

> I'm a huge fan of all things Disney, so it pains me a little to say that the highlight of our most recent trip was actually Universal Orlando. Not because Disney World isn't spectacular—it always is—but because Universal's themed Harry Potter experience is by far the most immersive I've ever had. Disney has to be a little nervous. Responding to Pottermania with an Avatar land just doesn't seem like a good move—Disney on the defensive! But hey, a little competition is healthy.

Or consider this, from a family of four from Kansas City:

> Our family loved our Universal experience better than Disney. . . . Universal is much more our style. The two parks are close together, so park-hopping doesn't require a shuttle ride. The streets are wide, so walking isn't such a crowded mess like Disney. The scenery is amazing.

We see the two Universal parks and the four Disney World parks as rough equals, and every one is world-class. Both Universal and Disney have splendid on-site hotels, with Universal offering more perks to its guests. There will always be those who miss the indescribable "magic" for which Disney World is famous. But here are five important arenas in which we think Universal currently has an advantage in the Orlando theme park wars:

MORE ADULT   If there's one distinguishing element that most separates Universal from Disney, it's the distinctly adult attitude that informs the resort's attractions and ambience. While Walt wanted to build a park that appealed equally to parents and their children, the majority of entertainments in today's Walt Disney World focus on themes and characters catering to little kids. (That's not to say that there aren't plenty of adults who enjoy singing "Let It Go" at the top of their lungs, but the less said about that the better.) The same goes for most Disney rides, which emphasize visual charm over physical intensity; aside from the half-dozen "mountains," you could probably take a nap on any given WDW attraction.

Universal, on the other hand, sets its sights slightly higher demographically, with a much higher proportion of attractions aimed at tweens, teens, and young (or young-at-heart) adults. Many of Universal's properties are based on PG-13 or R-rated movies; even their animated ambassadors, such as Shrek and *Despicable Me*'s Minions, are a bit edgier than Mickey and friends. Don't try to fall asleep on Universal's simulators and scream machines, which range in intensity from pleasantly discombobulating to, "Dear Lord, what have I done?"

This parent from the Dallas, Texas, area agrees:

> Universal is PG-13 regarding their rides, while Disney is PG. Universal's rides are amazing, while Disney's seem dated. We might not have noticed if we had visited Disney first. Also, our party consisted of teens; therefore, the thrill rides were the most important

experience for them. My teens tremendously enjoyed their time on their own at Universal.

Universal offers the CityWalk nightclub venue, just outside the park gates, for those with the energy to make a night of it; WDW's closest equivalent, the long-in-development Disney Springs complex, is far more sedate. And observant audience members will also notice the scripts at Universal have a subversively snarky, postmodern spin that flies over youngsters' heads but serves as a welcome antidote to pixie-dusted perfection. After all, as the host in *Universal Orlando's Horror Make-Up Show* jokes, "This isn't Disney. We don't have to be nice to you!"

All this isn't to imply that there's nothing for wee tykes to enjoy at Universal; on the contrary, the playgrounds in IOA's Seuss Landing and Jurassic Park are as good as any at WDW, and Universal's "child swap" policy is arguably more user-friendly than Disney's. But rather than spending the day focused on fulfilling their offspring's fantasies, parents at Universal get to realize some of their own along the way.

MORE ADVANCED   Universal has been technologically ascendant for several years, introducing revolutionary motion systems and special effects in both rides and theater performances. On the other hand, the Magic Kingdom's new and enlarged Fantasyland is a point in contrast: Though visually stunning, its attractions break little new ground. Neither the sophisticated animatronics of Under the Sea—Journey of the Little Mermaid nor the multi-motional ride vehicles of the Seven Dwarfs Mine Train come anywhere close to **Harry Potter and the Forbidden Journey** at Universal's Islands of Adventure or the new **Harry Potter and the Escape from Gringotts** at Universal Studios Florida. While Disney relies conservatively on a combination of highly detailed themed areas, beloved characters, and inspiration from classic animated features (that many young people under age 16 have never seen), Universal takes more technological swings for the fences.

Granted, Disney parks do have their share of high-tech attractions, and not all Universal attractions approach the creative genius of Forbidden Journey or Escape from Gringotts. But while guests at both Disney and Universal report high levels of satisfaction, it's the next-gen technology manifested in Universal's headliners that delivers true "Wow!" moments. Plus, **Port of Entry** and **Jurassic Park** at Islands of Adventure—along with **The Wizarding World of Harry Potter,** now encompassing both **Hogsmeade** at IOA and **Diagon Alley** at USF— clearly demonstrate that Universal can create exquisitely detailed and totally immersive themed areas.

MORE CURRENT   Doc Brown's time-traveling DeLorean from *Back to the Future* may be parked at USF, but Orlando's real time machine is found at Walt Disney World's theme parks. With the exception of über-trendy *Frozen,* WDW's recent top attractions are all inspired by pop-culture properties that date from the 1930s (Seven Dwarfs Mine Train) through the 1990s (Under the Sea and Toy Story Midway Mania!), and much of their older inventory is even more old-fashioned. Epcot is littered with celebrities (living and dead) whose peak popularity is two decades past, and only now are Hollywood Studios and Animal Kingdom finally inching forward with construction on lands themed to films that were popular in this millennium.

Universal, on the other hand, has been relentlessly aggressive about constantly updating its lineup with currently relevant characters. The best example of this is its Wizarding World of Harry Potter, the first phase of which debuted while the record-breaking film franchise was still in theaters. Despicable Me's Minions, Marvel's superheroes, and Jurassic Park's dinosaurs are also currently red-hot at the box office, and King Kong (one of the resort's original icons, resurrected for a brand-new ride in 2016) is poised for a big-screen comeback.

The downside to Universal's obsession with staying on the cultural cutting edge is a sense of impermanence that prevents the resort from retaining its rich history. Disney's blessing of size allows it to preserve the type of long-in-the-tooth attractions that space-squeezed Universal often sacrifices for the next generation. As a result, repeat visitors to WDW develop a sense of nostalgia over a lifetime of revisiting beloved rides, whereas those returning to Universal after a long absence are more likely to be befuddled; for a fun (and dangerous) drinking game, stand outside Diagon Alley and take a sip every time someone asks, "Where's Jaws?"

But Universal's weaker sense of tradition is offset by the thrill of the new; while the Magic Kingdom has now gone nearly a quarter century without a brand-new E ticket, you can count on a major attraction opening at Universal Orlando every year for the rest of this decade, and even bigger things—such as a fifth hotel, a heavily themed water park, and perhaps an expansion of the resort's borders—are on the horizon.

MORE COMPACT   While the lack of available elbow room hurts Universal in some ways, it's a huge advantage in others. Anyone who has stayed on-site at WDW (especially in a hotel not serviced by the monorail) can testify how arduous navigating Mickey's vast transportation system can be. Taking the Disney bus to Animal Kingdom sometimes seems to take longer than an actual African safari, and if you want to transfer from a theme park to Disney Springs, you'd better pack a lunch.

At Universal, on the other hand, you can go your whole vacation without ever taking a ride (other than the amusement kind) because everything is within easy walking distance. Even the most remote hotel room is only a 15- or 20-minute walk from the park gates, which are themselves separated by only a few hundred yards, making park-hopping at Universal a no-brainer. If your feet do get tired, a fleet of water taxis, pedicabs, and colorful buses are available to transport you, usually with much less waiting than their WDW equivalents.

In fact, if Universal Orlando closely compares to any Disney resort, it is not Walt Disney World but Disneyland in California. Both properties boast two first-rate theme parks in close proximity to each other, with an adjoining entertainment complex and nearby hotels for easy pedestrian access. If you've ever enjoyed the Disneyland Resort's intimacy, in contrast to Disney World's overwhelming scale, you'll feel right at home at Universal Orlando.

LESS COMPLEX   Universal's smaller scale also has both logistical and psychological benefits. Walt Disney World is so vast that there is no way to do it all, even if you were to stay for weeks. For some travelers, that overabundance of options creates anxiety and a sense of missing out or not getting your money's worth. Universal has plenty to occupy your attention—you could stay for a week without getting bored—but the list of choices is much more manageable.

unofficial **TIP**
If you visit central Florida and limit your choices to parks, hotels, restaurants, and nightspots with Disney labels, you'll be missing a lot.

More important, once you choose what you want to do at Universal, you can usually just go ahead and do it without jumping through the hoops now found at Disney World. Despite Disney's investment of well over a billion dollars, many guests find WDW's MyMagic+ vacation planning service—and the ability (read: necessity) to book FastPass+ attraction reservations weeks in advance—to be a royal hassle. Universal's Express line-cutting service, which is included free with every luxury hotel room, can be used at any time without prior arrangement, so you don't have to decide what time you want to ride Ripsaw Falls two months from now. Universal Express was a big hit with this Texas family:

> *Universal resorts' inclusion of the Express Pass [is] genius. My girls couldn't stop raving about the pass. They had gotten spoiled going to any ride and using the Express Pass with less than 10 minutes of wait time. They wished that all the rides had the Express Pass access. Disney's FastPass had mixed results with us.*

Likewise, WDW may have many more table-service restaurants inside and outside its parks, but good luck getting a seat in a popular eatery without booking your table six months in advance; at Universal, walk-ups are often accommodated, or you can simply make a reservation with your smartphone a few days (or even hours) before you want to eat.

UPCOMING AT UNIVERSAL ORLANDO RESORT

LOOKING TO THE FUTURE of Islands of Adventure, Marvel Super Hero Island is rumored to be ripe for an extensive makeover reflecting the Avengers cinematic series, with The Incredible Hulk Coaster receiving new launch mechanics as part of a major overhaul. Also, watch for the 3-D visuals that were installed in Japan's Harry Potter and the Forbidden Journey ride to be added to IOA's original version after Hollywood's Hogwarts opens in 2016.

At Universal Studios Florida, several older attractions are being eyed for replacement, though no official announcements have been made at press time. Also at press time, a new NBC Media Center was nearing completion in the Garden of Allah area, and *Lucy—A Tribute* is going under the knife. *Twister* is rumored to become a flight simulator starring *Tonight Show* host Jimmy Fallon, and *Disaster!* could make way for an expanded version of the *Fast & Furious: Supercharged* attraction added in 2015 to Universal Studios Hollywood's tram tour. And most of Woody Woodpecker's KidZone (including the Barney, Fievel, and Curious George attractions) may be closed by the time you read this, with the area becoming home to Nintendo video game characters such as Mario and Donkey Kong. Finally, look for upgrades to the park's parades and nighttime entertainment, along with an expansion of popular seasonal events such as Halloween Horror Nights, Mardi Gras, and the Macy's Holiday Parade.

UNIVERSAL-SPEAK POCKET TRANSLATOR AND GUIDE TO COMMON ABBREVIATIONS

IT MAY COME AS A SURPRISE to many, but Universal Orlando (like Walt Disney World) has its own somewhat peculiar language. The following table lists some terms and abbreviations you're likely to bump into, both in this guide and in the larger Universal (and Disney) community.

UNIVERSAL LEXICON IN A NUTSHELL
ATTRACTION   Ride or show
AUDIENCE   Crowd
BACKSTAGE   Behind the scenes, out of view of customers
CHARACTER   Cartoon or movie character impersonated by an employee
ANIMATED CHARACTER   A character who wears a head-covering costume (Scooby-Doo, the Minions, the Simpsons)
FACE CHARACTER   A "celebrity" character who doesn't wear a head-covering costume (Doc Brown, Marilyn Monroe, and the like)
COSTUME   Work attire or uniform
DARK RIDE   Indoor ride
DAY GUEST   Any customer not staying at a Universal resort
EARLY PARK ADMISSION (EPA)   Morning hour at Universal's theme parks for eligible hotel guests ("Early Entry," "Magic Morning," or "Extra Magic Hour" in Disney-speak)
GENERAL PUBLIC   Same as day guest
GREETER   Employee positioned at an attraction entrance
GUEST   Customer
ON-SITE   One of the Loews-operated resort hotels located on Universal Orlando property
ONSTAGE   In full view of customers
PRESHOW   Entertainment at an attraction before the feature presentation
QUICK-SERVICE RESTAURANT   Counter-service or fast food–style restaurant
RESORT GUEST   A customer staying at a Universal resort hotel
ROLE   A team member's job
TEAM MEMBER   Employee ("cast member" in Disney-speak)
TECHNICAL REHEARSAL   Opening a park or attraction before its stated opening date ("soft opening" in Disney-speak)

COMMON ABBREVIATIONS AND WHAT THEY STAND FOR	
AP	Annual Pass
EPA	Early Park Admission
I-4	Interstate 4 (main highway through central Florida)
I-DRIVE	International Drive (major Orlando thoroughfare)
IOA	Universal's Islands of Adventure theme park
TM	Team member
USF	Universal Studios Florida theme park
UOR	Universal Orlando Resort
UX OR UEx	Universal Express
WWoHP	Wizarding World of Harry Potter

WHAT IS THE WIZARDING WORLD?

UNIVERSAL HAS BEEN OPERATING ATTRACTIONS in central Florida for a quarter century, but if it only recently attracted your attention, a certain superstar boy wizard is likely responsible. In what may prove to be the competitive coup of all time between theme park arch-rivals Disney and Universal, the latter inked a deal with Warner Brothers Entertainment to create "fully immersive" Harry Potter–themed environments based on the best-selling children's books by J. K. Rowling and the companion blockbuster movies from Warner Brothers. The books have been translated into 74 languages, with more than 450 million copies sold in more than 200 territories around the world. The movies have made more than $7.7 billion worldwide, making Harry Potter the second highest-grossing film franchise in history. The project was blessed by Rowling, who is known for tenaciously protecting the integrity of her work. In the case of the films, she demanded that Warner Brothers be true, to an almost unprecedented degree, to the books on which the films were based.

"WHAT A LONG STRANGE TRIP IT'S BEEN"

THAT GRATEFUL DEAD LYRIC IS awfully appropriate when recounting the evolution of The Wizarding World—Hogsmeade. A Harry Potter theme park (or themed area) had been the chop-licking dream of the amusement industry for a decade. First, of course, there were the books, which against all odds trumped texting and TV to lure a broad age range of youth back to the printed page. Next came the movies. In securing the film rights, Warner Brothers, along with several unsuccessful suitors, learned the most important thing about exploiting the Harry Potter phenomenon: J. K. Rowling is boss.

As the Potter juggernaut took the world by storm, entertainment conglomerates began approaching Rowling about theme park rights. When she spurned a Universal Studios Florida concept for a show based on the Potter characters, industry observers were certain that she had struck a deal with Disney. In fact, Disney was in talks with Rowling about a stand-alone Harry Potter theme park. For her part,

Rowling had no problem visualizing what she wanted in a theme park, but from Disney's point of view, what Rowling wanted was operationally problematic, if not altogether impossible. Never an entity to concede control, Disney walked.

Universal caught Rowling on the rebound and brought her to Orlando to tour Islands of Adventure. Among other things, they squired her around the Lost Continent section of the park, impressing her with its detailed theme execution and showing her how, with a little imagination, it could be re-themed. Rowling saw the potential but wasn't much more flexible with Universal than she was with Disney. From her perspective, getting a themed area right couldn't be any harder than getting a movie right, so she insisted that Stuart Craig, her trusted production designer for the films, be responsible for faithfully re-creating sets from the movies. Universal, on fire to land Harry Potter, became convinced that the collaboration could work.

But theme parks and movies are two very different things. With a film, a set has to look good only for a few moments and then it's on to something else. With a theme park, a set has to look good 12–16 hours a day, in all manner of weather, and with tens of thousands of tourists rambling through it in need of food, drink, restrooms, protection from rain, and places to rest. With The Wizarding World—Hogsmeade, Rowling's insistence on authenticity occasioned conundrums not anticipated by the theme park designers, who, for example, logically assumed that guests would like to see the interior of Hagrid's Hut. No problem—a walk-through attraction will serve nicely. Of course, there's the Americans with Disabilities Act, so we'll need ramps both in and out of the hut. No way, say the movie people: Hagrid's Hut in the films had steps, so the theme park version must have them too.

To be frank, Universal shot itself in the foot by initially promoting the original Wizarding World as a "theme park within a theme park." While arguable from the aspect of immersive theming, the phrase implied a lot more content than what guests got back in 2010: a single land with only three rides, two of which were repurposed roller coasters. It also created a false impression that admission to the Harry Potter area was separate from the existing parks, or involved an additional charge. Now that Diagon Alley has been added, along with a train attraction connecting the two areas, the "theme park within a theme park" moniker is perhaps more apropos. But though the Wizarding World will be the resort's top draw for many years to come, it still represents just a sliver of what Universal Orlando's theme parks have to offer.

BONE UP

WE DON'T HAVE ROOM to explain all the Potter allusions and icons incorporated into The Wizarding World. Because they so accurately replicate scenes from the books and films, it helps immeasurably to be well versed in all things Harry. If it's been a while since you've seen one of the movies or read one of the novels, you can brush up by watching the first four flicks in the series, in particular *Harry Potter and the Goblet of*

South Orlando

Orlando

429

Windermere

Lake Butler

Universal Studios Florida

Vineland Rd

Universal's Islands of Adventure

74-B

Wet 'n Wild

535

Winter Garden–Vineland Rd.

S. Apopka–Vineland Rd.

74-A

Universal Blvd

Orange County Convention Center

72

1

Magic Kingdom

SeaWorld Orlando

71

Discovery Cove

Fort Wilderness Campground

Aquatica

The Walt Disney World Resort

International Dr.

(future site of) Flamingo Crossings

Western Way

Downtown Disney (Disney Springs)

Lake Buena Vista

Epcot Center Dr.

World Dr.

Epcot

68

Disney's Hollywood Studios

Buena Vista Dr.

To 27 & Ocala

Disney's Animal Kingdom

Osceola Pkwy.

67

536

417

65

535

W. Irlo Bronson Memorial Hwy.

192

ESPN Wide World of Sports Complex

3

64

2

Celebration

192

429

Poinciana Blvd.

62

4

58

532

27

To Busch Gardens & Tampa

17

92

To Davenport

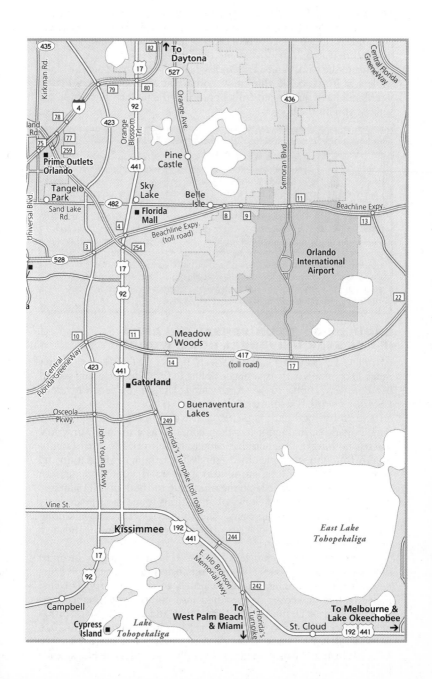

Fire and *Harry Potter and the Sorcerer's Stone* (*Harry Potter and the Philosopher's Stone* outside of India and the United States). The Gringotts ride is drawn directly from the first half of the final film, so you'll want to re-watch *Harry Potter and the Deathly Hallows: Part 2* before heading to the bank vaults. For an easy memory jog, check out the films' trailers at YouTube. If you know nothing at all about Harry Potter, you'll still have fun, but to truly appreciate the nuance and detail, we suggest you hit the books.

WIZARDING WORLD WHISPERS WITH JIM HILL

WHERE'S HARRY? At Disney World, it's easy enough to get your picture taken with Mickey. Likewise, in Springfield U.S.A. at Universal Studios Florida, you can get your photo taken with Bart and Homer. So why can't you snag a photo op with Harry and his crew at The Wizarding World? The answer begins and ends with J. K. Rowling: Because both Hogsmeade and Diagon Alley were created with her input and to her stringent specifications, the only true Harry would be the one played by Daniel Radcliffe. And with Radcliffe having moved on to other projects, Rowling has decreed that no look-alike ever be hired to stand in for him at the Universal Orlando parks. The same rule applies to all the other characters portrayed in the Potter movies. This is also why Hogsmeade and Diagon Alley are staffed by characters you've never heard of before.

SHOULD I GO TO UNIVERSAL ORLANDO IF I'VE SEEN UNIVERSAL HOLLYWOOD?

UNIVERSAL STUDIOS HOLLYWOOD IN CALIFORNIA shares much in common with its younger sibling in Orlando, including several headliner attractions. So is it worth visiting UOR if you've already done USH? In a word, "Absolutely!"

The Hollywood park is primarily a working movie studio with a park bolted on, making it less than cohesive as a themed attraction. There's nothing in Orlando that can compare to USH's justly famous Studio Tour, though some of its sights (the earthquake simulation and soon the 3-D King Kong encounter) have stand-alone analogues on the East Coast. But aside from the tram tour, the bulk of USH's limited lineup consists of virtual clones of attractions found in Orlando, only in less immersive environments. And though USH's CityWalk complex is larger than Orlando's, its offerings are less unique, featuring a number of familiar chains.

That's beginning to change, as Universal Hollywood is in the midst of an ambitious multiyear "Vision" expansion plan, which will bring new attractions, dining, and even hotels to the property. The first phase of this makeover has resulted in a colorfully re-themed area around the new Despicable Me attraction and an expansive Springfield district adjacent to The Simpsons Ride. It will culminate in 2016 with the debut of Harry Potter's West Coast digs. But even when USH's Wizarding World opens, it will only reproduce the Hogsmeade area from IOA; for the full Diagon Alley and Hogwarts Express experience, Orlando will continue to be your only option.

The bottom line is that Universal Studios Hollywood makes a fine daylong diversion from a Disneyland vacation, but it is not yet big enough by itself to build a trip around. Universal Orlando, on the other hand, has nearly everything USH has, plus a whole lot more.

CRITICAL COMPARISON OF ATTRACTIONS FOUND AT BOTH UNIVERSAL STUDIOS HOLLYWOOD AND UNIVERSAL ORLANDO

Animal Actors on Location   About the same at both parks.

Despicable Me Minion Mayhem   USH has an elaborate interactive exterior and much higher capacity; the ride itself is the same at both parks.

Jurassic Park River Adventure   IOA has fewer dinosaurs and some different effects; USH's version is much wetter in warm weather. Otherwise about the same at both parks.

Revenge of the Mummy—The Ride   Much longer with better effects at USF.

Shrek 4-D   About the same at both parks.

The Simpsons Ride   About the same at both parks.

Transformers: The Ride 3-D   USF has upgraded video projectors; otherwise, the same at both parks.

PART ONE

PLANNING *Before* YOU LEAVE HOME

GATHERING INFORMATION

IN ADDITION TO READING THIS GUIDE, we recommend that you visit our website, **touringplans.com,** which offers essential tools for planning your trip and saving you time and money. Our blog, **blog.touring plans.com,** lists breaking news for the Universal Orlando Resort and Universal theme parks worldwide.

The site also offers computer-optimized touring plans for Universal Studios Florida and Islands of Adventure. With these, you choose the attractions you want to experience, including character greetings, parades, shows, meals, and midday breaks, and we'll give you a step-by-step itinerary for your specific dates of travel, showing you how to see everything with minimal waits in line.

You can update the touring plans when you're in the parks too. Let's say that your touring plan calls for riding The Simpsons Ride next, but your family really needs a snack break and 30 minutes out of the sun. Get a Squishee or Duff Beer and take the break. When you're done, click the Optimize button on your plan, and it will be updated with what to do next. The ability to redo your plan allows you to recover from any situation while still minimizing your waits for the rest of the day.

Another really popular part of **touringplans.com** is our Crowd Calendar, which shows crowd projections for USF and IOA for every day of the year. Look up the dates of your visit, and the calendar will not only show the projected wait times for each day but also will indicate for each day which theme park will be the least crowded. Historical wait times are also available, so you can see how crowded the parks were last year for your upcoming trip dates.

The website has complete dining menus, including wine lists, for every food cart, stand, kiosk, counter-service restaurant, and sit-down restaurant in the Universal Orlando Resort. The whole thing is

Important Universal Addresses

THEME PARKS & CITYWALK PARKING GARAGE ADDRESS	
6000 Universal Boulevard, Orlando, FL 32819	
GPS COORDINATES FOR UNIVERSAL ORLANDO PARKING GARAGE	
Latitude: 28.47399° Longitude: -81.46228°	
GUEST SERVICES & CORPORATE OFFICES	
Universal Orlando Resort, 1000 Universal Studios Place, Orlando, FL 32819	
HARD ROCK HOTEL	
5800 Universal Boulevard, Orlando, FL 32819	
LOEWS PORTOFINO BAY HOTEL	
5601 Universal Boulevard, Orlando, FL 32819	
LOEWS ROYAL PACIFIC RESORT	
6300 Hollywood Way, Orlando, FL 32819	
LOEWS SAPPHIRE FALLS RESORT	
6601 Adventure Way, Orlando, FL 32819	
UNIVERSAL'S CABANA BAY BEACH RESORT	
6550 Adventure Way; Orlando, FL 32819	

searchable, too, so you can find every restaurant in IOA that serves steak (and its prices), or see which snacks are available in Diagon Alley.

Updated constantly, these menus represent the most accurate collection of Universal dining information available anywhere. The touring plans, menus, Crowd Calendar, and more are available in **Lines,** our mobile application, which provides continuous real-time updates on wait times at Universal Orlando. Using in-park staff and updates sent in by readers, Lines shows you the current wait times at every attraction in every park, as well as our estimated actual waits for these attractions for the rest of today. For example, Lines will tell you that the posted wait time for The Amazing Adventures of Spider-Man is 60 minutes, and that based on what we know about how Universal manages Spider-Man's queue, the actual time you'll probably wait in line is 48 minutes. Lines is the only Universal app that shows you both posted and actual wait times.

Lines also has an online chat feature, where folks can ask questions and give travel tips. Hundreds of "Liners" interact every day in discussions that stay remarkably on-topic for an Internet forum.

Lines is available free to **touringplans.com** subscribers for the Apple iPhone and iPad at the iTunes Store (search for "TouringPlans"; requires iOS 4.3 or later) and for Android devices at the Google Play Store (requires Android 2.1 Eclair or later). Owners of other phones can use the Web-based version at **m.touringplans.com.**

As long as you have that smartphone handy while visiting the parks, we and your fellow Unofficial Guide readers would love it if you could report on the actual wait times you get while you're there. Run Lines, log in to your user account, and click "+time" in the upper right corner to help everyone out. We'll use that information to update the wait times for everyone in the park and make everyone's lives just a little bit better.

Universal Orlando Phone Numbers

Universal Orlando Main Information	☎ 407-363-8000
Guest Relations	☎ 407-224-4233
Tickets by Mail	☎ 407-224-7840
Lost and Found (USF)	☎ 407-224-4244; press 2 to be connected
Lost and Found (IOA)	☎ 407-224-4245; press 2 to be connected
Merchandise	☎ 888-762-0820
Vacation Packages	☎ 877-801-9720
Vacation Packages Deaf or Hard of Hearing TDD	☎ 800-447-0672
On-Site Hotel Reservations	☎ 888-273-1311
Meeting Attendees/Individual Call-In for Group Blocks	☎ 866-360-7395
Universal In-Park Dining and Character Meals	☎ 407-224-3663
Universal Resort Dining and Character Meals	☎ 407-503-3463
Mandara Spa at Portofino Bay	☎ 407-503-1244
Hard Rock Hotel	☎ 407-503-ROCK (2000)
Loews Portofino Bay Hotel	☎ 407-503-1000
Loews Royal Pacific Resort	☎ 407-503-3000
Loews Sapphire Falls Resort	☎ 407-503-5000
Universal's Cabana Bay Beach Resort	☎ 407-503-4000

Much of our Web content—including the menus, resort photos and videos, and errata for this book—is completely free for anyone to use. Access to part of the site, most notably the Crowd Calendar, additional touring plans, and in-park wait times, requires a small subscription fee (current-book owners get a substantial discount). This nominal charge helps keep us online and costs less than lunch at the Leaky Cauldron restaurant in Diagon Alley. Plus **touringplans.com** offers a 45-day money-back guarantee.

UNIVERSAL ON THE WEB

IF, JUDGING FROM THE PLENITUDE of independent Disney World websites, you expect a similar number of such sites for Universal, you'd be wrong. Though some Disney-centric sites cover Universal in some (usually minimal) way, independent sites dedicated to Universal Orlando are much rarer. Of the independent Disney sites that deal with Universal, we recommend **mousesavers.com** for hotel and admission bargains.

For the latest Universal updates and rumors, try **parkscope.net, orlandoparksnews.com,** and the discussion boards at **orlandounited .com.** For crowd projections and touring tips, check our own **touring plans.com. Attractionsmagazine.com, themeparkinsider.com, scream scape.com,** and **behindthethrills.com** are all reliable sites covering central Florida attractions, including Universal. Local news and theme park developments are available at **orlandosentinel.com** and **orlando weekly.com**. **Jimhillmedia.com** offers insider information on attractions, new technologies, and changes in the parks. Finally, there's the official Universal Orlando website, **universalorlando.com**.

Universal also offers a free smartphone app for Apple and Android devices that displays wait times and interactive maps while you're inside the parks, using the resort's free Wi-Fi (connect to "xfinitywifi" and accept the legal terms to access).

BEST UNIVERSAL PODCASTS   The best podcast devoted to Universal is **"UUOP: The Unofficial Universal Orlando Podcast"** (**uuopodcast.libsyn .com**), which ironically is based not in Orlando but in the United Kingdom. **Parkscope** and **OrlandoUnited** also produce irreverent podcasts focusing on UOR. **"Pardon the Pixie Dust"** (**ptpdshow.cblogspot.com**) and the **"E-Ticket Report,"** both cohosted by irrepressible TouringPlans contributor Derek Burgan, frequently feature Universal content. **Orlando Tourism Report** (**centralfloridatop5.com**) often breaks local attraction news. **Seasonpasspodcast.com** and **coasterradio.com** have breaking news and in-depth interviews with theme park designers and executives from parks around the world. For Universal Studios Hollywood updates, check out the podcast from **insideuniversal.net.**

BEST UNIVERSAL TWITTER FEEDS   If you want your Universal news and rumors in 140 character bites, follow these prolific park Tweeters: @universalorl, @horrornightsorl, @parkscope, @orlandounited, @themepark, @attractions, @behindthrills, @orlando_parks, @hatetofly, @thrillgeek, @amusementbuzz, @touringplans, @derekburgan, and @skubersky.

◼▮ TIMING YOUR VISIT

TRYING TO REASON WITH THE TOURIST SEASON

CENTRAL FLORIDA THEME PARKS and attractions are busiest the last week or so of December and the first few days of January. Next busiest is the spring break period from mid-March through the week of Easter, then Thanksgiving week. Following those are the first few weeks of June, when summer vacation starts, and the week of Presidents' Day.

*un*_official_ **TIP**
Though crowds have grown in September and October as a result of promotions aimed at the international market and families without school-age children, these months continue to be good for touring.

The least busy time is from Labor Day in September through the beginning of October. Next slowest are the weeks in mid-January after the Martin Luther King Jr. holiday weekend up to Presidents' Day in February. The weeks after Thanksgiving and before Christmas are less crowded than average, as is mid-April to mid-May, after spring break, and before Memorial Day.

Late February, March, and early April are dicey. Crowds ebb and flow according to spring break schedules and the timing of Presidents' Day weekend. Besides being asphalt-melting hot, July brings throngs of South American tourists on their winter holiday.

THE DOWNSIDE OF OFF-SEASON TOURING

THOUGH WE STRONGLY RECOMMEND going to Universal Orlando in the fall, winter, or spring, there are a few trade-offs. The parks often close early during the off-season, either because of low crowds or special events such as the Halloween and Mardi Gras parties at Universal Studios Florida. This drastically reduces touring hours. Even when crowds are small, it's difficult to see everything at USF or IOA between 9 a.m. and 6 p.m. Early closing also usually means no evening fireworks. And because these are slow times, some rides and attractions may be closed. Finally, central Florida temperatures fluctuate wildly during late fall, winter, and early spring; daytime highs in the 40s and 50s aren't uncommon.

Given the choice, however, smaller crowds, bargain prices, and stress-free touring are worth risking cold weather or closed attractions. Touring in fall and other "off" periods is so much easier that our research team, at the risk of being blasphemous, would advise taking children out of school for an Orlando visit.

Most readers who've tried central Florida's attractions at various times agree. A New Hampshire parent writes:

> I took my grade-school children out of school for a few days to go during a slow time and would highly recommend it. We communicated with the teachers about a month before traveling to seek their preference for whether classwork and homework should be completed before, during, or after our trip. It's so much more enjoyable to be [in Orlando] when your children can experience rides and attractions . . . rather than standing in line. And traveling at a time of year when it's not unbearably hot makes such a difference as well. I would be hard-pressed to go during a hot or busy time ever again.

There's another side to this story, and we've received some well-considered letters from parents and teachers who don't think taking kids out of school is such a hot idea. From a father in Fairfax, Virginia:

> My wife and I are disappointed that you seem to be encouraging families to take their children out of school to avoid the crowds [in Orlando] during the summer months. My wife is an eighth-grade teacher of chemistry and physics. She has parents pull their children, some honor roll students, out of school for vacations, only to discover when they return that the students are unable to comprehend the material. Parents' suspicions about the quality of their children's education should be raised when children go to school for six hours a day yet supposedly can complete this same instruction with "less than an hour of homework" each night.

A Martinez, California, teacher offers this compelling analogy:

There are a precious 180 days for us as teachers to instruct our students, and there are 185 days during the year for [vacation]. I have seen countless students during my 14 years of teaching struggle to catch up the rest of the year due to a week of vacation during critical instructional periods. The analogy I use with my students' parents is that it's like walking out of a movie after watching the first 5 minutes, and then returning for the last 5 minutes and trying to figure out what happened.

But a teacher from Penn Yan, New York, sees things differently:

I've read the comments by teachers saying that they all think it's horrible for a parent to take a child out for a vacation. As a teacher and a parent, I disagree. If a parent takes the time to let us know that a child is going to be out, we help them get ready for upcoming homework the best we can. If the child is a good student, why shouldn't they go have a wonderful experience with their family? I also don't understand when teachers say they can't get something together for the time the student will be out. We all have to plan ahead, and we know what we are teaching days, if not weeks, in advance. Take 20 minutes out of your day and set something up. Learn to be flexible!

BE UNCONVENTIONAL Orlando's Orange County Convention Center hosts some of the largest conventions and trade shows in the world. Universal is far enough from the OCCC that it isn't usually affected by events, but hotel rooms anywhere around International Drive can be hard to find (and expensive) when there's a big convention. You can check the convention schedule at the Orlando Orange County Convention Center for the next seven months at **occc.net/global/calendar.**

DON'T FORGET AUGUST Kids go back to school pretty early in Florida (and in a lot of other places too). This makes mid- to late August a good time to visit Universal Orlando for families who can't vacation during the off-season. A New Jersey mother of two school-age children spells it out:

The end of August is the PERFECT time to go (just watch out for hurricanes; it's the season). There were virtually no wait times, 20 minutes at the most.

A mom from Rapid City, South Dakota, agrees:

School starts very early in Florida, so our mid-August visit was great for crowds but not for heat.

And from a family from Roxbury, New Jersey:

I recommend the last two weeks of August for anyone traveling there during the summer. We have visited twice during this time of year and have had great success touring the parks.

Though we recommend off-season touring, we realize that it's not possible for many families. We want to make it clear, therefore, that you can have a wonderful experience regardless of when you go. Our advice, irrespective of season, is to arrive early at the parks and avoid the crowds by using one of our touring plans. If attendance is light, kick back and forget the touring plans.

WE'VE GOT WEATHER! Long before theme parks, tourists visited Florida year-round to enjoy the temperate tropical and subtropical climates. The best weather months generally are October, November, March, and April. Fall is usually dry, whereas spring is wetter. December, January, and February vary, with average highs of 72°–73°F intermixed with highs in the 50°–65°F range. May is hot but tolerable. June, July, August, and September are the warmest months. Rain is possible anytime, usually in the form of scattered thunderstorms. An entire day of rain is unusual.

Universal Orlando Climate

	JAN	FEB	MAR	APR	MAY	JUN	JUL	AUG	SEP	OCT	NOV	DEC
AVERAGE DAILY LOW (°F)												
	47	50	54	59	65	71	73	73	72	66	58	51
AVERAGE DAILY HIGH (°F)												
	71	73	78	83	89	91	92	92	90	84	78	72
AVERAGE DAILY TEMPERATURE (°F)												
	60	61	67	71	77	81	82	83	81	75	68	62
AVERAGE DAILY HUMIDITY PERCENTAGES												
	62	73	71	70	68	70	74	76	76	75	74	73
AVERAGE RAINFALL PER MONTH (Inches)												
	2.9	2.7	4.0	2.3	3.1	8.3	7.0	7.7	5.1	2.5	2.1	2.9
NUMBER OF DAYS OF RAIN PER MONTH												
	6	7	8	6	8	14	17	16	14	9	6	6

A WORD ABOUT CROWDS

YOU'VE PROBABLY READ ABOUT THE HUGE CROWDS that inundate The Wizarding World outposts at both Universal parks. The reports are true, but they present an unbalanced view of the crowds at the Universal parks overall. To get a quantitative grip on crowding, let's look at attendance figures compared with the size of the parks. On a day of average attendance, USF and Disney's Hollywood Studios see about the same number of guests per acre. However, USF has 26 attractions, while DHS has only 17. Therefore, the crowds are distributed among more attractions at USF, making it seem less crowded. Contrasting the Magic Kingdom with IOA, the latter averages 203 guests per day, per acre, while the Magic Kingdom—the attendance leader of all the world's theme parks—registers a whopping 495 guests per day, per acre. Depending on how you define attractions, however, the Magic Kingdom has about 42, versus 26 at Islands of Adventure. Even so, there are still one-and-a-half as many guests for each Magic Kingdom attraction as for each IOA attraction.

HOW MUCH TIME TO ALLOCATE

PRIOR TO THE DEBUT OF THE WIZARDING WORLDS, some visitors found that they could see everything of note at both Universal parks within a single day. Not anymore: Touring Universal Studios Florida, including one meal and a visit to Diagon Alley, takes about 10–12 hours, while a comprehensive tour of Islands of Adventure will take a few hours less.

For that reason, we recommend devoting a minimum of a full day to each Universal Orlando theme park, especially if this is your first visit. Three days is ideal, particularly with a park-to-park pass, as it will allow you to fully explore each park and revisit your favorite attractions. An on-site stay of four or more days will allow you to sample the parks in smaller bites while taking full advantage of the resort's other amenities. One reader laments:

> There's a lot of standing at USF, and it isn't as organized as DHS. Many of the attractions don't open until 10 a.m. We weren't able to see nearly as many attractions at Universal as we were at DHS during the same amount of time.

*un*official **TIP**
Get to the park with your admission already purchased about 30–45 minutes before official opening time. Arrive 45–60 minutes before official opening time if you need to buy admission. Be aware that you can't do a comprehensive tour of both Universal parks in a single day.

As the reader observes, some Universal Orlando attractions don't open until 10 a.m. or later. Most theater attractions don't schedule performances until 11 a.m. or after. This means that early in the day, all park guests are concentrated among the limited number of attractions in operation.

As a postscript, you won't have to worry about any of this if you use our Universal Orlando touring plans. We'll keep you one jump ahead of the crowd and make sure that any given attraction is running by the time you get there.

SELECTING THE DAY OF THE WEEK FOR YOUR VISIT

WHEN READERS ASKED, "What is the best day to visit Universal Orlando?," we used to reply that Sunday was the least crowded day at the resort (presumably because people are starting their vacations at Walt Disney World), followed by Monday and Saturday, and that Thursday was the most crowded. While that still generally holds true, there are too many other variables—including weather and special events—to make this a reliable rule of thumb.

The best way to know which day to visit Universal Orlando is with our Crowd Calendar at **touringplans.com/universal-orlando /crowd-calendar.** No matter which day you visit, arriving early and following a touring plan makes a much bigger difference than what day of the week it is.

INTEGRATING A UNIVERSAL ORLANDO VISIT WITH A WDW VACATION

WHILE UNIVERSAL ORLANDO HAS RECENTLY MADE strides in convincing visitors to make UOR their primary destination, for many travelers a stop at Universal is still a side trip in their Walt Disney World–centric vacation. If you are devoting the bulk of your Orlando holiday to Disney but still want to make a detour to Universal, you have three primary options:

THE DAY TRIP   Most Disney guests who want to sample Universal take a single day out of their vacation to visit USF and/or IOA. This solution is simplest for guests with their own cars, or shuttle transportation between the resorts can be arranged (see page 129 in Part Three). The day trip has a couple of drawbacks: The per-day cost can be high, especially if you want to visit both UOR theme parks, and (depending on transportation arrangements) you'll probably arrive after rope drop and depart before closing.

THE WDW/UOR/WDW SANDWICH   An increasing number of guests take a night or two out of the middle of their WDW trip and stay on property at Universal. Again, transportation can be handled through a private car or shuttle bus. This method allows you to explore Universal over the course of two or three days and enjoy the perks of staying on-site, such as Early Park Admission to The Wizarding World. You can also use Disney's Magical Express for free transfers from and to the airport at the beginning and end of your trip. The main drawback is that you must check in and out (and back in again) to your Disney hotel, or pay for nights in a WDW bed you won't be using.

THE SPLIT TRIP   The best option if you want to divide your vacation roughly equally between Disney and Universal is a split trip, where you stay at one resort for the first half of your visit, and then transfer to the other for the remainder. You'll only be able to use Disney's Magical Express on one end of your vacation (arriving or departing), so look into the three-way transportation offered by outfits such as Quicksilver (see page 127). To decide which resort to visit first, check Touring Plans' Crowd Calendars for both properties, and visit Disney on the days it will be less busy, because crowds can make a bigger difference there than at Universal.

WHICH PARK TO VISIT?

UNIVERSAL ORLANDO'S PARKS ARE BOTH SPECTACULAR, so if you can only visit one, you can't really go wrong either way. If you've visited Universal since 2010, when the first Wizarding World opened, but have not yet seen Diagon Alley, you're going to want to go to Universal Studios Florida. If you've never been to Universal Orlando, or at least not in this decade, the decision is down to what type of attractions you prefer. If you are a fan of simulators, screen-based experiences, and live shows, then USF is right for you. If you prefer big outdoor roller coasters and wild water rides, IOA is your destination. Of course, if you are a Harry Potter devotee, you're going to have to visit both parks to get the full Wizarding World experience. Incidentally, USF is a much better park to visit during inclement weather, due to its larger percentage of indoor attractions.

OPERATING HOURS

THE UNIVERSAL ORLANDO WEBSITE PUBLISHES preliminary park hours up to six months in advance, but schedule adjustments can happen at any time, including the day of your visit. Check **universal orlando.com/resort-information/theme-park-hours.aspx** or call ☎ 407-363-8000 for the exact hours before you arrive. Off-season, parks may be open as few as eight hours (9 a.m.–5 p.m.). At busy times (particularly holidays), they may operate 8 a.m.–11 p.m.

Universal's website publishes the official operating hours, but on most days, the parks open earlier. If the official hours for both parks are 9 a.m.–9 p.m., for instance, turnstiles for the park (or parks) participating in Early Park Admission will open between 7:30 a.m. and 8 a.m., and the one not offering early entry may still open its gates as early as 8:30 a.m.

Queues to rides and attractions usually close to new guests at exactly the park's official closing time; if you are already in line at closing, you will be permitted to stay as long as it takes for you to ride, barring technical malfunctions. (One exception to that rule is Harry Potter and the Escape from Gringotts, which may close its queue an hour or more before the rest of the park, depending on how long the line is.) The main gift shops near the front of each park remain open 30 minutes to an hour after the rest of the park has closed.

▌▌ ALLOCATING MONEY

UNIVERSAL ORLANDO TICKETS

UNIVERSAL OFFERS TICKETS good for one to four days of admission to its theme parks. The basic ticket is called **Single Park admission** and includes entry to one theme park per day. If you buy a basic two-day ticket, you can visit Islands of Adventure on one day and Universal Studios Florida on the next. You may not use a basic two-day ticket to visit both parks in one day, but you can exit and return to the same park on the same day, in case you want to head back to your hotel for a nap.

If you want to visit both Universal Studios Florida and Islands of Adventure on the same day, purchase the **Park-to-Park admission** option, which allows you to move freely between both parks on the same day. It takes about 12–15 minutes to walk from one park to the next, or you can take the 4-minute Hogwarts Express trip between The Wizarding Worlds. Be aware that you *must* have park-to-park admission to ride

Universal vs. WDW Admissions

(PRICES INCLUDE TAX)	ADULTS	AGES 3-9
Universal One-Day Base Ticket	$109	$103
WDW One-Day Base Ticket (Magic Kingdom)	$112	$105
Universal Two-Day Base Ticket	$160	$149
WDW Two-Day Base Ticket	$204	$191
Universal Three-Day Base Ticket	$170	$160
WDW Three-Day Base Ticket	$293	$273
Universal Four-Day Base Ticket	$181	$170
WDW Four-Day Base Ticket	$325	$304
Universal One-Day Park-to-Park Ticket	$157	$151
WDW One-Day Park Hopper	$187	$180
Universal Two-Day Park-to-Park Ticket	$208	$197
WDW Two-Day Park Hopper	$285	$272
Universal Three-Day Park-to-Park Ticket	$218	$208
WDW Three-Day Park Hopper	$380	$359
Universal Four-Day Park-to-Park Ticket	$229	$218
WDW Four-Day Park Hopper	$414	$392
Universal Power Annual Pass *(no comparable WDW pass)*	$256	$256
Universal Preferred Annual Pass	$357	$357
Comparable WDW Annual Pass	$697	$697
Universal Premier Annual Pass	$511	$511
Comparable WDW Premium Annual Pass	$830	$830

BASE TICKETS / PARK-HOPPING / ANNUAL PASSES

the Hogwarts Express train between IOA and USF; single-park tickets may be upgraded at Guest Services or at the train stations.

A one-day, one-park Base Ticket is on par with those at the Disney parks; multiday single-park Base Tickets, however, are significantly less expensive at Universal. Park-hopping (or "park-to-park," in Universal parlance) tickets can be much more expensive at Disney, where, for example, a four-day Park Hopper ticket costs about 50% more than what you'd pay at Universal.

As at Disney, passes expire 14 days after the first use. Also as at Disney, kids under age 3 are free, but child tickets for ages 3–9 are only a few dollars discounted from the adult prices, despite the large number of rides with height requirements at Universal. Prices listed above are what you'd pay online and include tax.

The **Three-Park Unlimited** ticket is good for 14 consecutive days of park-to-park admission at both USF and IOA, plus Wet 'n Wild. Three-Park Unlimited tickets are sold by a number of third-party vendors but not directly by Universal itself at this time. Only a few dollars more than the four-day park-to-park ticket, this ticket is poorly publicized but a great value if you like water slides and aren't buying an annual pass for your extended stay.

The five-park, 14-day **Orlando Flex Ticket** allows unlimited entry to Universal Studios Florida, Universal's Islands of Adventure, SeaWorld,

Aquatica, and Wet 'n Wild; it costs $307 for adults and $291 for children ages 3–9, tax included. The six-park, 14-day **Orlando Flex Ticket Plus,** providing unlimited entry to USF, IOA, SeaWorld, Aquatica, Wet 'n Wild, and Busch Gardens, costs $349 for adults and $330 for children. Buy the tickets online at the websites of the participating parks, or get them at a third-party discounter. Flex Tickets are a good deal only if you visit all of the parks covered.

BUYING ADMISSION TO UNIVERSAL ORLANDO

ONE OF OUR BIG GRIPES ABOUT UNIVERSAL is that there are never enough ticket windows open in the morning to accommodate the crowds. Therefore, we strongly recommend that you buy your admission in advance. Passes are available directly from Universal at **universal orlando.com,** or by phone at ☎ 800-711-0080; at the concierge desks or attractions box offices of many Orlando-area hotels; and through Guest Services at the DoubleTree Universal hotel (☎ 407-351-1000), at the intersection of Major Boulevard and Kirkman Road.

Many hotels and some ticket brokers that sell Universal admissions don't issue actual passes. Instead, the purchaser gets a voucher that can be redeemed for a pass at the theme park. Fortunately, the voucher-redemption window is separate from the park's ticket-sales operation, but it's still quicker to get a ticket you can take straight to the gate.

SAVING MONEY ON ADMISSION
TO UNIVERSAL ORLANDO

UNIVERSAL'S ADMISSION DISCOUNTS CHANGE too rapidly to comprehensively cover in this guide. The best online clearing house for keeping up with the latest available offers is **mousesavers.com /universal-orlando-discounts-and-deals**.

Ticket Savings Direct from Universal Orlando

Unlike Disney, Universal offers discounts when you purchase passes online at **universalorlando.com,** including $20-per-pass discounts on multiday tickets plus other time-limited specials. Passes purchased online can be printed at home and used at the turnstiles without the need to exchange at a box office, or can be retrieved using the credit card they were purchased with from automated will-call kiosks outside each park. Passes purchased online (including annual passes) do not begin expiring until first activated at a park entrance. Though Universal discounts multiday tickets online, one-day admissions cost exactly the same as at the gate; nevertheless, they're probably worth ordering online for the convenience.

Multiday tickets purchased online directly from Universal include a coupon booklet with "up to $150 in savings" on food, merchandise, and hotel services. Universal also offers a best-price guarantee: If you buy park tickets through Universal's website, and then find them cheaper online within seven days, Universal Orlando will give you a gift card (good at restaurants and shops around the resort) refunding the price difference. The price guarantee is only on regular admission tickets (not

Express or special-event tickets) available to the general public from US-based websites, and excludes time-share promotions, group rates, or other special discounts. To claim your refund, call ☎ 877-589-4783 or send an e-mail via **visitorsatisfaction.com/contactus.**

Florida (and sometimes Georgia) residents can take advantage of an ever-changing array of price breaks, often tied to a fast-food chain or soft drink promotion. These specials require valid photo ID proving residency to redeem, so don't try using one if you aren't eligible. Current annual pass holders get a modest 10%–15% price break when buying additional multiday tickets at the gate but may do better with the standard online discount.

Universal Orlando frequently offers online-only specials that are usually superior to any other available discount. For example, from late 2014 through June 7, 2015, Universal's website was selling three-day tickets for the two-day price; these tickets had to be used by June 20, 2015, and blackout days applied, but it was still a substantial savings.

Ticket Savings from Third-Party Vendors

The lowest possible prices on electronically delivered Universal tickets that we're aware of are through **Orlando Ticket Connection** (**orlando ticketconnection.com**), which undercuts Universal's online prices on park-to-park tickets by $5–$10. We'd love to hear from readers who have had experiences (good or bad) with Orlando Ticket Connection. **Parksavers** (**parksavers.com**) sells Universal tickets for a few dollars more than Orlando Ticket Connection, but be aware that their buyers receive a printable voucher that must be redeemed at the park with a photo ID, instead of going straight to the turnstiles.

Dreams Unlimited Travel (**dreamsunlimitedtravel.com**) charges the same for Universal tickets as the official website, but it does offer exclusive one- and two-day park-to-park passes bundled with discounted round-trip transportation from Disney-area hotels via Mears (see page 129). Its tickets are purchased directly through Universal's secure website and can be printed at home or retrieved from will-call kiosks.

Universal charges $14 for domestic FedEx shipping of tickets ($19 for international delivery). If you want physical tickets mailed to you for the cheapest price and can order at least two weeks before your trip, consider using an online ticket wholesaler, such as **The Official Ticket Center** (**officialticketcenter.com**) or **Undercover Tourist** (**undercover tourist.com**). Official Ticket Center advertises all its prices inclusive of tax and USPS Certified shipping, and it has the lowest bottom-line cost on physical Universal Orlando tickets that we've found, usually within pennies of Orlando Ticket Connection's e-delivery price.

UNIVERSAL ORLANDO ANNUAL PASSES

UNIVERSAL ORLANDO'S ANNUAL PASSES ARE SOME of the best deals in town, not only for locals but also for anyone visiting the resort more than four days out of the year. The entry-level annual pass costs only $25 more than a four-day park-to-park ticket (or $35 more than

Chris Eliopoulos

a three-day ticket for Florida residents), and Universal's most expensive annual pass is about 60% of the price of Walt Disney World's Premium Annual Pass. Of course, Disney has several more theme parks included in its annual passes, but Universal throws in some great perks (depending on pass level) to compensate.

All Universal Orlando annual passes include park-to-park admission to both Universal Studios Florida and Islands of Adventure, including all special events that do not require a separate ticket, such as Mardi Gras, Grinchmas, and Macy's Holiday Parade, as well as discounts on those that cost extra, such as Halloween Horror Nights and Rock the Universe. All annual pass holders also receive up to 30% off room rates at on-site hotels, and a number of other discounts as detailed below.

Here are the three types of annual passes offered by Universal Orlando:

Power Pass

- Valid for one year, but with a few weeks of blackout dates, including Christmas week at both parks, and mid-June to mid-August at USF only
- No free parking
- No in-park food or merchandise discounts
- 10%-20% off food and merchandise at select CityWalk locations

Preferred Annual Pass

- Valid 365 days
- Free standard self-parking, and discounted preferred self-parking and valet
- 10% off most in-park restaurants and merchandise (outdoor carts and alcohol excluded)
- 10%-20% off food and merchandise at select CityWalk locations
- Additional discounts at CityWalk and the resort hotels

Premier Annual Pass

- Valid 365 days
- Free preferred self-parking and valet, and discounted Red Carpet Valet
- 15% off most in-park restaurants and 20% off in-park merchandise (outdoor carts and alcohol excluded)
- Free Universal Express after 4 p.m. every day (one time per participating attraction)
- One free non-peak Halloween Horror Nights ticket (valid select Sunday–Thursday nights only)
- 8 free bottles of Nestlé bottled water per year ($22 value)
- 15%-20% off food and merchandise at select CityWalk locations
- Free admission to CityWalk clubs, and free admission for one guest on Sunday–Thursday nights (excludes concerts and special events)
- Free access to hotel fitness centers and complimentary room upgrades when staying on-site

In addition, all annual pass holders get a quarterly newsletter with announcements of special limited-time perks, such as Early Park Admission on weekdays during the off-season. And if you can't handle the cost of a pass in one big bite, Universal's FlexPay service will (after a substantial down payment) split the remaining bill into interest-free payments as low as $11 per month.

So, should you buy a Universal Orlando annual pass, and if so, which one? If you are making only one trip to Universal within the year, are staying off-site, and plan to spend four days or fewer in the parks, then you should stick with standard tickets. If, however, you plan to spend five or more days at Universal's parks, anticipate returning to Universal within the year, or want to stay at an on-site hotel for more than one night, it is well worth your while to run the numbers on an annual pass.

As for which one to buy, first double-check the current Power Pass blackout dates on Universal's website to ensure they don't conflict with your trip. Even if you're in the clear, at least one member of your party will want to pick up at least a Preferred Annual Pass for its discounts, especially if you are driving to the resort; five days of self-parking at $17 per day adds up to $85, about the difference in price between the Power Pass and Preferred. (Note that free parking only applies after your first visit; you must activate your annual pass at a park gate first before receiving free parking.)

If—and only if—you take advantage of all its amenities, the Premier Annual Pass is an amazing value. At a $12-per-month up-charge from the Preferred Pass, Seth gets more than his money's worth in free valet parking alone, and the free Express after 4 p.m. is especially useful when the parks are open late. (Even though it's officially valid only once per attraction per day, we've rarely been denied a re-ride and can usually bring a companion along.) The free Halloween Horror Nights pass isn't valid Fridays or Saturdays and can't be upgraded, which limits its value, but once redeemed it can be transferred to another person.

DISCOUNTS AT UNIVERSAL ORLANDO

UNIVERSAL ORLANDO PROVIDES DISCOUNTS ON TICKETS, dining, and lodging to members of many travel organizations, including automobile clubs such as AAA and CAA. Discounts are also available to Universal Orlando annual pass holders. This section is a guide to finding the best discounts for members of these groups and the general public.

Admission

In addition to the previously mentioned admission discounts, AAA members save $4–$5 on multiday tickets at the gate. Some regional AAA offices also sell discounted Universal Orlando passes to members in advance, but prices vary by area. The closest Auto Club South office to Universal Orlando is at 7339 West Sand Lake Road, Ste. 424, in Bay Hill; call ☎ 407-351-5610 for hours and directions. AAA South members can buy discounted tickets, annual passes, and vacation packages online at **aaa.com/universal**. *Note:* Effective 2015, you must purchase your park admission through AAA and show the Discounts and Rewards voucher included with your ticket to receive any AAA food or merchandise discounts inside Universal's parks.

*un*official **TIP**
If you're trying to book a room on the Universal Orlando website with an annual pass discount, enter promo code "APH" on the search screen to see passholder rates.

Costco Warehouse clubs sometimes sell discounted Universal Orlando tickets to members.

Active duty and retired members of the United States armed forces should visit **universalorlando.com/military** for exclusive deals on tickets and hotel packages. Universal Orlando tickets are available at most base Leisure Travel offices, as well as at Shades of Green at Disney World.

Resorts

Annual pass holders receive discounts of up to 30% on resort lodging, depending on availability. If you're staying at a Universal resort for two or more days, you may save enough on lodging to offset the cost of an annual pass for the adult booking the room. AAA members can book on-site rooms and vacation packages at a modest discount, usually between 5% and 25%. You must call AAA or Loews directly to get the discount; it cannot be applied online.

Cheaptickets.com and **orbitz.com** often offer discount codes for up to 20% their already-discounted Universal Orlando room rates; Google "Orlando hotel promo codes" or use a site such as **retailme not.com** to find the latest offers.

Check the **mousesavers.com** website, which lists seasonal and specialized discounts for Universal's resorts, such as discounts available to residents of certain states.

The Loews free YouFirst frequent-stay program doesn't provide cheaper prices, but it does feature free faster Internet access and room upgrades after a couple of visits. A similar program is offered at Hard Rock Hotel as Hard Rock Rewards. Note that the perks sometimes cannot be used in conjunction with discounted rates.

Dining

AAA members receive 10% off food and nonalcoholic beverages at most USF, IOA, and CityWalk restaurants (Emeril's and Bubba Gump excluded), as well as 10% off at the Hard Rock Hotel's Palm Restaurant for groups of up to seven. *Note:* Effective 2015, you must purchase your park admission through AAA and show the Discounts and Rewards voucher included with your ticket to receive any AAA food or merchandise discounts inside Universal's parks.

Universal Orlando Preferred Annual Pass holders receive 10% off food and nonalcoholic beverages at all theme park restaurants (except carts and kiosks), and at most CityWalk and Universal Orlando resort restaurants. Premier Annual Pass holders receive 15% off at all theme park restaurants (except carts and kiosks) and at most CityWalk restaurants, and 10% off at most Universal Orlando resort restaurants.

American Express members save 10% off all food and nonalcoholic beverage purchases on their AmEx card at Universal-owned quick- and table-service locations, excluding carts and kiosks.

Restaurant.com sometimes sells cut-price gift certificates to restaurants at Universal Orlando and in the surrounding area. Search the website for ZIP code 32819 to see what's currently available. Be sure to read the fine print before purchasing, as restrictions apply.

Merchandise

AAA members receive 10%–15% off most merchandise (excluding carts and kiosks) at Universal's theme parks and resorts. *Note:* Effective 2015, you must purchase your park admission through AAA and show the Discounts and Rewards voucher included with your ticket to receive any AAA food or merchandise discounts inside Universal's parks.

Universal Orlando Preferred Annual Pass holders receive 10% off all Universal-owned merchandise stores and carts throughout the resort. Premier Annual Pass holders receive 20% off.

American Express members save 10% off merchandise with a $50 minimum purchase, or 15% off on $75 or more, when using their AmEx card at Universal-owned shops (restrictions apply).

Entertainment and Other Discounts

AAA members receive 15% off spa treatments of $100 or more at Portofino's Mandara Spa. Preferred Annual Pass holders receive 15% off services, and Premier Pass holders save 20% (Monday–Thursday only; some services excluded).

AAA members receive 10% off Blue Man Group tickets in Tier 1 seating, while all annual pass holders (including Power Pass) receive 20% off; limit six seats per transaction.

AAA members get "buy one, get one free" on CityWalk Party Passes. Preferred Pass holders save 20% on party passes; Premier Pass holders get Party Passes free for themselves, and for one guest on Sunday–Thursday nights.

All annual pass holders (including Power Pass) receive 15% off an 18-hole round at Hollywood Drive-In Mini-Golf for up to five players.

All annual pass holders (including Power Pass) receive $3 off admission to AMC Universal Cineplex 20 with IMAX (valid after 4 p.m.).

At Universal Orlando's kennel, Premier Annual Pass holders receive 50% off the cost of boarding one pet per day. Additional pets stay at regular price (subject to availability).

Preferred and Premier Annual Pass holders save 25% off a standard one-day admission to Wet 'n Wild for themselves, or $20 off per regular annual pass for up to six people. They also save 10% in the Breakers Beach Shop (excluding sundries and beverages).

Finally, one sure way *not* to save money at Universal Orlando is by booking a package with tickets and lodging through Universal Orlando Vacations (☎ 877-801-9720; **universalorlandovacations .com**), the official travel company of Universal Orlando. It advertises packages with attractive-sounding rates, like "only $99 per adult per night," but when you break down the component parts, you'll find that you are breaking even, or even paying a few bucks more, for the convenience of having a single point of contact for your booking.

Occasionally, packages may include perks like a Harry Potter souvenir or breakfast reservations, but you are usually paying list price for extras that could be purchased à la carte. An exception is during special events such as the Celebration of Harry Potter convention, when private parties are only available bundled with a vacation package. The only other time that booking through Universal Orlando Vacations provides a genuine benefit is with the Early Park Admission offered for guests of partner off-site hotels; if you can't afford on-site accommodations, this is the best way to enter The Wizarding World early.

MAKING *the* MOST *of* YOUR TIME *and* MONEY *at* UNIVERSAL ORLANDO

THE CARDINAL RULES FOR SUCCESSFUL TOURING

MANY VISITORS DON'T HAVE three or four days to devote to Universal Orlando. Some are en route to other destinations or are visiting Universal as a sideline to their Disney World vacation. For these visitors, efficient touring is a must.

Even the most time-effective touring plan won't allow you to comprehensively cover both Universal theme parks in one day. Plan to allocate an entire day to each park. An exception to this is when the parks close at different times, allowing you to tour one park until closing and then proceed to another.

One-Day Touring

A comprehensive tour of *both* Universal Orlando parks in one day is virtually impossible. A comprehensive one-day tour of Universal Studios Florida *or* Islands of Adventure is possible but requires knowledge of the park, good planning, good navigation, and plenty of energy and endurance. One-day touring leaves little time for sit-down meals, prolonged browsing in shops, or lengthy breaks. One-day touring can be fun and rewarding, but allocating at least three full days to enjoy the resort is preferable.

Successfully touring USF or IOA in one day hinges on three rules:

1. Determine in Advance What You Really Want to See

Which attractions appeal to you most? Which ones would you like to experience if you have time left? What are you willing to forgo?

To help you set your touring priorities, we describe the theme parks and their attractions in detail in Parts Seven and Eight. In each description, we include the authors' evaluation of the attraction and the opinions of Universal Orlando guests expressed as star ratings. Five stars is the highest rating.

Finally, because attractions range from midway-type rides and walk-through exhibits to high-tech extravaganzas, we have developed a hierarchy of categories to pinpoint an attraction's magnitude:

SUPER-HEADLINERS   The best attractions the theme park has to offer. Mind-boggling in size, scope, and imagination. Represent the cutting edge of attraction technology and design.

HEADLINERS   Multimillion-dollar, full-scale, themed adventures and theater presentations. Modern in technology and design and employing a full range of special effects.

MAJOR ATTRACTIONS   More modestly themed adventures, but ones that incorporate state-of-the-art technologies. Or larger-scale attractions of older design.

MINOR ATTRACTIONS   Midway-type rides, small dark rides (cars on a track, zigzagging through the dark), small theater presentations, transportation rides, and elaborate walk-through attractions.

DIVERSIONS   Exhibits, both passive and interactive. Includes playgrounds, video arcades, and street theater.

Though not every attraction fits neatly into these descriptions, the categories provide a comparison of attraction size and scope. Remember that bigger and more elaborate doesn't always mean better or more popular. Flight of the Hippogriff, a kiddie coaster in The Wizarding World of Harry Potter–Hogsmeade, often attracts a longer line than the larger Dragon Challenge nearby. Likewise, for many young children, no attraction, regardless of size, surpasses the Caro-Seuss-el merry-go-round.

2. Arrive Early! Arrive Early! Arrive Early!

This is the single most important key to efficient touring and avoiding long lines. First thing in the morning, there are no lines and fewer people. The same four rides you experience in one hour in early morning can take as long as three hours after 10:30 a.m. Eat breakfast before you arrive; don't waste prime touring time sitting in a restaurant.

The earlier a park opens, the greater your advantage. This is because most vacationers won't rise early and get to a park before it opens. Fewer people are willing to make an 8 a.m. opening than a 9 a.m. opening. If you visit during midsummer, arrive at the turnstile 30–45 minutes before you are eligible to enter. During holiday periods, arrive 45–60 minutes early.

3. Avoid Bottlenecks

Helping you avoid bottlenecks is what *The Unofficial Guide* is about. This involves being able to predict where, when, and why bottlenecks occur. Concentrations of hungry people create gridlocks at restaurants during lunch and dinner; concentrations of people moving toward the exit near closing time cause gift shops en route to clog; concentrations of visitors at new and popular rides, and at rides slow to load and unload, create logjams and long lines.

Our solution for avoiding bottlenecks: touring plans for the Islands of Adventure and Universal Studios Florida. We also provide detailed information on rides and performances, enabling you to estimate how long you may have to wait in line and allowing you to compare rides for their crowd capacity. All touring plans are in the back of this book, following the index. Plans for Universal Studios Florida begin on page 368, and for Islands of Adventure, on page 371. One-day and two-day touring plans for both USF and IOA are provided for those with park-to-park admission.

WHAT'S A QUEUE?

THOUGH IT'S NOT COMMONLY USED IN THE UNITED STATES, *queue* (pronounced "cue") is the universal English word for a line, such as one in which you wait to cash a check at the bank or to board a ride at a theme park. Queuing theory, a mathematical area of specialization within the field of operations research, studies and models how lines work. Because *The Unofficial Guide* draws heavily on this discipline, we use some of its terminology. In addition to the noun, the verb *to queue* means "to get in line," and a *queuing area* is a "waiting area that accommodates a line." When guests decline to join a queue because they perceive that the wait is too long, they're said to balk.

OF UTMOST IMPORTANCE: READ THIS!

IN ANALYZING READER SURVEYS, we were astonished by the percentage of readers who *don't* use our touring plans. Scientifically tested and proven, these plans can save you four entire hours or more of waiting in line in a single day—four fewer hours of standing, four hours freed up to do something fun. Our groundbreaking research that created the touring plans has been the subject of front-page articles in *The Dallas Morning News* and *The New York Times* and has been cited in numerous scholarly journals. So why would you not use them?

We get a ton of reader mail—98% of it positive—commenting on our touring plans. From an Edmonds, Washington, family who used our touring plans for Islands of Adventure:

> *It worked like a charm! I've always wondered how it feels to follow your plans not ever having seen the park before, and now I know— it was easy!*

TOURING PLANS: WHAT THEY ARE AND HOW THEY WORK

FROM THE FIRST EDITION OF The Unofficial Guide, minimizing our readers' waits in line has been a top priority. We know from our research and that of others that theme park patrons measure overall satisfaction based on the number of attractions they're able to experience during a visit: the more attractions, the better. Thus, we developed and offered our readers field-tested touring plans that allow them to experience as many attractions as possible with the least amount of waiting in line.

Our touring plans have always been based on theme park traffic flow, attraction capacity, the maximum time a guest is willing to wait (called a balking constraint), walking distance between attractions, and waiting-time data collected at every attraction in every park, every day of the year. The plans are derived from a combinatorial model (for anyone who cares) that married the well-known assignment problem of linear programming with queuing (waiting-line) theory. The model approximated the most time-efficient sequence in which to visit the attractions of a specific park.

As sophisticated as our model may sound, we recognized that it was cumbersome and slow, and it didn't approximate the "perfect" touring plan as closely as we desired. Moreover, advances in computer technology and science, specifically in the field of genetic algorithms, demonstrated that it wouldn't be long before a model, or program, was created that would leave ours in the dust.

Our response was to team up during the mid-1990s with Len Testa, a scientist and computer programmer who was working in the field of evolutionary algorithms and who, coincidentally, was a Disney junkie. Marrying our many years of collecting theme park observations and data to Len's vision and programming expertise, we developed a state-of-the-art program for creating nearly perfect touring plans. It has been a process of evolution and refinement, but in each year of its development, the new program came closer to beating, and eventually surpassed, the results of our long-lived model.

The Unofficial Guide touring plan program contains two algorithms that allow it to quickly analyze tens of millions of possible plans in a very short time. (An algorithm is to a computer what a recipe is to a chef. Just as a chef takes specific steps to make a cake, a computer takes specific steps to process information. Those steps, when grouped, form an algorithm.) The program can analyze standby wait times and estimate the time saved by using Universal Express Passes. The software can also schedule rest breaks throughout the day and estimate walking times to meals if you specify a preferred restaurant. Numerous other features are available, many of which we'll discuss in the next section.

Over the years, this research has been recognized by the travel industry and academe, having been cited by such diverse sources as *The New York Times, USA Today, Travel Weekly, Bottom Line, Money, Operations Research Forum,* CBS News, Fox News, the BBC, the Travel Channel, *The Dallas Morning News,* and *The Atlanta Journal-Constitution.* The methodology behind our touring plans was also used as a case study in the 2010 book *Numbers Rule Your World* by Kaiser Fung.

The program, however, is only part of what's needed to create a good touring plan. Good data is also important. With the introduction of our Lines mobile app, we've been able to collect wait times from every theme park every day of the year—more than 5 million to date. We supplement this data with actual wait times submitted by Lines users too, and use all of it to calibrate our touring-plan models.

Customize Your Touring Plans

The attractions included in our touring plans are the best and most popular as determined by our expert team and reader surveys. If you've never been to Universal Orlando, we suggest using the plans in this book. They'll ensure that you see the best Universal attractions with as little waiting in line as possible.

If you're a return visitor, your favorite attractions may be different. One way to customize the plans is to go to **touringplans.com** or use our Lines app to create personalized versions. Tell the software the date, time, and park you've chosen to visit, along with the attractions you want to see. The plan will tell you, for your specific travel date and time, the exact order in which to visit the attractions to minimize your waits in line. Lines also supports "child swap" (see page 173) on thrill rides. Besides rides, you can schedule shows, meals, breaks, character greetings, and more. You can even tell Lines how fast you plan to walk, and whether or not you'll be using Universal Express, and it will make the necessary adjustments.

Alternatively, some changes are simple enough to make on your own. If a plan calls for an attraction in which you're not interested, simply skip it and move on to the next one. You can also substitute similar attractions in the same area of the park. If a plan calls for, say, riding Cat in the Hat and you'd rather not, but you would enjoy the Caro-Seuss-el (which is not on the plan), then go ahead and substitute that for Cat. As long as the substitution is a similar attraction—substituting a show for a ride won't work—and is pretty close by the attraction called for in the touring plan, you won't compromise the plan's overall effectiveness.

OVERVIEW OF THE TOURING PLANS

OUR TOURING PLANS ARE STEP-BY-STEP GUIDES for seeing as much as possible with a minimum of standing in line, and without needing Universal Express Passes. They're designed to help you avoid crowds and bottlenecks on any day of the year. The plans will save time on days when attendance is lighter (see "Trying to Reason with the Tourist Season," page 28), but on those days, they won't be as critical to successful touring.

What You Can Realistically Expect from the Touring Plans

Though we present one-day/two-park plans for Universal Orlando, Universal Studios Florida and Islands of Adventure together have more attractions than you can reasonably expect to see in one day. You can either see all of The Wizarding World in depth, or highlights of the rest of the resort, but not both in a single visit. Because our two-day plans for Universal Orlando are the most comprehensive, efficient, and relaxing, we strongly recommend them over the one-day/two-park plans. However, if you must cram your visit to both parks into a single day, the one-day plans will allow you to see as much as is humanly possible.

Variables That Affect the Success of the Touring Plans

The plans' success will be affected by how quickly you move from ride to ride; when and how many refreshment and restroom breaks you take; when, where, and how you eat meals; and your ability (or lack thereof) to find your way around. Smaller groups almost always move faster than larger groups, and parties of adults generally cover more ground than families with young children. Child swap (page 173), also known as rider swap, baby swap, or switching off, inhibits families with little ones from moving as expeditiously as possible among attractions.

Plus, some folks simply cannot conform to the plans' "early to rise" conditions, as this reader from Cleveland Heights, Ohio, recounts:

> Our touring plans were thrown totally off by one member who could not be on time for opening. Even in October, this made a huge difference in our ability to see attractions without waiting.

And a family from Centerville, Ohio, says:

> The toughest thing about your touring plans was getting the rest of the family to stay with them. Getting them to pass by attractions to hit something across the park was no easy task.

If you have young children, the appearance of a cartoon character (especially Dora the Explorer or the Minions) can stop a touring plan in its tracks, and even adults will detour to snap a selfie with Optimus Prime or the Hogwarts Express conductor. While some characters stroll the parks, it's equally common that they assemble in a specific venue where families queue up for photos and autographs. Meeting characters and getting autographs aren't as popular pastimes at Universal as at Disney, but can still burn valuable touring time. If your kids collect character autographs, you need to anticipate these interruptions by including character greetings when creating your online touring plans, or else negotiate some understanding with your children about when you'll collect autographs.

Some things are beyond your control. Chief among these are the manner and timing of bringing a particular ride to capacity. For example, Harry Potter and the Escape from Gringotts, an indoor roller coaster in Universal Studios Florida, has nine trains, one of which is kept as a spare. On any given morning, it may begin operation with four or five trains running, and then add up to seven or eight as needed. If the waiting line builds rapidly before operators go to full capacity, you could have a long wait, even in early morning.

A variable that can give your touring plans a boost is the singles line (see page 62), as this English reader explains:

We used the touring plans to the letter and found that not only did they work, but they worked even better in conjunction with single-rider queues. The only rides that we queued up for normally were ones with a 20-minute-or-less queue time and wet rides.

Another variable is your arrival time for a theater show. You'll wait from the time you arrive until the end of the presentation in progress. Thus, if a show starts every 30 minutes and you arrive 1 minute after it has begun, your wait will be 29 minutes. Conversely, if you arrive just before the next show begins, your wait will be only a minute or two.

While we realize that following the plans isn't always easy, we nevertheless recommend continuous, expeditious touring until around noon. After that, breaks and diversions won't affect the plans significantly.

What to Do if You Lose the Thread

We suggest sticking to the plans religiously, especially in the mornings, if you're visiting during busy times. The consequence of touring spontaneity in peak season is hours of standing in line. When using the plans, however, relax and always be prepared for surprises and setbacks. If unforeseen events interrupt a plan:

1. If you're following a touring plan in our **Lines** app (**touringplans.com /lines**), just press "Optimize" when you're ready to start touring again. Lines will figure out the best possible plan for the remainder of your day.

2. If you're following a printed touring plan, skip a step on the plan for every 20 minutes' delay. For example, if you lose your wallet and spend an hour hunting for it, skip three steps and pick up from there.

3. Forget the plan and organize the remainder of the day using the standby wait times listed in the Lines app.

Clip-Out Touring Plans

For your convenience, we've prepared graphical clip-out copies of all touring plans. These pocket versions combine touring-plan itineraries with maps and directions. Select the plan appropriate for your party, and get familiar with it. Then clip the pocket version from the back of this guide and carry it with you as a quick reference at the theme park.

Will the Plans Continue to Work Once the Secret Is Out?

Yes! First, all the plans require that a patron be there when a park opens. Many Universal Orlando patrons simply won't get up early while on vacation. Second, less than 2% of any day's attendance has been exposed to the plans—too few to affect results. Last, most groups tailor the plans, skipping rides or shows according to taste.

How Frequently Are the Touring Plans Revised?

We revise them every year, and updates are always available at **touringplans.com.** Be prepared for surprises, though: Opening procedures and showtimes may change, for example, and you can't predict when an attraction might break down.

Tour Groups on Steroids

We've discovered that tour groups of up to 200 people sometimes use our plans. Unless your party is as large as that tour group, this development shouldn't alarm you. Because tour groups are big, they move slowly and have to stop periodically to collect stragglers. The tour guide also has to accommodate the unpredictability of five dozen or so bladders. In short, you should have no problem passing a group after the initial encounter.

"Bouncing Around"

Some readers object to crisscrossing a theme park as our touring plans sometimes require. A woman from Decatur, Georgia, told us she "got dizzy from all the bouncing around." Believe us, we empathize.

We've worked hard over the years to eliminate the need to crisscross a theme park in our touring plans. (In fact, our customized software can minimize walking instead of waiting in line, if that's important to you.) Occasionally, however, it's possible to save a lot of time in line with a few extra minutes of walking.

The reasons for this are varied. Sometimes a park is designed intentionally to require walking. In Universal Studios Florida, for example, the most popular attraction (Harry Potter and the Escape from Gringotts in Diagon Alley) is placed at the farthest corner from the front gate, so that guests are more evenly distributed throughout the day. Other times, you may be visiting just after a new attraction has opened that everyone wants to try. In that case, a special trip to visit the new attraction may be required earlier in the day than normal, to avoid longer waits later. And live shows, especially at USF, sometimes have performance schedules so at odds with each other (and the rest of the park's schedule) that orderly touring is impossible.

If you want to experience headliner attractions in one day without long waits, you can see those first (requires crisscrossing the park), use Universal Express and single-rider lines (if available), or hope to squeeze in visits during parades and the last hour the park is open (may not work).

If you have two days to visit Universal Orlando, use the two-day touring plans (see pages 374–381). These spread the popular attractions over two mornings and work great even when the parks close early.

Touring Plan Rejection

Some folks don't respond well to the regimentation of a touring plan. If you encounter this problem with someone in your party, roll with the punches as this Maryland couple did:

> *The rest of the group was not receptive to the use of the touring plans. I think they all thought I was being a little too regimented about planning this vacation. Rather than argue, I left the touring plans behind as we ventured off for the parks. You can guess the outcome. We took our camcorder with us and watched the movies when we returned home. About every 5 minutes or so, there's a shot of us all gathered around a park map trying to decide what to do next.*

Finally, as a Connecticut woman alleges, the touring plans are incompatible with some readers' bladders as well as their personalities:

> *When you write those day schedules next year, can you schedule bathroom breaks in there too? You expect us to be at a certain ride at a certain time and with no stops in between. The schedules are a problem if you are a laid-back, slow-moving, careful detail noticer. What were you thinking when you made these schedules?*

Before you injure your urinary tract, feel free to deviate from the touring plan as necessary to heed the call of nature. If you are using a customized plan in Lines, you can build in as many breaks (bathroom or otherwise) as you like, and the optimizer will plan around them.

WHAT TO EXPECT WHEN YOU ARRIVE AT THE PARKS (ROPE DROP)

BECAUSE MOST TOURING PLANS ARE BASED ON being present when the theme park opens, you need to know about opening procedures. Universal Orlando on-site resort transportation to the parks via buses and water taxis begins two hours before official opening, or one hour before Early Park Admission (see page 54). Guests staying on-site during peak periods will want to catch the first ride of the morning (or start walking around the time it leaves) to be the first into The Wizarding World during the early-entry period. Off-season visitors should arrive at the gates 10–20 minutes before Early Park Admission begins.

The parking garage also opens two hours before official opening, but on days of exceptional attendance (like the grand opening of Diagon Alley, or the free One Direction concert in 2014), the garage has opened as early as 3 a.m. If you are driving to the resort and not eligible for Early Park Admission, plan to arrive at the Universal parking garage 45–60 minutes prior to official opening. If you need to purchase park admission, add another 15 minutes to that. It takes approximately 10–15 minutes to walk from the parking garage to the parks' entrance turnstiles, so you should arrive at the turnstiles 30–45 minutes before the park opens.

There are fewer turnstiles at Universal Studios Florida and Islands of Adventure than at Disney's Magic Kingdom or Epcot, and the turnstiles are not spread out over as much ground. Consequently, lines tend to be evenly distributed at each turnstile. If you see a shorter line, however, get in it, especially if portable ticket scanners (which are usually faster than the fixed turnstiles) have been set up in front of the center gate.

Universal's turnstiles use a biometric scanner that will record your fingerprint when using your ticket for the first time. Be sure to remember which finger you used to speed reentry. You'll also be asked to sign your pass, so that you don't mix it up with those of other family members. Universal's finger scanners don't seem nearly as efficient as the ones Disney uses, so be prepared for slowdowns at entry.

Rope Drop at Universal Studios Florida

USF team members select a "first family" from the early risers at the turnstiles each morning, and usher them in a few minutes early to open the park with an old-fashioned movie clapboard. It's no Magic Kingdom character welcome, but it is a cute moment worth catching if you can.

Once the gates open, there is no mad dash for Diagon Alley, nor is a literal rope dropped. When USF's turnstiles open for Early Park Admission, resort guests walk straight toward Despicable Me and are escorted to The Wizarding World via San Francisco. Day guests are diverted to the right down Hollywood, where they are held until shortly before the official opening. At that time, they are walked to Diagon Alley through Springfield.

On days when USF does not officially offer Early Park Admission, the gates may still open 30 minutes before opening, with Despicable Me, *Shrek 4-D,* and possibly Rip Ride Rockit running for all early guests. Hotel guests are permitted to walk to Diagon Alley as soon as they enter the park, while day guests are held near *Shrek*'s exit until about 15 minutes before park opening. Guests can enter the Escape from Gringotts queue before official opening, but the ride may not begin running until park opening (or a few minutes before) on non-EPA mornings.

Most of the crowd will head for The Wizarding World of Harry Potter's Gringotts ride, which usually sees its longest waits between opening and early afternoon. Despicable Me, located a short distance past the entrance, also attracts large crowds, as do Transformers: The Ride 3-D and Hollywood Rip Ride Rockit. A smaller number of visitors will head for The Simpsons Ride or Revenge of the Mummy, but these attractions usually don't get crowded until an hour or two after the park has opened.

Rope Drop at Islands of Adventure

At the end of Port of Entry, hotel guests are walked to the right through Seuss Landing to Hogsmeade, while day guests are sent to Marvel

Super Hero Island until opening time. Once released into the park, most guests turn counterclockwise through Seuss Landing and make a beeline for The Wizarding World of Harry Potter–Hogsmeade as soon as the park is open. Locals who've already had their fill of Potter, as well as coaster fans, will head clockwise for The Incredible Hulk Coaster and The Amazing Adventures of Spider-Man.

Unless you have early entry, our advice is to see Hulk and Spider-Man first and save The Wizarding World until late in the day. Note that when one park opens before the other, guests arriving on the first Hogwarts Express train from the early-entry park will reach the opposite Wizarding World at the same time or slightly after those entering from the front gates.

EARLY PARK ADMISSION (EARLY ENTRY)

THE MOST VALUABLE PERK AVAILABLE to all Universal on-site resort hotel guests is Early Park Admission (EPA, also sometimes referred to as Early Entry), which grants entry to The Wizarding World of Harry Potter one hour before the general public. This perk is given for free to all guests staying at a Universal Orlando on-site hotel, including those staying at Cabana Bay. In addition, guests holding certain designated vacation packages purchased through Universal Orlando Vacations (☎ 877-801-9720; **universalorlandovacations.com**) and including both accommodations at an off-site Universal partner hotel *and* theme park admission are also allowed in early.

Which park you may enter on any particular day, and which attractions will be operating, are at Universal's discretion and will vary with the attendance seasons. The turnstiles to the park(s) participating in early entry will open 60–90 minutes before the official opening time. Both hotel and day guests will be admitted to the park, and each EPA-eligible guest (including children) will need to show his or her own room key to pass beyond the park's entry plaza during the early admission hour. Guests not eligible for Early Park Admission will be held in an alternative area to await the official opening time.

During Early Park Admission, all of the attractions, shops, and restaurants in the participating Wizarding World area should be open, along with select attractions outside the Harry Potter area. Early Park Admission, when available at Universal Studios Florida, is by far the best time to ride Escape from Gringotts without waiting more than an hour in the standby queue, as this father from New York City experienced:

We got to the Universal Studios turnstiles at 10 minutes before 6 [for 7 a.m. Early Park Admission] and had only five people in front of us. Soon there were plenty behind us, however! They let us in at about 6:20, and we were among the first 100–150 people to enter Diagon Alley and subsequently Gringotts. . . . We essentially walked onto the ride, slowed only by our amazed awe at walking through the Gringotts lobby and seeing all the astonishing attractions in the line.

We were through so quickly that we immediately got in the singles line and literally walked on the ride a second time, and then a third time with the singles line, which by this time was backed up a bit toward the steps leading to the loading platform, resulting in about a 20-minute wait. It was now 8 a.m. and we had been on the ride three times. The non-resort guests were now streaming into Diagon Alley to be welcomed by a standby entrance to Gringotts, which was marked 180 minutes.

However, if the Gringotts or Forbidden Journey attractions are not operational when early entry begins, skip them and try again late in the day; by the time it begins running in the morning, there will be a huge backlog of riders.

Early Park Admission procedures seem to change often and arbitrarily with no warning. Ask at your hotel's front desk to find out what opening procedures are in effect during your visit.

IOA-Only Early Park Admission (Off-Season Standard)

During most of the year, only Islands of Adventure (and not Universal Studios Florida) will admit eligible guests for Early Park Admission.

The following attractions should be available during IOA-only Early Park Admission:

- Dragon Challenge
- Flight of the Hippogriff
- Harry Potter and the Forbidden Journey
- Ollivanders Wand Shop (Hogsmeade)

In addition, on days that USF does not offer Early Park Admission, it will still unofficially open 30 minutes before the scheduled time, with the following attractions open for all guests (hotel and off-site alike):

- Despicable Me Minion Mayhem
- Hollywood Rip Ride Rockit (seasonally)
- *Shrek 4-D* (seasonally)
- Transformers: The Ride 3-D (seasonally)

Guests entering USF early may also enter the queue for Escape from Gringotts, though the ride itself usually won't begin running until just before the park officially opens.

The Hogwarts Express train from Hogsmeade Station should begin operating up to 30 minutes before USF officially opens for the day. The first trainload of guests riding from IOA will enter Diagon Alley around the same time or shortly after the first guests entering through USF's front gates.

USF-Only Early Park Admission (Off-Season Alternate)

During some off-peak periods, Early Park Admission may be confined to Universal Studios Florida. USF-only early entry was offered for the first few months after Diagon Alley's debut summer but is not currently scheduled to return, though it could be reinstated without warning at Universal's whim.

The following attractions should be available during USF-only Early Park Admission:

- Despicable Me Minion Mayhem
- Harry Potter and the Escape from Gringotts
- Ollivanders Wand Shop (Diagon Alley)

The Hogwarts Express train from King's Cross Station will not begin running to The Wizarding World of Harry Potter–Hogsmeade in Islands of Adventure until 10 minutes before both parks have officially opened for the day. The first trainload of guests riding from USF will enter Hogsmeade around the same time or shortly after the first guests entering through IOA's front gates.

Two-Park Early Park Admission (Peak Season)

Universal Orlando only guarantees early admission to one park per day, but during the busiest times of the year—primarily the weeks around Easter, Thanksgiving, and Christmas—Universal offers Early Park Admission to The Wizarding World of Harry Potter areas at both Universal Studios Florida (Diagon Alley) and Islands of Adventure (Hogsmeade).

However, at times, only the front gates of one park may open during Early Park Admission. To enter the other park during Early Park Admission, guests may be required to use a park-to-park ticket to ride the Hogwarts Express train from one Wizarding World to the other. When both parks are scheduled to open at the same time, the Hogwarts Express will begin running when Early Park Admission starts. When one park opens later than the other, the train will begin running up to 30 minutes before the second park opens for Early Park Admission.

The following attractions should be available during peak season Early Park Admission:

UNIVERSAL STUDIOS FLORIDA

- Despicable Me Minion Mayhem
- Harry Potter and the Escape from Gringotts
- Hogwarts Express (King's Cross Station) (only if IOA is open)
- Ollivanders Wand Shop (Diagon Alley)

ISLANDS OF ADVENTURE

- The Cat in the Hat Ride (seasonally)
- Dragon Challenge
- Flight of the Hippogriff
- Harry Potter and the Forbidden Journey
- Ollivanders Wand Shop (Hogsmeade)
- Hogwarts Express: Hogsmeade Station (only if USF is open)

Annual Pass Holder Early Park Admission

On certain days during slower times of year, Universal Orlando histori-cally has allowed its annual-pass holders to enjoy some form of Early Park Admission. Check Universal's annual-pass holder website for cur-rent promotions.

In late 2014–mid-2015, all pass holders could use Early Park Admission to The Wizarding World of Harry Potter Monday–Friday during the following dates: September 1–30, November 3–14, Novem-ber 18–21, December 1–18, and May 1–29 (except Memorial Day).

UNIVERSAL EXPRESS

LIKE DISNEY WORLD'S FASTPASS+, Universal Express is a system whereby guests can "skip the line" and experience an attraction via a special queue with little or no waiting. Guests approach the marked Universal Express entrance at participating attractions, present their Universal Express Pass, and proceed to ride with a significantly reduced wait—usually 20% or less of the posted standby time, or no more than a 15–20 minute wait.

There are three major differences between Disney's FastPass+ and Universal Express. While Disney's system requires scheduling your ride reservation hours or days ahead of time, Universal Express involves no advance planning; simply visit any eligible operating attraction whenever you choose, no return time windows required. Also, FastPass+ is only offered at a select list of designated attrac-tions, while more than 90% of rides at Universal (with a couple of high-profile exceptions, as discussed on page 58) accept Express. Finally, unlike FastPass+, Universal Express is not free.

unofficial **TIP**
Universal Express is not valid at the headliner Harry Potter attractions: Forbidden Journey, Escape from Gringotts, and Hogwarts Express.

Three versions of Universal Express are available, all of which require you to cough up more money beyond your park admission:

UNIVERSAL EXPRESS PASS   Available for pur-chase online or in the parks, allowing one person one ride on each attraction that participates in Universal Express.

UNIVERSAL EXPRESS UNLIMITED PASS   Available for purchase online or in the parks (either bundled with admission or separately), allowing one person an unlimited number of rides on any attraction that participates in Universal Express.

ON-SITE HOTEL UNIVERSAL EXPRESS UNLIMITED PASS   Included for all guests at the three luxury Universal Resort hotels (Cabana Bay Beach Resort and Sapphire Falls excluded) at no extra cost, allowing each person staying on-site an unlimited number of rides on any attrac-tion that participates in Universal Express.

No matter which version of Universal Express you use, it works the same: Present your pass to a greeter at each attraction entrance, get it scanned for verification, and enjoy your expedited entertainment. At shows, you can show your pass for priority seating 15 minutes before showtime, but that's less of a perk because Universal's large theaters rarely fill up.

It's worth noting that, while almost all the Express queues are themed, in a few cases (Revenge of the Mummy and Men in Black Alien Attack at USF; Doctor Doom's Fearfall and Dragon Challenge at IOA), they sacrifice significant scenic elements and story setup that the standby line sees.

Finally, be aware that neither Harry Potter and the Forbidden Journey nor Pteranodon Flyers at IOA is a Universal Express attraction, nor is Harry Potter and the Escape from Gringotts at USF or the interpark Hogwarts Express train. Further, all of the Express types (including the free passes for resort guests) are valid only during regular operating hours and not during separately ticketed events. Separate Express Passes are available at additional cost for special events such as Rock The Universe and Halloween Horror Nights.

Universal Express and Express Unlimited for Purchase

Anyone can purchase Universal Express for one or both parks and for either single (one ride only on each participating attraction) or unlimited use, and from one to four days. The number of Express Passes is limited each day, and they can sell out. Increase your chances of securing passes by buying and printing them at home from Universal's website. They are available up to eight months in advance at **tickets.universalorlando .com/ticket-store/purchasetickets.aspx.** You'll need to know when you plan on using it, though, because prices vary depending on the date.

Universal Express Pass prices range from $35 for a one-park single-use pass in slow season to $150 for a two-park unlimited pass on a holiday; the top-tier passes are significantly cheaper when bundled with a park-to-park multiday pass. Incidentally, the online calendar of Express Pass prices is a great indicator of how crowded Universal will be on any given day. Visit the above link and click "choose dates"; the more expensive the passes, the more packed the park will be.

You can also buy Universal Express at the theme parks' ticket windows, just outside the front gates, but it's faster to do so inside the parks. At Universal Studios Florida, it's available at Super Silly Stuff; at Islands of Adventure, you can buy Universal Express at Jurassic Outfitters, Toon Extra, and the Marvel Alterniverse Store. Universal also sells Express from freestanding kiosks that seem to proliferate around the parks like mushrooms during peak seasons.

Universal Express for Resort Guests

This program allows guests at Universal's three original luxury resorts (Cabana Bay and Sapphire Falls excluded) to bypass the regular line and use the Express entrance any time and as often as desired. Guests must first use their room keys at a computerized kiosk in their hotel lobby to obtain photo-bearing On-Site Hotel Universal Express Unlimited Pass cards.

Universal Express for resort guests is available from the moment of check-in until closing time on the day of checkout. And even though check-in time at Universal's on-site hotels isn't until 4 p.m., guests can retrieve room keys and Express Passes as early in the morning as they are able to arrive, and may drop their luggage in the lobby and head to the parks until their room is ready. Therefore, a single night's stay on-site yields two full days of Universal Express access. This perk far surpasses any benefit accorded to guests of Disney resorts; combined with the hour of Early Park Admission to The Wizarding World, it helps make touring Universal Orlando a remarkably low-stress experience for on-site guests, even during peak attendance periods.

A father from Snellville, Georgia, did the math and discovered that it was cheaper for his family to stay at a Universal resort than buy Universal Express:

> The benefits of staying on-property are worth it, with early entry to The Wizarding World and unlimited Express privileges at both parks. We got a room at the Royal Pacific Resort for $349 on a Saturday night, which allowed us to use Universal Express Saturday and Sunday. The room cost $43.63 per person per day, while an [à la carte] Express Pass this same weekend would have cost $56 per person per day, and we still would have had to pay for a hotel.

Is Universal Express Worth It?

No matter when you use it, Universal Express will significantly reduce the amount of time you spend waiting in queues at Universal Orlando. But whether or not that time saving is "worth it" depends on the season you visit, hours of park operation, and crowd levels.

During busy periods, Universal Express users should wait no more than 15–20 minutes for a ride, even when the standby wait is well more than an hour; the one exception is Despicable Me Minion Mayhem, whose Express queue can approach an hour at peak times due to its limited guest capacity. That's a significant time savings and may make the difference between seeing all your favorite headliners in a single day or going home disappointed.

During slow periods, Express users should experience little to no wait at most attractions and can practically walk on to most rides. However, the standby waits will typically top out between 15 and 30 minutes at these times, making the total minutes saved with Express much less impressive.

Attendance has jumped at both parks since the opening of each Harry Potter land, especially at Universal Studios Florida now that Diagon Alley has opened. However, the big-ticket Harry Potter rides in Hogsmeade and Diagon Alley don't participate in Universal

Express, so you don't get to cut in line at Universal's most in-demand attractions.

If you want to sleep in and arrive at a park after opening, Express is an effective, albeit expensive, way to avoid long lines at the non-Potter headliner attractions, especially during holidays and busy times. If, however, you arrive 30 minutes before park opening and you use our touring plans (see pages 368–381), you should experience the lowest possible waits at both USF and IOA.

If you are not eligible for free Express Passes, we encourage you to try the touring plans first, but if waits for rides become intolerable, you can always buy Express in the parks (provided they haven't sold out, an infrequent occurrence).

A New York mom had a trouble-free experience, but she questions the value of the investment:

> We bought Universal Express, but it was neither necessary nor consistently effective. By arriving at park opening, we were able to see many attractions right away without needing the passes at all. They helped on about three attractions between the two parks—a poor return for an investment of $156, but it was like life insurance: good to have just in case. On Dudley Do-Right, we still had to wait 30 minutes even with Express, whereas with Disney's free FastPass+ we never waited more than 5 minutes for an attraction. The only aspect of UE that was better than FP+ is that touring order was unaffected: UE could be used whenever you first approached an attraction instead of your having to come back later.

On the other hand, this Kansas City family thought very highly of the Unlimited Express Passes included in their Royal Pacific Resort stay:

> The Express Pass that you get free by staying at one of the resorts is a lifesaver. We never waited in line more than 15 minutes, and it was usually closer to 5. For my roller coaster–loving family, this was great. We didn't have a scheduled time to ride anything like Disney, so we could stray from our plan and re-ride Hulk or Rockit over and over again, which we did. Once again, I cannot say enough about the Express Pass.

Finally, you'll want to devise a convenient way to keep track of your pass, as this Bluffton, Indiana, dad found out a little too late:

> I wish I'd known ahead of time to bring a lanyard to hang our Universal Express Pass on.

How Universal Express Affects Crowd Conditions at Attractions

Guests using Universal Express don't have to modify their touring behavior in any way; simply visit any attraction at will, and enjoy the shorter waits. However, the Express effect can be somewhat less salutatory for guests without Express. The standby and Express queues at each attraction meet up shortly before the boarding area, and attendants are supposed to merge them so that Express guests wait 15 minutes or less, without the standby guests' wait being inflated beyond the estimate posted outside.

Typically, this means about half of each ride's capacity is dedicated to Express guests, which ordinarily keeps both queues flowing smoothly. The catch is that, because Universal Express guests (unlike Disney FastPass+ users) don't schedule ride times in advance, the number of them waiting in a queue at any given time is highly variable and unpredictable. As a result, an unexpected backlog of Express guests—either because of a sudden influx of pass users or a temporary technical breakdown that pauses the line—can force Universal to increase the ratio of Express to standby, slowing non-Express guests' progress to a crawl.

While great news for Universal Express users, this can dramatically affect crowd movement (and touring-plan usage) for those without it, as a woman from Yorktown, Virginia, writes:

> People in the Express line were let in at a rate of about 10 to 1 over the regular-line folks. This created bottlenecks and long waits for people who didn't have the Express privilege at the very times when it's supposed to be easier to get around!

If you encounter this situation while waiting standby, simply grit your teeth and take some deep yoga breaths; the situation normally clears up quickly, and your total wait should still be approximately as originally advertised. In case of a major traffic jam where the standby line stops moving altogether, calculate how much time you've invested already, and consider hopping out of line and returning later when things are running more smoothly. And for those who really can't stand watching Express guests pass them by: If you can't beat 'em, join 'em.

U-BOT

THIS RIDE-RESERVATION SYSTEM also works much like Disney's FastPass+ but incorporates the small U-Bot device. These water-resistant egg-shaped gadgets (provided by Accesso, the same company behind the FlashPass and Q-Bot services at Six Flags and other regional parks) closely resemble the Tamagotchi virtual pet toys that were briefly popular in the 1990s.

Guests can purchase access to the device at an Express kiosk near the front of each park (buying access online is currently not an option). Once you have your U-Bot, you can use the small built-in screen to reserve ride times for any Universal Express attraction. Note that you can make only one reservation at a time; you must use or cancel your first reservation before making another.

Your minimum wait time before you can experience an attraction with U-Bot will be the same as the ride's current standby wait; that is, if a ride's posted wait time is one hour, you can enter the attraction any time one hour or more after making your reservation. The U-Bot will vibrate and display a message telling you when it's time to ride. Next, you take your U-Bot to the ride's Express entrance, where the attraction greeter will scan your device and admit you to the Express queue.

U-Bot costs considerably less than an Express Pass (usually by about $10–$20 per person), and a single U-Bot can be used by up to six guests, though the full per-person price still applies. U-Bot can be rented for either park and can be activated for one reservation per ride per day, or for unlimited reservations per ride (at an additional cost, of course). When renting a U-Bot, you'll be asked to provide a credit card, which will be charged $50 if you fail to return your device to a designated location near the park exit at the end of the day.

Despite the lower price and geeky tech appeal of the U-Bots, they aren't nearly as popular as Universal Express Passes, largely because they lack the latter's "use anytime" ease. If managed efficiently, U-Bot can help cut time spent standing in queues, but only if you can slip into another attraction while waiting for your next reservation time to come around. Otherwise, most visitors are better off saving their money, or investing a little more in Express.

SINGLE-RIDER LINES

ONE TIME-SAVING OPTION available to all Universal Orlando guests without extra charge is the single-rider (or "singles") line. Several attractions at USF and IOA have this special line for guests traveling alone, or at least willing to be temporarily separated from their companions. Single riders wait in a separate queue and are slipped into vacant seats left by large groups without (theoretically) impacting the other lines. Disney also offers single-rider queues, but at fewer attractions across all four WDW parks than Universal has in their two, making it a great alternative for those unable or unwilling to cough up the dough for Universal Express Passes.

The singles line is often just as fast as the Express line. However, because the speed of the singles line is highly dependent on the flow of odd-numbered parties through the other queues, the wait time can be extremely unpredictable. At some times we've walked onto Forbidden Journey via the singles line when the standby wait time was more than an hour; at others we've stood longer in Hollywood Rip Ride Rockit's singles line than the posted standby wait.

Single-rider lines open at the discretion of the ride attendants and may temporarily close if crowds are very light (because they aren't needed) or very heavy (when the singles queue becomes filled to capacity, which happens frequently at Gringotts). In the latter case, try hanging around the entrance for 15 or 20 minutes, which is usually how long it takes for the singles line to shrink enough to be reopened.

Also note that some queues (particularly those of Forbidden Journey and Escape from Gringotts) are attractions in themselves and deserve to be experienced during your first ride. Even so, we strongly recommend using the singles line whenever possible—it will decrease your overall wait and leave more time for repeat rides or just bumming around the parks.

Single-rider lines are almost always available at the following attractions:

SINGLE-RIDER LINES AT UNIVERSAL STUDIOS FLORIDA	SINGLE-RIDER LINES AT ISLANDS OF ADVENTURE
Harry Potter and the Escape from Gringotts	The Amazing Adventures of Spider-Man
Hollywood Rip Ride Rockit	Doctor Doom's Fearfall
Men in Black Alien Attack	Harry Potter and the Forbidden Journey
Revenge of the Mummy	
Transformers: The Ride 3-D	

In addition, IOA intermittently offers single-rider access at Dudley Do-Right's Ripsaw Falls, The Incredible Hulk Coaster, and Jurassic Park River Adventure, but don't count on them being open every day.

VIP TOURS

FOR THE ULTIMATE no-expenses-spared Universal Orlando experience, book a VIP tour of one or both parks. VIP guests are given the red-carpet treatment at both parks and never have to worry about waiting in line. And don't worry if you aren't a genuine VIP—or even a social media pseudo-celebrity—because at Universal, anyone can be treated like the rich and famous . . . for a price.

Universal offers two types of VIP tours: nonexclusive and private. On nonexclusive tours, your party will be paired with other guests to form a group of up to 12. Nonexclusive tours begin at 10 a.m. and last five to seven hours. Your guide will expedite you onto a minimum of 8 attractions (10 if you take the two-park option) based on group consensus.

Private tours give you free reign to set your start time and make your own itinerary because the guide is dedicated to only your party for a full eight hours. You can even ride your favorite ride over and over all day, if you like. Private tours also include a table-service meal (shared appetizer, entrée, dessert, and nonalcoholic beverage) and Photo Connect digital pictures of your day.

Either way, your VIP experience begins with free valet parking and a complimentary Continental breakfast in the private guest services lounge. In addition to backdooring you into rides—bypassing even the Universal Express queues—and getting you reserved seating at shows, VIP tour guides are a font of trivia about the history and operations of the parks, and can even grant backstage access to see how some of the magic is done, like a glimpse underneath Revenge of the Mummy's ride track, or inside *Twister*'s special effects control booth. At the end of the tour, your souvenir VIP lanyard serves as an unlimited Express Pass for the rest of the day and offers discounts on food and merchandise.

Perhaps most important, VIP tours are currently the only way to skip the queues at the headlining Harry Potter attractions: Forbidden Journey, Escape from Gringotts, and Hogwarts Express. The value of this perk during peak times can't be overstated; during the height of Diagon Alley's opening summer, when guests were waiting more than four hours just for Gringotts, Bob and Len were able to experience everything in both Wizarding Worlds (including lunch and ice cream) plus other park highlights in a little more than five hours.

Of course, this kind of star treatment doesn't come cheap. A one-day, one-park nonexclusive VIP tour of USF or IOA will run you $299 per person; a one-day tour of both parks is $329. During peak pricing times (the weeks around Christmas and Easter), those rates jump up to $369 and $389.

Private-tour pricing approaches "if you have to ask, you can't afford it" territory, starting at $2,599 for a day in one park or $2,899 for both. That flat rate is good for one to five guests; additional guests (up to a total of 10) cost another $325 each for one park, or $349 each for two parks. During peak times, those base prices increase to $2,899 for one park and $3,199 for two parks. Finally, if you splurge on the ultimate two-day, two-park private tour, you'll be poorer by $4,799 ($4,999 during peak periods).

Before you break out your credit card, there's one final catch: In addition to not including tax, the above prices are on top of admission tickets, which are required and not included with any VIP tour.

Whether the VIP tours are "worth it" depends largely on your net worth and your tolerance for any type of wait. Having taken them many times over the years, we can say that the experience is a dream come true for theme park junkies, who will get their money's worth in insider info alone, as well as anyone allergic to rubbing elbows with unwashed hordes. If you were already planning to pony up for unlimited Express Passes, the extra couple hundred per person (depending on the season) could seem a bargain in the heat of summer. For most visitors, a stay at a luxury on-site hotel (with free unlimited Express included) is probably a more economical investment, but no one we know who has taken a VIP tour has regretted it.

Nonexclusive tours can be booked online through an interactive calendar with availability and pricing at **universalorlando.com/theme-park-tickets/vip-experience.aspx,** but private tours must be booked by phone at ☎ 866-346-9350. If you want to take a VIP tour, order early because they can fill up quickly at busier times.

Note that all of the previously mentioned tours are offered only during regular daytime operating hours. Different VIP tours with their own pricing may be available during separately ticketed special events such as Halloween Horror Nights (see page 282).

TECHNICAL REHEARSALS

TECHNICAL REHEARSALS, OR SOFT OPENINGS as they are commonly called, are when Universal uses its paying guests as guinea pigs and allows them to preview an attraction that isn't yet ready for prime time. Technical rehearsals may be held anywhere from a few weeks to a few days before a new ride officially opens, but they are never pre-announced or guaranteed; frontline employees may be instructed to deny that any opening is possible until the moment they open the queue. In exchange for bragging rights that they were the first inside a hot new attraction, technical rehearsal participants must accept the possibility of waiting a long time without ever getting to ride, as the soft opening may end at any moment.

For theme park junkies who live in the area, technical rehearsals can be both a blessing and a curse; some folks stood in front of Diagon Alley for more than 30 consecutive days waiting for a soft opening, and even then the Gringotts ride never had a public preview before grand opening. Unless you are a local with lots of time on your hands, or on an extended vacation and obsessed with the about-to-open attraction, avoid spending any of your valuable time waiting for a ride that may or may not open. Instead, enjoy everything else the parks have to offer, and keep your ears open (and an eye on our @touringplans Twitter feed) just in case.

QUITTING TIME

BECAUSE THE DAY PARKING for both Universal theme parks and the CityWalk shopping, dining, and entertainment complex is consolidated in the same parking structures, chaos can ensue on days when both parks close at the same time, resulting in an epic flood of humanity heading to the parking garages.

An Orlando woman, obviously very perturbed, comments:

> Both Universal Studios and Islands of Adventure share the same parking lot. IT MAKES NO SENSE for the two theme parks to close at the same time (especially since Islands has no night finale). I cannot even explain the amount of people. It was insane at closing (and other people were coming IN to go to CityWalk, so it was SUCH a big mess)!

If you are unlucky enough to find yourself in such a situation, we suggest taking a side trip to CityWalk and sitting out the stampede with a snack or drink. If you haven't yet exited the park, you can try lingering inside the gates as long as possible, browsing the shops that remain open past closing time. Security guards will eventually gently shoo you out, but not until most of the parking mess has cleared.

PART TWO

ACCOMMODATIONS

The BASIC CONSIDERATIONS

WHILE YOU'LL SURELY HAVE FUN inside Universal's theme parks wherever you spend the night, your choice of hotel is critical to the overall success of your vacation. Visitors to Disney face the basic question of whether to stay inside Walt Disney World—where room rates range from about $100 on an off-season weeknight at a Value resort, to more than $1,300 per night for a peak-season luxury property—or outside WDW, where rooms are as low as $35 a night. Affordability and easier access to non-Disney attractions must be weighed against the convenience and comfort of staying on Disney property.

Universal Orlando guests face a similar decision but with a few twists. For one, while Walt Disney World has more than 30,000 rooms spread across nearly 30 hotels, Universal currently operates only four on-site resorts, totaling just 4,200 rooms. (A fifth hotel will bring the count up to 5,200 in 2016, and NBCUniversal CEO Steve Burke has said that the resort could someday support 10,000–20,000 rooms.) That makes your choice of an on-site hotel a lot simpler, but it also means that you may find limited room availability during busy times. Many off-site hotels are within walking distance of the Universal theme parks, unlike off-site options near Disney.

On the other hand, Universal's hotels (all operated by the highly regarded Loews chain) boast service and amenities equal to or better than Disney's hotels for a significantly lower cost; Universal's Deluxe rooms are often priced like Disney's Moderates, and its Value resort outshines Disney's All-Star hotels. You should also consider the superior benefits granted to Universal's on-site guests, a couple of which can make the difference between a marvelous vacation and a miserable one.

Whether you decide to stay on-site or off, this chapter will help you get a grip on the multitude of lodging options in the Universal Orlando area and find the property that fits your family's needs.

THE TAX MAN COMETH

SALES AND LODGING TAXES can add a chunk of change to the cost of your hotel room. Cumulative tax in Orange County, which includes the Universal Orlando area and International Drive, is 12.5%.

ABOUT HOTEL RENOVATIONS

WE INSPECT SEVERAL HUNDRED HOTELS in the Orlando area to compile *The Unofficial Guide*'s list of lodging choices. Each year we call each hotel to verify contact information and inquire about renovations or refurbishments. If a hotel has been renovated or has refurbished its guest rooms, we reinspect it, along with any new hotels, for the next edition of the guide. Hotels reporting no improvements are rechecked every two years. We inspect most Universal-owned hotels every 6–12 months and no less than once every two years.

Many hotels more than five years old refurbish 10%–20% of their guest rooms each year. This incremental approach minimizes disruption, but it makes your room assignment a crapshoot—you might luck into a newly renovated room, or you might be assigned a threadbare one.

Universal reservationists won't guarantee you a recently refurbished room but will note your request and try to accommodate you. On the other hand, off-site hotels will often guarantee you an updated room when you book.

BENEFITS OF STAYING ON-SITE AT UNIVERSAL ORLANDO

UNIVERSAL OFFERS PERKS TO GET THEME PARK visitors into its hotels. All guests at any Universal Orlando Resort on-site hotel can take advantage of the following:

- Early Park Admission to The Wizarding World one hour before the public (see page 54)
- The ability to charge in-park purchases to the hotel-room key
- Free package delivery to the hotel room for any items purchased in the theme parks
- Free parking at the main CityWalk parking garage
- Free transportation to the theme parks and CityWalk
- Pool-hopping privileges to use any hotel's recreational facilities
- Free Wi-Fi Internet in all hotel rooms and public areas (faster speeds available for a fee)
- Free scheduled transportation to SeaWorld, Aquatica, and Wet 'n Wild via the Super Star Shuttle (see page 129)
- Free rental golf clubs, range balls, and transportation (for foursomes) to participating golf courses.

In addition, every guest staying at the three deluxe hotels (Porto-fino Bay, Hard Rock, and Royal Pacific) get the following benefits:

- Free Universal Express Unlimited Passes for both parks (see page 57)
- Priority seating at select restaurants in the parks and CityWalk

All these benefits are available from the moment you arrive until midnight on the day you check out. Even if your room won't be ready until the afternoon, you can register at your hotel as early in the morning as you like, leaving your bags and retrieving your Express Passes (if eligible) in time for the Early Park Admission hour. Then linger at the resort after your checkout time, taking advantage of your pool privileges until late in the evening.

The most valuable of these perks is the admission to The Wizarding World of Harry Potter one hour before the general public each morning, followed by the Universal Express Unlimited Passes for deluxe guests. It's hard to put a dollar value on the Early Park Admission, but two-park Universal Express Unlimited Passes are sold to the general public for $80–$160 per day, per person, excluding tax, depending on the time of year you visit. Universal says the pass is "a value of up to $89," which works out to $356 per day for a family of four. One night at Universal's Royal Pacific hotel costs anywhere from $234 to $404, excluding tax, depending on the season. If you were planning on staying at a comparable off-site deluxe hotel anyway, staying at the Royal Pacific gets your family two days of Universal Express Unlimited at little to no cost. During busy season, this can be a huge boon for parties of four or five. If you are traveling solo or as a couple, or are visiting at a slow time of year, calculate the cost of staying at Cabana Bay or Sapphire Falls and buying Express Passes upon arrival if they turn out to be necessary.

Some of the benefits are of questionable value. Free parking at the theme parks, for example, is of little use to anyone staying at the resort because it's probably just as much walking from the resort as it is from the garages.

Having stayed at each of Universal's hotels, we think a sometimes-overlooked benefit is the ability to walk to the parks from your hotel. And it's not just the convenience—the walkways are pretty and almost serene at night, if you can ignore the whooshing noise from The Incredible Hulk Coaster.

This Dallas-area family found foot accessibility to the parks to be Universal's biggest advantage over Walt Disney World's on-site hotels:

The simple convenience of being able to walk everywhere whenever you wanted was definitely worth the expense. Disney's shuttle or parking system is extensive. We tried the bus, but it gets bogged down by the stops. Parking your own vehicle meant parking and then using a tram to get to the gate. Magic Kingdom was the worst with its parking off-site; thereby, you cannot hop from park to park quickly. At Universal, with one parking area, everything was easily and quickly reachable. The girls discovered that they could enjoy the park early (with little wait time), walk back to the hotel to nap, and then go back to the park or CityWalk. They felt very grown up being able to be on their own without us adults to slow them down. This was inconvenient at Disney due to the transport time.

UNIVERSAL ORLANDO RESORT HOTELS 101

UNIVERSAL HAS FOUR RESORT HOTELS. The 750-room **Portofino Bay Hotel** is a gorgeous property set on an artificial bay and themed like an Italian coastal town. The 650-room **Hard Rock Hotel** is an ultracool "Hotel California" replica, and the 1,000-room, Polynesian-themed **Royal Pacific Resort** is sumptuously decorated and richly appointed. All three are on the pricey side. The retro-style **Cabana Bay Beach Resort,** Universal's newest and largest hotel, has 1,800 moderate- and value-priced rooms, plus amenities (bowling alley, lazy river) not seen at comparable Disney resorts. A fifth hotel, the Caribbean-styled **Sapphire Falls Resort,** opens in 2016 with 1,000 rooms priced between Royal Pacific and Cabana Bay.

Before you make any decisions, understand these basics regarding Universal Orlando Resort hotels.

UNIVERSAL ORLANDO RESORT HOTEL POLICIES

Resort Classifications

While Disney loves to categorize and has developed a five-level hierarchy of resort classifications, Universal's hotels fall into just three categories. The original three on-site hotels—Portofino Bay Hotel, Hard Rock Hotel, and Royal Pacific Resort—are all **Deluxe resorts.** Portofino is the swankiest, and Royal Pacific the least pricey, but all are AAA Four Diamond–awarded hotels.

The Cabana Bay Beach Resort currently represents both the **Moderate resort** category and **Value resorts,** with the family suites falling into the former classification, and the standard rooms in the latter. Sapphire Falls Resort will be classified a Moderate when it opens in 2016. Despite the classification, all Cabana Bay guests receive amenities that surpass any Disney Moderate or Value resort and compete with some Disney Deluxe hotels.

Seasonal Rates

Universal (like Disney) uses so many adjectives—"Value," Regular," "Summer," "Holiday," and "Peak"—to describe its seasonal calendar that it's hard to keep up. Plus, Universal also changes the price of its hotel rooms with the day of the week, charging more for the same room on Friday and Saturday nights. Visit **universalorlando.com/Hotels /Onsite-Hotel-Rates-and-Offers/Seasonal-Rates.aspx** for a current breakdown of Universal's hotel seasons and the corresponding rack (or non-discounted) rates. These prices are for a weeknight stay in a basic room with a standard view, usually of a "garden" or parking lot; upgrades to pool or bay views start at $25–$50. Rack rates do not include taxes or parking, but no hidden resort fees are tacked on at Universal's hotels.

These were Universal's starting seasonal rack rates for 2015:

SEASON 2015 TRAVEL DATES	CABANA BAY BEACH RESORT	ROYAL PACIFIC RESORT	HARD ROCK HOTEL	PORTOFINO BAY HOTEL
Value Season 1 Jan. 4-15; Jan. 19-Feb. 12; Sept. 7-Oct. 1; Nov. 29-Dec. 17	$119	$234	$259	$294
Value Season 2 Aug. 16-Sept. 6	$129	$244	$279	$304
Regular Season Jan. 16-18; April 12-May 21; May 25-June 4; Oct. 2-Nov. 24	$139	$269	$304	$324
Summer 1 June 5-20; Aug. 2-15	$154	$304	$369	$369
Summer 2 June 21-Aug. 1	$169	$329	$394	$394
Peak Season 1 Feb. 22-Mar. 12; May 22-24; Nov. 25-28	$169	$319	$389	$399
Peak Season 2 Feb. 13-21; Mar. 13-26	$179	$334	$409	$414
Holiday Season Jan. 1-3; Mar. 27-April 11; Dec. 18-31	$199	$404	$464	$479

Discounts

Universal hotel rack rates are just the starting point, and most clever visitors can save substantially on their stay with a little legwork. Unlike Disney, which prefers to use inducements like "free dining" rather than discounts per se, Universal frequently offers sizable percentage-off deals to fill its rooms.

Start by reviewing the resort discount information in Part One (see page 41), and then visit **universalorlando.com/hotels/onsite-hotel-rates-and-offers.aspx** to view the latest deals. Use the booking tool on the right side of that page to select your dates, and enter "APH" in the Promotion/Group Code box to see annual-pass-holder discounts, or "FLO" for Florida resident discounts. You don't have to prove eligibility to book with these codes, but you will need to show appropriate ID upon check-in.

If you are staying for multiple nights, Universal's "Stay More, Save More" pricing structure kicks in. Stays in a Value or Moderate room of four to seven nights save 10%–20% during holiday, peak, and summer seasons, and stays of three to seven nights save 15%–25% during regular and value seasons. At the Deluxe hotels, four to seven nights save 10%–25% during holiday, peak, and summer seasons, and three to seven nights save 10%–30% during regular and value seasons.

Making Reservations

The easiest way to book a room at Universal Orlando is online through **uo.loewshotels.com,** or by phone at ☎ 888-273-1311. If you are attending a meeting or event, call ☎ 866-360-7395 for your group block room.

Cancellations

A credit card deposit equal to one night's room rate (plus tax) is required when booking. Cancellations made six or more days prior to check-in receive a full refund. Cancellations five or fewer days before check-in forfeit the deposit. However, Universal's "No Questions Asked" severe-weather policy says that if you are not able to travel to Orlando due to an "active named storm impacting your travel," you can reschedule your vacation or receive a full refund.

Check-In and Checkout

Check-in time at all Universal hotels is 4 p.m., and checkout is 11 a.m.; if you ask nicely, you can usually get a noon checkout for free. Remember that all on-site hotel benefits—including Early Park Admission and Express Unlimited Passes for Deluxe guests—begin the first morning of your stay and last until midnight after you check out. So even if you can't get into your room, you can preregister as early as you like, leave your luggage, grab your Express Passes (at Deluxe hotels), and hit the parks at rope drop. Checkout can be done at the front desk, through the interactive television system, or via Express with your bill e-mailed to you.

Age Requirements

The minimum age to book a hotel room at Universal Orlando is 21, and valid ID is required at check-in. At least one guest staying in the room must be age 21 or older.

Accessibility

All Universal Orlando hotels have wheelchair-accessible public areas and offer designated accessible rooms for both mobility-impaired and sight/hearing-impaired guests. Accessibility features include 36-inch-wide entry doors, peepholes at 3.5 feet from the floor, closets with rods at 48 inches high, toilets with hand bar, and roll-in shower stalls or combination shower/tubs with adjustable showerheads. Sight- and hearing-impaired features include Braille room numbers, closed-caption televisions, smoke detectors with lights, and Hearing-Impaired Kits, including a TDD-relay service that may be used in any guest room.

Pets

Loews "loves pets" and is one of the few luxury chains to allow cats and dogs in its rooms. It even has a special (and expensive) room service menu for four-legged guests. There are some restrictions, starting with a $50 fee per night for a maximum of two pets per guest room. Guests will be assigned to a pet-friendly room category on arrival, which includes garden- and bay-view rooms at the Portofino Bay, garden-view rooms at the Hard Rock, and standard rooms at the Royal Pacific. Club rooms don't participate in the pet program, nor does Cabana Bay Beach Resort.

Dogs may be walked only in designated areas and are not allowed in the pool/lounge or restaurant areas. Arrangements must be made with housekeeping for daily room cleaning, and there is a $10 per-hour fee if they find your pet left unattended. If other guests complain about your pet's behavior, you may be asked to board it outside. You must provide current vaccination records from a licensed veterinarian on request.

Smoking

All Universal Orlando Resort hotels are smoke-free. Smoking is only permitted outdoors in designated locations. If you light up in your room, you'll be burned with a $200 cleaning fee.

YouFirst and Hard Rock Rewards

The Loews-branded hotels (excluding Cabana Bay and Hard Rock) participate in the YouFirst loyalty reward program, which offers complimentary upgrades and faster Internet access to return guests. Hard Rock Hotel accepts the similar Hard Rock Rewards card. Be warned that discounted room bookings may not qualify for reward program benefits, and YouFirst is not valid at Cabana Bay. Ask about the programs at check-in, or call ☎ 800-563-9712 or visit **loewshotels.com/youfirst** for Loews YouFirst; visit **hardrock.com/rewards** for Hard Rock Rewards.

UNIVERSAL ORLANDO RESORT HOTEL SERVICES *and* AMENITIES

DINING

TO KEEP YOU FED, EVERY UNIVERSAL ON-SITE hotel has multiple restaurants, a spot for coffee and grab-and-go snacks, and at least three bars. The Deluxe properties each have several sit-down restaurants, including one fine-dining venue and one family-friendly eatery, while Cabana Bay has a counter-service food court, as well as table-service munchies in the bowling alley. Sapphire Falls' eateries will include a waterside sit-down restaurant, a grab-and-go marketplace, a poolside grill, and a lobby lounge. The Deluxe hotels also offer extensive room service menus, while Cabana Bay has pizza delivery to the rooms and occasionally hosts local food trucks in the north pool courtyard.

The primary downside to staying on-site at Universal is the cost of food at the Deluxe hotels' restaurants, which seems priced as if everyone staying at the hotels was on a corporate expense account. Fortunately, many good, cheaper restaurant choices are within a few minutes' drive of the hotels on Major Boulevard, International Drive, and Sand Lake Road—much more so than at Disney's hotels. Hotel guests also have easy access to CityWalk, which has some cheaper choices for dining.

POOLS AND RECREATION

SWIMMING IS MANY GUESTS' NUMBER one priority (after the theme parks, of course), so you'll find some of Orlando's best pools at Universal's hotels. Each resort has at least one themed swimming facility for guests. The main pool is the more active, family-centric one where you'll find playground equipment and organized activities, both for kids (water-based games and contests) and adults (free smoothies and cool towels). Each resort (except for Royal Pacific) has a waterslide, and Cabana Bay has a lazy river. On most nights (weather permitting) a PG-rated "dive-in" movie is projected on an outdoor screen.

The secondary pools at Portofino and Cabana Bay are usually slightly more sedate and attract a more adult clientele. All pools are staffed with trained lifeguards during operating hours (which vary seasonally, typically 8 a.m.–10 p.m.) and have adjacent whirlpools, changing facilities, and drink services. Towels are free with resort ID, and hotel guests are free to pool-hop from one resort to another; ask an attendant for access if your room key won't open another hotel's security gate.

Each hotel's main pool has private cabanas for rent, which start around $100 per day. Aside from providing shade and cushioned lounge chairs, cabanas come with ceiling fans, TVs, a refrigerator, free soft drinks, food and drink delivery, and a personal safe. Reserve a cabana by calling ☎ 407-503-4175 at Cabana Bay, ☎ 407-503-3235 at Royal Pacific, ☎ 407-503-2236 at Hard Rock, or ☎ 407-503-1200 at Portofino Bay. Same-day cancellations incur a 50% penalty fee. You'll also find a variety of recreational activities around the pools, from a bocce court at Portofino Bay to a croquet lawn at the Royal Pacific; free equipment can be checked out to play.

KIDS' ACTIVITIES AND KIDS' SUITES

THE LOEWS LOVES KIDS PROGRAM means that there's always something at the hotel to keep the rug rats occupied when your family isn't in the parks. Free lending libraries of games and sports equipment are available at every hotel, and a schedule of supervised activities is offered at each main pool (or indoors on rainy days). Universal's characters make regular meet-and-greet appearances at each hotel on a weekly schedule. In addition, the kids' clubs at the three Deluxe hotels offer evening child care for a fee (see page 179), and every hotel has an arcade with video games; Cabana Bay's Game-O-Rama is the newest and best.

If you want to go all out and amaze the kids (at the expense of your bank account), reserve one of the Deluxe resorts' elaborately decorated **Kids' Suites.** Portofino Bay's Despicable Me suites look like Gru's laboratory, with missile-shaped beds and vaultlike doors. Royal Pacific's Jurassic Park suites have appropriately dinosaurish decor, with high-tech headboards and jungle graphics. The Hard Rock's Kids' Suites have a separate kids' room with TV and child-size furniture but no whimsical theming. All the Kids' Suites have separate bedrooms for the kids that only open on the parents' room (not the hallway). You'll get some extra privacy but pay a hefty price with the resort's highest room rates (outside the outrageous presidential suites). Still, these rooms are almost always booked up, so someone is willing to pay for them.

PARKING

UNIVERSAL CHARGES A $20 PER-NIGHT self-parking fee ($27 for valet) at its luxury resorts for registered guests; day guests pay $22 for self-parking and $32 for valet. Cabana Bay charges $12 for overnight guests (self-parking only) and $20 for day visitors. Several of the hotel restaurants (including Tchoup Chop at Royal Pacific and The Palm at Hard Rock) will validate diners for free valet parking. There are no annual pass discounts on parking at the hotels. The hotels charge for another night starting at 11 a.m., so move your car before checkout time to avoid paying extra.

INTERNET

ALL UNIVERSAL ORLANDO HOTELS offer free Wi-Fi in their public areas and guest rooms for up to four devices. The service is somewhat spotty but good enough for e-mail and social media. If you plan to stream videos or upload large photos, you may want to pay $15 per 24 hours for Premium Plus Internet, which affords higher bandwidth (we've achieved more than 30 megabits-per-second downloads) on up to eight devices.

BUSINESS CENTERS

EACH OF THE HOTELS (excluding Cabana Bay) has a fully equipped business center offering Internet-connected computers with printers, copy and fax services, and mail facilities through FedEx and UPS. Portofino Bay's business center is open 7 a.m.–6 p.m., Monday–Friday, and 9 a.m.–3 p.m., Saturday (closed Sunday). Royal Pacific's center is open 7 a.m.–4 p.m., Monday–Friday (closed Saturday–Sunday). Hard Rock Hotel's business center is open 24-7, and the others may be accessed during off hours by contacting the front desk. Fees apply for certain services such as copying and faxing. Cabana Bay's diner has a quiet corner with phone booths and a couple touch screens for printing boarding passes.

CRIBS AND ROLLAWAY BEDS

COMPLIMENTARY CRIBS ARE AVAILABLE in all rooms. Rollaway beds can be requested on a first-come, first-serve basis for $25 per day, plus 12.5% sales tax. Only one rollaway per room is allowed.

LAUNDRY

ALL THE HOTELS EXCEPT PORTOFINO BAY offer self-service Laundromats. Machines take quarters or credit cards and cost $3 per load to wash, and the same to dry. At all the Deluxe hotels, you can also avail yourself of valet laundry, dry cleaning, quick pressing, and shoe-shines, with express same-day service available daily, 9 a.m.–7 p.m.; pricing and instructions can be found inside your closet.

MICROWAVES AND REFRIGERATORS

ROOMS IN THE PORTOFINO BAY HOTEL come with a small refrigerator pre-stocked with expensive drinks and snacks. Microwaves and empty refrigerators are available on a first-come, first-serve basis for $15 each per day, plus 12.5% sales tax. If you tell the front desk you have medical needs, the fridge will be free. The newly renovated rooms at the Hard Rock Hotel and Royal Pacific Resort include small refrigerators that can be used by guests for no extra fee. All rooms at Cabana Bay include a mini-fridge, and the family suites have kitchenettes with a microwave and sink.

TRANSPORTATION AND CAR RENTAL

ALL FOUR UNIVERSAL HOTELS OFFER free transportation via bus and/or water taxi to CityWalk and the theme parks, as well as well-lit landscaped walking paths connecting the resort. Water taxis depart from each of the Deluxe hotels every 15–20 minutes, while the bus from Cabana Bay runs even more frequently. Either transportation method takes about 15 minutes to reach the park entrances, while walking takes between less than 5 minutes from Hard Rock Hotel to 15 or 20 minutes from Cabana Bay and Portofino Bay.

Free daily transportation for hotel guests to Wet 'n Wild, SeaWorld, Discovery Cove, and Aquatica is available on the Super Star Shuttle (see page 129). There are a limited number of departures and returns; check with the ticket desk for the schedule and to book a seat. For a fee, the concierge desk will also arrange for Mears Transportation to take you to Walt Disney World or the airport. If you want to rent a car, Hertz rental-car service desks operate inside each hotel.

FITNESS CENTERS AND MANDARA SPA

IF YOU WANT TO STAY IN SHAPE while vacationing, every Universal hotel has a well-appointed fitness center filled with the latest in exercise equipment. The expansive Jack LaLanne–themed workout room at Cabana Bay Beach Resort, as well as the somewhat smaller workout rooms in the other hotels, are free for all hotel guests to use.

Whether you are staying at a Universal hotel or not, you may book services at Portofino Bay's Mandara Spa, which is attached to the hotel's fitness center. Access to the spa's shower and sauna facilities costs $10 per day for guests of the resort and is free for club-level guests, loyalty-club members, Premier Annual Pass holders, or anyone purchasing spa services. If you aren't staying on-site, you can get access to the spa (though not the nearby Beach Pool) with a $25 day pass, which also includes free self-parking or $5 valet parking at the hotel entrance.

Universal Orlando's Mandara Spa was renovated in 2013, retaining its Asian ambience despite its location in an Italy-themed resort. We like the contrast, though, and find it slightly exotic. Waiting areas are decorated in comforting earth tones; treatment rooms feature silk-draped ceilings. Changing and bathroom areas are spacious and clean, but they also include less-than-subtle advertisements for products sold on premises. The remodeled treatment rooms feature additional decorative lighting and accessories.

The emphasis on tranquility extends to the stellar spa services, which include free self-heating oil for massages. Men and women enjoy separate steam and sauna facilities; the whirlpool is unisex. The Portofino's sand-bottom pool is conveniently located near the entrance to the spa, as are nail services. The fitness center is still on the other side of the glass wall, however, so you may feel a bit like that doggy in the window.

We rate the Mandara Spa at Portofino Bay as 4.5 stars, just behind the spas at Disney's Grand Floridian and the Waldorf Astoria, and equivalent to the spas at the Ritz-Carlton, Saratoga Springs, and Gaylord Palms. Prices range from $70 for a 25-minute reflexology massage to $595 for a 6-plus-hour Day of Bliss package. Hair salon and makeup services are also on the menu. A 20% automatic gratuity applies to all services, and annual-pass holders can save 10%–20%. Groupon often offers half-price Mandara Spa packages, but you'll be charged gratuity based on the full value. Purchase of most massages and treatments also includes access to the fitness center for the day. Call ☎ 407-503-1244 for reservations, or visit **mandaraspa.com/spa/orlando-loews-portofino-bay-hotel-at-universal-orlando.aspx** to preview the price list.

CLUB LEVEL

ALL THE HOTELS EXCEPT CABANA BAY offer club-level rooms or suites that allow access to an exclusive lounge, where you'll find a complimentary Continental breakfast, afternoon snacks, hot and cold evening hors d'oeuvres with free beer and wine, and after-dinner desserts. Club-level guests also get free fitness-center access, discounted poolside cabana rentals, personal concierge service, evening turndown service, and other luxurious touches. Hard Rock Hotel's Rock Royalty and Royal Pacific's Royal Club Lounges are on the seventh floor, while Portofino Bay's Portofino Club Lounge is in the lobby; all are open 7 a.m.–10 p.m. daily. Most of our readers who stay in a club-level room seem happy with their choice, like this family from Kansas City:

> We stayed on the club level of the Royal Pacific. Absolutely worth the money. It not only includes breakfast every morning, which saved us money, but also includes sodas all day and cocktails in the evening with heavy appetizers, which we usually made a meal out of. There was always a salad and then something hot. One night it was beef stew, then fried rice, and then chicken potpie. And if you weren't full, they put out dessert 8–9 p.m. This ended up saving us money, and we were usually tired from the day, so just walking down the hall was fabulous.

WEDDINGS

SEEING HOW SUCCESSFUL THE NUPTIAL BUSINESS has been for Disney, it was only a matter of time before Universal got into the matrimony game. There is no dedicated wedding pavilion at Universal (yet), but each hotel has facilities for staging fairy-tale ceremonies, large or small. Intimate weddings with 50 or fewer guests start at $1,000 for a simple ceremony, plus $250 for a cake and $70 per guest for a one-hour cocktail reception. A Signature wedding for more than 50 guests starts at $2,500–$3,000 for the ceremony and $150-plus per plate for a dinner reception. To Universal's credit, it doesn't quote an hourly rate for having Minions attend your bachelorette party, but this is Orlando: Money talks. Visit **universalorlando.com/hotels/weddings.aspx** to download brochures with pricing and menus, and start planning your Universal union today.

UNIVERSAL ORLANDO RESORT HOTEL PROFILES

Hard Rock Hotel ★★★★½

Rate per night $259–$464. **Pool** ★★★★. **Fridge in room** Yes. **Shuttle to parks** Yes (Universal, SeaWorld, Discovery Cove, Aquatica, and Wet 'n Wild). **Maximum number of occupants per room** 5 (double/queen) or 3 (king). **Special comments** Character dinner on Saturday. Pets welcome (2 per room, $50 per night [$150 maximum per stay]).

5800 Universal Blvd.
Orlando
☎ 407-503-2000 or
888-464-3617
hardrockhotelorlando.com

FOR YOUNGER ADULTS AND FAMILIES WITH older kids, the Hard Rock Hotel is the hippest place to lay your head. Opened in 2001, the Hard Rock Hotel is both Universal Orlando's least expensive (but second most expensive) on-site resort and the closest resort to Universal's theme parks. The exterior has a California Mission theme, with white stucco walls, arched entryways, and rust-colored roof tiles. Inside, the lobby is a tribute to rock-and-roll style, all marble, chrome, and stage lighting. The lobby's walls are decorated with enough concert posters, costumes, and musical instruments to start another wing of Cleveland's Rock and Roll Hall of Fame; ask the front desk for information about a self-guided memorabilia tour.

The eight floors hold 650 rooms and 29 suites, with the rooms categorized into standard, deluxe, and club-level tiers. Standard rooms are 375 square feet, slightly larger than rooms at Disney's Moderate resorts and a bit smaller than most Disney Deluxe rooms. The Hard Rock Hotel completed a top-to-bottom "remastering" of its rooms in early 2015, giving the formerly masculine decor a major makeover, with light-gray walls and linens, pastel furniture, and colorful retro-inspired accents, such as throw pillows crocheted with phrases such as "Quiet Please" and "Be Nice." To be frank, the style looks more bubblegum-pop than hard rock, but the brighter look is a bit more soothing after you stumble back from a fatiguing day in the parks.

Standard rooms are furnished with two queen beds, with smooth, plush, comfortable linens and more pillows than you'll know what to do with. Rooms also include a flat-panel LCD TV, refrigerator, coffeemaker, and an alarm clock with a 30-pin iPhone docking port.

A six-drawer dresser and separate closet with sliding doors ensure plenty of storage space. In addition, most rooms have a reading chair and a small desk with two chairs. An optional rollaway bed, available at an extra charge, allows standard rooms to sleep up to five people.

Each room's dressing area features a sink and hair dryer. The bathroom is probably large enough for most adults to get ready in the morning while another person gets ready in the dressing area.

Guests staying in standard rooms can choose from one of three views: standard, which can include anything from walkways and parking lots to lawns and trees; garden view, which includes the lawn, trees, and (in some rooms) the waterway around the resort; and pool view, which includes the Hard Rock's expansive pool.

A step up from standard rooms are deluxe rooms. Deluxe rooms with king beds are around 500 square feet and can accommodate up to three people with an optional rollaway bed rental. These rooms feature a U-shaped sitting area in place of the second bed, and the rest of the amenities are the same as in standard rooms. Deluxe queen rooms are also 500 square feet and can hold up to five people using a pullout sofa, located in a small cubby just off the room's entrance.

The zero-entry pool is an attraction unto itself; it is the place to see and be seen. Situated in the middle of the resort's C-shaped main building, the 12,000-square-foot pool includes a 250-foot waterslide (the longest on Universal property), a sand beach, and underwater speakers so you can hear the music while you swim. Adjacent to the pool are a fountain play area for small children, a sand volleyball court, hot tubs, and a pool-side bar. The entire pool area is lined with tall palm trees, but if they don't provide enough shade (or you just want to make an impression), private cabanas are available for rent. The Hard Rock also has a small, functional fitness center, but for spa services you'll have to go to the Mandara at Universal's nearby Portofino Bay. Like all Universal Orlando Resort hotels, the Hard Rock has a business center and video arcade.

On-site dining includes The Kitchen, a casual full-service restaurant open for breakfast, lunch, and dinner, featuring American food such as burgers, steaks, and salads. The Kitchen hosts character dinners every Saturday, along with strolling magicians on Friday, Kids Can Cook activities on Tuesday–Thursday, and random celebrity-chef sightings. The Palm Restaurant is an upscale steak house available for dinner only. There is also an Emack & Bolio's ice cream shop and grab-and-go marketplace on the lower level; the stylish Velvet Bar in the lobby for drinks after dark and monthly Velvet Sessions rock-and-roll cocktail parties (visit **velvet sessions.com** for the schedule and to request an invitation); and the BeachClub bar and grill by the pool. And, of course, the Hard Rock Cafe is just a short distance away at Universal CityWalk.

If all that musical immersion puts you in the mood to jam, you can borrow 1 of 20 Fender guitars—including Stratocasters, Telecasters, and even bass guitars—with amp and headphones for free (after a $1,000 credit card deposit) through the hotel's The Sound of Your Stay program; ask the front desk for details.

After its much-needed refurbishment, we rate the rooms at Hard Rock slightly ahead of the more-expensive Portofino Bay. While not exactly cheap, Hard Rock is a good value compared to, say, Disney's Yacht & Beach Clubs. What you're paying for at the Hard Rock is a short walk to the theme parks and Universal Express Unlimited first, and the room second.

While the hotel can get a bit loud, especially in areas facing the pool, it gets high marks from families with teenagers, like this Texas parent with two daughters ages 15 and 17:

> One word: "WOW!" My group loved it! We splurged for a club room. My teenagers liked the club lounge . . . allowing them to pop in for food whenever they wanted. The beds were super comfortable, soft instead of firm mattresses. The pool was a big hit with the girls. We all liked the convenience of being so close to walk to the parks.

Loews Portofino Bay Hotel ★★★★½

5601 Universal Blvd. Orlando
☎ 407-503-1000 or 888-464-3617
loewshotels.com /portofino-bay-hotel

Rate per night $294–$479. **Pools** ★★★★. **Fridge in room** Mini-bar; fridge available for $15/day. **Shuttle to parks** Yes (Universal, SeaWorld, Discovery Cove, Aquatica, and Wet 'n Wild). **Maximum number of occupants per room** 5 (double/queen) or 3 (king). **Special comments** Character dinner on Friday. Pets welcome (2 per room, $50 per night [$150 maximum per stay]).

IF YOU ARE IN SEARCH OF the ultimate European-style, spare-no-expense on-site experience, look no further than the Portofino Bay Hotel. Universal's top-of-the-line hotel evokes the Italian seaside city of Porto-fino, complete with a man-made Portofino Bay past the lobby. To Univer-sal's credit, the layout, color, and theming of the guest room buildings are a good approximation of the architecture around the harbor in the real Portofino (Universal's version has fewer yachts, however).

The front of the Portofino continues the theme, with a trio of Vespa-like scooters parked next to a convertible red Fiat, all around a burbling foun-tain. Deep-green tapestries hang from the sand-colored porte cochere, whose formal arched opening is flanked on either side by narrower recessed arches. It's a convincing transition from the nearby parking deck.

Inside, the lobby is decorated with pink marble floors, white wood columns, and arches. The space is both airy and comfortable, with side rooms featuring seats and couches done in bold reds and deep blues.

Portofino Bay was refurbished in 2013. Most guest rooms are 450 square feet, larger than most at Disney's Deluxe resorts, and have either one king bed or two queen beds. King rooms sleep up to three people with an optional rollaway bed; the same option allows queen rooms to sleep up to five. Two room-view options are available: Garden rooms look out over the landscaping and trees (many of these are the east-facing rooms in the resort's east wing; others face one of the three pools); bay-view rooms face either west or south and overlook Portofino Bay, with a view of the piazza behind the lobby too. A very small number of rooms have working balconies; you can request one, but there are no guarantees.

Rooms come furnished with a 32-inch LCD flat-panel TV, a refrigerator, a coffeemaker, and an alarm clock with a 30-pin iPhone docking port.

Other amenities include a small desk with two chairs, a comfortable reading chair with lamp, a chest of drawers, and a standing closet. Beds are large, plush, and comfortable. You'll have a hard time in the morning convincing yourself that getting out of them and going to a theme park is the best option you have.

Guest bathrooms at Portofino Bay are the best on Universal property. We've seen smaller New York apartments! Speakers inside the bathroom transmit the audio from whatever is playing on the room's television. The best thing is the shower, which has enough water pressure to strip paint from old furniture, not to mention an adjustable spray nozzle that varies the water pulses to simulate everything from monsoon season in the tropics to the rhythmic thumps of wildebeest hooves during migrating season. We love it.

Portofino Bay has three pools, the largest of which is the Beach Pool, on the west side of the resort. Two smaller quiet pools sit at the far end of the east wing and to the west of the main lobby. The Beach Pool has a zero-entry design and a waterslide themed after a Roman aqueduct, plus a children's play area, hot tubs, and a poolside bar and grill. The Villa Pool has private cabana rentals for that Italian Riviera feeling and a bocce ball court with free equipment for that Jersey shore feeling. Rounding out the luxuries are the full-service Mandara Spa; a complete fitness center with weight machines, treadmills, and more; a business center; and a video arcade.

On-site dining includes three sit-down restaurants serving Italian cuisine; a deli; a pizzeria; and a café serving coffee and gelato. Two bars round out the food offerings at Portofino. The Portofino has 10 separate convention meeting rooms and is a popular destination for small to mid-size groups. Perhaps because Universal figures that most guests have an expense account, some of the food prices go well beyond what we'd consider reasonable, even for a theme park hotel.

While we think Portofino Bay has some of Universal's best rooms, the prices put it on par with the Ritz-Carlton, something its good points can't quite justify. On the other hand, the Ritz isn't a short walk from Harry Potter, and the Portofino is significantly cheaper than the Grand Floridian at Disney. If you're going to stay at the Portofino for two nights or more, consider getting an annual pass to the Universal parks, which gives substantial discounts on rooms (often more than $100 per night) and can more than offset the cost of the room.

If you still can't swing a stay here, at least take a complimentary sunset water taxi ride to the harbor for Musica della Notte, the free mini-concert of romantic operatic pop tunes belted from Portofino's bayside balconies daily at dusk (weather permitting). Several times each year, Harbor Nights are held on the plaza, with wine tasting, hors d'oeuvres, and live music. Tickets are $45 (plus tax) in advance, $55 if purchased at the event, and $75 for VIP admission with reserved seating. See Loews's event page at **loewshotels.tix.com** for details on the next date.

Loews Royal Pacific Resort ★★★★½

Rate per night $234–$404. **Pools** ★★★★. **Fridge in room** Yes. **Shuttle to parks** Yes (Universal, SeaWorld, Discovery Cove, Aquatica, and Wet 'n Wild). **Maximum number of occupants per room** 5 (double/queen) or 3 (king).

6300 Hollywood Way
Orlando
☎ 407-503-1000 or
888-464-3617
loewshotels.com
/royal-pacific-resort

Special comments Character breakfast on Sunday; character dinners on Monday, Wednesday, and Thursday. Pets welcome (2 per room, $50 per night [$150 maximum per stay]).

A FAVORITE OF YOUNG FAMILIES and solo travelers alike, the Royal Pacific is the least expensive and most relaxing of Universal's Deluxe hotels. You may be tempted, as we were initially, to write off the Royal Pacific, which opened in 2002, as a knockoff of Disney's Polynesian Village Resort. There are indeed similarities, but the Royal Pacific is attractive enough, and has enough strengths of its own, for us to recommend that you try a stay there to compare for yourself.

The South Seas–inspired theming is both relaxing and structured. Guests enter the lobby from a walkway two stories above an artificial stream that surrounds the resort. Once you're inside, the lobby's dark teakwood accents contrast nicely with the enormous amount of light coming in from the windows and three-story A-frame roof. Palms line the walkway through the lobby, which surrounds an enormous outdoor fountain.

The Royal Pacific's 1,000 guest rooms are spread among three Y-shaped wings attached to the resort's main building. Standard rooms are 335 square feet (about the size of a room at Disney's Moderate resorts) and feature one king or two queen beds. The beds, fitted with 300-thread-count sheets, are very comfortable.

The rooms and hallways of Royal Pacific's first tower were refurbished in early 2015 (and the remainder will be made over by early 2016) with modern monochrome wall treatments and carpets, accented with boldly colored floral graphics. Rooms include a 32-inch flat-panel LCD TV, a refrigerator, a coffeemaker, and an alarm clock with a 30-pin iPhone docking port. Other amenities include a small desk with two chairs, a comfortable reading chair, a chest of drawers, and a large closet.

As at the Hard Rock, rooms at the Royal Pacific have a dressing area with sink, separated from the rest of the room by a wall. Adjacent to the dressing area is the bathroom, with a tub, shower, and toilet. While they're acceptable, the bathroom and dressing areas at the Royal Pacific are our least favorite in the Universal resorts.

The Royal Pacific was one of the first Orlando hotels to offer themed rooms for kids with its Jurassic Park Kids Suite. These two-room suites have a door connecting the kid's room to the main hotel room, but only the main room has a door out to the hallway. The kid's room has two twin beds with light-up raptor slash marks on the headboards, while the rest of the room is fully themed to the *Jurassic Park* film, including on-set photos.

Some standard-view rooms look out over the Royal Pacific's green landscape, while others see the parking lot or nearby roads. Water-view rooms facing the pool or lagoon are also available, many of which have a great look at Hogwarts Castle. Guests in north- and west-facing rooms in Tower 1 are closest to the attractions at Islands of Adventure and can hear the roar from IOA's Incredible Hulk Coaster throughout the day and night. East-facing rooms in Towers 1 and 2 are exposed to traffic noise from Universal Boulevard and, more distantly, I-4. Quietest are south-facing pool-view rooms in Tower 1 and south-facing rooms in Tower 3.

Like the Hard Rock, the Royal Pacific's zero-entry pool includes a sand beach, volleyball court, play area for kids, hot tub, and cabanas for rent, plus a poolside bar and grill. Designed to look like a cross between a tropical island and cruise-ship pool (complete with faux exhaust tower and observation deck), the swimming complex pool is huge; it does not, however, have a waterslide. Lounge chairs line most of the walkway around the pool, and portable folding umbrellas provide shade where the palm trees and lush green plants can't. A free torch-lighting ceremony with Polynesian dance, music, and fire juggling is held by the pool around sunset on select nights (usually Tuesday, Friday, and Saturday during the summer). For the full island experience, the Wantilan Luau is held every Saturday night year-round, plus select Tuesdays seasonally; see the review on page 227.

The Royal Pacific includes a 5,000-square-foot fitness facility, with free weights and machines, treadmills, stair-climbers, elliptical machines, and exercise bikes, plus separate lockers, dressing areas, and sauna rooms for men and women. In 2015 the Royal Pacific expanded its already-expansive convention facilities to 141,000 square feet, which will be connected to the new Sapphire Falls Resort by an air-conditioned bridge. A business center and video arcade round out the on-site amenities.

On-site dining includes two full-service restaurants, three bars, and a luau. Of the table-service restaurants, only the Islands Dining Room is open daily for breakfast. Its buffet is stocked with the usual eggs, bacon, pancakes, and French toast. At dinner, Islands has better-than-average international cuisine, with character dining three nights a week. Another breakfast option is the grab-and-go Continental-style breakfast in the Orchid Court Lounge near the hotel lobby. Jake's American Bar hosts a character breakfast on Sundays and serves a casual sit-down menu all day, along with late-night bar snacks. Emeril's Tchoup Chop is the final table-service option; it serves Asian-inspired food and is open for lunch and dinner (reservations recommended through **opentable.com**). Several casual bar areas—including Jake's American Bar, the Orchid Court Lounge & Sushi Bar, and the poolside Bula Bar & Grille with neighboring ice cream stand—are located in the resort.

Though nice, the rooms alone aren't worth the rates, but adding in Universal Express Unlimited and a short walk to the parks makes it the best deal among Universal's Deluxe hotels.

Loews Sapphire Falls Resort (opens 2016)

Fridge in room Yes. **Shuttle to parks** Yes (Universal, SeaWorld, Discovery Cove, Aquatica, and Wet 'n Wild). **Maximum number of occupants per room** 5 (double/queen) or 3 (king).

6601 Adventure Way
Orlando
☎ 407-503-5000 or
888-464-3617
**loewshotels.com
/sapphire-falls-hotel**

UNIVERSAL'S FIFTH ON-SITE LOEWS HOTEL, the Sapphire Falls Resort, will seek to bring a sunny Caribbean island vibe to the Moderate market when its 1,000 rooms (including 77 suites) open in summer 2016. Sandwiched between Royal Pacific and Cabana Bay—both physically and price-wise—Sapphire Falls will sport all of the amenities of Universal's three Deluxe hotels, including water taxi transportation to the parks, with the crucial exception of complimentary Express Passes.

Water figures heavily at Sapphire Falls, whose namesake waterfalls form the scenic centerpiece of the resort. The 15,600-square-foot zero-entry main pool features 3,500 square feet of white-sand beaches, a waterslide, children's play areas, fire pits, and cabanas for rent. A fitness room holds a sauna and hot tub. For dinner, Amatista Cookhouse offers table-service Caribbean dining, with an open kitchen and waterfront views. Club Katine serves tapas-style small plates near the pool bar's fire pit. New Dutch Trading Co., an island-inspired grab-and-go marketplace, has ice cream, coffee, and packaged snacks, and Strong Water Tavern in the lobby has rum tastings and table-side ceviche.

The rooms range from 364 square feet in a standard queen or king to 529 square feet in the 36 Kids' Suites, up to 1,358 square feet in the 15 Hospitality Suites. All rooms include a 49-inch flat-panel HDTV, mini-fridge, and coffeemaker.

Sapphire Falls also contains 131,000 square feet of meeting space and a business center. Covered walkways connect to a parking structure, which in turn connects to the meeting facilities at Royal Pacific, making the new sister properties ideal for conventions.

Universal will begin accepting reservations in the spring of 2016. At press time, no official pricing information was available, but we expect rates to rest between Royal Pacific and Cabana Bay.

Universal's Cabana Bay Beach Resort ★★★★

6550 Adventure Way
Orlando
☎ 407-503-4000 or
888-464-3617
**loewshotels.com
/cabana-bay-hotel**

Rate per night $119–$210. **Pools** ★★★★. **Fridge in room** Yes. **Shuttle to parks** Yes (Universal, SeaWorld, Discovery Cove, Aquatica, and Wet 'n Wild). **Maximum number of occupants per room** 6 (family suites) or 4 (standard room). **Special comments** Character greeting in lobby on Friday. Pets not permitted.

IF YOU'RE OBSESSED WITH VINTAGE 1950s and 1960s designs, and with finding a good value (we're guilty on both accounts), you may just fall in love with Cabana Bay Beach Resort, Universal's first on-site hotel aimed at the Value and Moderate markets. The mid-century modern aesthetic starts with the neon signage that welcomes you outside and continues inside with lots of windows, bright colors, and period-appropriate lighting and furniture. The designers were inspired by classic seaside hotels such as the doo-wop Caribbean Motel in Wildwood, New Jersey, and Loews's original Americana Hotel in Bal Harbour, Florida. We think that the resort would be right at home in the deserts of Palm Springs or Las Vegas, while our British friends say that the decor reminds them of Butlin's Bognor Regis resort circa 1985.

Whatever Cabana Bay reminds you of, we think you'll like it. Kids will love the two large and well-themed pools (one with a lazy river), the amount of space they have to run around in, the vintage cars parked outside the hotel lobby, and the video arcade. Adults will appreciate the sophisticated kitsch of the decor, the multiple lounges, the business center, and the on-site Starbucks. We think Cabana Bay is an excellent choice for price- and/or space-conscious families visiting Universal.

The hotel's closest competitor in the Orlando area is Disney's Art of Animation Resort, and the two share many similarities. Both have standard rooms and family suites. At 430 square feet per suite, Cabana Bay suites are about 135 square feet smaller than comparable suites at Art of Animation and have only one bathroom. We found them well appointed for two to four people per room (though not for the six Loews claims as its capacity). Rates for the suites are about $140–$300 per night less than Art of Animation's. Standard rooms can frequently be had for less than $90 a night with discounts, undercutting Disney's cheapest rooms.

Each family suite has a small bedroom with two queen beds, divided from the living area and kitchenette by a sliding screen; a pullout sofa in the living area offers additional sleeping space. The bath is divided into three sections: toilet, sink area, and shower room with additional sink; all are separated by doors, so three people can theoretically get ready at once. Retro theming even extends to the toiletries, which feature the fondly remembered Zest and VO5 brands. The kitchenette has a microwave, coffeemaker, and mini-fridge. A bar area allows extra seating for quick meals, and a large closet has enough space to store everyone's luggage. Built-in USB charging outlets for your devices are a thoughtful touch. Standard rooms have the same two queen beds but without the living area, kitchenette, or three-way bathroom. Instead, they get a mini-fridge with coffeemaker and an average-size single bathroom.

Cabana Bay's two large pools both have artificial beaches and zero-entry sloping bottoms. The Cabana Courtyard Pool is more active, with a splash-pad playground and 100-foot waterslide wrapped around a central diving tower (which you can't actually dive off of, for safety reasons). The Lazy River Courtyard is a little more laid-back, with oldies music (as opposed to the top 40 usually played around the Cabana Courtyard) and a lushly landscaped circular stream in which to relax; flotation toys are sold for $3–$12, inflation and deflation included.

Indoor recreational options include the Game-O-Rama arcade (well stocked with late-model machines) and the 10-lane Galaxy Bowl, modeled after the Hollywood Star Lanes featured in *The Big Lebowski.* Bowling costs $15 per adult, $9 per kid age 12 and under, for 60–90 minutes of play with shoe rental. Other diversions include poolside table tennis and billiards, as well as a large Jack LaLanne fitness center for free. (Fitness centers aren't found at any Disney Value or Moderate resort except Coronado Springs.) An activity room with board games and beanbag chairs opens on rainy days. Finally, outdoor movies are shown nightly near both pools, and the food court sells $8 s'mores kits to roast over the gas-fueled fire pits.

In addition to the lobby's full-service Starbucks, there is the Bayliner Diner food court, with Coke Freestyle dispensers and giant screens in the seating area showing 1960s TV clips. Swizzle Lounge in the lobby, two pool bars (one with an attached counter-service grill), in-room pizza delivery, and table-service snacks and sandwiches at the Galaxy Bowl round out the on-site dining options. You'll find more restaurants and clubs nearby at the Royal Pacific Resort and Universal CityWalk. The Universal Gift Shop is the largest hotel store in the resort and stocks candy and clothes exclusive to Cabana Bay.

Unlike the other Universal resorts, Cabana Bay offers no watercraft service to the parks—it's either take the bus or walk. Colorful buses (with faux wood paneling and surfboards painted on the roof) depart to the parks' main parking hub from outside Cabana Bay's food court. The bus service is amazingly efficient; we've never waited more than 5 minutes for one to arrive, and the total transit time to the attractions is usually less than 15 minutes. It takes about the same amount of time to walk to CityWalk along the landscaped garden walkway, which passes the Sapphire Falls construction site before joining up with the walking path to Royal Pacific.

Self-parking is $12 for overnight guests, which is significantly less than other Universal hotels, but there is no valet, and hourly parking is steep for visitors ($8 for 5–30 minutes, $20 for 24 hours). Day guests who want to check out Cabana Bay should take the bus there from the parking hub because the garden walk's gate requires a key card for hotel access. Take care when driving into and out of the hotel's driveway on Adventure Way. If you miss the entrance, or make a right when exiting, you'll find yourself on a one-way road to I-4 West toward Disney, and you won't be able to make a U-turn until the FL 528 expressway.

Remember, Cabana Bay guests are eligible for Early Park Admission at Universal but do not receive complimentary Express Passes.

UNIVERSAL ORLANDO VACATION PACKAGES

UNIVERSAL FREQUENTLY OFFERS VACATION packages including hotel accommodations and theme park tickets via its in-house travel company, Universal Orlando Vacations. You can book a package yourself by calling ☎ 877-801-9720, or by visiting **universalorlando vacations.com** or your preferred travel agent. Universal Orlando Vacations booked more than 45 days in advance require only a $50 per-person deposit (airfare fully due at time of booking) that is fully refundable until 45 days out; after that, the penalty is $200 per package, though some event tickets may be nonrefundable.

Universal Orlando Vacations also handles group sales; if you want to organize a family reunion at Cabana Bay, call ☎ 800-224-4489 and choose option 3, or visit **res.universalorlandovacations.com /group-vacations/group-vacation-deals.**

Universal advertises its packages with enticing taglines like, "The Wizarding World from only $109 a night!" You've got to do the math, though, because sometimes it's difficult to see how buying the package can save money over buying each component separately.

Here's an example. A Wizarding World of Harry Potter Vacation Package in early 2015 offered a family of four (two adults and two kids under age 10) these components:

1. Four nights at a Universal on-site hotel (or off-site partner hotel)
2. Three days of park-to-park admission
3. Breakfast at The Three Broomsticks (one per person)
4. Breakfast at The Leaky Cauldron (one per person)
5. Special themed welcome parcel with owl plush, welcome letter, and home delivery of tickets
6. Early Park Admission to The Wizarding World of Harry Potter one hour before the general public

Staying at the Royal Pacific Resort, the package started at $1,726, including tax, during the value season, and cost $1,852 during regular season (April and May). There were significant restrictions, including blackout dates around spring break, Easter, and Memorial Day, and the stay had to occur on a Sunday–Thursday to qualify for that low rate; weekend nights were more expensive.

Here's the first thing to recognize: The last item—early admission to The Wizarding World—is automatically given to everyone who stays at a Universal resort. That is already included in the package, so it doesn't have any value by itself.

There are only three components to price: the hotel, tickets, and the breakfasts at The Three Broomsticks and Leaky Cauldron. Universal normally charges $14 for FedEx ticket delivery (discount ticket vendors deliver for free), and the stuffed toy would retail for around $15; the welcome letter has no monetary value. We checked Universal's website for the cost of the other components using various dates in early 2015 and ensured those dates would also qualify for the package above. Here's a typical cost per component:

- $968.40 for four nights (using "Stay More, Save More" discount) at Royal Pacific Resort, including tax (regular seasonal rate $1,210.52, including tax)
- $691.96 for the same three-day tickets from **undercovertourist.com**
- $120.90 for breakfast for four at The Three Broomsticks and Leaky Cauldron, including tax

The total cost if you bought each component separately is $1,781.26, a savings of almost $75 off the online package. You can still reserve breakfast in The Wizarding World through your hotel's ticket desk even without a package. Universal's price for the breakfast is $16 per adult and $12.39 per child, so it's easy enough to figure out what it costs. And you can always have lunch at The Three Broomsticks too, with the money you'll save by buying each item separately.

While it won't save you money, there are a few reasons why you might still want to book a Universal Orlando Vacations package. The first is if you can't afford to stay on-site but still want Early Park Admission to The Wizarding World. Booking a room at a Universal-area partner hotel as part of a package through Universal Orlando Vacations is the *only* way to get guaranteed early entry to the Harry Potter attractions, other than staying in an on-site hotel.

Another reason is if you are attending a special event at Universal Orlando that offers exclusive experiences for package buyers. For example, the Celebration of Harry Potter fan convention in January holds an after-hours party in The Wizarding World just for vacation-package purchasers. Occasionally, packages are offered with truly unique perks: Before the openings of Hogsmeade and Diagon Alley, a limited number of package holders were allowed into the new Wizarding Worlds weeks before the general public. These rare opportunities are only for the diehards because uncontrollable technical delays can always preempt previews without refunds.

One worthwhile package to consider is the Volunteer Vacation, which combines two-day park tickets with a four-hour volunteer opportunity at Give Kids the World Village, a nonprofit resort for kids with serious illnesses and their families. Universal will provide round-trip transportation to your volunteer shift and donate $100 to the organization per package purchased. Visit **universalorlando.com /vacation-packages/volunteer-vacations** for details.

Finally, if you are a big fan of Walt Disney World's Disney Dining Plan and insist on prepaying for your table-service meals, the Universal Dining Plan is available exclusively as an add-on to any Universal Orlando Vacations package. The adult plan costs $52 per person, per day, and includes one table-service meal (entrée, nonalcoholic beverage, and select dessert), one quick-service meal (entrée and nonalcoholic beverage), one snack, and a third nonalcoholic beverage. The child plan costs $18 and includes one table-service meal and one quick-service meal from the kids' menu, plus a regular snack and soft drink. Neither plan's price includes tax or gratuities, which are expected at table-service restaurants based on the value of your meal. Eligible table-service restaurants are restricted to the two sit-down restaurants at each park, plus a handful of CityWalk locations, the best of which are The Cowfish, Vivo Italian Kitchen, and Antojitos Authentic Mexican Food. Bafflingly, none of the restaurants inside the resort's hotels accept the dining plan, making it even more pointless for on-site guests.

Suffice to say that there are much better ways to spend $60-plus bucks a day on dining at Universal, and that you'll have to order very carefully to get your $32 value back from every table-service meal. A quick service-only dining plan ($20 for adults, $13 for kids, plus tax) is also sold to the general public; there's no real benefit to buying it in advance in a package. For more information on Universal's dining plans, see page 185, and visit **universalorlando.com/restaurants /universal-dining-plan.aspx.**

OFF-SITE LODGING OPTIONS
SELECTING AND BOOKING A HOTEL

LODGING COSTS IN ORLANDO vary incredibly. If you shop around, you can find a clean motel with a pool for as low as $40 a night. Because of hot competition, discounts abound, particularly for AAA and AARP members. There are four primary areas to consider:

1. UNIVERSAL STUDIOS AREA   In the triangular area bordered by I-4 on the southeast, Vineland Road on the north, and Turkey Lake Road on the west are Universal Orlando and the hotels most convenient to it. Running north–south through the middle of the triangle is Kirkman Road, which connects to I-4. On the east side of Kirkman are a number of independent hotels and restaurants. Universal hotels, theme parks, and CityWalk are west of Kirkman. Traffic in this area is not nearly as congested as on nearby International Drive, and there are good interstate connections in both directions.

2. INTERNATIONAL DRIVE AREA   This area, about 5 minutes from Universal, parallels I-4 on its eastern side and offers a wide selection of hotels and restaurants. Prices range from $56 to $400 per night. The chief drawbacks of this area are its terribly congested roads, countless traffic signals, and inadequate access to I-4 West. While International's biggest bottleneck is its intersection with Sand Lake Road, the mile between Kirkman and Sand Lake Roads is almost always gridlocked.

Regarding traffic on International Drive (known locally as I-Drive), a convention-goer from Islip, New York, weighed in with this:

> When I visited Orlando with my family last summer, we wasted huge chunks of time in traffic on International Drive. Our hotel was in the section between the big McDonald's [at Sand Lake Road] and Wet 'n Wild [at Universal Boulevard]. There are practically no left-turn lanes in this section, so anyone turning left can hold up traffic for a long time.

Traffic aside, a man from Ottawa, Ontario, sings the praises of his I-Drive experience:

Continued on page 93

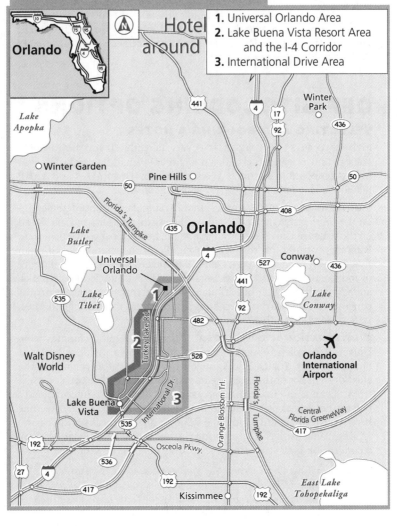

Hotel Concentrations Around Universal Orlando

1. Universal Orlando Area
2. Lake Buena Vista Resort Area and the I-4 Corridor
3. International Drive Area

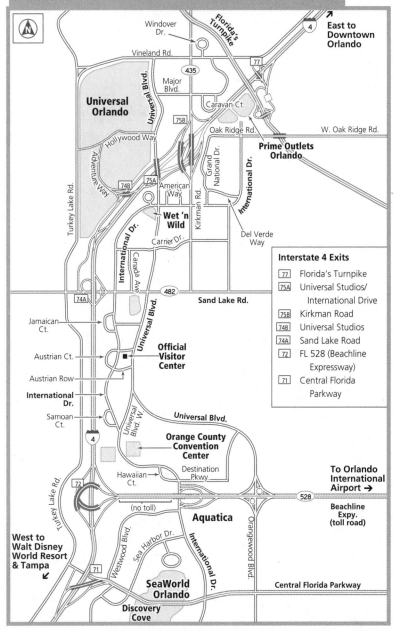

International Drive & Universal Areas

Windover Dr.

Florida's Turnpike

4 East to Downtown Orlando

Vineland Rd.

77

435

Major Blvd.

Universal Orlando

Universal Blvd.

Caravan Ct.

75B

Oak Ridge Rd.

W. Oak Ridge Rd.

Hollywood Way

Prime Outlets Orlando

Adventure Way

74B

75A

American Way

Grand National Dr.

International Dr.

Turkey Lake Rd.

Wet 'n Wild

Kirkman Rd.

Del Verde Way

International Dr.

Carrier Dr.

Canada Ave.

74A

482

Sand Lake Rd.

Jamaican Ct.

Universal Blvd.

Austrian Ct.

Official Visitor Center

Austrian Row

International Dr.

Samoan Ct.

Universal Blvd.

4

Universal Blvd. W.

Orange County Convention Center

Turkey Lake Rd.

72

Hawaiian Ct.

Destination Pkwy.

To Orlando International Airport →

528

Beachline Expy. (toll road)

(no toll)

Aquatica

Orangewood Blvd.

West to Walt Disney World Resort & Tampa ↙

Westwood Blvd.

Sea Harbor Dr.

International Dr.

71

SeaWorld Orlando

Central Florida Parkway

Discovery Cove

Interstate 4 Exits

77	Florida's Turnpike
75A	Universal Studios/ International Drive
75B	Kirkman Road
74B	Universal Studios
74A	Sand Lake Road
72	FL 528 (Beachline Expressway)
71	Central Florida Parkway

Lake Buena Vista Resort Area & the I-4 Corridor

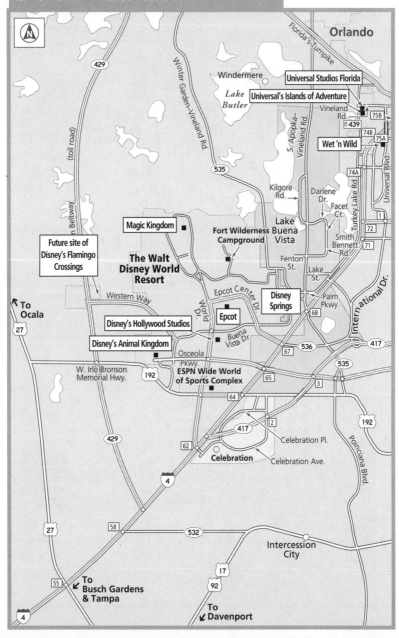

Continued from page 89

> *International Drive is the place to stay in Orlando. Your description of this location failed to point out that there are several discount stores, boutiques, restaurants, mini-putts, and other entertainment facilities all within walking distance of remarkably inexpensive accommodations and a short drive away from the attractions.*

International Drive hotels are listed in the *Official Visitor Guide*. To obtain a copy, call ☎ 800-972-3304 or 407-363-5872, or go to **visitorlando.com**.

3. LAKE BUENA VISTA AND THE I-4 CORRIDOR   A number of hotels are along FL 535 and west of I-4 between Disney World and I-4's intersection with Florida's Turnpike. They're easily reached from the interstate and are near many restaurants, including those on International Drive. Traffic on I-4 can be a real slog, so avoid it during rush hours.

4. WDW   We've also included a few hotels that are on the northeast side of Walt Disney World property, due to their proximity to Universal Orlando. We have not included other hotels on Disney property, nor have we included hotels along US 192 or those in Kissimmee.

HOTEL SHOPPING ON THE INTERNET: WELCOME TO THE WILD WEST

UNMATCHED AS AN EFFICIENT AND TIMELY distributor of information, the Internet has become the primary resource for travelers seeking to shop for and book their own air travel, hotels, rental cars, entertainment, and travel packages. It's by far the best direct-to-consumer distribution channel in history.

INTERNET ECONOMICS 101   The evolution of selling travel on the Web has radically altered the way airlines, hotels, cruise lines, rental-car companies, and the like do business. Before the Internet, these entities depended on travel agents or direct contact with customers by phone. Transaction costs were high because companies were obligated to pay commissions and fund labor-intensive in-house reservations departments. With the advent of the Internet, inexpensive e-commerce transactions became possible: Airlines and rental-car companies began using their own websites to effectively cut travel agents out of the sales process. Hotels also developed websites but continued to depend on wholesalers and travel agents as well.

It didn't take long before independent websites sprang up that sold travel products from a wide assortment of suppliers, often at deep discounts. These sites, called online travel agencies (OTAs), include such familiar names as Travelocity, Orbitz, Priceline, Expedia, Hotels.com, and Hotwire. Those mentioned and others like them attract huge numbers of customers shopping for hotels.

OTAS AND THE MERCHANT MODEL   In the beginning, hotels paid OTAs about the same commission that they paid travel agents, but then the OTAs began applying the thumbscrews, forcing hotels to make the transition from a simple commission model to what's called a merchant model. Under this model, hotels provide an OTA with a deeply discounted room rate that the OTA then marks up and sells. The difference between the marked-up price and the discounted rate paid to the hotel is the OTA's gross profit. If, for example, a hotel makes $120 rooms available to an OTA at a 33% discount, or $80, and the OTA sells the room at $110, the OTA's gross profit is $30 ($110-$80=$30).

The merchant model, originally devised for wholesalers and tour operators, has been around since long before the Internet. Wholesalers and tour operators, then and now, must commit to a certain volume of business, commit to guaranteed room allotments, pay deposits, and bundle the discounted rates with other travel services so that the actual hotel rate remains hidden within the bundle. This is known as opaque pricing. The merchant model costs the hotel two to three times the normal travel agent commission—considered justifiable because the wholesalers and tour operators also promote the hotel through brochures, websites, trade shows, print ads, and events.

OTAs now demand the equivalent of a wholesale commission or higher but are subject to none of the requirements imposed on wholesalers and tour operators. For instance, they don't have to commit to a specified volume of sales or keep discounted room rates opaque. In return, hotels give up 20%–50% of gross profit and are rewarded by having their rock-bottom rates plastered all over the Internet, with corresponding damage to their image and brand.

What's more, doing business with OTAs is very expensive for hotels. A hotel's cost of a multiday booking on its own website is $10–$12, including site hosting and analytics, marketing costs, and management fees. This is 10–20 times cheaper than the cost of the same booking through an OTA. Let's say a hotel sells a $100 room for six nights on its own website. Again, the booking would cost the hotel around $12, or $2 per night. If an OTA books the same room having secured it from the hotel at a 30% discount, the hotel receives $70 per night from the OTA. Thus the hotel's cost for the OTA booking is $30 per night, or $180 for six nights—15 times as costly as selling the room online with no middleman.

In the hotel industry, occupancy rates are important, but simply getting bodies into beds doesn't guarantee a profit. A more critical metric is revenue per available room (RevPAR). For a hotel full of guests booked through an OTA, RevPAR will be 20%–50% lower than for the same number of guests who booked the hotel directly, either through the hotel's website or by phone.

It's no wonder, then, that hotels and OTAs have a love/hate relationship. Likewise, it's perfectly understandable that hotels want to maximize direct bookings through their own websites and minimize OTA bookings. The problem is that the better-known OTAs draw a lot more Web traffic than a given hotel's (or even hotel chain's) website.

So the challenge for the hotel becomes how to shift room-shoppers away from the OTAs and channel them to its website. A number of hotel corporations, including Choice, Hilton, Hyatt, InterContinental, Marriott, and Wyndham, have risen to that challenge by forming their own OTA called Room Key (**roomkey.com**). The participating chains hope that working together will generate enough visitor traffic to make Room Key competitive with the Expedias and Travelocities of the world.

MORE POWER TO THE SHOPPER   Understanding the market dynamics we've described gives you a powerful tool for obtaining the best rates for the hotel of your choice. It's why we tell you to shop the Web for the lowest price available and then call your travel agent or the hotel itself to ask if they can beat it. Any savvy reservationist knows that selling you the room directly will both cut the hotel's cost and improve gross margin. If the reservationist can't help you, ask to speak to his or her supervisor. (We've actually had to explain hotel economics to more than a few clueless reservation agents.)

As for travel agents, they have clout based on the volume of business they send to a particular hotel or chain and can usually negotiate a rate even lower than what you've found on the Internet. Even if the agent can't beat the price, he or she can often obtain upgrades, preferred views, free breakfasts, and other deal sweeteners. If you enjoy cyber-shopping, have at it, but hotel shopping on the Internet isn't as quick or convenient as handing the task to your travel agent. When we bump into a great deal on the Web, we call our agent. Often she can beat the deal or improve on it, perhaps with an upgrade. *Reminder:* Except for special arrangements agreed to by you, the fee or commission due to your travel agent will be paid by the hotel.

THE SECRET   The key to shopping on the Internet is, well, shopping. When we're really hungry for a deal, there are a number of sites that we always check out (see the table below).

OUR FAVORITE ONLINE HOTEL RESOURCES
HOTELCOUPONS.COM   Self-explanatory
FLORIDAKISS.COM   Primarily US 192–Kissimmee area hotels
ORLANDOVACATION.COM   Great rates for condos and home rentals
VISITORLANDO.COM   Good info; not user-friendly for booking

We scour these sites for unusually juicy hotel deals that meet our criteria (location, quality, price, amenities). If we find a hotel that fills the bill, we check it out at other websites and comparative travel search engines such as Kayak (**kayak.com**) and Mobissimo (**mobissimo.com**) to see who has the best rate. (As an aside, Kayak used to be purely a search engine but now sells travel products, raising the issue of whether products not sold by Kayak are equally likely to come up in a search. Mobissimo, on the other hand, only links potential buyers to provider websites.) Your initial shopping effort should take about 15–20 minutes, faster if you can zero in quickly on a particular hotel.

Next, armed with your insider knowledge of hotel economics, call the hotel or have your travel agent call. Start by asking about specials. If there are none, or if the hotel can't beat the best price you've found on the Internet, share your findings and ask if the hotel can do better. Sometimes you'll be asked for proof of the rate you've discovered online—to be prepared for this, go to the site and enter the dates of your stay, plus the rate you've found to make sure it's available. If it is, print the page with this information and have it handy for your travel agent or for when you call the hotel. (*Note:* Always call the hotel's local number, not its national reservations number.)

INDEPENDENT AND BOUTIQUE HOTEL DEALS   While chain hotels worry about sales costs and profit margins, independent and so-called boutique hotels are concerned about discoverability—making themselves known to the traveling public. The market is huge, and it's increasingly hard for these hotels to get noticed, especially when they're competing with major chains. Independent and boutique hotels work on the premise that if they can get you through the front door, you'll become a loyal customer. For these hotels, substantially discounting rates is part of their marketing plan to build a client base. Because such hotels get lost on the big OTA sites and on search engines such as Kayak and Google, they've jumped on the flash-sale bandwagon. Offering almost irresistible rates on daily-coupon sites such as Groupon and LivingSocial, the independents can get their product in front of thousands of potential guests.

These offers are very generous but also time-limited. If you're in the market, though, you'll be hard-pressed to find better deals. While an OTA such as Expedia generally obtains rooms at a 20%–35% discount off the hotel's published rate, flash sites cut deals at an extra-deep discount. This allows their subscribers to bid on or to secure coupons for rooms that are often as much as 50% lower than the hotel's standard rate, and the coupons frequently include perks such as meals, free parking, waived resort fees, shopping vouchers, spa services, and entertainment. On Groupon's home page, click "Getaways" or just wait for Getaway coupons by e-mail as part of your free subscription. On LivingSocial you have to specifically subscribe to "Adventures" and "Escapes"; otherwise, you'll receive only non-travel-related offers.

ANOTHER WRINKLE   Finally, a quick word about a recent trend: bidding sites. On these sites you enter the type of accommodation you desire and your travel dates, and hotels will bid for your reservation. Some sites require that you already have a confirmed booking from a hotel before you can bid. A variation is that you reserve a room at a particular hotel for a set rate. If the rate drops subsequently, you get money back; if the rate goes up, your original rate is locked in.

TripAdvisor's Tingo (**tingo.com**) and Montreal-based BackBid (**backbid.com**) both claim to be able to beat rates offered by hotel websites and OTAs.

Simply put, bidding sites work best when hotels are dumping inventory—something that is rare among the better properties. Two-star hotels can always be booked for two-star prices, so nobody bids on the hotels with fewer than three stars.

IS IT WORTH IT?   You might be asking yourself if it's worth all this effort to save a few bucks. Saving $10 on a room doesn't sound like a big deal, but if you're staying six nights, that adds up to $60. Earlier we referred to unusually juicy deals, deep discounts predicated by who-knows-what circumstances that add up to big money. They're available every day, and with a little perseverance, you'll find them. Good hunting!

TWO OTHER DISCOUNT SOURCES WORTH MENTIONING

ORLANDO MAGICARD   This discount program is sponsored by Visit Orlando. Cardholders are eligible for discounts of 12%–50% at about 50 hotels. The Magicard is also good for discounts at some area attractions, three dinner theaters, museums, performing arts venues, restaurants, shops, and more. Valid for up to six persons, the card isn't available for larger groups or conventions.

To obtain a free Magicard and a list of participating hotels and attractions, call ☎ 800-643-9492 or 407-363-5872. On the Web, go to **visitorlando.com/magicard**; the Magicard and accompanying brochure can be printed from a computer. If you miss getting one before you leave home, obtain one at the Convention and Visitors Bureau Information Center at 8723 International Dr. When you call for your Magicard, also request the *Official Visitor Guide*.

HOTELCOUPONS.COM FLORIDA GUIDE   This book of coupons for lodging statewide is free in many restaurants and motels on main highways leading to Florida. Because most travelers make reservations before leaving home, picking up the book en route doesn't help much. To view it online or sign up for a free monthly guide sent by e-mail, visit **hotelcoupons.com**. For a hard copy ($3 for handling, $5 if shipped to Canada), call ☎ 800-222-3948 Monday–Friday, 8 a.m.–5 p.m. Eastern time.

SCRATCH THAT ITCH . . . FOR INFORMATION

GRANTED, IT WON'T HELP YOU FIND good deals on hotels, but The Bedbug Registry (**bedbugregistry.com**) is nonetheless a useful resource, allowing you to peruse reports of bedbug and other insect infestations at any hotel in the United States. Simply enter the name, city, and state of the property in question; you can also submit a report of your own. Understand that bedbug outbreaks are usually confined to particular rooms and that the creepy-crawlies were probably brought in by previous guests. If you suspect an infestation, report it to management immediately.

CONDOMINIUMS AND VACATION HOMES

VACATION HOMES ARE FREESTANDING, while condominiums are essentially one- to three-bedroom accommodations in a larger building housing a number of similar units. Because condos tend to be part of large developments (frequently time-shares), amenities such as swimming pools, playgrounds, game arcades, and fitness centers often rival those found in the best hotels. Generally speaking, condo developments don't have restaurants, lounges, or spas. In a condo, if something goes wrong, there will be someone on hand to fix the problem. Vacation homes rented from a property-management company likewise will have someone to come to the rescue, though responsiveness tends to vary vastly from company to company. If you rent directly from an owner, correcting problems is often more difficult, particularly when the owner doesn't live in the same area as the rental home.

In a vacation home, all the amenities are contained in the home (though in planned developments, there may be community amenities available as well). Depending on the specific home, you might find a small swimming pool, hot tub, two-car garage, family room, game room, and even a home theater. Features found in both condos and vacation homes include full kitchens, laundry rooms, TVs, DVD players, and frequently stereos. Interestingly, though almost all freestanding vacation homes have private pools, very few have backyards. This means that, except for swimming, the kids are pretty much relegated to playing in the house.

Time-share condos are clones when it comes to furniture and decor, but single-owner condos and vacation homes are furnished and decorated in a style that reflects the taste of the owner. Vacation homes, usually one- to two-story houses in a subdivision, very rarely afford interesting views (though some overlook lakes or natural areas), while condos, especially the high-rise variety, sometimes offer exceptional ones.

The Price is Nice

The best deals in lodging in the Orlando area are vacation homes and single-owner condos. Prices range from about $65 a night for two-bedroom condos and town homes to $200–$500 a night for three- to seven-bedroom vacation homes. Forgetting about taxes to keep the comparison simple, let's compare renting a vacation home to staying at the Cabana Bay Beach Resort, a Value resort. A family of two parents, two teens, and two grandparents would need two hotel rooms at Cabana Bay. At the lowest rate obtainable, that would run you $119 per night, per room, or $238 total. Rooms are 300 square feet each, so you'd have a total of 600 square feet. Each room has a private bath and a television.

Renting at the same time of year from All Star Vacation Homes (no relation to Disney's All-Star Resorts), you can stay at a 2,001-square-foot, three-bedroom, two-bath condo 3.5 miles from Universal Orlando for $159.

The home comes with the following features and amenities: a big-screen TV with surround sound, a computer, three additional TVs (one in each bedroom, all with DVD players and one with a PlayStation 2), a fully equipped kitchen, a full-size washer and dryer, and a fully furnished private patio.

The home is in a community with a 24-hour gated entrance. At the community center are a large swimming pool, a kiddie pool, a hot tub, a poolside refreshments bar, a fitness center, a theater, a game room, a basketball court, a business center, and a convenience store.

One thing we like about All Star Vacation Homes is that its website (**allstarvacationhomes.com**) offers detailed information, including a dozen or more photos of each specific home. When you book, the home you've been looking at is the actual one you're reserving. If you want to see how the home previously described is furnished, for instance, go to the home page, scroll down to "Select Code," and look for a small search window in the upper-right side of the photograph that reads "Search a Property Code." Enter 5-5024 SL-VC #305 in the search window. You'll be taken to another page with a description of the home, a slide show, a floor plan, a virtual tour, and more.

On the other hand, some vacation-home companies, like rental-car agencies, don't assign you a specific home until the day you arrive. These companies provide photos of a "typical" home instead of making information available on each of the individual homes in their inventory. In this case, you have to take the company's word that the typical home pictured is representative and that the home you'll be assigned will be just as nice.

How the Vacation-Home Market Works

In the Orlando area, there are more than 25,000 rental homes, including stand-alone homes, single-owner condos (that is, not time-shares), and town homes. The same area has about 114,000 hotel rooms. Almost all the rental homes are occupied by their owners for at least a week or two each year; the rest of the year, the owners make the homes available for rent. Some owners deal directly with renters, while others enlist the assistance of a property-management company.

Incredibly, about 700 property-management companies operate in the Orlando market. Most of these are mom-and-pop outfits that manage an inventory of 10 homes or fewer (probably fewer than 70 companies oversee more than 100 rental homes).

Homeowners pay these companies to maintain and promote their properties and handle all rental transactions. Some homes are made available to wholesalers, vacation packagers, and travel agents in deals negotiated either directly by the owners or by property-management companies on the owners' behalf. A wholesaler or vacation packager will occasionally drop its rates to sell slow-moving inventory, but more commonly the cost to renters is higher than when dealing directly with owners or management companies: Because most wholesalers and packagers sell their inventory through travel agents, both the whole-saler/packager's markup and the travel agent's commission are passed along to the renter. These costs are in addition to the owner's cut and/or the fee for the property manager.

Along similar lines, logic may suggest that the lowest rate of all can be obtained by dealing directly with owners, thus eliminating middle-men. Though this is sometimes true, it's more often the case that property-management companies offer the best rates. With their mar-keting expertise and larger customer base, these companies can produce a higher occupancy rate than the owners themselves can. What's more, management companies, or at least the larger ones, can achieve econo-mies of scale not available to owners regarding maintenance, cleaning, linens, and even acquiring furniture and appliances (if a house is not already furnished). The combination of higher occupancy rates and economies of scale adds up to a win-win situation for owners, manage-ment companies, and renters alike.

Location, Location, Location

The best vacation home is one that is within easy commuting distance of the theme parks. If you plan to spend some time at Walt Disney World and SeaWorld, in addition to the Universal parks, you'll want something just to the southwest of Universal Orlando (between Walt Disney World and Orlando).

Zoning laws in Orange County (which also includes most of Orlando, Universal Studios, SeaWorld, Lake Buena Vista, and the International Drive area) used to prohibit short-term rentals of homes and single-owner condos, but in recent years the county has loosened its zoning restrictions in a few predominantly tourist-oriented areas. So far, practically all of the vacation-rental homes in Orange County are in the Floridays and Vista Cay developments.

By our reckoning, about half the rental homes in Osceola County and all the rental homes in Polk County are too far away for commuting to be practical. You might be able to save a few bucks by staying farther out, but the most desirable homes to be found are in Vista Cay and in developments no more than 4 miles from Disney World's main entrance on US 192 (Irlo Bronson Memorial Highway), in Osceola County.

To get the most from a vacation home, you need to be close enough to commute in 20 minutes or less to your Orlando destination. This will allow for naps, quiet time, swimming, and dollar-saving meals you prepare yourself.

Shopping for a Vacation Home

The only practical way to shop for a rental home is on the Web. This makes it relatively easy to compare different properties and rental com-panies; on the downside, there are so many owners, rental companies, and individual homes from which to choose that you could research yourself into a stupor. There are three main types of websites in the home-rental game: those for property-management companies, which showcase a given company's homes and are set up for direct bookings; individual owner sites; and third-party listings sites, which advertise properties available through different owners and sometimes management companies as well. Sites in the last category will usually refer prospective renters to an owner's or management company's site for reservations.

We've found that most property-management sites are not very well designed and will test your patience to the max. You can practically click yourself into old age trying to see all the homes available or figure out where on earth they are. Nearly all claim to be "just minutes from Universal [or Disney]." (By that reasoning, we should list Bob's home; it's also just minutes from Universal . . . 570 minutes, to be exact!)

Many websites list homes according to towns (such as Auburndale, Clermont, Davenport, Haines City, and Winter Garden) or real estate developments (including Eagle Pointe, Formosa Gardens, Indian Ridge, and Windsor Palms) in the general Disney–Universal area, none of which you're likely to be familiar with. The information that counts is the distance of a vacation home or condo from Universal; for that, you often must look for something like "4 miles from Universal" embedded in the home's description.

The best websites provide the following:

- Numerous photos and in-depth descriptions of individual homes to make comparisons quick and easy
- Overview maps or text descriptions that reflect how far specific homes or developments are from your Orlando destination
- The ability to book the specific rental home of your choice on the site
- An easy-to-find phone number for bookings and questions

The best sites are also easy to navigate, let you see what you're interested in without your having to log in or divulge any personal information, and list memberships in such organizations as the Better Business Bureau and the Central Florida Vacation Rental Managers Association (visit **cfvrma.com** for the association's code of ethics).

Recommended Websites

After checking out dozens upon dozens of sites, here are the ones we recommend. All of them meet the criteria listed above. If you're stunned that there are so few of them, well, so were we. (For the record, we elected not to list some sites that met our criteria but whose homes are too far away from the Orlando-area attractions.)

All Star Vacation Homes (**allstarvacationhomes.com**) is easily the best of the management-company sites, with easily accessible photos and plenty of details about featured homes. All the company's rental properties are within either 3 miles of Universal Studios or 4 miles of Walt Disney World.

#1 Dream Homes (**floridadreamhomes.com**) has a good reputation for customer service and now has photos of and information about the homes in its online inventory.

Orlando's Finest Vacation Homes (**orlandosfinest.com**) represents both homeowners and property-management companies. Offering a broad inventory, the Orlando's Finest website features photos and information on individual homes. Though the info is not as detailed as that offered by the All Star Vacation Homes site, friendly sales agents can fill in the blanks.

Vacation Rentals by Owner (**vrbo.com**) is a nationwide vacation-homes listings service that puts prospective renters in direct contact with owners. The site is straightforward and always lists a large number of rental properties in Celebration, Disney's planned community situated about 15–20 minutes from the Universal theme parks. Two similar listings services with good websites are Vacation Rentals 411 (**vacationrentals411.com**) and Last Minute Villas (**lastminutevillas.net**).

The website for Visit Orlando (**visitorlando.com**) is the place to go if you're interested in renting a condominium at one of the many time-share developments (click on "Places to Stay" at the site's home page). You can call the developments directly, but going through this website allows you to bypass sales departments and escape their high-pressure invitations to sit through sales presentations. The site also lists hotels and vacation homes. For all types of accommodations, you can sort by distance from where you'll spend your touring time. Distance-sorting categories include Walt Disney World, Universal, the Orange County Convention Center, and downtown Orlando, among others. If you select Universal, for example, the list of accommodations will be ordered from the closest to the most distant.

Making Contact

Once you've found a vacation home you like, check around the website for a Frequently Asked Questions (FAQ) page. If there's not an FAQ page, here are some of the things you'll want to check out on the phone with the owner or rental company.

1. How close is the property to your vacation destination?
2. Is the home or condominium that I see on the Internet the one I'll get?
3. Is the property part of a time-share development?
4. Are there any specials or discounts available?
5. Is everything included in the rental price, or are there additional charges? What about taxes?
6. How old is the home or condo I'm interested in? Has it been refurbished recently?
7. What is the view from the property?
8. Is the property near any noisy roads?
9. What is your smoking policy?
10. Are pets allowed? This consideration is as important to those who want to avoid pets as to those who want to bring them.
11. Is the pool heated?

12. Is there a fenced backyard where children can play?

13. How many people can be seated at the main dining table?

14. Is there a separate dedicated telephone at the property?

15. Is high-speed Internet access available?

16. Are linens and towels provided?

17. How far are the nearest supermarket and drugstore?

18. Are child-care services available?

19. Are there restaurants nearby?

20. Is transportation to the parks provided?

21. Will we need a car?

22. What is required to make a reservation?

23. What is your change/cancellation policy?

24. When is checkout time?

25. What will we be responsible for when we check out?

26. How will we receive our confirmation and arrival instructions?

27. What are your office hours?

28. What are the directions to your office?

29. What if we arrive after your office has closed?

30. Whom do we contact if something goes wrong during our stay?

31. How long have you been in business?

32. Are you licensed by the state of Florida?

33. Do you belong to the Better Business Bureau and/or the Central Florida Vacation Rental Managers Association?

We frequently receive letters from readers extolling the virtues of renting a condo or vacation home. This endorsement by a family from Ellington, Connecticut, is typical:

> Our choice to stay in a vacation home was based on cost and sanity. We've found over the last couple of years that our children can't share the same bed. We have also gotten tired of having to turn off the lights at 8 p.m. and lie quietly in the dark waiting for our children to fall asleep. With this in mind, we needed a condo/suite layout. We decided on the Sheraton Vistana Resort. We had a two-bedroom villa with full kitchen, living room, three TVs, and washer/dryer. I packed for half the trip and did laundry almost every night. The facilities offered a daily children's program and several pools, kiddie pools, and play-scapes. Located on FL 535, we had a 5- to 10-minute drive to most attractions, including SeaWorld, Disney, and Universal.

A New Jersey family of five echoes the above:

> I cannot stress enough how important it is if you have a large family (more than two kids) to rent a house for your stay! We had visited Orlando several times in the past by ourselves when we were

newlyweds. Fast-forward 10 years later, when we took our three kids, ages 6 years, 4 years, and 20 months. We stayed at Windsor Hills Resort, which I booked through globalresorthomes.com. *I was able to see all the homes and check availability when I was reserving the house.*

The BEST HOTELS *for* FAMILIES NEAR UNIVERSAL ORLANDO

WHAT MAKES A SUPER FAMILY HOTEL? Roomy accommodations, in-room fridge, great pool, complimentary breakfast, child-care options, and programs for kids are a few of the things *The Unofficial Guide* hotel team researched in selecting the top hotels for families from among hundreds of properties in the Universal Orlando area. Some of our picks are expensive, others are more reasonable, and some are a bargain. Regardless of price, be assured that these hotels understand a family's needs.

Though all of the following hotels offer some type of shuttle to the theme parks, some offer very limited service. Call the hotel before you book and ask what the shuttle schedule will be when you visit. Because families, like individuals, have different wants and needs, we haven't ranked the following properties here; they're listed alphabetically.

INTERNATIONAL DRIVE AND UNIVERSAL AREA HOTEL PROFILES

Castle Hotel ★★★½

8629 International Dr.
Orlando
☎ 407-345-1511 or
877-317-5753
castlehotelorlando.com

Rate per night $149–$219. **Pool** ★★★. **Fridge in room** Yes ($15/day). **Shuttle to parks** Yes (Universal, SeaWorld, and Wet 'n Wild). **Maximum number of occupants per room** 4. **Special comments** For an additional fee ($12 for adults, children age 12 and under free with paying adult), up to 4 people receive a full breakfast. Pets up to 50 pounds welcome ($150 nonrefundable fee).

YOU CAN'T MISS THIS ONE: it's the only castle on I-Drive. Previously a Holiday Inn and before that a DoubleTree, the Castle is now part of Marriott's Autograph Collection. A recent $6.5-million renovation left the hotel's over-the-top ambience refreshed but largely unchanged: Inside you'll find the same royal colors (purple predominates), opulent fixtures (antlers are a recurring motif), European art, and Renaissance music.

The 216 rooms and suites also retain the royal treatment, but the decor is a bit more tasteful and streamlined after the renovation. All rooms are fairly large and well equipped with flat-panel TV, minibar (fridge is available at an extra charge), free Wi-Fi, coffeemaker, iron and board, hair dryer, and safe. The Garden Bistro & Bar off the lobby serves full or Continental breakfast. For lunch or dinner, you might walk next door to Vito's Chop House (dinner only) or Café Tu Tu Tango (an Unofficial favorite). The heated circular pool is 5 feet deep and features a fountain in the center, a poolside bar, and a hot tub. There's no separate kiddie pool. Other amenities include the Poseidon Spa, a fitness center, gift shop, lounge, valet laundry service and facilities, and guest services desk with park passes for sale and babysitting recommendations. Security feature: Elevators require an electronic key card.

CoCo Key Hotel and Water Resort–Orlando ★★★½

Rate per night $75–$108. **Pools** ★★★★. **Fridge in room** Yes. **Shuttle to parks** Yes (Aquatica, SeaWorld, Universal, Wet 'n Wild). **Maximum number of occupants** per room 4. **Special comments** Daily $22 resort fee for use of the water park; day guests may use the water park for $23/person Monday–Friday ($25 Saturday–Sunday and $20 for Florida residents).

7400 International Dr. Orlando
☎ 407-351-2626 or 877-875-4681
cocokeyorlando.com

NOT FAR FROM THE UNIVERSAL ORLANDO theme parks, CoCo Key combines a tropical-themed hotel with a canopied water park featuring three pools and 14 waterslides, as well as poolside food and arcade entertainment. A full-service restaurant serves breakfast and dinner; a food court offers family favorites such as burgers, chicken fingers, and pizza.

A unique feature of the resort is its cashless payment system, much like that on a cruise ship. At check-in, families receive bar-coded wristbands that allow purchased items to be easily charged to their room.

The unusually spacious guest rooms include 37-inch flat-panel TVs, free Wi-Fi, granite showers and countertops, and plenty of accessible outlets for guests' electronics.

DoubleTree by Hilton Orlando at SeaWorld ★★★★½

Rate per night $129–$179. **Pools** ★★★½. **Fridge in room** Standard in some rooms; available in others for $10/day. **Shuttle to parks** Yes. **Maximum number of occupants per room** 4. **Special comments** Good option if you're visiting SeaWorld or Aquatica. Pets welcome (1 per room, 25-pound limit, $75).

10100 International Dr. Orlando
☎ 407-352-1100 or 800-327-0363
doubletreeorlando idrive.com

ON 28 LUSH, TROPICAL ACRES WITH a Balinese feel, the DoubleTree is adjacent to SeaWorld and Aquatica water park. The 1,094 rooms and suites—classified as resort or tower—are suitable for business travelers or families. We recommend the tower rooms for good views and the resort rooms for maximum convenience. The Bamboo Grille serves steak and seafood, along with breakfast; you can also get a quick bite at Bangli Lounge, the deli, or the pool bar. Relax and cool off at one of the three pools (there are two more just for kids), or indulge in a special spa treatment. A fitness center, mini-golf course and putting green, children's day camp, and game area afford even more diversions.

The resort is about a 12-minute drive to Universal, a 15-minute drive to Walt Disney World, or a short walk to SeaWorld.

Nickelodeon Suites Resort ★★★½

14500 Continental Gateway Orlando
☎ 407-387-5437 or 877-NICK-111
(877-642-5111)
nickhotel.com

Rate per night $149–$209. **Pools** ★★★★. **Fridge in room** Yes. **Shuttle to parks** Yes. **Maximum number of occupants per room** 8. **Special comments** Daily character breakfast; resort fee of $30/night.

SPONGEBOB SQUAREPANTS, EAT YOUR HEART OUT. This resort is as kid-friendly as they come. Decked out in all themes Nickelodeon, the hotel is sure to please any fan of the TV shows *SpongeBob, Dora the Explorer,* and *Avatar: The Last Airbender*, to name a few. Nickelodeon characters from the channel's many shows hang out in the resort's lobby and mall area, greeting kids while parents check in.

Guests can choose from among 777 suites—one-bedroom Family Suites and two- and three-bedroom KidSuites—executed in a number of different themes—all very brightly and creatively decorated. All suites include kitchenettes or full kitchens; also standard are a microwave, fridge, coffeemaker, TV, iron and board, hair dryer, and safe. KidSuites feature a semiprivate kids' bedroom with bunk or twin beds, pullout sleeper bed, 32-inch TV, CD player, and activity table. The master bedroom offers ample storage space that the kids' bedroom lacks.

Additional amenities include a video arcade, Studio Nick—a game show studio that hosts several game shows a night for the entertainment of a live studio audience, a buffet (kids age 3 and younger eat free with a paying adult), a food court offering Subway and other choices, the full-service Nicktoons Cafe (offers character breakfasts), a convenience store, a lounge, a gift shop, a fitness center, a washer and dryer in each courtyard, and a guest activities desk (buy Disney tickets and get recommendations on babysitting). Not to be missed—don't worry, your kids won't let you—are the resort's two pools, Oasis and Lagoon. Oasis features a water park complete with water cannons, rope ladders, geysers, and dump buckets, as well as a hot tub for adults (with a view of the rest of the pool so you can keep an eye on little ones) and a smaller play area for younger kids. Kids will love the huge, zero-entry Lagoon Pool with 400-gallon dump bucket, plus a nearby basketball court and nine-hole mini-golf course. Pool activities for kids are scheduled several times a day, seasonally; some games feature the infamous green slime. Whatever you do, avoid letting your kids catch you saying the phrase "I don't know" while you're here—trust us.

Rosen Shingle Creek ★★★★

9939 Universal Blvd. Orlando
☎ 407-996-9939 or 866-996-6338
rosenshinglecreek.com

Rate per night $179–$190. **Pools** ★★★★. **Fridge in room** Yes. **Shuttle to parks** Yes (Universal, Wet 'n Wild, Discovery Cove, Aquatica, and SeaWorld only). **Maximum number of occupants per room** 4.

BEAUTIFUL ROOMS (EAST-FACING ONES HAVE GREAT VIEWS) and excellent restaurants distinguish this mostly meeting- and convention-oriented resort. The pools are large and lovely and include a lap pool, a family pool, and a kiddie wading pool. There's an 18-hole golf course on-site, as well as a superior spa and an adequate fitness center. Child care is provided as well.

Though a state-of-the-art video arcade will gobble up your kids' pocket change, the real kicker, especially for the 8-years-and-up crowd, is a natural area encompassing lily ponds, grassy wetlands, Shingle Creek, and an adjacent cypress swamp. Running through the area is a nature trail complete with signs to help you identify wildlife. Great blue herons, wood storks, coots, egrets, mallard ducks, anhingas, and ospreys are common, as are sliders (turtles), chameleons, and skinks (lizards). Oh yeah, there are alligators and snakes too—real ones, but that's part of the fun.

If you stay at Shingle Creek and plan to visit the theme parks, you'll want a car. Shuttle service is limited, departing and picking up at rather inconvenient times and stopping at three other hotels before delivering you to your destination.

HOTELS AND MOTELS:
Rated and Ranked

IN THIS SECTION, WE COMPARE HOTELS in four main areas outside Universal Orlando (see page 89) with those inside the resort. Additional hotels can be found at the intersection of US 27 and I-4, on US 441 (Orange Blossom Trail), and in downtown Orlando. Most of these require more than 30 minutes of commuting to the Orlando-area attractions and thus are not rated. We also haven't rated lodging along US 192.

WHAT'S IN A ROOM?

EXCEPT FOR CLEANLINESS, STATE OF REPAIR, and decor, travelers pay little attention to hotel rooms. There is, of course, a clear standard of quality and luxury that differentiates Motel 6 from Holiday Inn, Holiday Inn from Marriott, and so on. Many guests, however, fail to appreciate that some rooms are better engineered than others. Making the room usable to its occupants is an art that combines both form and function.

Decor and taste are important. No one wants to stay in a room that's dated, garish, or ugly. But beyond decor, how "livable" is the room? In Orlando, for example, we've seen some beautifully appointed rooms that aren't well designed for human habitation. Even more than decor, your room's details and design elements are the things that will make you feel comfortable and at home.

ROOM RATINGS

TO EVALUATE PROPERTIES FOR THEIR QUALITY, tastefulness, state of repair, cleanliness, and size of their standard rooms, we have grouped the hotels and motels into classifications denoted by stars—the overall star rating. Star ratings in this guide apply only to Orlando-area properties and don't necessarily correspond to ratings awarded by Frommer's, Mobil, AAA, or other travel critics. Because stars have little relevance when awarded in the absence of recognized standards of comparison, we have tied our ratings to expected levels of quality established by specific American hotel corporations.

Overall star ratings apply only to room quality and describe the property's standard accommodations. For most hotels, a standard accommodation is a room with one king bed or two queen beds. In an all-suite property, the standard accommodation is either a studio or a one-bedroom suite. In addition to standard accommodations, many hotels offer luxury rooms and special suites, which aren't rated in this guide. Star ratings for rooms are assigned without regard to whether a property has restaurant(s), recreational facilities, entertainment, or other extras.

OVERALL STAR RATINGS		
★★★★★	Superior rooms	Tasteful and luxurious by any standard
★★★★	Extremely nice rooms	What you'd expect at a Hyatt Regency or Marriott
★★★	Nice rooms	Holiday Inn or comparable quality
★★	Adequate rooms	Clean, comfortable, and functional without frills—like a Motel 6
★	Super-budget	These exist but are not included in our coverage

In addition to stars (which delineate broad categories), we use a numerical rating system—the room quality rating. Our scale is 0–100, with 100 being the best possible rating and zero (0) the worst. Numerical ratings show the difference we perceive between one property and another. For instance, rooms at both the Best Western Plus Universal Inn and the Fairfield Inn & Suites Near Universal Orlando Resort are rated 3.5 stars (★★★½). In the supplemental numerical ratings, the former is a 75 and the latter an 80. This means that within the 3.5-star category, Fairfield Inn & Suites has slightly nicer rooms than Best Western Plus.

The location column identifies the area where you'll find a particular property. A 1 means it's in the Universal Orlando area. A 2 means it's on or near International Drive. All others are marked with 3 and for the most part are along FL 535 and the I-4 corridor, though some are in nearby locations that don't meet any other criteria. WDW, of course, indicates hotels located inside Walt Disney World property.

*un*official **TIP**
The key to avoiding disappointment is to snoop in advance. Ask how old the hotel is and when its guest rooms were last renovated.

LODGING AREAS *(see map on page 90)*	
1 Universal Orlando Area	**2** International Drive
3 Lake Buena Vista and I-4 Corridor	**WDW** Walt Disney World Resort

Names of properties along US 192 also designate location (for example, Holiday Inn Main Gate East). The consensus in Orlando seems to be that the main entrance to Disney World is the broad interstate-type road that runs off US 192. This is called the Maingate. Properties along US 192 call themselves Maingate East or West to differentiate their positions along the highway. So, driving southeast from Clermont or Florida's Turnpike, the properties before you reach the Maingate turnoff are called Maingate West, while the properties after you pass the Maingate turnoff are called Maingate East.

Cost estimates are based on the hotel's published rack rates for standard rooms. Each $ represents $50. Thus a cost symbol of $$$ means that a room (or suite) at that hotel will be about $150 a night; amounts more than $200 are indicated by $ x 5 and so on.

We've focused on room quality and excluded consideration of location, services, recreation, or amenities. In some instances, a one- or two-room suite is available for the same price or less than that of a single standard hotel room.

If you've used another guidebook in this series, you'll notice that new properties have been added and many ratings and rankings have changed, some because of room renovation or improved maintenance or housekeeping. Lax housekeeping or failure to maintain rooms can bring down ratings.

Before you shop for a hotel, consider this letter from a man in Hot Springs, Arkansas:

> We canceled our room reservations to follow the advice in your book and reserved a hotel highly ranked by The Unofficial Guide. We wanted inexpensive but clean and cheerful. We got inexpensive but also dirty, grim, and depressing. The room spoiled the holiday for me aside from our touring.

This letter was as unsettling to us as the bad room was to the reader—our integrity as travel journalists is based on the quality of the information we provide. When rechecking the hotel, we found our rating was representative, but the reader had been assigned one of a small number of threadbare rooms scheduled for renovation.

Be aware that some chains use the same guest room photo in promotional literature for all their hotels and that the rooms at a specific property may bear no resemblance to the photo in question. When you or your travel agent calls, ask how old the property is and when the guest room you're being assigned was last renovated. If you're assigned a room that is inferior to your expectations, demand to be moved.

A **WORD** *About* **TOLL-FREE TELEPHONE NUMBERS**

AS WE'VE REPEATED SEVERAL TIMES in this chapter, it's essential to communicate with the hotel directly when shopping for deals and stating your room preferences. Most toll-free numbers are routed directly to a hotel chain's central reservations office, and the customer service agents there typically have little or no knowledge of the individual hotels in the chain or of any specials those hotels may be offering. In our Hotel Information Chart (pages 115–121), therefore, we list the toll-free number only if it connects directly to the hotel in question; otherwise, we provide the hotel's local phone number.

The **30 BEST HOTEL VALUES**

IN THE CHART ON THE OPPOSITE PAGE, we look at the best combinations of quality and value in a room. Rankings are made without consideration for location or the availability of restaurant(s), recreational facilities, entertainment, and/or amenities.

A reader wrote to complain that he had booked one of our top-ranked rooms in terms of value and had been very disappointed in the room. We noticed that the room the reader occupied had a quality rating of 2.5. Remember that the list of top deals is intended to give you some sense of value received for dollars spent. A 2.5 room at $40 may have the same value as a 4.0 room at $115, but that doesn't mean the rooms will be of comparable quality. Regardless of whether it's a good deal, a 2.5 room is still a 2.5 room.

THE 30 BEST HOTEL VALUES

	HOTEL	LODGING AREA	OVERALL QUALITY	ROOM QUALITY	($ = $50)
1.	Monumental Hotel	2	★★★★½	94	$$-
2.	Extended Stay America Orlando Lake Buena Vista	3	★★★★	83	$$-
3.	Extended Stay America Convention Center/Westwood	2	★★★★	84	$$-
4.	Monumental MovieLand Hotel	2	★★★	68	$+
5.	Motel 6 Orlando–I-Drive	2	★★★	66	$+
6.	Hilton Grand Vacations Club at SeaWorld	2	★★★★½	95	$$$-
7.	Extended Stay America Deluxe Orlando Theme Parks	1	★★★½	75	$$-
8.	Extended Stay America Orlando Theme Parks	1	★★★½	75	$$-
9.	Rosen Inn at Pointe Orlando	2	★★★½	75	$$-
10.	Hilton Orlando Bonnet Creek	2	★★★★	88	$$+
11.	Four Points by Sheraton Orlando Studio City	2	★★★★½	90	$$$-
12.	Quality Suites Turkey Lake	3	★★★	74	$+
13.	Extended Stay America Orlando Convention Center	2	★★★	72	$+
14.	La Quinta Inn Orlando I-Drive	2	★★★	73	$$-
15.	Ramada Convention Center I-Drive	2	★★★	65	$+
16.	Comfort Inn Orlando–Lake Buena Vista	3	★★★½	80	$$
17.	Rosen Centre Hotel	2	★★★★½	95	$$$+
18.	Best Western Plus Universal inn	1	★★★½	75	$$-
19.	Hawthorn Suites Lake Buena Vista	3	★★★★	85	$$+
20.	Wyndham Orlando Resort I-Drive	2	★★★★	85	$$+
21.	Hilton Orlando Lake Buena Vista	WDW	★★★★	87	$$$-
22.	Courtyard Orlando LBV in Marriott Village	3	★★★½	82	$$+
23.	Residence Inn Orlando at SeaWorld	3	★★★★	85	$$$-
24.	Stay Sky Suites I-Drive Orlando	2	★★★½	82	$$+
25.	DoubleTree by Hilton Orlando at SeaWorld	2	★★★★½	92	$$$+
26.	WorldQuest Orlando Resort	2	★★★★	88	$$$-
27.	CoCo Key Water Resort–Orlando	2	★★★★½	82	$$+
28.	Comfort Inn–I-Drive	2	★★★★	66	$$-
29.	DoubleTree Universal	1	★★★★½	89	$$$-
30.	Hawthorn Suites Orlando I-Drive	2	★★★★	75	$$+

How the Hotels Compare

HOTEL	LOCATION	OVERALL QUALITY	ROOM QUALITY	($ = $50)
Four Seasons Resort Orlando at Walt Disney World Resort	WDW	★★★★★	98	$ x 9
Hilton Grand Vacations Club at SeaWorld	2	★★★★½	95	$$$−
Rosen Centre Hotel	2	★★★★½	95	$$$+
Monumental Hotel	2	★★★★½	94	$$−
Ritz-Carlton Orlando, Grande Lakes	2	★★★★½	94	$+ x 5
Waldorf Astoria Orlando	3	★★★★½	93	$$$$+
JW Marriott Orlando Grande Lakes	2	★★★★½	93	$+ x 5
Hard Rock Hotel	1	★★★★½	93	$ x 8
DoubleTree by Hilton Orlando at SeaWorld	2	★★★★½	92	$$$+
Marriott's Grande Vista	2	★★★★½	92	$$$+
Westgate Lakes Resort & Spa	3	★★★★½	92	$$$+
Hilton Orlando	2	★★★★½	92	$$$$+
Villas of Grand Cypress	3	★★★★½	92	$− x 5
Hyatt Regency Grand Cypress	3	★★★★½	92	$− x 5
Marriott's Sabal Palms	3	★★★★½	92	$+ x 6
Loews Portofino Bay Hotel	1	★★★★½	92	$+ x 8
Four Points by Sheraton Orlando Studio City	2	★★★★½	90	$$$−
Rosen Plaza Hotel	2	★★★★½	90	$$$+
Renaissance Orlando at SeaWorld	2	★★★★½	90	$$$+
Marriott's Harbour Lake	3	★★★★½	90	$$$$−
Hyatt Regency Orlando	2	★★★★½	90	$$$$−
Grand Beach	2	★★★★½	90	$$$$−
Orlando World Center Marriott Resort	3	★★★★½	90	$$$$+
Wyndham Bonnet Creek Resort	3	★★★★½	90	$$$$+
Loews Royal Pacific Resort	1	★★★★½	90	$+ x 6
Disney's Saratoga Springs Resort & Spa	WDW	★★★★½	90	$+ x 8
DoubleTree Universal	1	★★★★	89	$$$−
Courtyard Orlando Lake Buena Vista at Vista Centre	3	★★★★	89	$$$−
Sheraton Vistana Resort Villas	3	★★★★	89	$$$$−
Hilton Orlando Bonnet Creek	2	★★★★	88	$$+
WorldQuest Orlando Resort	2	★★★★	88	$$$−
Caribe Royale All-Suite Hotel & Convention Center	2	★★★★	88	$$$+
Hilton Garden Inn Lake Buena Vista/Orlando	3	★★★★	88	$$$+
Hilton Grand Vacations Club on I-Drive	2	★★★★	88	$$$+
Sheraton Lake Buena Vista Resort	3	★★★★	88	$$$+
Rosen Shingle Creek	2	★★★★	88	$$$+
Universal's Cabana Bay Beach Resort	1	★★★★	88	$$$$−

How the Hotels Compare

HOTEL	LOCATION	OVERALL QUALITY	ROOM QUALITY	($ = $50)
Hilton Orlando Lake Buena Vista	WDW	★★★★	87	$$$-
Westin Orlando Universal Boulevard	2	★★★★	87	$$$$+
Embassy Suites Orlando–Lake Buena Vista Resort	3	★★★★	86	$$$+
Floridays Resort Orlando	2	★★★★	86	$$$$
Marriott's Cypress Harbour	2	★★★★	86	$ x 6
Marriott's Imperial Palms	2	★★★★	86	$- x 9
Hawthorn Suites Lake Buena Vista	3	★★★★	85	$$+
Wyndham Orlando Resort I-Drive	2	★★★★	85	$$+
Residence Inn Orlando at SeaWorld	3	★★★★	85	$$$-
Legacy Vacation Club Lake Buena Vista	3	★★★★	85	$$$-
Homewood Suites by Hilton LBV-Orlando	3	★★★★	85	$$$$-
Marriott's Royal Palms	2	★★★★	85	$- x 6
Extended Stay America Convention Center/ Westwood	2	★★★★	84	$$-
Hyatt Place Orlando/Universal	1	★★★★	84	$$$+
Extended Stay America Orlando Lake Buena Vista	3	★★★★	83·	$$-
Buena Vista Suites	2	★★★★	83	$$$+
Courtyard Orlando LBV in Marriott Village	3	★★★½	82	$$+
Stay Sky Suites I-Drive Orlando	2	★★★½	82	$$+
CoCo Key Water Resort–Orlando	2	★★★½	82	$$+
Point Universal Orlando Resort, The	2	★★★½	82	$$+
Holiday Inn Resort Lake Buena Vista	3	★★★½	82	$$+
Radisson Hotel Orlando Lake Buena Vista	3	★★★½	82	$$$-
Castle Hotel	2	★★★½	82	$$$+
B Resort	WDW	★★★½	82	$$$+
Nickelodeon Suites Resort	2	★★★½	82	$$$$
Homewood Suites by Hilton I-Drive	2	★★★½	81	$$$$-
Comfort Inn Orlando–Lake Buena Vista	3	★★★½	80	$$
Hilton Garden Inn Orlando I-Drive North	2	★★★½	80	$$+
Hawthorn Suites Orlando Convention Center	2	★★★½	80	$$+
Fairfield Inn & Suites Near Universal Orlando Resort	1	★★★½	80	$$$-
Hilton Garden Inn Orlando at SeaWorld	2	★★★½	80	$$$-
Embassy Suites Orlando I-Drive/ Jamaican Court	2	★★★½	80	$$$-
Residence Inn Orlando Convention Center	2	★★★½	80	$$$-
Buena Vista Palace Hotel & Spa	WDW	★★★½	80	$$$-
SpringHill Suites Orlando Convention Center	2	★★★½	80	$$$$-
Fairfield Inn & Suites Orlando Lake Buena Vista	3	★★★½	79	$$+

How the Hotels Compare *(Continued)*

HOTEL	LOCATION	OVERALL QUALITY	ROOM QUALITY	($ = $50)
Holiday Inn in the Walt Disney World Resort	WDW	★★★½	79	$$$+
Courtyard Orlando I-Drive	2	★★★½	78	$$+
Hampton Inn Orlando/Lake Buena Vista	3	★★★½	76	$$$-
Quality Suites Lake Buena Vista	3	★★★½	76	$$$-
Extended Stay America Deluxe Orlando Theme Parks	1	★★★½	75	$$-
Extended Stay America Orlando Theme Parks	1	★★★½	75	$$-
Rosen Inn at Pointe Orlando	2	★★★½	75	$$-
Best Western Plus Universal Inn	1	★★★½	75	$$-
Hawthorn Suites Orlando I-Drive	2	★★★½	75	$$+
Fairfield Inn & Suites Orlando LBV in Marriott Village	3	★★★½	75	$$+
Embassy Suites Orlando I-Drive	2	★★★½	75	$$#-
Holiday Inn & Suites Orlando Universal	1	★★★½	75	$$$-
Wyndham Lake Buena Vista Resort	WDW	★★★½	75	$$+
DoubleTree Guest Suites	WDW	★★★½	75	$$$
Residence Inn Orlando Lake Buena Vista	3	★★★½	75	$$$+
Sonesta ES Suites Orlando	2	★★★½	75	$$$+
Quality Suites Turkey Lake	3	★★★	74	$+
Fairfield Inn & Suites Orlando I-Drive/ Convention Center	2	★★★	74	$$+
Best Western Lake Buena Vista Resort Hotel	WDW	★★★	74	$$$+
La Quinta Inn Orlando I-Drive	2	★★★	73	$$-
International Palms Resort & Conference Center	2	★★★	73	$$+
Extended Stay America Orlando Convention Center	2	★★★	72	$+
Ramada Plaza Resort and Suites Orlando I-Drive	2	★★★	72	$$+
Staybridge Suites Lake Buena Vista	3	★★★	72	$$$+
SpringHill Suites Orlando LBV in Marriott Village	3	★★★	71	$$$+
Hampton Inn I-Drive/Convention Center	2	★★★	70	$$+
Comfort Suites Universal	1	★★★	70	$$+
Monumental MovieLand Hotel	2	★★★	68	$+
Westgate Palace	2	★★★	68	$$$$-
Enclave Hotel & Suites	2	★★★	67	$$$-
Hampton Inn Universal	1	★★★	67	$$$-
Motel 6 Orlando–I-Drive	2	★★★	66	$+
Comfort Inn I-Drive	2	★★★	66	$$-
Ramada Convention Center I-Drive	2	★★★	65	$+
Rosen Inn International Hotel	2	★★★	65	$$+
Best Western I-Drive	2	★★★	65	$$+

How the Hotels Compare *(Continued)*

HOTEL	LOCATION	OVERALL QUALITY	ROOM QUALITY	($ = $50)
Clarion Inn & Suites at I-Drive	2	★★½	64	$+
Clarion Inn Lake Buena Vista	3	★★½	64	$$-
Hampton Inn South of Universal	2	★★½	64	$$$-
Floridian Hotel & Suites	2	★★½	63	$$-
La Quinta Inn Orlando–Universal Studios	1	★★½	63	$$-
Country Inn & Suites Orlando Universal	2	★★½	63	$$
Avanti Resort Orlando	2	★★½	62	$$+
Red Roof Inn Orlando Convention Center	2	★★	58	$+
Extended Stay Orlando Convention Center	2	★★	58	$$-

Hotel Information Chart

Avanti Resort Orlando
★★½
8738 International Dr.
Orlando, FL 32819
☎ 407-313-0100
avantiresort.com
LOCATION 2
ROOM RATING 62
COST ($=$50) $$+

B Resort   ★★★½
1905 Hotel Plaza Blvd.
Lake Buena Vista, FL 32830
☎ 407-828-2828
bresortlbv.com
LOCATION WDW
ROOM RATING 82
COST ($=$50) $$$+

Best Western I-Drive
★★★
8222 Jamaican Ct.
Orlando, FL 32819
☎ 407-345-1172
tinyurl.com/bwidrive
LOCATION 2
ROOM RATING 65
COST ($=$50) $$+

Best Western Lake Buena Vista Resort Hotel   ★★★
2000 Hotel Plaza Blvd.
Lake Buena Vista, FL 32830
☎ 407-828-2424
lakebuenavistaresorthotel.com
LOCATION WDW
ROOM RATING 74
COST ($=$50) $$$+

Best Western Plus Universal Inn   ★★★½
5618 Vineland Rd.
Orlando, FL 32819
☎ 407-226-9119
tinyurl.com/bwuniversal
LOCATION 1
ROOM RATING 75
COST ($=$50) $$-

Buena Vista Palace Hotel & Spa   ★★★½
1900 E. Buena Vista Dr.
Lake Buena Vista, FL 32830
☎ 407-827-2727
buenavistapalace.com
LOCATION WDW
ROOM RATING 80
COST ($=$50) $$$-

Buena Vista Suites
★★★★
8203 World Center Dr.
Orlando, FL 32821
☎ 407-239-8588
bvsuites.com
LOCATION 2
ROOM RATING 83
COST ($=$50) $$$+

Caribe Royale All-Suite Hotel & Convention Center   ★★★★
8101 World Center Dr.
Orlando, FL 32821
☎ 407-238-8000
cariberoyale.com
LOCATION 2
ROOM RATING 88
COST ($=$50) $$$+

Castle Hotel
★★★½
8629 International Dr.
Orlando, FL 32819
☎ 407-345-1511
castlehotelorlando.com
LOCATION 2
ROOM RATING 82
COST ($=$50) $$$+

Clarion Inn & Suites at I-Drive   ★★½
9956 Hawaiian Ct.
Orlando, FL 32819
☎ 407-351-5100
tinyurl.com/clarionidrive
LOCATION 2
ROOM RATING 64
COST ($=$50) $+

Clarion Inn Lake Buena Vista   ★★½
8442 Palm Pkwy.
Lake Buena Vista, FL 32836
☎ 407-996-7300
clarionlbv.com
LOCATION 3
ROOM RATING 64
COST ($=$50) $$-

CoCo Key Water Resort–Orlando   ★★★½
7400 International Dr.
Orlando, FL 32819
☎ 407-351-2626
cocokeyorlando.com
LOCATION 2
ROOM RATING 82
COST ($=$50) $$+

Hotel Information Chart *(Continued)*

Comfort Inn I-Drive
★★★
8134 International Dr.
Orlando, FL 32819
☎ 407-313-4000
tinyurl.com/comfortidrive
LOCATION 2
ROOM RATING 66
COST ($=$50) $$-

Comfort Inn Orlando–Lake Buena Vista ★★★½
8686 Palm Pkwy.
Orlando, FL 32836
☎ 407-239-8400
tinyurl.com/comfortinnlbv
LOCATION 3
ROOM RATING 80
COST ($=$50) $$

Comfort Suites Universal
★★★
5617 Major Blvd.
Orlando, FL 32819
☎ 407-363-1967
tinyurl.com/csuniversal
LOCATION 1
ROOM RATING 70
COST ($=$50) $$+

Country Inn & Suites Orlando Universal ★★½
7701 Universal Blvd.
Orlando, FL 32819
☎ 407-313-4200
countryinns.com
/orlandofl_universal
LOCATION 2
ROOM RATING 63
COST ($=$50) $$

Courtyard Orlando I-Drive
★★★½
8600 Austrian Ct.
Orlando, FL 32819
☎ 407-351-2244
tinyurl.com/courtyardidrive
LOCATION 2
ROOM RATING 78
COST ($=$50) $$+

Courtyard Orlando Lake Buena Vista at Vista Centre ★★★★
8501 Palm Pkwy.
Lake Buena Vista, FL 32836
☎ 407-239-6900
tinyurl.com/courtyardlbv
LOCATION 3
ROOM RATING 89
COST ($=$50) $$$-

Courtyard Orlando LBV in Marriott Village ★★★½
8623 Vineland Ave.
Orlando, FL 32821
☎ 407-938-9001
tinyurl.com
/courtyardlbvmarriottvillage
LOCATION 3
ROOM RATING 82
COST ($=$50) $$+

Disney's Saratoga Springs Resort & Spa ★★★★½
1960 Broadway
Lake Buena Vista, FL 32830
☎ 407-827-1100
tinyurl.com/saratogawdw
LOCATION WDW
ROOM RATING 90
COST ($=$50) $+ x 8

DoubleTree by Hilton Orlando at SeaWorld
★★★★½
10100 International Dr.
Orlando, FL 32821
☎ 407-352-1100
doubletreeorlandoidrive.com
LOCATION 2
ROOM RATING 92
COST ($=$50) $$$+

DoubleTree Guest Suites ★★★½
2305 Hotel Plaza Blvd.
Lake Buena Vista, FL 32830
☎ 407-934-1000
doubletreeguestsuites.com
LOCATION WDW
ROOM RATING 75
COST ($=$50) $$$

DoubleTree Universal ★★★★
5780 Major Blvd.
Orlando, FL 32819
☎ 407-351-1000
doubletreeorlando.com
LOCATION 1
ROOM RATING 89
COST ($=$50) $$$-

Embassy Suites Orlando I-Drive ★★★½
8978 International Dr.
Orlando, FL 32819
☎ 407-352-1400
embassysuitesorlando.com
LOCATION 2
ROOM RATING 75
COST ($=$50) $$$-

Embassy Suites Orlando I-Drive/Jamaican Court ★★★½
8250 Jamaican Ct.
Orlando, FL 32819
☎ 407-345-8250
orlandoembassysuites.com
LOCATION 2
ROOM RATING 80
COST ($=$50) $$$-

Embassy Suites Orlando–Lake Buena Vista Resort ★★★★
8100 Lake Ave.
Orlando, FL 32836
☎ 407-239-1144
embassysuiteslbv.com
LOCATION 3
ROOM RATING 86
COST ($=$50) $$$+

The Enclave Hotel & Suites
★★★
6165 Carrier Dr.
Orlando, FL 32819
☎ 407-351-1155
enclavesuites.com
LOCATION 2
ROOM RATING 67
COST ($=$50) $$$-

Extended Stay America Convention Center/ Westwood ★★★★
6443 Westwood Blvd.
Orlando, FL 32821
☎ 407-351-1982
tinyurl.com
/extendedstaywestwood
LOCATION 2
ROOM RATING 84
COST ($=$50) $$-

Extended Stay America Deluxe Orlando Theme Parks ★★★½
5610 Vineland Rd.
Orlando, FL 32819
☎ 407-370-4428
tinyurl.com/esvineland
LOCATION 1
ROOM RATING 75
COST ($=$50) $$-

Extended Stay America Orlando Convention Center ★★★
6451 Westwood Blvd.
Orlando, FL 32821
☎ 407-352-3454
tinyurl.com/extendedstayocc
LOCATION 2
ROOM RATING 72
COST ($=$50) $+

Hotel Information Chart *(Continued)*

Extended Stay America Orlando Lake Buena Vista ★★★★
8100 Palm Pkwy.
Orlando 32836
☎ 407-239-4300
tinyurl.com/extendedlbv
LOCATION 3
ROOM RATING 83
COST ($=$50) $$-

Extended Stay America Orlando Theme Parks ★★★½
5620 Major Blvd.
Orlando, FL 32819
☎ 407-351-1788
tinyurl.com/extendeduniversal
LOCATION 1
ROOM RATING 75
COST ($=$50) $$-

Extended Stay Orlando Convention Center ★★½
8750 Universal Blvd.
Orlando, FL 32819
☎ 407-903-1500
tinyurl.com/esccuniversal
LOCATION 2
ROOM RATING 58
COST ($=$50) $$-

Fairfield Inn & Suites Near Universal Orlando Resort ★★★½
5614 Vineland Rd.
Orlando, FL 32819
☎ 407-581-5600
tinyurl.com/fairfielduniversal
LOCATION 1
ROOM RATING 80
COST ($=$50) $$$-

Fairfield Inn & Suites Orlando I-Drive/ Convention Center ★★★
8214 Universal Blvd.
Orlando, FL 32819
☎ 407-581-9001
tinyurl.com/fairfieldocc
LOCATION 2
ROOM RATING 74
COST ($=$50) $$+

Fairfield Inn & Suites Orlando Lake Buena Vista ★★★½
12191 S. Apopka-Vineland Rd.
Lake Buena Vista, FL 32836
☎ 407-239-1115
tinyurl.com/fairfieldlbv
LOCATION 3
ROOM RATING 78
COST ($=$50) $$+

Fairfield Inn & Suites Orlando LBV in Marriott Village ★★★½
8615 Vineland Ave.
Orlando, FL 32821
☎ 407-938-9001
tinyurl.com
/fairfieldlbvmarriottvillage
LOCATION 3
ROOM RATING 75
COST ($=$50) $$+

Floridays Resort Orlando ★★★★
12562 International Dr.
Orlando, FL 32821
☎ 407-238-7700
floridaysresortorlando.com
LOCATION 2
ROOM RATING 86
COST ($=$50) $$$$

The Floridian Hotel & Suites ★★½
7531 Canada Ave.
Orlando, FL 32819
☎ 407-212-3021
thefloridianhotel.com
LOCATION 2
ROOM RATING 63
COST ($=$50) $$-

Four Points by Sheraton Orlando Studio City ★★★★½
5905 International Dr.
Orlando, FL 32819
☎ 407-351-2100
fourpointsorlandostudiocity.com
LOCATION 2
ROOM RATING 90
COST ($=$50) $$$-

Four Seasons Resort Orlando at Walt Disney World Resort ★★★★★
10100 Dream Tree Blvd.
Golden Oak, FL 32836
☎ 407-313-7777
fourseasons.com/orlando
LOCATION WDW
ROOM RATING 98
COST ($=$50) $ x 9

Grand Beach ★★★★½
8317 Lake Bryan Beach Blvd.
Orlando, FL 32821
☎ 407-238-2500
diamondresorts.com
/grand-beach
LOCATION 2
ROOM RATING 90
COST ($=$50) $$$$-

Hampton Inn I-Drive/ Convention Center ★★★
8900 Universal Blvd.
Orlando, FL 32819
☎ 407-354-4447
tinyurl.com/hamptonocc
LOCATION 2
ROOM RATING 70
COST ($=$50) $$+

Hampton Inn Orlando/ Lake Buena Vista ★★★½
8150 Palm Pkwy.
Orlando, FL 32836
☎ 407-465-8150
tinyurl.com/hamptonlbv
LOCATION 3
ROOM RATING 76
COST ($=$50) $$$-

Hampton Inn South of Universal ★★½
7110 S. Kirkman Rd.
Orlando, FL 32819
☎ 407-345-1112
tinyurl.com/hamptonkirkman
LOCATION 2
ROOM RATING 64
COST ($=$50) $$$-

Hampton Inn Universal ★★★
5621 Windhover Dr.
Orlando, FL 32819
☎ 407-351-6716
tinyurl.com/hamptonuniversal
LOCATION 1
ROOM RATING 67
COST ($=$50) $$$-

Hard Rock Hotel ★★★★½
5800 Universal Blvd.
Orlando, FL 32819
☎ 407-503-2000
hardrockhotelorlando.com
LOCATION 1
ROOM RATING 93
COST ($=$50) $ x 8

Hawthorn Suites Lake Buena Vista ★★★★
8303 Palm Pkwy.
Orlando, FL 32836
☎ 407-597-5000
hawthornlakebuenavista.com
LOCATION 3
ROOM RATING 87
COST ($=$50) $$+

Hotel Information Chart *(Continued)*

Hawthorn Suites Orlando Convention Center
★★★½
6435 Westwood Blvd.
Orlando, FL 32821
☎ 407-351-6600
hawthornsuitesorlando.com
LOCATION 2
ROOM RATING 80
COST ($=$50) $$+

Hawthorn Suites Orlando I-Drive ★★★½
7975 Canada Ave.
Orlando, FL 32819
☎ 407-345-0117
tinyurl.com/hawthornidrive
LOCATION 2
ROOM RATING 75
COST ($=$50) $$+

Hilton Garden Inn Lake Buena Vista/ Orlando ★★★★
11400 Marbella Palm Ct.
Orlando, FL 32836
☎ 407-239-9550
tinyurl.com/hgilakebuenavista
LOCATION 3
ROOM RATING 88
COST ($=$50) $$$+

Hilton Garden Inn Orlando at SeaWorld ★★★½
6850 Westwood Blvd.
Orlando, FL 32821
☎ 407-354-1500
tinyurl.com/hgiseaworld
LOCATION 2
ROOM RATING 80
COST ($=$50) $$$-

Hilton Garden Inn Orlando I-Drive North ★★★½
5877 American Way
Orlando, FL 32819
☎ 407-363-9332
tinyurl.com/hiltonidrive
LOCATION 2
ROOM RATING 80
COST ($=$50) $$+

Hilton Grand Vacations Club at SeaWorld
★★★★½
6924 Grand Vacations Way
Orlando, FL 32821
☎ 407-239-0100
tinyurl.com/hgvseaworld
LOCATION 2
ROOM RATING 95
COST ($=$50) $$$-

Hilton Grand Vacations Club on I-Drive ★★★★
8122 Arrezzo Way
Orlando, FL 32821
☎ 407-465-2600
tinyurl.com/hgvidrive
LOCATION 2
ROOM RATING 88
COST ($=$50) $$$+

Hilton Orlando
★★★★½
6001 Destination Pkwy.
Orlando, FL 32819
☎ 407-313-4300
thehiltonorlando.com
LOCATION 2
ROOM RATING 92
COST ($=$50) $$$$+

Hilton Orlando Bonnet Creek ★★★★
14100 Bonnet Creek Resort Ln.
Orlando, FL 32821
☎ 407-597-3600
hiltonbonnetcreek.com
LOCATION 2
ROOM RATING 88
COST ($=$50) $$+

Hilton Orlando Lake Buena Vista ★★★★
1751 Hotel Plaza Blvd.
Lake Buena Vista, FL 32830
☎ 407-827-4000
hilton-wdwv.com
LOCATION WDW
ROOM RATING 87
COST ($=$50) $$$-

Holiday Inn & Suites Orlando Universal
★★★½
5905 Kirkman Rd.
Orlando, FL 32819
☎ 407-351-3333
hiuniversal.com
LOCATION 1
ROOM RATING 75
COST ($=$50) $$$-

Holiday Inn in the Walt Disney World Resort
★★★½
1805 Hotel Plaza Blvd.
Lake Buena Vista, FL 32830
☎ 407-828-8888
hiorlando.com
LOCATION WDW
ROOM RATING 79
COST ($=$50) $$$+

Holiday Inn Resort Lake Buena Vista ★★★½
13351 FL 535
Orlando, FL 32821
☎ 407-239-4500
hiresortlbv.com
LOCATION 3
ROOM RATING 82
COST ($=$50) $$+

Homewood Suites by Hilton I-Drive ★★★½
8745 International Dr.
Orlando, FL 32819
☎ 407-248-2232
homewoodsuitesorlando.com
LOCATION 2
ROOM RATING 81
COST ($=$50) $$$$-

Homewood Suites by Hilton LBV-Orlando
★★★★
11428 Marbella Palm Ct.
Orlando, FL 32836
☎ 407-239-4540
tinyurl.com/homewoodsuiteslbv
LOCATION 3
ROOM RATING 85
COST ($=$50) $$$$-

Hyatt Place Orlando/ Universal ★★★★
5895 Caravan Ct.
Orlando, FL 32819
☎ 407-351-0627
orlandouniversal.place.hyatt.com
LOCATION 1
ROOM RATING 84
COST ($=$50) $$$+

Hyatt Regency Grand Cypress ★★★★½
1 Grand Cypress Blvd.
Orlando, FL 32836
☎ 407-239-1234
grandcypress.hyatt.com
LOCATION 3
ROOM RATING 92
COST ($=$50) $- x 5

Hyatt Regency Orlando
★★★★½
9801 International Dr.
Orlando, FL 32819
☎ 407-284-1234
orlando.regency.hyatt.com
LOCATION 2
ROOM RATING 90
COST ($=$50) $$$$-

Hotel Information Chart *(Continued)*

International Palms Resort & Conference Center ★★★	**JW Marriott Orlando Grande Lakes** ★★★★½	**La Quinta Inn Orlando I-Drive** ★★★
6515 International Dr.	4040 Central Florida Pkwy.	8300 Jamaican Ct.
Orlando, FL 32819	Orlando, FL 32837	Orlando, FL 32819
☎ 407-351-3500	☎ 407-206-2300	☎ 407-351-1660
internationalpalms.com	jw-marriott.grandelakes.com	tinyurl.com/lqidrive
LOCATION 2	LOCATION 2	LOCATION 2
ROOM RATING 73	ROOM RATING 93	ROOM RATING 73
COST ($=$50) $$+	COST ($=$50) $+ x 5	COST ($=$50) $$-
La Quinta Inn Orlando– Universal Studios ★★½	**Legacy Vacation Club Lake Buena Vista** ★★★★	**Loews Portofino Bay Hotel** ★★★★½
5621 Major Blvd.		5601 Universal Blvd.
Orlando, FL 32819	8451 Palm Pkwy.	Orlando, FL 32819
☎ 407-313-3100	Lake Buena Vista, FL 32836	☎ 407-503-1000
tinyurl.com/lquniversal	☎ 407-238-1700	tinyurl.com/portofinobay
LOCATION 1	legacyvacationresorts.com	LOCATION 1
ROOM RATING 63	LOCATION 3	ROOM RATING 92
COST ($=$50) $$-	ROOM RATING 85	COST ($=$50) $+ x 8
	COST ($=$50) $$$-	
Loews Royal Pacific Resort ★★★★½	**Marriott's Cypress Harbour** ★★★★	**Marriott's Grande Vista** ★★★★½
6300 Hollywood Way	11251 Harbour Villa Rd.	5925 Avenida Vista
Orlando, FL 32819	Orlando, FL 32821	Orlando, FL 32821
☎ 407-503-3000	☎ 407-238-1300	☎ 407-238-7676
tinyurl.com/royalpacific	tinyurl.com/cypressharbourvillas	tinyurl.com/marriottsgrandevista
LOCATION 1	LOCATION 2	LOCATION 2
ROOM RATING 90	ROOM RATING 86	ROOM RATING 92
COST ($=$50) $+ x 6	COST ($=$50) $ x 6	COST ($=$50) $$$+
Marriott's Harbour Lake ★★★★½	**Marriott's Imperial Palms** ★★★★	**Marriott's Royal Palms** ★★★★
7102 Grand Horizons Blvd.	8404 Vacation Way	8404 Vacation Way
Orlando, FL 32821	Orlando, FL 32821	Orlando, FL 32821
☎ 407-465-6100	☎ 407-238-6200	☎ 407-238-6200
tinyurl.com/harbourlake	tinyurl.com/imperialpalmvillas	tinyurl.com/marriottsroyalpalms
LOCATION 3	LOCATION 2	LOCATION 2
ROOM RATING 90	ROOM RATING 86	ROOM RATING 85
COST ($=$50) $$$$-	COST ($=$50) $- x 9	COST ($=$50) $- x 6
Marriott's Sabal Palms ★★★★½	**Monumental Hotel** ★★★★½	**Monumental MovieLand Hotel** ★★★
8805 World Center Dr.	12120 International Dr.	6233 International Dr.
Orlando, FL 32821	Orlando, FL 32821	Orlando, FL 32819
☎ 407-238-6200	☎ 407-239-1222	☎ 407-351-3900
tinyurl.com/marriottssabalpalms	monumentalhotelorlandofl.com	monumentalmovielandhotel.com
LOCATION 3	LOCATION 2	LOCATION 2
ROOM RATING 92	ROOM RATING 94	ROOM RATING 68
COST ($=$50) $+ x 6	COST ($=$50) $$-	COST ($=$50) $+
Motel 6 Orlando–I-Drive ★★½	**Nickelodeon Suites Resort** ★★★½	**Orlando World Center Marriott Resort** ★★★★
5909 American Way	14500 Continental Gateway	8701 World Center Dr.
Orlando, FL 32819	Orlando, FL 32821	Orlando, FL 32821
☎ 407-351-6500	☎ 407-387-5437	☎ 407-239-4200
tinyurl.com/motel6idrive	nickhotel.com	marriottworldcenter.com
LOCATION 2	LOCATION 2	LOCATION 3
ROOM RATING 61	ROOM RATING 82	ROOM RATING 89
COST ($=$50) $+	COST ($=$50) $$$$	COST ($=$50) $$$$+

Hotel Information Chart *(Continued)*

The Point Orlando Resort ★★★½ 7389 Universal Blvd. Orlando, FL 32819 ☎ 407-956-2000 thepointorlando.com **LOCATION** 2 **ROOM RATING** 82 **COST ($=$50)** $$+	**Quality Suites Lake Buena Vista** ★★★ 8200 Palm Pkwy. Orlando, FL 32836 ☎ 407-465-8200 qualitysuiteslbv.com **LOCATION** 3 **ROOM RATING** 74 **COST ($=$50)** $$$–	**Quality Suites Turkey Lake** ★★★ 9350 Turkey Lake Rd. Orlando, FL 32819 ☎ 407-351-5050 qualitysuitesorlandolbv.com **LOCATION** 3 **ROOM RATING** 74 **COST ($=$50)** $+
Radisson Hotel Orlando Lake Buena Vista ★★★½ 12799 Apopka-Vineland Rd. Orlando, FL 32836 ☎ 407-597-3400 tinyurl.com/radissonlbv **LOCATION** 3 **ROOM RATING** 82 **COST ($=$50)** $$$–	**Ramada Convention Center I-Drive** ★★★ 8342 Jamaican Ct. Orlando, FL 32819 ☎ 407-363-1944 tinyurl.com/ramadaidrive **LOCATION** 2 **ROOM RATING** 65 **COST ($=$50)** $+	**Ramada Plaza Resort and Suites Orlando I-Drive** ★★★ 6500 International Dr. Orlando, FL 32819 ☎ 407-345-5340 tinyurl.com/ramadaplazaidrive **LOCATION** 2 **ROOM RATING** 72 **COST ($=$50)** $$+
Red Roof Inn Orlando Convention Center ★★½ 9922 Hawaiian Ct. Orlando, FL 32819 ☎ 407-352-1507 tinyurl.com/redroofkiss **LOCATION** 2 **ROOM RATING** 58 **COST ($=$50)** $+	**Renaissance Orlando at SeaWorld** ★★★★½ 6677 Sea Harbor Dr. Orlando, FL 32821 ☎ 407-351-5555 tinyurl.com/renorlandoseaworld **LOCATION** 2 **ROOM RATING** 93 **COST ($=$50)** $$$+	**Residence Inn Orlando at SeaWorld** ★★★★ 11000 Westwood Blvd. Orlando, FL 32821 ☎ 407-313-3600 tinyurl.com /residenceinnseaworld **LOCATION** 3 **ROOM RATING** 85 **COST ($=$50)** $$$–
Residence Inn Orlando Convention Center ★★★½ 8800 Universal Blvd. Orlando, FL 32819 ☎ 407-226-0288 tinyurl.com /resinnconventioncenter **LOCATION** 2 **ROOM RATING** 80 **COST ($=$50)** $$$–	**Residence Inn Orlando Lake Buena Vista** ★★★½ 11450 Marbella Palm Ct. Orlando, FL 32836 ☎ 407-465-0075 tinyurl.com/residenceinnlbv **LOCATION** 3 **ROOM RATING** 75 **COST ($=$50)** $$$+	**Ritz-Carlton Orlando, Grande Lakes** ★★★★½ 4012 Central Florida Pkwy. Orlando, FL 32837 ☎ 407-206-2400 grandelakes.com **LOCATION** 2 **ROOM RATING** 94 **COST ($=$50)** $+ x 5
Rosen Centre Hotel ★★★★½ 9840 International Dr. Orlando, FL 32819 ☎ 407-996-9840 rosencentre.com **LOCATION** 2 **ROOM RATING** 95 **COST ($=$50)** $$$+	**Rosen Inn at Pointe Orlando** ★★★½ 9000 International Dr. Orlando, FL 32819 ☎ 407-996-8585 roseninn9000.com **LOCATION** 2 **ROOM RATING** 75 **COST ($=$50)** $$–	**Rosen Inn International Hotel** ★★★ 7600 International Dr. Orlando, FL 32819 ☎ 407-996-1600 roseninn7600.com **LOCATION** 2 **ROOM RATING** 65 **COST ($=$50)** $$+
Rosen Plaza Hotel ★★★★½ 9700 International Dr. Orlando, FL 32819 ☎ 407-996-9700 rosenplaza.com **LOCATION** 2 **ROOM RATING** 90 **COST ($=$50)** $$$+	**Rosen Shingle Creek** ★★★★ 9939 Universal Blvd. Orlando, FL 32819 ☎ 407-996-9939 rosenshinglecreek.com **LOCATION** 2 **ROOM RATING** 88 **COST ($=$50)** $$$+	**Sheraton Lake Buena Vista Resort** ★★★★ 12205 S. Apopka-Vineland Rd. Orlando, FL 32836 ☎ 407-239-0444 sheratonlakebuenavistaresort .com **LOCATION** 3 **ROOM RATING** 88 **COST ($=$50)** $$$+

Hotel Information Chart *(Continued)*

Sheraton Vistana Resort Villas ★★★★½
8800 Vistana Centre Dr.
Orlando, FL 32821
☎ 407-239-3100
tinyurl.com/vistanavillas
LOCATION 3
ROOM RATING 95
COST ($=$50) $$$$-

Sonesta ES Suites Orlando ★★★½
8480 International Dr.
Orlando, FL 32819
☎ 407-352-2400
sonesta.com/orlando
LOCATION 2
ROOM RATING 75
COST ($=$50) $$$+

SpringHill Suites Orlando Convention Center ★★★½
8840 Universal Blvd.
Orlando, FL 32819
☎ 407-345-9073
tinyurl.com/shsconventioncenter
LOCATION 2
ROOM RATING 80
COST ($=$50) $$$$-

SpringHill Suites Orlando LBV in Marriott Village ★★★
8601 Vineland Ave.
Orlando, FL 32821
☎ 407-938-9001
tinyurl.com/springhillmarriottvillage
LOCATION 3
ROOM RATING 71
COST ($=$50) $$$+

Staybridge Suites Lake Buena Vista ★★★
8751 Suiteside Dr.
Orlando, FL 32836
☎ 407-238-0777
tinyurl.com/staybridgelbv
LOCATION 3
ROOM RATING 72
COST ($=$50) $$$+

Stay Sky Suites I-Drive Orlando ★★★½
7601 Canada Ave.
Orlando, FL 32819
☎ 407-581-2151
stayskysuitesidriveorlando.com
LOCATION 2
ROOM RATING 82
COST ($=$50) $$+

Universal's Cabana Bay Beach Resort ★★★★
6550 Adventure Way
Orlando, FL 32819
☎ 407-503-2000
tinyurl.com/cabanabay
LOCATION 1
ROOM RATING 83
COST ($=$50) $$$$-

Villas of Grand Cypress ★★★★½
1 N. Jacaranda
Orlando, FL 32836
☎ 407-239-4700
grandcypress.com
LOCATION 3
ROOM RATING 92
COST ($=$50) $- x 5

Waldorf Astoria Orlando ★★★★½
14200 Bonnet Creek Resort Ln.
Lake Buena Vista, FL 32830
☎ 407-597-5500
waldorfastoriaorlando.com
LOCATION 3
ROOM RATING 93
COST ($=$50) $$$$+

Westgate Lakes Resort & Spa ★★★★½
10000 Turkey Lake Rd.
Orlando, FL 32819
☎ 407-345-0000
westgateresorts.com/lakes
LOCATION 3
ROOM RATING 92
COST ($=$50) $$$+

Westgate Palace ★★★
6145 Carrier Dr.
Orlando, FL 32819
☎ 407-996-6000
westgateresorts.com/palace
LOCATION 2
ROOM RATING 68
COST ($=$50) $$$$-

Westin Orlando Universal Boulevard ★★★★
9501 Universal Blvd.
Orlando, FL 32819
☎ 407-233-2200
westinorlandouniversal.com
LOCATION 2
ROOM RATING 87
COST ($=$50) $$$$+

WorldQuest Orlando Resort ★★★★
8849 Worldquest Blvd.
Orlando, FL 32821
☎ 407-387-3800
worldquestorlando.com
LOCATION 2
ROOM RATING 88
COST ($=$50) $$$-

Wyndham Bonnet Creek Resort ★★★★½
9560 Via Encinas
Lake Buena Vista, FL 32830
☎ 407-238-3500
wyndhambonnetcreek.com
LOCATION 3
ROOM RATING 90
COST ($=$50) $$$$+

Wyndham Lake Buena Vista Resort ★★★½
1850 Hotel Plaza Blvd.
Lake Buena Vista, FL 32830
☎ 407-828-4444
wyndhamlakebuenavista.com
LOCATION WDW
ROOM RATING 75
COST ($=$50) $$+

Wyndham Orlando Resort I-Drive ★★★★
8001 International Dr.
Orlando, FL 32819
☎ 407-351-2420
wyndham.com/hotels/MCOWD
LOCATION 2
ROOM RATING 83
COST ($=$50) $$+

PART THREE

ARRIVING *and* GETTING AROUND

▎ GETTING THERE

DIRECTIONS TO UNIVERSAL ORLANDO

UNIVERSAL ORLANDO IS LOCATED WITHIN the Orlando city limits, a short distance from I-4 and Florida's Turnpike. You can access the resort from I-4 East by taking Exit 75A and turning left at the top of the ramp onto Universal Boulevard. If you're traveling on I-4 West, use Exit 74B and then turn right on Hollywood Way. Entrances are also located off Kirkman Road (Exit 75B) to the east, Turkey Lake Road to the west, and Vineland Road to the north. Universal Boulevard connects the International Drive area to Universal via an overpass bridging I-4. Turkey Lake and Vineland Roads are particularly good alternatives when I-4 is gridlocked. See pages 10–11 for a map of the area.

Signs for Universal's hotels and theme parks are easy to find and read as soon as you've left the highway. Once on Universal property, follow the signs to the parking garage or your hotel.

FROM THE ORLANDO INTERNATIONAL AIRPORT (MCO) Take FL 528/Beachline Expressway, a toll road, west for about 12 miles to the intersection with I-4. Bear right and go east 2 miles on I-4 to Exit 75A, marked UNIVERSAL/INTERNATIONAL DRIVE, and make a left at the end of the exit ramp. Tolls should cost less than $4 one-way, and we advise bringing $2 in quarters in case you encounter an unstaffed tollbooth along the way.

FROM WALT DISNEY WORLD Go east on I-4, take Exit 75A (marked UNIVERSAL/INTERNATIONAL DRIVE), and make a left at the end of the exit ramp.

FROM DAYTONA, SANFORD INTERNATIONAL AIRPORT (SFB), OR ORLANDO Head west on I-4 through Orlando. Take Exit 74B toward Universal Orlando.

FROM MIAMI, FORT LAUDERDALE, OR SOUTHEASTERN FLORIDA
Head north on Florida's Turnpike to Exit 259, and merge onto I-4 West toward Tampa. Take Exit 74B toward Universal Orlando.

FROM TAMPA AND SOUTHWESTERN FLORIDA　Take I-75 North to I-4. Go east on I-4, take Exit 75A (marked UNIVERSAL/INTERNATIONAL DRIVE), and make a left at the end of the exit ramp.

FROM FLORIDA'S TURNPIKE SOUTH　Take Exit 259 to merge onto I-4 West toward Tampa, and then take Exit 74B toward Universal Orlando.

FROM I-10　Take I-10 East across Florida to I-75 South at Exit 296A/Tampa; then take Florida's Turnpike (toll road) southbound at Exit 328 (on the left) toward Orlando. Take Exit 259 to merge onto I-4 West toward Tampa; then take Exit 74B toward Universal Orlando.

FROM I-75 SOUTH　Take I-75 South onto Florida's Turnpike via Exit 328 (on the left) toward Orlando. Take Exit 259 to merge onto I-4 West toward Tampa, and then take Exit 74B toward Universal Orlando.

FROM I-95 SOUTH　Take Exit 260B to merge onto I-4 West, and then take exit 74B toward Universal Orlando.

Universal Orlando Exits off I-4

West to east (in the direction of Tampa to Orlando), six I-4 exits serve Universal Orlando.

Exit 74A (Sand Lake Road) serves the southern edge of Universal's property, with access to the resort from Turkey Lake Road, which lies just west of the exit. This exit also provides access to the attractions on the southern end of International Drive, heading toward the convention center, as well as the "Restaurant Row" dining options on west Sand Lake Road. Be warned that this exit can get quite congested with I-Drive traffic.

Exit 74B (Adventure Way) is only accessible from I-4 West and serves as the primary entrance to Universal Orlando Resort from that direction. The exit ramp leads directly to the Cabana Bay Beach and Sapphire Falls Resorts. Make a right at the light past the hotels to reach the Universal Orlando parking garage. Note that you can't return to I-4 East via this exit.

Exit 75A (Universal Boulevard/International Drive) serves as the primary entrance to Universal Orlando Resort from I-4 East. Make a left at the end of the ramp into Universal property, and the parking garage will be ahead on your right. Make a right off this exit to take Universal Boulevard south across International Drive; it then parallels that busy road, making it a perfect bypass to south International Drive and the convention center.

Exit 75A (Kirkman Road South) is the confusingly numbered exit accessible from I-4 West, which leads drivers to Kirkman Road just south of Universal, and several blocks east of the other 75A. It does not provide direct access to Universal Orlando, but it is the closest exit to the shopping and attractions on north International Drive.

Exit 75B (Kirkman Road North) leads drivers north past the Kirkman Road entrance on the east side of Universal Orlando Resort. This is the closest exit to the Portofino Bay and Hard Rock Hotels, as well as most off-site hotels within walking distance. Drivers coming from I-4 East take a left-hand exit and make an immediate left into the resort. Those coming from I-4 West have a barrier preventing the left turn directly into the resort but can make a right onto Major Boulevard, followed by a quick U-turn back toward Universal. Alternatively, make the next left onto Vineland Road, and then turn left onto Universal Boulevard to enter the resort from the north.

Exit 78 (Conroy Road/Millenia) is an option for westbound drivers when traffic is backed up approaching the Turnpike. Make a right off the exit (at the Holy Land Experience religious theme park), and then make an immediate left onto Vineland Road. Universal will be on your left immediately after crossing Kirkman Road.

THE I-4 BLUES

OVER MANY YEARS OF COVERING Orlando's attractions, we've watched I-4 turn from a modern interstate highway into a parking lot. The greatest congestion used to be between the Universal Orlando–International Drive area and downtown Orlando, but the section to the southwest serving the Disney World exits has become the new choke point, seemingly irrespective of the time of day. If you're going from Walt Disney World toward Universal Orlando (east), the jam usually breaks up after you've passed the FL 535 exit. As you head west toward Tampa, traffic calms down after the US 192 interchange.

Ameliorating (or complicating) the situation, the state of Florida is renovating a 21-mile stretch of I-4, from FL 434 in the northeast to Kirkman Road in the southwest to improve traffic flow and capacity in these areas. The construction project will renovate 15 of the busiest interchanges, build 56 new bridges, and replace more than 70 overpasses, plus add four variable-charge toll lanes to help pay for the $2-billion estimated cost. The bad news is that construction is likely to last through 2021, assuming everything goes according to schedule.

On long road trips, we always use a GPS device that's smart enough to accept traffic updates and route us around delays. Our TomTom GPS unit, for example, has a $5 accessory cable that picks up traffic signals from HD radio broadcasts. If you have a newer smartphone, the free mobile app Waze (**waze.com**; iOS, Android, and Windows Phone) also does this trick.

If the I-4 traffic becomes intolerable, it's pretty easy to commute from the Universal Orlando–International Drive area to Walt Disney World via Turkey Lake Road, connecting to Palm Parkway and FL 535 on the northwest side of I-4, or on the southernmost section of I-Drive, connecting to FL 536 on the southeast side of the interstate.

SECURITY AT ORLANDO INTERNATIONAL AIRPORT

THIS AIRPORT HANDLES about 35 million passengers a year. It's not unusual to see lines from the checkpoints snaking out of the terminal and into the main shopping corridor and food court. Airport officials sometimes actually shut down moving sidewalks to use them for more queuing space. A number of passengers have reported missing their flights even when they arrived at the airport 90 minutes before departure. System improvements have alleviated some, but by no means all, of the congestion. Most waits to clear security are 25 minutes on average, compared with as many as 55 minutes before the improvements. Even so, there are substantial fluctuations, with peak waits nearing an hour.

unofficial **TIP**
We recommend arriving at MCO 90 minutes–2 hours before your scheduled departure.

ALTERNATIVE AIRPORTS

A SHORT DISTANCE NORTHEAST OF ORLANDO is **Sanford International Airport** (SFB; **orlandosanfordairport.com**). Small, convenient, and easily accessible, it's low hassle compared with the huge Orlando International Airport (MCO) and its block-long security-checkpoint lines.

The primary domestic carrier serving Sanford International is **Allegiant Air** (☎ 702-505-8888; **allegiantair.com**), with service from large and small airports throughout the Eastern and Midwestern United States. European carriers include **ArkeFly** (Netherlands: ☎ 855-808-4015; **arkefly.nl**), **Icelandair** (Iceland: ☎ 800-223-5500; **icelandair.com**), **Jetairfly** (Belgium: **jetairfly.com**), **Monarch** (UK: ☎ 0871 940 5040; **flymonarch.com**), and **Thomson Airways** (UK: ☎ 0871 231 4787; **thomson.co.uk**). Finally, **SST Air** (☎ 407-288-8820; **sstair.com**) offers seasonal charter flights between Sanford and various cities in Brazil.

A reader from Roanoke, Virginia, uses Sanford frequently, writing:

The 45-minute drive to [Orlando] is more than made up for by avoiding the chaos at Orlando International, and it's stress free.

Other readers, like this couple from White Township, New Jersey, prefer flying into Tampa instead:

We've found that flying from Newark to Tampa instead of Orlando saves us money and our sanity. It means significantly lower fares, fewer children on the plane, and shorter security lines.

(Note that it's an 84-mile drive from Tampa International Airport to Universal Orlando—about an hour and 20 minutes.)

GETTING TO UNIVERSAL ORLANDO FROM THE AIRPORT

YOU HAVE FIVE OPTIONS FOR GETTING from Orlando International to Universal Orlando:

1. TAXI Mears Transportation Group (☎ 888-983-3... transportation.com) has a near monopoly on taxi service in c... and operates multiple brands (Yellow Cab Company, Chec... pany, and City Cab Company) with identical rates. Taxis ... eight passengers (depending on vehicle type). Rates vary according ... distance. If your hotel is on Universal property, or nearby on International Drive or Major Boulevard, your fare will be about $45–$50, plus tip.

2. SHUTTLE SERVICE Mears Transportation Group (☎ 888-983-3346; **mearstransportation.com**) also dominates shared shuttle service and provides the transportation for most vacation packages that include airport transfers. Non-package travelers can also use the service. The shuttles collect passengers until a van (or bus) is filled. The vehicles are then dispatched. Mears charges *per-person* rates (children under age 3 ride free). A one-way adult fare is $20 ($15 for children); round-trip is $32 for adults ($24 for children). Mears's competitor **SuperShuttle** (☎ 800-258-3826; **supershuttle.com**) also offers shared vans to Universal for a flat $20 per person each way; book online to save $2.

You might have to wait at the airport until a vehicle fills. Once under way, the shuttle will probably stop several times to discharge passengers before reaching your hotel. Obviously, it takes less time to fill a van than a bus, and less time to deliver and unload those passengers.

From your hotel to the airport, you will likely ride in a van (unless you're part of a tour group, for which Mears might send a bus). Because shuttles make several pickups, they ask you to leave much earlier than you'd depart if you were taking a cab or returning a rental car.

3. TOWN CAR SERVICE Like a taxi, town car service will transport you directly from the airport to your hotel. The driver will usually be waiting for you in your airline's baggage-claim area. If saving time and hassle is worth the money, book a town car.

Each town car service we surveyed offers large, well-appointed late-model sedans, such as the Lincoln Town Car series, or limousines. These hold four persons; trunks easily hold golf bags. Some services also offer roomier luxury SUVs and vans for an extra fee. To reserve a child's car seat, call ahead.

Tiffany Towncar Service (☎ 888-838-2161 or 407-370-2196; **tiffanytowncars.com**) provides a prompt, clean ride. The round-trip fee to the Universal area in a town car is $126 plus tip; one-way is $68. Tiffany offers a free 30-minute stop at a supermarket en route to your hotel with a round-trip booking.

Quicksilver Tours & Transportation (☎ 888-GO-TO-WDW [468-6939] or 407-299-1434; **quicksilver-tours.com**) offers eight-person limos and ten-person vans in addition to four-person town cars. Round-trip in a town car from MCO to the Universal area and back (with a free 30-minute grocery stop on the way) is $125; round-trip in a van costs $140; the round-trip limo rate is $240. Quicksilver also offers a "3 Way Trip" from the airport to Walt Disney World, then to

Universal Orlando, and finally back to the airport, starting at $170—perfect for those splitting their vacation between the two resorts.

Mears Transportation Group (☎ 407-423-5566; **mearstransportation .com**) also offers a town car service for $120–$145 round-trip, as does **SuperShuttle** (☎ 800-258-3826; **supershuttle.com**) for $70 each way.

4. RENTAL CARS   Short- and long-term rentals are available. Most companies allow drop-off at certain hotels or subsidiary locations in the Universal area if you don't want the vehicle for your entire stay. Likewise, any time during your stay, you can pick up a car at those hotels and locations. Check **mousesavers.com** for rental-car discount codes.

The preferred routes to Universal Orlando (as well as Walt Disney World, International Drive, and US 192) all involve toll roads. Some roads require exact change to enter or exit via automated gates, and manned tollbooths will not accept any denomination bill higher than $20. So before you leave the airport, make sure you're armed with at least $2 in quarters and some lower-denomination currency.

5. RIDE-SHARE SERVICES   This new and somewhat controversial option is represented in Orlando by the companies Uber and Lyft, both of which were successfully established in other cities before spreading to central Florida in 2014. You start by downloading a service's app to your smartphone (Apple or Android) and registering an account with a form of payment. When you want to hail a ride, the app shows you what available drivers are nearby and estimates the time and cost to your destination. You can follow your car's progress via GPS, and the tip is built into the price.

In other cities, the advantage to Uber and Lyft is that they charge about 40%–30% less than a traditional taxi. Orlando, however, has mandated that ride-sharing services charge the same per-mile as taxis, negating their price advantage. (At press time, Uber was still charging its lower rates while it negotiates with the city.) In addition, the ride-share companies are not currently authorized to operate on Orlando International Airport property (as scary signage warns arriving visitors on their way to baggage claim) and are in litigation with the airport authority over their status.

If you've used Uber or Lyft elsewhere and are comfortable with them, consider using them for transportation around Orlando or back to the airport. We've had nothing but positive experiences with them so far, but your mileage may vary.

Dollars and Sense

Which option is the best deal depends on how many people are in your party and how much you value your time. If you're traveling solo or have only two in your party and you're pretty sure that you won't need a rental car, the shuttle is your least-expensive bet.

A cab for two makes sense if you want to get to your hotel faster than the shuttle can arrange. The cab will cost about $50–$55, including tip. That's $25–$28 per person. The shuttle will cost $20 each (one-way), saving $5–$8 per person. You must decide whether the cab's timeliness and convenience are worth the extra bucks.

A one-day car rental costs $40–$70, plus you have to take time to complete the paperwork, get the vehicle, and fill the tank before you return it. The more people you have in your group, the more economical the cab becomes over the shuttle. Likewise with the rental car, though the cab or ride share will get you there faster.

GETTING TO UNIVERSAL ORLANDO FROM WALT DISNEY WORLD

DRIVING FROM WALT DISNEY WORLD to Universal Orlando along I-4 takes about 15 minutes with light traffic, or as much as 40 minutes during rush hour. If you're staying at Walt Disney World and you don't have a car, **Mears Transportation** will shuttle you from your hotel to Universal and back for $20. Pickup and return times are at your convenience. To schedule a shuttle, call ☎ 855-463-2776.

Taxis and ride-share services (**Uber** and **Lyft**) are also readily available to and from the resorts. A one-way taxi ride is $35–$45 (plus tip), depending on which Disney hotel you are leaving from, and may be cheaper than a shuttle if you have three to five people. An Uber ride will cost about half that, and you can usually get picked up from any WDW hotel in less than 15 minutes. All transportation services drop off at and pick up from the lower level of Universal's main parking hub, from which you can walk to CityWalk and the parks.

SUPER STAR SHUTTLE

UNIVERSAL OFFERS FREE SCHEDULED TRANSPORTATION to SeaWorld, Wet 'n Wild, and Aquatica for its on-site hotel guests via the Super Star Shuttle. Departure and return times are limited and are based on regular park operating hours; typically there are up to a half-dozen trips each way to SeaWorld, and only a couple in either direction to the water parks, but during slow season, there may be only a single trip scheduled each way. Boarding passes are required and available at the ticket desk in each hotel lobby, between one day in advance and 30 minutes prior to departure. The Super Star Shuttle picks up guests directly at Universal's three luxury hotels; guests at Cabana Bay must transfer to the parking hub and catch the shuttle there.

OFF-SITE HOTEL SHUTTLES

MANY INDEPENDENT HOTELS AND MOTELS near Universal Orlando provide free shuttle buses to the resort. Some properties participate in the same Super Star Shuttle program that services Universal's on-site hotels, while others operate their own transportation. The shuttles are fairly carefree, depositing you at the parking garages' central hub and saving you parking fees. The rub is that they might not get you there as early as you desire (a critical point if you take our touring advice) or be available when you wish to return to your lodging. Each service is different; check details before you make reservations.

Some shuttles go directly to Universal, while others stop at other hotels en route. This can be a problem if your hotel is the second or third stop on the route. During periods of high demand, buses frequently fill up at the first stop, leaving little or no room for passengers at subsequent stops. Before booking, inquire how many hotels are on the route and the sequence of the stops. The different hotels are often so close together that you can easily walk to the first hotel on the route and board there. Similarly, if there's a large hotel nearby, it might have its own dedicated bus service that is more efficient. Use it instead of the service provided by your hotel. The majority of Universal-area shuttles work on a fixed schedule, typically with three or four departures in the morning, and a similar or smaller number of returns around closing. Knowing exactly when a bus will depart makes it easier to plan your day.

At closing or during a hard rain, more people will be waiting for the shuttle than it can hold, and some will be left behind. Most shuttles return for stranded guests, but guests may wait 20 minutes to more than an hour.

If you're depending on shuttles, leave the park at least 45 minutes before closing. If you stay until closing and don't want the hassle of the shuttle, take a cab or request a ride share. Cab stands and guest pickup/drop-off are located on the lower level of the main parking hub, near the bus stops.

I-RIDE TROLLEY

THE I-RIDE TROLLEY (☎ 407-248-9590; **iridetrolley.com**) is a cheap, convenient transportation system servicing the International Drive area. Cheerful trolley-shaped buses circulate from the Orlando Vineland Premium Outlets on the south side of town up to the hotels near Universal on Major Boulevard, with stops at SeaWorld, the Orange County Convention Center, and Wet 'n Wild along the way.

A single one-way fare costs $2 for adults ($1 for kids ages 3–9; $0.25 for seniors age 65 and older) and must be paid in cash using exact change. You can prepurchase unlimited ride passes for 1 day ($5) to 14 days ($18) via the website or at participating hotels and attractions listed at **iridetrolley.com/passes.asp.**

The only problem with the I-Ride Trolley is that it doesn't stop at Universal Orlando. The closest stop is at the DoubleTree hotel on the corner of Kirkman Road and Major Boulevard (marked G4 on the trolley route map). From there you can walk to the Universal parks (see below).

WALKING TO UNIVERSAL ORLANDO

UNLIKE DISNEY WORLD, UNIVERSAL ORLANDO has a number of nearby off-site hotels that are within walking distance of the resort's attractions. The closest off-site hotels to Universal are along Major Boulevard near the intersection with Kirkman Road, at the eastern entrance to Universal property. The DoubleTree hotel on this corner isn't much farther from Universal's parks than the on-site Portofino Bay. To reach the parks from this area, cross Kirkman at Major from the northeast corner, and follow the sidewalks to Universal Boulevard. Cross Universal Boulevard and turn left, and then walk to the escalators leading up to CityWalk from the valet parking circle. You should be able to walk the half mile from the DoubleTree to CityWalk in about 15 minutes.

Farther away, but still within walking distance, are the hotels and motels on International Drive near Universal Boulevard, just south of the resort. This route requires walking north along Universal Boulevard, over the I-4 overpass, and into the bus and taxi parking loop on the lower level of the parking hub. While there are sidewalks and pedestrian traffic signals the entire way, this is at least a 0.75-mile walk alongside busy traffic and isn't recommended for families with young children.

THE PUBLIC TRANSPORTATION ALTERNATIVE

SOME OFF-SITE HOTEL SHUTTLES don't operate early enough to get you to the parks before opening. An alternative is the **LYNX** public bus system, which costs $2 (exact change required) for a single one-way fare, with discounted all-day, weekly, and monthly passes available for advance purchase online.

If you're staying in downtown Orlando, you can take the LYNX #21 or #40 bus from the central bus station to Universal's parking garage. To reach Walt Disney World, take LYNX #8 from Wet 'n Wild (or the I-Ride Trolley from Kirkman and Major) to SeaWorld, and then transfer to LYNX #50 to the Magic Kingdom's Transportation and Ticket Center (TTC). The buses run daily, from hours before the parks open until long past closing, to accommodate commuting employees. Precise hours of service vary depending on where along the route you are. Use the online trip planner at **golynx.com** or call ☎ 407-841-LYNX (5969) for travel information.

GETTING ORIENTED

*un*official **TIP**
When the tollbooths before the garages are backed up, the farthest left one is often the swiftest.

PARKING AT UNIVERSAL ORLANDO

UNIVERSAL IS HOME to two massive multistory parking garages, holding a combined total of 20,000 cars. According to Forbes, they form the world's largest parking complex, dwarfing Disney Springs's 6,000-space garages. Signs route you from each of the five resort entrances to the parking structures.

The two rectangular garages lie along a north–south axis, with the pedestrian walkways leading to the theme parks running along the west, or long, side of each building. Sections are named for classic Universal movies and characters found in the parks: Jurassic Park, King Kong, and Jaws in the north garage, and E.T., Spider-Man, and Cat in the Hat in the south structure. The first numeral following the section name tells you on which deck level you are located, and the remaining numbers specify the row. So if a sign tells you that you're on King Kong 409, you're in the King Kong section on the fourth floor in row nine. We strongly recommend that you take a photo of the name and number of your section, level, and row.

Guests driving to Universal Orlando's attractions have three parking options:

SELF PARKING   Parking in the main garage costs $17 for cars and $22 for RVs, trailers, and other large rigs. Regular parking drops to $5 between 6 p.m. and 10 p.m. and is free after 10 p.m. (Evening discounts start later during Halloween and other event nights.) Parking is free for Preferred and Premier Annual Pass holders, and Florida residents with photo ID get free parking from 6 p.m. on.

PREFERRED SELF PARKING   For $25, you will be parked on the garages' central level in the closest available section to the central hub. These spots are supposed to be the second closest to the parks, after the handicapped parking section. However, we've scored spaces just as good or better using the regular parking, especially when we've arrived before 10:30 a.m. Because the garages are two-thirds as wide as they are long, the farther your parking place is from the west side, the worse it will be. This is why preferred parking is often not as close as regular parking—with the former, you'll be closer to the covered walkways to the parks, but if your particular space is toward the east side of the garage, you'll end up farther away than a guest who chose regular parking and was assigned a space closer to the west side of the structure.

An advantage of preferred parking, however, is that you'll park faster because the ratio of cars choosing preferred to regular is about 1 to 13. Preferred parking is free for Premier Annual Pass holders and costs $8 for Preferred Pass holders.

VALET PARKING   In addition to the self-parking garages, valet parking is available at CityWalk for $15 for a visit of up to two hours, or $35 for longer than that ($30 if arriving after 6 p.m.). Red Carpet Valet costs $45 and guarantees that your car will be kept close for a quick exit at the end of your evening. The entrance to the valet parking circle is on Universal Boulevard, across the street from the parking garages' taxi and bus loop. After dropping off your car, ascend the escalator adjacent to the miniature golf course and turn right to enter the CityWalk complex.

Premier Pass holders valet park for free (tip not included; not valid July 4, Mardi Gras and Halloween event nights, or December 31) or can upgrade to Red Carpet for $15; Preferred Pass holders can valet for $15, or use Red Carpet for $25. Select CityWalk restaurants will validate for up to two hours of valet if you eat lunch between 11 a.m. and 2 p.m. Monday–Friday. Stay past two hours and you'll be charged full freight. And be warned that if you imbibe too much and have to leave your car at valet overnight, you'll have to pay a $50 fine in the morning.

Guest Drop-Off

If you aren't parking at the resort but only dropping off passengers, find the Universal Boulevard entrance to the taxi and bus loop beneath the central parking hub, across the street from valet parking. This is also the best spot to pick up departing guests at the end of the day. Some guests try to use the valet parking circle for this purpose, but it is officially not permitted.

Another option is to drop off at the lobby of the Hard Rock Hotel, which is a short walk from USF's front gates if you cut through the pool. However, you can't backtrack through the pool at the end of the day without a resort key card.

Speaking of the hotels, don't attempt to save money by parking at one of the resorts. Unless you are eating at a hotel restaurant that validates for valet, off-site guests are charged a hefty fee for parking at the hotels.

FINDING YOUR WAY AROUND

UNLIKE AT DISNEY PARKS, there are no parking trams, so depending on where in the garage your car is parked, you'll have an 8- to 20-minute hike to the theme park entrances. From the garages, (sometimes) moving sidewalks deliver you first to the central hub between the two garages. In this area, you'll find wheelchair rentals, a snack and souvenir stand, and escalators leading down to bus and taxi parking. To proceed to CityWalk and the parks, you'll need to pass through a security-screening checkpoint; stay to the left if you have no bags that need inspection.

Upon exiting the parking structure, you'll pass the AMC Universal Cineplex on your right and Starbucks (always open early for that essential morning caffeine jolt) on your left before reaching CityWalk's central plaza. From here, you walk straight toward the lighthouse to reach the main entrance of Islands of Adventure, or bear right at the Fossil store toward the big globe for Universal Studios Florida's front gate.

unofficial **TIP**
You can cut through the Quiet Flight Surf Shop (which exits into The Island Clothing Company) as a shortcut to USF.

TRANSPORTATION BETWEEN UNIVERSAL RESORTS AND THEME PARKS

UNIVERSAL OFFERS WATER TAXI SERVICE between each of its on-site hotels (except Cabana Bay) and the two theme parks. The boat service uses a dock in CityWalk near the bridge to USF as a hub, which is great if you're going from one of the hotels to a theme park. If you're traveling between hotels for a meal, however, you'll need to switch boats. Boats depart about every 15 minutes, from one hour before Early Park Entry begins until after CityWalk shuts down at 2 a.m.; allow 20–25 minutes for each leg of your journey by boat.

Universal also offers a shuttle bus service that circulates between its luxury hotels, which is often faster than its boats for getting from one resort to another; tell the driver your destination when boarding.

In addition, nicely themed buses frequently run between Cabana Bay Beach Resort and the parking hub, from which you must walk to CityWalk or the theme parks.

Finally, walking from any resort hotel to either theme park takes a maximum of about 15 minutes using the resort's beautifully landscaped (though frustratingly winding) garden pathways. Hard Rock Hotel is the closest to the parks, being only steps away from Universal Studios Florida's front gates, while Portofino and Cabana Bay are the farthest. To walk between the two hotels farthest apart, Portofino and Cabana Bay, takes 25–35 minutes.

You'll find more about Universal Orlando resort transportation in the Accommodations chapter (see page 76).

LEAVING UNIVERSAL ORLANDO

AT THE END OF YOUR VISIT, retrace your steps to your vehicle and follow directional signage to depart the resort. From the south garage, you have little option but to follow the arrows to I-4 or International Drive. If you exit the north garage onto Universal Boulevard, you can reach I-4 West by turning right onto Major Boulevard and then right onto Kirkman Road; reach I-4 East by making a U-turn onto Universal Boulevard southbound at Major Boulevard, and then turn left onto the interstate after passing the garage.

PART FOUR

BARE NECESSITIES

MONEY, ETC.

ATMS AND BANKING SERVICES

UNIVERSAL STUDIOS FLORIDA ONCE had a full-service bank inside its gates, but today, banking at Universal Orlando is limited to ATMs, which are marked on the park maps. There are a half dozen ATMs in each park, plus three in CityWalk and one in each hotel. Most major banking networks are accepted.

The closest full-service bank to Universal Orlando is the Regions Bank at the corner of Kirkman and Vineland Roads (5401 S. Kirkman Road).

UNIVERSAL STUDIOS FLORIDA ATM LOCATIONS	ISLANDS OF ADVENTURE ATM LOCATIONS	CITYWALK ATM LOCATIONS
Outside the park entrance to the right of the Guest Services window	Outside the park entrance to the right of the Guest Services window	Downstairs to the left of the Guest Services window
Front Lot near First Aid and Lost and Found	Marvel Super Hero Island near The Amazing Adventures of Spider-Man	Upstairs by the second-level exit of the movie theater
New York near Revenge of the Mummy	Jurassic Park by the Jurassic Park River Adventure exit	To the left of The Groove
Outside Diagon Alley to the right of King's Cross Station	Hogsmeade outside of Three Broomsticks	
World Expo at the *Fear Factor Live* restrooms	Lost Continent outside Mythos Restaurant	
World Expo along Fast Food Boulevard		

CHECKS

UNIVERSAL ORLANDO ONLY ACCEPTS PERSONAL CHECKS that are preprinted, drawn on US banks, and are made out for the exact amount of the purchase, and they are only accepted at the front gate. A valid photo ID is required, and your check will be submitted to an online verification system.

Traveler's checks in US currency are accepted throughout the resort but must be signed by the bearer in front of the cashier and be presented with photo ID.

Business checks, cashier's checks, and school checks are only accepted if they are drawn on US banks, are preprinted, are made out for the exact amount of purchase, and are presented with photo ID.

CREDIT CARDS

AMERICAN EXPRESS, DINERS CLUB, DISCOVER, MASTERCARD, and Visa are accepted throughout the Universal Orlando Resort. The hotels also accept Japanese Credit Bureau and Carte Blanche.

American Express is the official card of Universal Orlando, and members get several discounts and perks, including access to a private **American Express VIP Lounge** hidden behind the Classic Monsters Cafe near the front of Universal Studios Florida; look for the door to the left of the Shrek meet-and-greet. Inside you'll find free bottled water, potato chips, granola bars, and smartphone charging stations, as well as air-conditioning and a respite from the crowds. In addition, a full-time concierge inside can assist you with information or reservations. The lounge is open daily, noon–5 p.m., and up to six people can enter per American Express card. Technically, you must have purchased your Universal admission (park-to-park tickets or annual pass) with your American Express, but we have only ever been asked to show our admission and AmEx card, not receipts. For additional details and current discounts, visit **universalorlando.com /theme-park-tickets/special-offers/american-express.aspx.**

CURRENCY EXCHANGE

EXCHANGE YOUR EUROS, KRONER, OR ZLOTYS for good old American greenbacks (the only form of cash accepted at Universal Orlando) at either theme park's Guest Services window, or at any hotel front desk. There may be a daily limit on how much you can exchange (around $500), and a nominal transaction surcharge applies.

A LICENSE TO PRINT MONEY

AFTER DECADES OF WATCHING DISNEY literally mint money with its **Disney Dollars,** Universal got into the currency game with **Gringotts Wizarding Bank Notes.** Available exclusively at the Gringotts Money Exchange shop in USF's Diagon Alley, these handsome bills are available in $10 or $20 denominations, and there is no extra fee to exchange your Muggle money for some.

The bank notes can be redeemed virtually anywhere on Universal Orlando property (even for valet parking) at a one-for-one exchange rate. While you won't lose any money on Wizarding currency as long as you spend it before leaving the resort, most guests (intentionally or unintentionally) take them home as souvenirs, making a healthy profit for Universal's goblin accountants. Less magical credit card–style Universal Orlando gift cards with various designs are also sold (in $5 increments up to $500) and accepted all around the resort; online you can buy them at **universalorlando.com/gift-cards.aspx.**

SALES TAX

A COMBINED STATE AND LOCAL SALES TAX of 6.5% applies to all purchases made at Universal Orlando. Hotels also charge a 6% Orange County occupancy tax, for a total of 12.5%. All prices listed in this book are before tax, unless otherwise noted.

PROBLEMS *and* UNUSUAL SITUATIONS

ATTRACTION CLOSURES

FIND OUT IN ADVANCE WHAT RIDES and attractions are scheduled to be closed for repair during your visit. For complete refurbishment schedules, check online at Universal's official operating calendar (**universalorlando.com/resort-information/theme-park-hours.aspx**) and our own Universal Orlando closures page (**touringplans.com/universal-orlando/closures**), or use our mobile app, Lines.

Universal's attractions are technically complex, so it's almost inevitable that you will experience some unscheduled downtime during your visit. If a ride is temporarily closed, ask the attendants outside if there is an estimated reopening time (usually they can't tell you) and continue with your touring, returning later if possible. If a ride stops running while you are already in the queue, decide whether to stay based on how long the posted wait was when you entered, and how much time you've already invested. Most "brief operational delays" are resolved in about 15 minutes, but there are no guarantees.

If a ride halts unexpectedly while you are on it, remain calm and rest assured that Universal has extremely safe evacuation procedures for every contingency. Stay seated and listen for announcements, and be patient because employees may need to evacuate ride vehicles one at a time in a specific order. On the plus side, you may get an exclusive backstage view of how the ride operates, and you should be offered either an immediate re-ride (if the attraction resumes operating) or a return ticket to let you skip the standby line later on.

CAR TROUBLE

UNIVERSAL ORLANDO OFFERS COMPLIMENTARY vehicle assistance—including battery jumps—to guests parked in its garage.

Raise your car's hood (if possible) and flag down a parking attendant, or use one of the security call boxes located in each parking section.

If you have more serious car trouble, the nearest repair facility is the **Universal Service Center** in the Hess Express gas station located on the west side of Universal property at 5989 Turkey Lake Road (☎ 407-345-4860, **universalservicecenter.net**).

CELL PHONE SNAFUS

CELL PHONE SERVICE CAN BE SPOTTY at Universal Orlando, especially on days of high attendance. A woman from Leawood, Kansas, tells it like it is:

In our group, we were using three different carriers, and we all had problems sending and receiving texts and calls.

The problem of signal strength is compounded by crowd noise and the ambient music played throughout the parks. Even if you have a decent signal, it's an exasperating challenge to find some place quiet enough to have a conversation. When possible, opt for texting.

Smartphone data speeds can be especially sluggish when the park is packed with guests trying to Facebook over LTE. Luckily, Universal's Wi-Fi service is free and fairly stable throughout the parks and CityWalk; you can even get decent reception inside Gringotts' vaults. Log into "xfinitywifi" and accept the nonsubscriber agreement before opening your browser or social media apps. You may have to log in again every day or so.

GASOLINE

THERE IS ONE HESS EXPRESS GAS STATION on Universal property. It is on the west side of the resort, adjacent to the corporate offices and employee parking lot. The address is 5981 Turkey Lake Road. From the guest parking garages, take Hollywood Way west to Turkey Lake Road; turn right, and the station will be ahead on your right.

LOST AND FOUND

IF YOU LOSE (OR FIND) SOMETHING in Universal Studios Florida, go to the Lost and Found counter to the right of the main gate as you enter. At Islands of Adventure, visit Guest Services at the front of the park. If you discover your loss after you've left the park(s), call ☎ 407-224-4233 and choose option 2.

It's better not to lose anything in the first place, but if you do, there is hope: We've had an excellent track record with Universal's Lost and Found, which has recovered errant hats and car keys for us over the years.

MEDICAL MATTERS

HEADACHE RELIEF Sample sizes of some over-the-counter medications are available for free from the First Aid stations. For the locations of the **First Aid** centers in the theme parks and CityWalk, see page 142. Aspirin and other sundries are sold at the Universal Studios Store in USF and at Islands of Adventure Trading Co. at IOA; they are held behind the counter, so you must ask an employee for them.

ILLNESSES REQUIRING MEDICAL ATTENTION Off property, the closest walk-in clinic is **Mt. Sinai Urgent Care** (5979 Vineland Road, Ste. 109; ☎ 407-730-3113). It's open 10 a.m.–6 p.m. daily. **Centra Care** (8014 Conroy Windermere Road; ☎ 407-291-9960) is open 8 a.m.– 8 p.m., Monday–Friday, and 8 a.m.–5 p.m., Saturday–Sunday; Centra Care also operates a 24-hour physician house call service and runs a free shuttle (call ☎ 407-938-0650 to arrange pickup).

The **Medical Concierge** (☎ 855-932-5252; **themedicalconcierge .com**) has board-certified physicians available 24-7 for house calls to your hotel room. It offers in-room X-rays and IV therapy service, as well as same-day dental and specialist appointments. It also rents medical equipment. Insurance receipts, insurance billing, and foreign-language interpretation are provided. Walk-in clinics are also available. You can also inquire about transportation arrangements.

DOCS (Doctors on Call Service; ☎ 407-399-3627; **doctorson callservice.com**) offers 24-hour house call service. All physicians are certified by the American Board of Medical Specialties. A father of two from O'Fallon, Illinois, gives them a thumbs-up:

My wife's cold developed into an ear infection that required medical attention, and DOCS was able to respond in 40 minutes. The doctor had medicine with him and was very professional and friendly.

Physician Room Service (☎ 407-238-2000; **physicianroom service.com**) provides board-certified doctor house calls to Universal Orlando–area guest rooms for adults and children.

DENTAL NEEDS Call **Celebration Dental Group** (☎ 407-351-7904), located at 6001 Vineland Road, Ste. 106.

PRESCRIPTION MEDICINE The nearest pharmacy to Universal Orlando is **Walgreens** (☎ 407-238-0600) at 5501 Kirkman Road, in the shopping plaza across from the resort. Google will tell you that there is a Walgreens at 1000 Universal Studios Plaza, but that is a backstage clinic for employees only. **Turner Drugs** (☎ 407-828-8125) charges $10–$15 to deliver a filled prescription to your hotel's front desk ($7.50 for Disney hotels).

SERGEANT BLISTERBLASTER'S GUIDE TO HAPPY FEET

1. ON YOUR FEET! Get up, La-Z-Boy rider: When you go to Universal Orlando, you'll have to walk a lot farther than to the refrigerator. You can log 5–12 miles a day at the parks, so now's the time to shape up them dogs. Start with short walks around the neighborhood. Increase your distance gradually until you can do 6 miles without CPR.

2. A-TEN-SHUN!   During your training program, pay attention when those puppies growl. They'll give you a lot of information about your feet and the appropriateness of your shoes. Listen up! No walking in flip-flops, loafers, or sandals. Wear well-constructed, broken-in running or hiking shoes. If you feel a hot spot, that means a blister is developing. The most common sites for blisters are heels, toes, and balls of the feet. If you develop a hot spot in the same place every time you walk (a clue!), cover it with a Johnson & Johnson blister bandage before you set out.

3. SOCK IT UP, TRAINEE!   Good socks are as important as good shoes. When you walk, your feet sweat like a mule in a peat bog, and the moisture only increases friction. To minimize friction, wear a pair of socks, such as SmartWool or CoolMax, that wick perspiration away from your feet (SmartWool makes socks of varying thicknesses). To further combat moisture, dust your dogs with antifungal talcum powder.

4. WHO DO YOU THINK YOU ARE? JOHN WAYNE?   Don't be a hero. Take care of a foot problem the minute you notice it. Carry a small foot-emergency kit for your platoon. Include gauze, Betadine antibiotic ointment, moleskin or Johnson & Johnson blister bandages, scissors, a sewing needle or such (to drain blisters), and matches to sterilize the needle. Extra socks and talcum powder are optional.

5. BITE THE BULLET!   If you develop a hot spot, cover it ASAP with a blister bandage. Cut the material large enough to cover the skin surrounding the spot. If you develop a blister, air out and dry your foot. Next, drain the fluid, but don't remove the top skin. Clean the area with Betadine and place a blister bandage over the blister. The bandages come in several sizes, including specially shaped ones for fingers and toes; they're also good for covering hot spots. If you don't have blister bandages, don't cover the hot spot or blister with Band-Aids; they'll slip and wad up.

6. TAKE CARE OF YOUR PLATOON.   If you have young, green troops in your outfit, they might not sound off when a hot spot develops. Stop several times a day and check their feet. If you forgot your emergency kit and a problem arises, visit the park's First Aid. It will have all the stuff you need to keep your command in action.

RAIN

WEATHER BAD? GO TO THE PARKS ANYWAY. The crowds are lighter, and most attractions and waiting areas are under cover. Showers, especially during warmer months, are short and frequently occur in the late afternoon around 4 p.m.

unofficial **TIP**
Raingear isn't always displayed in shops, so you may have to ask for it.

If picking between the two parks, know that USF is a much better park to tour in the rain, as almost all its headliner attractions (except for Hollywood Rip Ride Rockit) are indoors. While the many outdoor attractions at IOA can operate in a moderate downpour, they must all shut down when lightning is in the vicinity. That leaves Forbidden Journey, Spider-Man, and Cat in the Hat as virtually the only rides at IOA that can operate during severe weather.

Ponchos are $8 for adults and $7 for children; umbrellas are about $15. All ponchos sold at Universal Orlando are made of clear plastic (though ones sold within the Wizarding World have a special insignia), so picking out somebody in your party on a rainy day can be tricky. Stores such as Target sell inexpensive solid-color ponchos that will make your family bright beacons in a plastic-covered sea of humanity.

A Wilmington, North Carolina, mom thinks high-quality raingear is worth the investment:

> We're outdoor-sports people, so we have very good raincoats. It rained every day on this trip, driving many people out of the parks and leaving others looking miserable in their ponchos. Meanwhile, we hardly noticed the rain from inside our high-end jackets as we walked right onto many of the attractions.

Some unusually heavy rain precipitated (no pun intended) dozens of reader suggestions for dealing with soggy days. The best came from this Memphis, Tennessee, mom:

1. *Raingear should include ponchos and umbrellas. When rain isn't beating down on your ponchoed head, it's easier to ignore.*

2. *Buy blue ponchos at Walgreens. We could keep track of each other more easily because we had blue ponchos instead of clear ones.*

3. *If you're using a stroller, bring a plastic sheet or extra poncho to protect it from rain. (Ponchos cover only single strollers.) Carry a towel in a plastic bag to wipe off your stroller after experiencing an attraction during a rainfall.*

Unofficial Guide researcher Connie Wolosyk adds, "It helps to wear a baseball cap under the poncho hood—without it, the hood never covers your head properly, and your face always gets wet."

HOW TO LODGE A COMPLAINT WITH UNIVERSAL

GUEST SERVICES AT THE FRONT of each Universal park will be happy to listen to any complaints, and will be even happier to pass along praise for any exceptional employees you encounter. Minor problems are often addressed with a sincere apology and a pass to skip an attraction queue. You usually will find Universal folks highly responsive to guests' issues. However, a more global gripe, or one beyond an on-site manager's ability to resolve, is likely to founder in the labyrinth of Universal bureaucracy. To contact Guest Services after your trip, use the e-mail contact form at **visitorsatisfaction.com/contactus**.

■ SERVICES

CELEBRATION BUTTONS

CELEBRATING A BIRTHDAY, ANNIVERSARY, honeymoon, engagement, or bat mitzvah at Universal? Or just celebrating the fact that its your first visit to the parks? Stop by Guest Services for a free celebration button to wear during your special day. Buttons come in "It's My Birthday!" and more generic "I'm Celebrating!" varieties. At a minimum, you'll have employees (and fellow guests) shouting you warm wishes all day long. And if you're lucky, you might find yourself treated to preferred seating, a special meet-and-greet, or other unexpected perks.

CELL PHONE CHARGING

UNLIKE WALT DISNEY WORLD, UNIVERSAL ORLANDO has not yet installed any dedicated cell phone charging stations in the parks, so pack a power cable and wall plug if you want to steal juice from accessible outlets you find along the way. The exception is the American Express VIP Lounge discussed previously, which stocks charging adapters for most Apple and Android devices (including micro-USB and Lightning). If you prefer to charge on the go, we use Mophie and New Trent external batteries for our devices. Both are available on **amazon.com.**

FIRST AID

EACH THEME PARK has a Walgreens-sponsored first-aid center. In Universal Studios Florida, it's located on Canal Street to the left of the *Beetlejuice* show, on the border between New York and San Francisco. In Islands of Adventure, it is in the Lost Continent near the *Sindbad* show; look for the red cross behind the coin vendor. In both parks, the Family Services nursing facilities and companion restroom are right next to First Aid. CityWalk's first-aid facility is located near Guest Services, at the end of the hallway behind Cold Stone Creamery. Guests who use the service are generally very positive about it; Seth once sought treatment for a minor flesh wound and was patched up and riding rides again in a matter of minutes.

GROCERIES

EACH UNIVERSAL RESORT HOTEL has a shop or food court selling sundries, snacks, and grab-and-go breakfast foods. While their locations make them undeniably convenient, the selection is poor, and you'll find the prices higher and more frightening than Doctor Doom's Fearfall. For down-to-earth prices, try **Publix,** located north of Universal at the intersection of Kirkman and Conroy Roads (4606 S. Kirkman Road; ☎ 407-293-7673), or for fancier fare visit **Whole Foods,** located southwest of Universal on Sand Lake Road near I-4 (8003 Turkey Lake Road; ☎ 407-355-7100).

If you don't have a car or you don't want to take the time to go to the supermarket, **GardenGrocer** (**gardengrocer.com**) will shop for you and deliver your groceries. The best way to compile your order is on GardenGrocer's website before you leave home. It's simple, and the selection is huge. If there's something you want that's not on the list of available items, the service will try to find it for you (including alcohol). Delivery arrangements are per your instructions. If you're staying at a hotel, you can arrange for your groceries to be left with bell services. Currently, GardenGrocer can only deliver to Portofino Bay Hotel and Royal Pacific Resort, not Hard Rock Hotel or Cabana Bay Beach

Resort. For the sake of order-fulfillment accuracy and customer service, GardenGrocer is primarily set up for online ordering. If you can't get online, though, you can order by phone (☎ 866-855-4350). For orders of $200 or more, there's a $2 delivery fee; for orders less than $200, the delivery charge is $14. A minimum order of $40 is required. It pays to plan ahead: You'll get a 5% discount for ordering at least 15 days in advance, 7% off for 30 days, and 10% off for 60 days. Note that GardenGrocer's delivery schedule may fill completely around holidays, at which point it will stop accepting orders for delivery on those dates.

We get lots of positive reader feedback about GardenGrocer. The following review from an Eagan, Minnesota, family is representative:

> GardenGrocer was fabulous. I ordered our groceries online about one week before our arrival. I had a few questions, so I called and actually spoke with a human who was very helpful! Our flight got in about 7 p.m., and I called to let them know we were on our way. They arrived about 20 minutes after we did with everything we ordered.

LOCKERS

WHEN VISITING UNIVERSAL'S THEME PARKS, we try to pare down our gear to a bare minimum and only bring those necessities that fit comfortably in our pockets: admission, ID, a credit card or cash, and a cell phone. Many guests keep their tickets handy in a plastic lanyard (readily available around the resort for $5 and up), and Seth swears by cargo shorts with zippered pockets, for function if not fashion. However, many guests (especially those accompanying young children or those with special needs) find that they simply can't travel that light. When your burden becomes too much to bear, make a beeline for a bank of lockers and lighten your load.

Incidentally, Universal is rather liberal in what it allows guests to bring into its parks. Obviously, any form of weapon or illegal substance is prohibited, as is clothing with "offensive language or content" or that "represents someone as emergency personnel." You are also disallowed from entering with large duffel bags, folding chairs, beach umbrellas, or hard-sided coolers. You may, however, bring food and snacks for your personal consumption, along with any medically necessary nutritional items and baby food, as long as it is nonalcoholic, is not in glass containers, and carried in a soft-sided cooler or bag no bigger than 8.5 inches by 6 inches by 6 inches. There are also no facilities for refrigerating or reheating outside food in the park. Keep in mind that all items are subject to inspection before entering CityWalk, so be prepared to open your bags at the security checkpoint (or use the "no bags" line to speed your entry if unencumbered).

All of Universal Orlando's lockers are automated and use a biometric locking system. The locker banks are easy to find, and each bank has a small touch screen computer in the center. Begin by approaching a locker computer, selecting your language, and touching RENT A LOCKER. (When the sun is bright, the screen is almost impossible to read, so have someone block the sun or use a different computer.) After selecting your language and locker size (if applicable), press your thumb onto the keypad and have your fingerprint scanned. We've seen people walk away cursing at this step, having repeated it over and over with no success. Don't press down too hard—the computer can't read your thumbprint that way. Instead, take a deep breath and lightly place your thumb on the scanner.

After your do your thumb scan, you'll receive a locker number. Commit it to memory, or write it down! Place your property in the indicated locker, which should have a flashing green light, and press the illuminated button after you have closed the door to lock it.

When you are ready to retrieve your belongings, go to the same kiosk machine, select REOPEN YOUR LOCKER, enter your locker number, and scan your thumb again. Remember that only the person who used his or her thumb to get the locker can retrieve anything from it. The locker should relinquish its contents; if you have any trouble, find a nearby employee to assist.

Universal Orlando offers three types of lockers:

Paid All-Day Lockers

These lockers charge one flat rate for a full day and can be opened and relocked by the original user as many times as you like during your visit. All-day lockers come in two categories: regular (approximately 9.5 inches wide by 17 inches high by 17 inches deep) for $8 per day, or roomier "family size" (approximately 12.5 inches wide by 17 inches deep by 25 inches deep or larger) for $10 per day.

All-day lockers can be found in the following locations:

UNIVERSAL STUDIOS FLORIDA ALL-DAY LOCKERS
• Next to the Studio Audience Center inside the front gate (regular size)
• Behind the restrooms near the Studio Audience Center (family size)
• Near the exit turnstiles, next to wheelchair and stroller rental (regular size)
• Outside the park to the far right of the entrance, around the corner from Guest Services (jumbo family size, up to 23 inches high by 35 inches deep)
ISLANDS OF ADVENTURE ALL-DAY LOCKERS
• Outside the exit turnstiles at Group Sales (jumbo family size, up to 15.5 inches wide by 17 inches or 23 inches high by 35 inches deep)
• Inside the front gate near wheelchair and stroller rental (regular and family size)

Free Short-Term Lockers

Universal enforces a mandatory locker system at its big thrill rides. Small lockers (approximately 9.5 inches wide by 11.5 inches high by 17 inches deep) outside these attractions are free for an amount of time that varies with the length of the standby line. So if the line is 30 minutes, for example, and the ride itself is 10 minutes, you get 40 minutes plus a small cushion of about 15 minutes. The lockers then cost $3 for each 30 minutes after that, with a $20 daily maximum.

Free short-term lockers are located at the following attractions:

UNIVERSAL STUDIOS FLORIDA FREE SHORT-TERM LOCKERS
• Harry Potter and the Escape from Gringotts   • Hollywood Rip Ride Rockit • Men in Black Alien Attack   • Revenge of the Mummy

ISLANDS OF ADVENTURE FREE SHORT-TERM LOCKERS
• Dragon Challenge   • Harry Potter and the Forbidden Journey • The Incredible Hulk Coaster

On most of the aforementioned rides, all bags, purses, and other objects too large to be secured in a pocket must be placed in a free locker during your ride; wallets, cell phones, and compact cameras are generally permitted, as are small hip belts or fanny packs that can be securely fastened and tucked beneath a shirt.

In 2015 Universal began strictly enforcing a "no loose items" policy at The Incredible Hulk Coaster, Hollywood Rip Ride Rockit, and Dragon Challenge. At these rides, guests are required to pass through an airport-style security screening (complete with walk-through metal detectors and electronic scanning wands) to ensure no phones, keys, or even spare change enter the queue. You should be permitted to keep your prescription eyeglasses and ticket lanyard.

If the ride breaks down while you are in line and you exceed your free usage period through no fault of your own, a locker attendant can override the charge on request.

When you want to ride a thrill ride but don't want to bother with a locker, you can use each attraction's child-swap area (see page 173) as a bag swap, and leave a non-rider with your belongings. This is an especially useful technique for the Harry Potter rides because the free lockers are too small to hold wand boxes from Ollivanders, and the locker banks for Forbidden Journey and Gringotts are frequently overcrowded.

Paid Short-Term Lockers

Universal does not enforce mandatory locker usage on its water rides, but it does conveniently (or capitalistically) provide paid short-term lockers outside each attraction that is likely to soak you and your belongings. The lockers are the same size as the free ones (approximately 9.5 inches wide by 11.5 inches high by 17 inches deep) and operate identically. The difference is that they cost $4 for the first 90 minutes, and $3 for each additional hour after that, with a $20 daily maximum.

Paid short-term lockers are located only at IOA at the following attractions:

ISLANDS OF ADVENTURE PAID SHORT-TERM LOCKERS
• Dudley Do-Right's Ripsaw Falls   • Jurassic Park River Adventure • Popeye & Bluto's Bilge-Rat Barges

PACKAGE PICKUP AND DELIVERY

COMPLIMENTARY PACKAGE PICKUP is available at both parks. Ask the salesperson to send your purchases to Package Pickup. When you leave the park, they'll be waiting for you. At USF, Package Pickup is at the gift shop immediately adjacent to the exit turnstiles. At IOA, it is outside Islands of Adventure Trading Co. in the open-air market across from Croissant Moon Bakery.

If you're staying at a Universal Orlando resort, you can also have the packages delivered directly to your hotel room by the following day for free. If you're leaving within 24 hours, however, take them with you or use the in-park pickup location.

If you get home and realize you missed an essential souvenir, shop for Universal Orlando tchotchkes online at **universalorlando.com /merchandise/merchandisehome.aspx.**

PET CARE

UNIVERSAL ORLANDO'S KENNEL FACILITY BOARDS dogs and cats (no exotic or native species allowed) on a first-come, first-serve basis. You can find the facility by following the signs to RV and camper parking after passing through the tollbooths; the kennel is located on the corner of the oversize parking lot. The kennel opens at 8 a.m. and does not take reservations. The cost is $15 per pet, per day; Premier Pass holders save 50% on their first pet.

An attendant remains on duty at the kennel until two hours after the last park closes, but you can retrieve your pet until 3 a.m. by using the phone outside the kennel to call for assistance. The kennel provides water, but you need to bring your own food and toys and return to walk your dog at least once during the day.

Note: You must provide written proof from a veterinarian of current vaccination (rabies, Bordetella, and DHPP for dogs; rabies, calicivirus, panleukopenia, and rhinotracheitis for cats) either at check-in or by fax at ☎ 407-224-9516. Call ☎ 407-224-9509 for more information.

PHOTO CONNECT

WHILE SOME GUESTS STILL FIND their point-and-shoot or camera phone sufficient for documenting their vacation, Universal (in partnership with Colorvision's Amazing Pictures) has capitalized on advancing digital photo and social media technology with its Photo Connect program. All the images captured during your day by Universal—either by roving paparazzi near the park entrances, at organized character meet-and-greets, or inside attractions—can be collected on plastic cards (distributed free from every photo location) and retrieved at the end of the day at the photography shops at the front of either park.

Photos can be printed à la carte, which quickly gets expensive at $20-plus each. A better value are the Star Card packages, which offer 1, 3, or 14 days of unlimited digital photos and a souvenir lanyard to hold your Star Card. If you have a Star Card package, you receive deep discounts on videos ($20 for Hollywood Rip Ride Rockit; $5 for The Incredible Hulk Coaster) and prints ($2 for 4-by-6; $5 for 5-by-7; $10 for 8-by-10), along with 20% off Amazing Pictures green screen photo ops. The package includes all street photographers, on-ride still images, and even unique photo ops such as the Simpson's couch gag and E.T.'s flying bicycle.

The digital images can be downloaded at **universalphotoconnect.com** or through the free Apple or Android app (search for "Amazing Pictures Mobile" in your app store), from where they can be e-mailed, shared on Facebook and Twitter, or saved at a resolution good enough for printing (though not poster-size enlargements).

To use the Star Card, simply present it to every Universal photographer you approach, or at the photo counters at the exits of rides. Ride photos can be edited to zoom in on your party, and some photographers can set up special effects shots. Universal also has automated Star Card kiosks at the exits of Revenge of the Mummy, Men in Black Alien Attack, and The Incredible Hulk Coaster, so you can register your photos without waiting in line, though Photo Connect team members are still available to help find and edit your photos if you don't want to use the self-service stations. You get two cards per Star Card package, in case your party splits up, and any additional images you get on other Photo Connect cards can be added to your Star Card account at any photo service center.

If you prepurchase your Photo Connect Star Card package online at **presale.amazingpictures.com/photoconnect.aspx,** it won't begin expiring until you activate it upon visiting the parks; once activated, Star Card packages are valid for the purchased number of consecutive days. Online prices are $40 for a single day, $60 for 3 days, and $90 for a 14-day package. Annual-pass holders can get a full year of Star Card service for the 14-day price. A package combining a three-day Star Card with a video session at Shutterbutton's costs $100 online. The 3- to 14-day Star Cards and annual pass–holder packages cost considerably more if purchased inside the park.

We're big fans of Photo Connect, especially the yearlong Star Card for annual-pass holders, though a recent 50% price hike makes it a bit less attractive. If you're the type of person who buys ride and character photos, you'll save big, and if not, the freedom of unlimited snapshots may seduce you. And Universal's offer is significantly cheaper than Disney World's similar Memory Maker package. But you should be aware of some deficits and gotchas to the Star Card before buying.

For starters, Photo Connect photographers can be found at each park's entrance, and occasionally at an impromptu character greeting, but they aren't on every corner like at Disney World. You certainly should not leave your camera at home with the expectation that Photo Connect will be able to capture all your vacation memories.

Second, if you want to purchase any photos, you must do so (or buy and activate a Star Card package) before you leave the park; once you exit at the end of the day, photos not paid for or not connected to an active Star Card account will be erased. Also, if you want digital copies of your photos, you must have a Star Card package, as à la carte digital photos are no longer offered.

Finally, a few specific attractions have their own quirks. All still photos in The Wizarding Worlds are included with the Star Card, but if you want to use your included free prints for the Forbidden Journey or Gringotts ride, you must get your photo printed at those attractions. All other attraction pictures may be printed at any photo-service location. Also, Hollywood Rip Ride Rockit's photos are free for Star Card purchasers, but their computer system is separate, and the photos will not automatically be added to your online account. Instead, you'll be given a paper receipt with a code number that can be redeemed at **universal photoconnect.com.** For the record, here is where you can always find Photo Connect locations throughout Universal's two parks:

UNIVERSAL STUDIOS FLORIDA PHOTO CONNECT LOCATIONS	ISLANDS OF ADVENTURE PHOTO CONNECT LOCATIONS
• Park entrance	• Park entrance
• Meet-and-greet near *Shrek 4-D* exit	• The Incredible Hulk Coaster on-ride photo
• SpongeBob StorePants in KidZone	• The Amazing Adventures of Spider-Man queue photo (standby only)
• Transformers meet-and-greet	• Spider-Man meet-and-greet
• E.T. Toy Closet	• Dudley Do-Right's Ripsaw Falls on-ride photo
• Men in Black Alien Attack on-ride photo	• Jurassic Park photo op
• Simpsons couch gag	• Jurassic Park River Adventure on-ride photo
• Revenge of the Mummy on-ride photo	• Jurassic Park Raptor Encounter
• Hollywood Rip Ride Rockit on-ride photo	• Harry Potter and the Forbidden Journey on-ride photo
• Harry Potter and the Escape from Gringotts queue photo	• The High in the Sky Seuss Trolley Train Ride! queue photo (standby only)

RELIGIOUS SERVICES

THE CLOSEST CHURCHES TO UNIVERSAL ORLANDO are the nondenominational storefront Church of Life (7436 Universal Blvd.; ☎ 407-394-1967; **thechurchoflife.com**) and the enormous First Baptist Orlando (3000 John Young Pkwy.; ☎ 407-425-2555; **firstorlando.com**). The nearest Catholic Mass is held at Holy Family at 5125 S. Apopka-Vineland Road (☎ 407-876-2211; **holyfamilyorlando.org**), and the nearest synagogue is Southwest Orlando Jewish Congregation at 11200 S. Apopka-Vineland Road (☎ 407-239-5444; **sojc.org**). For a complete list of religious services in the Orlando tourist area, see **allears.net/btp /church.htm** and **wdwinfo.com/tips_for_touring/churchservices.htm.** Christian visitors may also be interested in the Rock the Universe religious music weekend held in early September (see page 281).

VACATION SERVICES

THROUGHOUT BOTH PARKS, you'll spot stands marked VACATION SERVICES, staffed by chatty team members who will ask you where you're from as you pass. Most guests hurry by, assuming—correctly—that these outposts serve as sales pitches for time-shares (or "fractional vacation ownership opportunities," as George Orwell might have put it). But unlike the similar Disney Vacation Club kiosks found around Walt Disney World, Universal's Vacation Services actually serves a number of other useful functions. In addition to selling Universal Orlando gift cards, meal plans, Express Passes, and Blue Man Group tickets, they can help book dining reservations and answer many Guest Services questions. If you have an issue, stop by one of these locations before walking back to the front of the park.

WINE, BEER, AND LIQUOR

ALCOHOL IS WIDELY AVAILABLE by the pint, glass, or shot throughout Universal's theme parks, hotels, and CityWalk. Bars in Islands of Adventure and CityWalk even hold daily happy hours each afternoon to save you a few bucks on booze. You can also buy wine by the bottle in the resort's table-service restaurants and some hotel shops. Note that while you can walk freely with a drink within either of the parks or City-Walk, due to liquor-license laws, you may not pass from CityWalk into a park or hotel (or vice versa) with an open container in hand.

Wine and beer are also sold off property in grocery stores, convenience stores, and liquor stores. The best range of adult beverages is sold at the **ABC Fine Wine & Spirits** at 7611 International Dr. (☎ 407-351-5165). The **Walgreens** across Kirkman Road from Universal also has a decent, if slightly expensive, liquor selection.

Remember that the minimum age to buy or consume alcohol in Florida is 21, and anyone who looks 30 or younger should plan to present government-issued photo ID (valid driver's license or passport) when purchasing. At CityWalk you'll be tagged with a paper bracelet while drinking, to take home as a hair-snagging reminder of your debauched revels.

UNIVERSAL ORLANDO *for* GUESTS *with* SPECIAL NEEDS

LIKE ITS COMPETITORS, UNIVERSAL ORLANDO makes efforts to accommodate every visitor, in accordance with the Americans with Disabilities Act (ADA). The resort offers a free **"Rider's Guide for Rider Safety & Guests with Disabilities"** describing each attraction's restrictions and requirements in detail at **universalorlando.com/resort-information/accessibility-information.aspx.** You can download the booklet in PDF format before your visit (which we highly recommend) or get a printed copy at Guest Services, at resort front desks, or at wheelchair-rental locations inside the parks. The limitations you will face at Universal Orlando, and the accommodations you can take advantage of, will vary according to the nature of your special needs.

MOBILITY RESTRICTIONS

UNIVERSAL ORLANDO IS FAIRLY FRIENDLY for nonambulatory guests to navigate, and the resort has recently repaved some bumpy streets (such as the faux cobblestones along USF's New York waterfront) to be more comfortable for wheelchair users.

Universal provides close(er)-in parking for disabled visitors; ask for directions when you pay your parking fee. These spots are located on the main level of each parking garage, nearest to the central hub. You'll still have a substantial trip to CityWalk and the parks from even the best handicapped parking spot.

The entire Universal Orlando Resort transportation system is also disabled-accessible. Water taxis have roll-on ramps for easy boarding, and bus routes are served by vehicles with wheelchair lifts that can accommodate all but the largest motorized scooters.

All park shopping, dining, and restroom facilities at the theme parks, CityWalk, and hotels are generally ADA compliant for wheelchair access. Some fast-food queues and shop aisles (especially in The Wizarding World of Harry Potter) are too narrow for wheelchairs. At these locations, ask a team member for assistance. All shows and performances (including parades) also have designated disability sections for guests in wheelchairs and their parties.

In addition, all attraction queues (with the exception of Pteranodon Flyers in IOA) are fully wheelchair accessible, so you can enjoy the full preshow experience. Alternative routes (such as elevators to bypass stairs at Harry Potter and the Escape from Gringotts, Revenge of the Mummy, and Men in Black Alien Attack) and accessible boarding procedures (such as the stationary loading station at Harry Potter and the Forbidden Journey) are provided wherever necessary; be sure to read the specific instructions posted outside each attraction, and bring your needs to the attention of the first attendant to greet you for further instructions.

Strollers are not normally permitted inside most attractions, so if your child's stroller doubles as his or her wheelchair, swing by Guest Services for a special pass that will allow you to roll it through queues.

None of Universal's ride vehicles are able to accommodate electric convenience vehicles (ECVs) or motorized wheelchairs, though a handful have special cars that can carry a manual wheelchair. At those rides, guests can transfer from their powered chair to a standard one that will be provided at each applicable attraction. Even if an attraction doesn't accommodate wheelchairs of any kind, nonambulatory guests may ride if they can transfer from their wheelchair to the ride's vehicle. Universal's staff, however, aren't trained or permitted to assist with transfers—guests must be able to board the ride unassisted or have a member of their party assist them. Either way, members of the nonambulatory guest's party will be permitted to ride with him or her.

Wheelchair Rentals

Any guest may rent a wheelchair, with no proof of medical need required. Most rides, shows, attractions, restrooms, and restaurants accommodate the nonambulatory disabled. If you're in a park and need assistance, go to Guest Services. Be aware that, as all attraction queues are wheelchair accessible, using one does not automatically allow you to skip the standby line or shorten your wait.

Wheelchairs rent for $12 per day (tax included) with a fully refundable $50 deposit (cash or credit card) required. Standard wheelchairs are available at the central parking hub before you reach CityWalk and inside both theme parks near the front gates.

A limited number of ECVs are available for rent. Easy to drive, they give nonambulatory guests tremendous freedom and mobility. ECVs are $50 per day, plus the same $50 refundable deposit (prices do not include tax). An upgraded model with a canopy is an extra $65. ECVs are popular and tend to sell out by midmorning on peak days, so call Guest Services (☎ 407-224-4233, option 3) at least a week in advance to reserve one. ECVs are only available inside the parks; you can rent a standard wheelchair at the parking hub and upgrade to an ECV once you reach the park.

SERVICE ANIMALS

SERVICE ANIMALS ARE WELCOME at the Universal Orlando Resort, and the luxury Loews hotels even accommodate non-service pets. Working companion animals are allowed inside all Universal restaurant and merchandise locations, attraction queues, and most other locations throughout the resort. Specific guidelines for each attraction are posted at the queue entrance and listed in the "Rider's Guide." For attractions where the service animal cannot safely enter, portable kennels are provided.

When nature calls, service-animal relief areas are marked on the park map. There are two designated walking areas in USF (Central Park across from Cafe La Bamba and World Expo between Men in Black Alien Attack and *Fear Factor Live*) and three in IOA (Marvel Super Hero Island between The Amazing Adventures of Spider-Man and Doctor Doom's Fearfall, Jurassic Park behind Pizza Predattoria, and Seuss Landing behind One Fish, Two Fish, Red Fish, Blue Fish).

DIETARY RESTRICTIONS

UNIVERSAL ORLANDO RESTAURANTS WORK very hard to accommodate guests' special dietary needs. If properly informed, Universal's chefs can prepare food that is vegetarian or vegan; kosher or halal; dairy-free, gluten-free, or nut-free. When you make a dining reservation, either online at **opentable.com** or by phone (☎ 407-224-DINE [3463] for restaurants in the parks and CityWalk; ☎ 407-503-DINE [3463] for hotel dining), you'll be asked about food allergies and the like. The host or hostess and your server will also ask about this and send the chef out to discuss the menu; if you're not asked, just talk to your server when you're seated.

At counter-service restaurants, ask to see the menu book with ingredient and allergen info. Unfortunately, one place that does not get high marks for dietary accommodation is the Leaky Cauldron in Diagon Alley. There is virtually nothing on the menu that's vegan, and not much more for the gluten-free or lactose intolerant. In general, those on restricted diets will find many more options at Universal's table-service eateries.

Be aware, also, that Universal Orlando does not have separate kitchen facilities in which to prepare allergen-free foods, so there is always a slight possibility of inadvertent allergen contamination before or during preparation. You are welcome to bring your own food into the resort, as long as you follow the restrictions on items permitted inside the parks (no glass containers nor large or hard coolers). If you are staying on-site, a refrigerator can be rented in rooms that do not provide one as standard for $15 per day.

For more information, e-mail your specific dietary requests to **foodservicecuf@universalorlando.com.**

HEARING IMPAIRMENT

GUEST SERVICES AT THE PARKS PROVIDES FREE assistive-technology devices to hearing-impaired guests with a refundable deposit (depending on the device). Hearing-impaired guests can benefit from amplified audio on many attractions, and closed-captioning is available upon request for queue video monitors. Select shows offer reflective captioning as well. Guest Services can also provide a printed script to many of the attractions for you to peruse.

In addition, Universal provides complimentary sign language interpretations of live shows at the theme parks daily. There is typically only one interpreted performance of each show per day, so check the show schedule in the park map as soon as you arrive and plan your visit accordingly. Even if you don't understand sign language, it's well worth seeing for how animated and expressive the interpreters are—they truly steal the show.

VISION IMPAIRMENT

PARK INFORMATION GUIDES, RESTAURANT MENUS, and attraction scripts are available at Guest Services in large print and embossed Braille. Some rides can accommodate guests with white canes (a collapsible cane is recommended), while at others an attendant will hold the cane and return it to the guest immediately at the unload area.

MISSING AND PROSTHETIC LIMBS

ALL GUESTS MUST BE ABLE TO HOLD THEMSELVES upright and continuously grasp a safety restraint with at least one extremity to experience most rides. Guests with prosthetic limbs may ride with them securely attached on most rides. Those with prosthetic arms or hands may need to demonstrate that they can grip the safety restraints. Those with prosthetic legs or feet will need to remove them before riding Dragon Challenge, Harry Potter and the Forbidden Journey, or

Pteranodon Flyers. No prosthetic limbs may be worn on Hollywood Rip Ride Rockit. Consult the "Rider's Guide" for details.

LARGER GUESTS

THRILL-SEEKING GUESTS OF SIZE WILL DISCOVER that several of Universal's rides are unfriendly toward those of generous girth. The Harry Potter headliners are the most notorious for excluding plus-size riders, though both have certain seats—the outside seats on Harry Potter and the Forbidden Journey, and rows three and six on Harry Potter and the Escape from Gringotts—that are more accommodating to most body shapes. Likewise, the big roller coasters at Islands of Adventure have designated seats in rows three and six with double seat belts designed for bigger guests, and row three at Revenge of the Mummy offers extra leg room.

In all cases, these safety restrictions are based less on weight than torso circumference; some guests with large chests who would not otherwise be considered overweight may find the restraint harnesses challenging to lock properly. Before getting into line for any attraction, check out the sample ride vehicle at the entrance, and discuss your concerns with the attraction's greeter. If you wait to ride but are rejected because the restraints won't fit, the employees will be very polite but can't compensate your time.

NONAPPARENT DISABILITIES

WE RECEIVE MANY LETTERS FROM READERS whose traveling companion or child requires special assistance but who, unlike a person in a wheelchair, is not visibly disabled. Autism, for example, makes it very difficult or impossible for someone with the disorder to wait in line for more than a few minutes or in queues surrounded by a crowd.

A trip to Universal Orlando can be nonetheless positive and rewarding for guests with autism and similar conditions. And while any theme park vacation requires planning, a little extra effort to accommodate the affected person will pay large dividends.

Our first suggestion is to visit the website **autismattheparks.com,** and study its extensive information on visiting Universal Orlando. It's the best independent source we know for dealing with neurological or sensory issues at the attractions, and it is filled with practical first-hand advice.

Next, you'll want to familiarize yourself with two programs Universal offers to make your visit a little smoother:

Universal's Attractions Assistance Pass (AAP)

For years, Universal has been offering assistance to impaired guests through its Attractions Assistance Pass (AAP), a program that's remarkably similar to the Disability Access Service (DAS) system Disney famously switched to in late 2013, following reports from the national media that its then-current Guest Assistance Card (GAC) program was being rampantly abused.

Universal's AAP is designed to accommodate guests who can't wait in regular standby lines. You must first obtain an AAP card at the Guest Services of the first theme park you visit. AAP cards are good for parties of up to six people. The same card is valid in both parks for the length of your vacation, or up to 14 days for annual-pass holders.

When you get to Guest Services, you'll need to present identification and describe your or your family member's limitations. You don't need to disclose a disease or medical condition—by federal privacy law, they are forbidden to ask. Rather than an attempt to have you prove your condition, the goal here is to get you the right level of assistance.

Be as detailed as possible in describing limitations. For instance, if your child is on the autism spectrum, has trouble waiting in long lines, and has sensory issues that make it difficult for him or her to stand or be subjected to loud noises, you need to let the team member know each of these things. "He doesn't wait in lines" isn't enough to go on. A doctor's note explaining the necessary accommodations can be very helpful.

AAP cards can be used at any ride or attraction, even if it doesn't have a Universal Express entrance. Present the card to a team member at the attraction you want to ride. If the ride's standby wait time is less than 30 minutes, you'll usually be escorted through the Universal Express entrance or through an alternate queue in the case of non-Express rides such as Hogwarts Express, Harry Potter and the Forbidden Journey, and Harry Potter and the Escape from Gringotts. If the standby time is higher than 30 minutes, the team member will enter on the AAP card the attraction name, time of day, wait time, and a return time for you to come back to ride. The return time will be based on the current wait time, so if you get to The Amazing Adventures of Spider-Man at 12:20 p.m. and the standby time is 40 minutes, your return time will be 40 minutes later, at 1 p.m.

You may return at the specified time or at any time thereafter, but you can't get another AAP return time until you have used or forfeited the first. When you return, you'll be given access to the Universal Express line, where you should face a wait of 15 minutes or less. The card holder need not be present to obtain a return time but must be present with his or her party for anyone to gain admission.

Universal's Guest Assistance Pass (GAP) Entry Cards

If the AAP doesn't meet your family's needs, Universal makes a small number of Guest Assistance Pass (GAP) Entry cards available on a strictly limited basis. Basically, a GAP Entry card is identical to a one-day/two-park unlimited Universal Express Pass and provides immediate entry to any attraction's Universal Express queue, regardless of the standby wait. Like the Universal Express Pass, GAP Entry is only valid at attractions that offer Universal Express, which excludes the big Harry Potter rides, so you'll still want an AAP card for those attractions.

If you want a GAP because long standby lines are rendering the AAP unworkable for your party, be prepared to plead your case to a Guest Services supervisor and endure some time-consuming scrutiny. If you're turned down, or prefer not to deal with the hassle, you can always purchase Express Passes (subject to availability).

FRIENDS OF BILL W.

THE NEAREST ALCOHOLICS ANONYMOUS meetings to Universal Orlando are held daily (except Wednesday) at St. Luke Methodist Church (Room A113) at 4851 Apopka-Vineland Road; visit **cflinter group.org** for additional information. For information on **Al-Anon/ Alateen** meetings in the area, visit **alanon-orlando.com.**

INTERNATIONAL VISITORS

UNIVERSAL ORLANDO PROVIDES PARK MAPS in a number of different languages and maintains special websites designed for visitors from Brazil, Germany, Puerto Rico, and the United Kingdom. Visit **universalorlando.com/general-information/international-page.aspx** for further international information.

PART FIVE

UNIVERSAL ORLANDO *with* KIDS

IT'S *a* SMALL UNIVERSE, AFTER ALL

SINCE THE OPENING OF ISLANDS OF ADVENTURE'S coasters and CityWalk's nightclubs, Universal Orlando has positioned itself as an edgier, more adult alternative to the Mouse. Even Disney diehards will admit that Universal Orlando sports more attractions aimed at older teens and young adults than Walt Disney World currently does. But the commonly heard rejoinder is that there's "nothing" for little kids to do at Universal's parks.

That stereotype has seeds of truth. While the Magic Kingdom can claim more than a dozen rides with no height restrictions, USF and IOA combined have only seven rides that accommodate kids less than 34 inches tall. And as popular as Universal characters like the Minions and SpongeBob are with the single-digit set, it's tough to compete with the multibillion-dollar marketing machine behind Anna and Elsa. But numbers alone don't tell the tale because a vacation at UOR can actually be a better experience for the youngest visitors (and therefore the family members around them) than the equivalent WDW escape.

For starters, while Universal lacks many moving attractions for tots, it makes up for it with the best themed playgrounds in town, as well as a lineup of live shows sure to delight youngsters (assuming they have a tolerance for loud noises and purple dinosaurs). Second, without FastPass+ reservations and 180-day Advanced Dining Reservations to worry about, a stay at Universal Orlando requires much less preplanning, which means less damage to your day when the inevitable toddler tantrum derails your carefully laid touring plans. Universal's parks are more compact than Magic Kingdom and Epcot, which means that little legs won't tire as quickly. Also, on any given day, the crowds are likely to be lighter at UOR, welcome news for anyone shoving a stroller through the streets. Finally, it's far easier to travel from Universal's on-site hotels to its parks and back, a key benefit when heading back to your room for that essential midday nap.

Ideally, your kids should be at least 42 inches tall to experience the bulk of the parks' dark rides and simulators, or 54 inches tall to brave the biggest roller coasters. But traveling to Universal Orlando with a toddler, or even infant, can be equally rewarding, as long as you know what you're getting into and prepare thoroughly. The biggest danger is in dealing with a child who's barely under the minimum for something they'll "just die" without riding, so read up on height requirements (see page 173) in advance to avoid disappointment on the day.

When you're planning a Universal Orlando vacation with young children, consider the following:

AGE   Though Universal Orlando's color and festivity excite all children (with specific attractions that delight toddlers and preschoolers), and there's no admission fee for those under 3 years old, Universal's entertainment is generally oriented to older children and adults. Children should be a fairly mature 8 years old to appreciate Universal Studios Florida, and a bit older to tackle the thrill rides in Islands of Adventure. Note that Universal considers all kids ages 3–9 as children for pricing purposes, regardless of height or ability to experience rides.

WHEN TO VISIT   Avoid the hot, crowded summer months, especially if you have preschoolers. Go in October, November (except Thanksgiving), early December, January, February, or May. If you have children of varied ages and they're good students, take the older ones out of school and visit during the cooler and less congested off-season. Arrange special assignments relating to the educational aspects of Universal Orlando. If your children can't afford to miss school, take your vacation as soon as the school year ends. Alternatively, try late August before school starts. Please understand that you don't have to visit during one of the more ideal times of year to have a great vacation.

unofficial **TIP**
Coupled with a sense of humor and a little preparedness on your part, our touring plans and tips for families ensure a super experience at any time of year.

A Peterborough, England, woman agrees:

> *We visited at the end of August, and we expected that the crowds would be almost unbearable. However, we were surprised to find that because most local schools were back in session, we could walk on most headliner rides up until late afternoon, and even then there was only a short wait—some rides at Universal Studios didn't even open until 11 a.m. because we were visiting on a low-attendance day! We'd recommend that more people go this time of year, especially those people whose children don't return to school until later.*

BUILD NAPS AND REST INTO YOUR ITINERARY   The parks are huge: Don't try to see everything in one day. Tour in the early morning and return to your hotel around 11:30 a.m. for lunch, a swim, and a nap.

Even during off-season, when crowds are smaller and the temperature is more pleasant, the size of the parks will exhaust most children younger than age 8 by lunchtime. Return to the park in the late afternoon or early evening and continue touring. A family from Texas underlines the importance of naps and rest:

> Probably the most important tip your guide gave us was going to the hotel to swim and regroup during the day. The parks became unbearable by noon—and so did my husband and boys. The hotel was an oasis that calmed our nerves! After about three hours of playtime, we headed out to [the other park] for dinner and a cool evening of fun.

Regarding naps, this mom doesn't mince words:

> For parents of small kids: Take the book's advice, get out of the park, and take the nap, take the nap, TAKE THE NAP! Never in my life have I seen so many parents screaming at, ridiculing, or slapping their kids. (What a vacation!) [The parks can be] overwhelming for kids and adults.

If you plan to return to your hotel at midday and want your room made up, let housekeeping know.

WHERE TO STAY   The time and hassle involved in commuting to and from the theme parks will be less if your hotel is on Universal property. It's hard to overemphasize how convenient it is to commute between your room and the parks when staying at the luxury Loews resorts, and even the value-priced Cabana Bay is only a 15-minute stroller push away from IOA's front gates. A number of off-site hotels, along Major Boulevard and International Drive (see page 104), are also within walking distance, but you may not feel comfortable crossing busy roads with small kids in tow.

BE IN TOUCH WITH YOUR FEELINGS   When you or your kids get tired and irritable, call a time-out. Trust your instincts. What would feel best? Another ride, an ice cream break, or going back to the room for a nap?

LEAST COMMON DENOMINATORS   Somebody is going to run out of steam first, and when he or she does, the whole family will be affected. Sometimes a snack break will revive the flagging member. Sometimes, however, it's better to return to your hotel. Pushing the tired or discontented beyond their capacity will spoil the day for them—and you. Energy levels vary. Be prepared to respond to members of your group who poop out. *Hint:* "We've driven a thousand miles to take you to Harry Potter and now you're ruining everything!" is not an appropriate response.

BUILDING ENDURANCE   Though most children are active, their normal play usually doesn't condition them for the exertion required to tour an Orlando park. Start family walks four to six weeks before your trip to get in shape. A mother from Wescosville, Pennsylvania, reports:

> We had our 6-year-old begin walking with us a bit every day one month before leaving—when we arrived [in Orlando], her little legs could carry her, and she had a lot of stamina.

From a Middletown, Delaware, mom:

You recommended walking for six weeks prior to the trip, but we begal months in advance, just because. My husband lost 10 pounds, my daughter never once complained, and we met a lot of neighbors! We wouldn't have made it without you—thanks!

SETTING LIMITS AND MAKING PLANS To avoid arguments and disappointment, establish guidelines for each day and get everybody committed. Include the following:

1. Wake-up time and breakfast plans

2. When to depart for the park

3. What to take with you

4. A policy for splitting the group or for staying together

5. What to do if the group gets separated or someone is lost

6. What you want to see, including plans in the event an attraction is closed or too crowded

7. A policy on what you can afford for snacks

8. How long you plan to tour in the morning and what time you'll return to your hotel to rest

9. When you'll return to the park and how late you'll stay

10. Dinner plans

11. A policy for buying souvenirs, including who pays: Mom and Dad or the kids

12. Bedtimes

BE FLEXIBLE Any day at Universal Orlando includes surprises; be prepared to adjust your plan. Listen to your intuition, and take advantage of Lines's optimization tool to update your itinerary after any unexpected detours.

WHAT KIDS WANT According to the travel-research firm Yesawich, Pepperdine, Brown, and Russell, 71% of children between the ages of 6 and 17 say they need a vacation because school and homework get them down. The chart below shows what kids want and don't want when taking a vacation. Kids surveyed have a lot in common about what they do want, not as much concerning what they don't.

WHAT DO KIDS WANT?	WHAT DO KIDS NOT WANT?
To go swimming/have pool time 80%	To get up early 52%
To eat in restaurants 78%	To ride in a car 36%
To stay at a hotel or resort 76%	To play golf 34%
To visit a theme park 76%	To go to a museum 31%
To stay up late 73%	

ABOUT *The* UNOFFICIAL GUIDE TOURING PLANS

PARENTS WHO USE OUR TOURING PLANS are often frustrated by interruptions and delays caused by their young children. Here's what to expect:

1. CHARACTER ENCOUNTERS CAN WREAK HAVOC WITH THE TOURING PLANS.   Many children will stop in their tracks whenever they see a cartoon character like Dora the Explorer or Scooby-Doo. Attempting to haul your child away before he has satisfied his curiosity is likely to cause anything from whining to full-scale revolt. Either go with the flow or specify a morning or afternoon for photos and autographs. Luckily, queues for autographs at Universal aren't nearly as long as at Disney World.

2. OUR TOURING PLANS CALL FOR VISITING ATTRACTIONS IN A SEQUENCE, OFTEN SKIPPING ATTRACTIONS ALONG THE WAY. Children don't like to skip anything! If something catches their eye, they want to see it that moment. Some kids can be persuaded to skip attractions if parents explain their plans in advance. Other kids flip out at skipping something, particularly in Seuss Landing and The Wizarding Worlds.

3. IF YOU'RE USING A STROLLER, YOU WON'T BE ABLE TO TAKE IT INTO ATTRACTIONS OR ONTO RIDES.   You'll need to leave your stroller (personal or rented) outside each attraction, unless you have a special pass indicating a medical need (see page 153 in Part Four). An exception is the Hogwarts Express train, which provides transportation between the parks and accommodates personal strollers; rentals will be swapped for free at the stations. Well-marked stroller parking is available throughout the theme parks.

4. YOU PROBABLY WON'T FINISH THE TOURING PLAN.   Varying hours of operation, crowds, your group's size, your children's ages, and your stamina will all affect how much of the plan you'll complete. Tailor your expectations to this reality, or you'll be frustrated.

While our touring plans allow you to make the most of your time at the parks, it's impossible to define what *most* will be. It differs from family to family. If you have two young children, you probably won't see as much as two adults will. If you have four children, you probably won't see as much as a couple with only two children.

*un**official* TIP
Keep little ones well covered in sunscreen and hydrated with fluids. Don't count on hydrating young children with soft drinks and stops at water fountains. Carry refillable bottles of water. Bottles with screw caps are sold in both parks for about $3. *Remember:* Excited kids may not tell you when they're thirsty or hot.

STUFF *to* THINK ABOUT

OVERHEATING, SUNBURN, AND DEHYDRATION   These are the most common problems of younger children at Universal Orlando. Carry and use sunscreen. Apply it on children in strollers, even if the stroller has a canopy. To avoid overheating, stop for rest regularly—say, in the shade, in a restaurant, or at a show with air-conditioning.

BLISTERS AND SORE FEET   In addition to wearing comfortable shoes, bring along some blister bandages if you or your children are susceptible to blisters. These bandages (which are also available at First Aid, if you didn't heed our warnings) offer excellent protection, stick well, and won't sweat off. Remember, a preschooler may not say anything about a blister until it's already formed, so keep an eye on things during the day. For an expanded discussion, see page 139.

FIRST AID   If you or your children have a medical problem, go to a First Aid Center (see page 142 in Part Four). They're friendlier than most doctor's offices and are accustomed to treating everything from paper cuts to allergic reactions. And if your kid just needs some rehydration and a short nap, they can provide a quiet cot.

CHILDREN ON MEDICATION   Some parents of hyperactive children on medication discontinue or decrease the child's dosage at the end of the school year. If you have such a child, be aware that Universal Orlando might overstimulate him or her. Consult your physician before altering your child's medication regimen.

GLASSES AND SUNGLASSES   If your kids (or you) wear them, attach a strap or string to the frames so the glasses will stay on during rides and can hang from the child's neck while indoors.

THINGS YOU FORGOT OR RAN OUT OF   Raingear, diapers, baby formula, sunburn treatments, memory cards, and other sundries are sold at both theme parks, at Wet 'n Wild, and at CityWalk. If you don't see something you need, ask if it's in stock. Basic over-the-counter meds are often available free in small quantities at the First Aid Centers in the parks.

INFANTS AND TODDLERS AT THE THEME PARKS   Both Universal theme parks have centralized Family Services facilities for infant and toddler care adjacent to the first-aid stations. Everything necessary for changing diapers, preparing formulas, and warming bottles and food is available. Supplies are for sale, and rockers and special chairs for nursing mothers are provided. In Universal Studios Florida, Family Services is located in the Front Lot near Lost and Found, and on Canal Street to the left of *Beetlejuice Graveyard Revue,* on the border between New York and San Francisco. In Islands of Adventure, Family Services is in Port of Entry near Guest Services, and in the Lost Continent near *The Eighth Voyage of Sindbad Stunt Show*; look for the red cross behind the coin vendor. Dads are welcome at the centers and can use most services. In addition, most men's restrooms in the resort have changing tables.

RUNNING OUT OF GAS   When Bob was preparing to hike from the Colorado River to the rim of the Grand Canyon—a 5,000-foot ascent—a park ranger told him to mix an electrolyte-replacement powder in his water and eat an energy-boosting snack at least twice every hour. While there's not much ascending to do at Universal, battling the heat, humidity, and crowds contributes to poop-out, especially where kids are concerned. Limiting calorie consumption to mealtimes just won't get it, as an experienced and wise grandma points out:

> *Children who get cranky during a visit often do so from all that time and energy expended without food. Feed them! A snack at any price goes a long way to keeping the little ones happy and parents sane. Oh, and the security people are very nice about you taking snacks or drinks in, but DO NOT bring glass containers!*

STROLLERS

STROLLERS ARE AVAILABLE for rent inside both parks to the left of the front gates as you enter. A single stroller is $15 (tax included) per day, and a double stroller is $25. Kiddie cars have plastic steering wheels attached so your child can pretend he or she is driving; they come in single and double sizes and cost $3 more than the price of a standard stroller. A $50 deposit (cash or credit card) is required, which will be fully refunded when you return your stroller. If you leave the park and return, or switch parks during the day, you can get a fresh stroller for free by showing your receipt.

Strollers are a must for infants and toddlers, but we've seen many sharp parents rent strollers for somewhat older children—the stroller spares parents from having to carry kids when they sag, and it provides a convenient place to tote water and snacks.

A family from Tulsa, Oklahoma, recommends springing for a double stroller:

> *We rented a double for baggage room or in case the older child gets tired of walking.*

But a New Lenox, Illinois, family advocates not leaving anyone out:

> *If your kids are 8 or under, rent strollers for all of them! An 8-year-old will fit in a stroller, and you can fit up to four kids in two doubles. My husband suggested getting a stroller for our 6-year-old and the two "babies" (ages 4 and 3). We plowed through crowds, and the kids didn't get nearly as tired because they could be seated whenever they wanted.*

We've always advocated using strollers for any child who will fit; however, a McKean, Pennsylvania, reader thinks the situation has gotten out of hand:

Please tell parents their children don't have to be in strollers if (a) they're old enough to vote, (b) they've served in the armed services, (c) they smoke, and/or (d) they have kids of their own. It's gotten really ridiculous—this last visit we saw more 10-plus-year-olds in strollers than sub-10-year-olds. Strollers add congestion, especially with dingbat parents using them to blast through crowds like child-first battering rams. I never knew walking was bad for you.

A Charleston, West Virginia, mom recommends a backup plan:

Strollers are not allowed in lines for rides, so if you have a small child (ours was 4) who needs to be held, you might end up holding him a long time. If I had it to do over, I'd bring along some kind of child carrier for when he was out of the stroller.

Rental strollers are too large for all infants and many toddlers. If you plan to rent a stroller for your infant or toddler, bring pillows, cushions, or rolled towels to buttress him or her in. Bringing your own stroller is permitted. Your stroller is unlikely to be stolen, but mark it with your name.

STROLLER-RENTAL OPTIONS With Disney and Universal pricing their own stroller rentals so high, several Orlando companies have sprung up, able to undercut the parks' prices, provide more comfortable strollers, and deliver them to your hotel. Most of the larger companies offer the same stroller models (the Baby Jogger City Mini Single, for example), so the primary differences between the companies are price and service.

To rate stroller companies, we had Unofficial Guide researchers rent the same strollers from each company, use the strollers in the parks, and return them. Our evaluation covers the overall experience, from the ease with which the stroller was rented to the delivery of the stroller, its condition upon arrival, and the return process.

Baby Wheels Orlando (☎ 800-510-2480; **babywheelsorlando .com**) had the best combination of price and service. Upon request, Baby Wheels will include a rain cover and beverage cooler free—both of which are useful during Florida's summer months. At Universal on-site resorts (as at Disney) pickup and delivery must be done in person at your hotel. A two-day/one-night rental is $30, two nights are $35, three nights are $40, and five nights are $48. Thus, the break-even point for using Baby Wheels Orlando instead of Universal is three days/two nights. Drop-off and pickup went without incident, and customer service is excellent.

We also recommend **Orlando Stroller Rentals, LLC** (☎ 800-281-0884; **orlandostrollerrentals.com**), which has slightly higher prices and whose strollers have a few more miles on them. The service is excellent, though, and they can drop off and pick up your stroller without your presence at the on-site hotels (excluding Hard Rock).

STROLLER WARS Sometimes strollers disappear while you're enjoying a ride or show. Universal staff will often rearrange strollers parked outside an attraction. This may be done to tidy up or to clear a walkway. Don't assume that your stroller is stolen because it isn't where you left it. It may be neatly arranged a few feet away—or perhaps more than a few feet away, as this Skokie, Illinois, dad reports:

> The stroller reorganizations while you're on rides are a bit unnerving. More than once, our stroller was moved out of visible distance from the original spot. On one occasion, it was moved to a completely different stroller-parking area near another ride, and no sign or team member was around to advise where. We had to track down a team member, and she had to call in to find out where it had been moved. Be prepared for this.

Sometimes, however, strollers are taken by mistake or ripped off by people not wanting to spend time replacing one that's missing. Don't be alarmed if yours disappears. You won't have to buy it, and you'll be issued a new one.

While replacing a stroller is no big deal, it's inconvenient. Through our own experiments and readers' suggestions, we've developed a technique for hanging on to a rented stroller: Affix something personal (but expendable) to the handle. Evidently, most strollers are pirated by mistake (they all look alike) or because it's easier to swipe someone else's than to replace one that has disappeared. Because most stroller "theft" results from confusion or laziness, the average pram-pincher will hesitate to haul off a stroller containing another person's property. We tried several items and concluded that a bright, inexpensive scarf or bandanna tied to the handle works well as identification. A sock partially stuffed with rags or paper works even better (the weirder and more personal the object, the greater the deterrent). A multigenerational family from Utah went a step further:

> We decorated our stroller with electrical tape to make it stand out, and my son added a small cowbell to make it clang if moved.

STROLLERS AS LETHAL WEAPONS A middle-aged couple from Brunswick, Maine, lobbies for a temporary stroller ban:

> As an over-45 couple, we couldn't believe the number and sizes of strollers and those ubiquitous scooters. You had to be constantly vigilant or you would have your foot run over or path slowed down by them. We've decided that one day a week, in one theme park, there should be a "no wheels" day. (Ah, but we live in Fantasyland!)

You'd be surprised at how many people are injured by strollers pushed by parents who are driving aggressively or in a hurry. Given the number of strollers, pedestrians, and tight spaces, mishaps are inevitable on both sides. A simple apology and a smile are usually the best remediation.

*un*official **TIP** Don't try to lock your stroller to a fence, post, or anything else at Universal. You'll get in big trouble.

LOST CHILDREN

THOUGH IT'S AMAZINGLY EASY TO LOSE a child (or two) in the theme parks, it usually isn't a serious problem: Universal employees are schooled in handling the situation. If you lose a child in the resort, report it to the nearest Universal employee, and then check at Guest Services. Paging isn't used, but in an emergency, an all-points bulletin can be issued throughout the park(s) via internal communications.

Sew a label into each child's shirt that states his or her name, your name, the name of your hotel, and your cell phone number. Accomplish the same thing by writing the information on a strip of masking tape.

An easier and trendier option is a temporary tattoo with your child's name and your phone number. Unlike labels, ID bracelets, or wristbands, the tattoos cannot fall off or be lost. Temporary tattoos last about two weeks, won't wash or sweat off, and are not irritating to the skin. They can be purchased online from SafetyTat at **safety tat.com,** or from Tattoos with a Purpose at **tattooswithapurpose.com.** Special tattoos are available for children with food allergies or cognitive impairment such as autism.

A Kingston, Washington, reader recommends recording vital info for each child on a plastic key tag or luggage tag and affixing it to the child's shoe. This reader also snaps a photo of the kids each morning to document what they're wearing. A mother from Rockville, Maryland, reported a strategy one step short of a cattle brand:

> *Traveling with a 3-year-old, I was very anxious about losing him. I wrote my cell phone number on his leg with a permanent marker and felt much more confident that he'd get back to me quickly if he became lost.*

One way to better keep track of your family is to buy each person a Universal uniform—in this case, the same brightly and distinctively colored T-shirt. A Yuma, Arizona, family tried this with great success:

> *We all got the same shirts (bright red) so that we could easily spot each other in case of separation (VERY easy to do). It was a lifesaver when our 18-month-old decided to get out of the stroller and wander off. No matter what precautions you may try, it seems there are always those opportunities to lose a child, but the recognizable shirts helped tremendously.*

HOW KIDS GET LOST

CHILDREN GET SEPARATED from their parents every day at Universal theme parks under remarkably similar (and predictable) circumstances:

1. PREOCCUPIED SOLO PARENT The party's only adult is preoccupied with something like buying refreshments, reading a map, or using the restroom. Junior is there one second and gone the next.

2. THE HIDDEN EXIT Sometimes parents wait on the sidelines while two or more young children experience a ride together. Parents expect the kids to exit in one place and the youngsters pop out elsewhere. Exits from some attractions are distant from entrances. Know exactly where your children will emerge before letting them ride by themselves.

3. AFTER THE SHOW At the end of many shows and rides, a Universal staffer announces, "Check for personal belongings and take small children by the hand." When dozens, if not hundreds, of people leave an attraction simultaneously, it's easy for parents to lose their children unless they have direct contact.

4. RESTROOM PROBLEMS Mom tells 6-year-old Tommy, "I'll be sitting on this bench when you come out of the restroom." Three possibilities: One, Tommy exits through a different door and becomes disoriented (Mom may not know there's another door). Two, Mom decides she also will use the restroom, and Tommy emerges to find her gone. Three, Mom pokes around in a shop while keeping an eye on the bench but misses Tommy when he comes out.

If you can't find a companion- or family-accessible restroom, make sure there's only one exit. Designate a distinctive meeting spot and give clear instructions: "I'll meet you by this flagpole. If you get out first, stay right here." Have your child repeat the directions back to you.

5. PARADES There are many parades and shows at which the audience stands. Children tend to jockey for a better view. By moving a little this way and that, the child quickly puts distance between you and him before either of you notices.

6. MASS MOVEMENTS Be on guard when huge crowds disperse after fireworks or a parade, or at park closing. With 20,000–40,000 people at once in an area, it's very easy to get separated from a child or others in your party. Use extra caution after the afternoon Superstar Parade and evening *Cinematic Spectacular* fireworks in Universal Studios Florida. Plan where to meet in the event you get separated.

7. CHARACTER GREETINGS When the Universal characters appear, children can slip out of sight.

UNIVERSAL, KIDS,
and SCARY STUFF

THOUGH THERE'S PLENTY FOR YOUNGER children to enjoy at the Universal parks, most major attractions can potentially make kids under age 8 wig out. To be frank, they freak out a fairly large percentage of adults as well. On average, Universal's rides move more aggressively and feature more intense (some would say assaultive) audiovisual effects, than their Disney counterparts. There are attractions with menacing mummies, exploding tanker trucks, and man-eating dinosaurs—not to mention demonic soul-sucking Dementors and fire-breathing dragons. And while Walt Disney World rides always end on a happy note,

Universal is just as likely to send you out with a final scare or snarky parting shot, which is less likely to soothe shaken nerves. Universal also sets surprisingly strict minimum height requirements for some kid-centric rides, ruling out attractions such as Cat in the Hat and The High in the Sky Seuss Trolley Train Ride! for the infants who might enjoy them most.

You can reliably predict that a visit to Universal Orlando will, at one time or another, send a young child into system overload. Be sensitive, alert, and prepared for almost anything, even behavior that is out of character for your child. Most children take Universal's macabre trappings in stride, and others are easily comforted by an arm around the shoulder or a squeeze of the hand. Parents who know that their children tend to become upset should take it slow and easy, sampling milder adventures like the E.T. Adventure, gauging reactions, and discussing with the children how they felt about what they saw. If your child has difficulty coping with the cartoon creatures in Despicable Me and Men in Black Alien Attack, you should think twice before exposing him or her to the photo-realistic Lord Voldemort in Harry Potter and the Escape from Gringotts.

Sometimes young children will rise above their anxiety in an effort to please their parents or siblings. This doesn't necessarily indicate a mastery of fear, much less enjoyment. If children leave a ride in apparently good shape, ask if they would like to go on it again (not necessarily now, but sometime). The response usually will indicate how much they actually enjoyed the experience.

Evaluating a child's capacity to handle the visual and tactile effects of Universal Orlando requires patience, understanding, and experimentation. Each of us has our own demons. If a child balks at or is frightened by a ride, respond constructively. Let your children know that lots of people, adults and children, are scared by what they see and feel. Help them understand that it's OK if they get frightened and that their fear doesn't lessen your love or respect. Take pains not to compound the discomfort by making a child feel inadequate; try not to undermine self-esteem, impugn courage, or ridicule. Most of all, don't induce guilt by suggesting the child's trepidation might be ruining the family's fun. It's also sometimes necessary to restrain older siblings' taunting.

A visit to Universal Orlando is more than an outing or an adventure for a young child. It's a testing experience, a sort of controlled rite of passage. If you help your little one work through the challenges, the time can be immeasurably rewarding and a bonding experience for you both.

THE FRIGHT FACTOR

WHILE EACH YOUNGSTER IS DIFFERENT, following are seven attraction elements that alone or combined could push a child's buttons and indicate that a certain attraction isn't age appropriate for that child:

1. NAME OF THE ATTRACTION Young children will naturally be apprehensive about something called, say, *Disaster!* or *Horror Make-Up Show.*

2. VISUAL IMPACT OF THE ATTRACTION FROM OUTSIDE   The Incredible Hulk Coaster, Dragon Challenge, Dudley Do-Right's Ripsaw Falls, Doctor Doom's Fearfall, Harry Potter and the Forbidden Journey, Jurassic Park River Adventure, and Hollywood Rip Ride Rockit look scary enough to give adults second thoughts, and they terrify many young children.

3. VISUAL IMPACT OF THE INDOOR-QUEUING AREA   The dark forest inside E.T. Adventure and the castle dungeon of Harry Potter and the Forbidden Journey can frighten children.

4. INTENSITY OF THE ATTRACTION   Some attractions inundate the senses with sights, sounds, movement, and even smell. USF's *Shrek 4-D,* for example, combines loud sounds, lights, water spray, and moving seats with 3-D cinematography to create a total sensory experience.

A Johnston, Iowa, mom describes the situation well:

> *The 3-D and 4-D experiences are way too scary for even a very brave 5-year-old girl. The shows that blew things on her, shot smells in the air, had bugs flying, etc. scared the bejesus out of her.*

5. VISUAL IMPACT OF THE ATTRACTION   Sights in various attractions range from falling fish to flying cows, from grazing dinosaurs to gory body parts. What one child calmly absorbs may scare the bejabbers out of another the same age.

6. DARK   Many Universal attractions operate indoors in the dark. For some children, this triggers fear. A child who gets frightened on one dark ride (E.T. Adventure, for example) may be unwilling to try other indoor rides.

7. THE TACTILE EXPERIENCE   Some rides are wild enough to cause motion sickness, wrench backs, and discombobulate guests of any age.

As a footnote to the preceding, be aware that gaining the courage and confidence in regard to the attractions is not necessarily an upwardly linear process. A ride that delights a child at age 4 may scare them to death at 5; by 6 years old they may be fine again. As a dad from Maryland explains:

> *Just because a child loves a ride at one age doesn't mean that he or she will love it on the next trip.*

A BIT OF PREPARATION

WE RECEIVE MANY TIPS from parents telling how they prepared their young children for their theme park experience. A common strategy is to acquaint children with the characters and stories behind the park attractions by reading Universal-related books and watching movies at home.

Continued on page 172

SMALL-CHILD FRIGHT-POTENTIAL TABLE

This is a quick reference to identify attractions to be wary of, and why. The table represents a generalization, and all kids are different. It relates specifically to kids ages 3–7. On average, children at the younger end of the range are more likely to be frightened than children in their 6th or 7th year.

Universal Studios Florida

PRODUCTION CENTRAL

DESPICABLE ME MINION MAYHEM Universal's mildest simulator motion-wise, but the huge 3-D images and loud sound track may startle preschoolers. Stationary benches are available in the front row to avoid the moving seats.

HOLLYWOOD RIP RIDE ROCKIT The tallest roller coaster at Universal Orlando, with loud music to cover your screams. May terrify guests of any age.

SHREK 4-D Intense, loud, and disrespectful toward beloved fairy-tale icons. Stationary seating is available to avoid the jerky moving chairs.

TRANSFORMERS: THE RIDE 3-D Intense, bloodlessly violent virtual reality simulator may frighten younger children and deafen guests of any age.

NEW YORK

BEETLEJUICE GRAVEYARD REVUE Singing monsters and pyrotechnics may spook younger kids, and some parents may blush at the emcee's PG-13 banter.

THE BLUES BROTHERS SHOW Not frightening, but some loud R&B music and brief references to tobacco and alcohol.

DISASTER! The preshows are sedate and unintimidating, but the ride (which can be skipped) features loud explosions, rushing water, and violent shaking that may scare younger kids.

REVENGE OF THE MUMMY Very intense roller coaster in the dark with angry mummies, bugs, and fireballs. May frighten guests of any age.

TWISTER . . . RIDE IT OUT! Intense wind, rain, and explosions may frighten younger kids. Stationary area is available to avoid a startling floor drop. You must remain standing through the entire attraction.

THE WIZARDING WORLD OF HARRY POTTER–DIAGON ALLEY

CELESTINA WARBECK AND THE BANSHEES Not frightening in any respect.

HARRY POTTER AND THE ESCAPE FROM GRINGOTTS Visually intimidating with intense 3-D effects and brief moments of moderately fast roller coaster motion. Less frightening than Harry Potter and the Forbidden Journey or Revenge of the Mummy, but may still rattle some riders.

HOGWARTS EXPRESS: KING'S CROSS STATION Brief encounter with Dementors may scare some preschoolers; otherwise, not frightening.

OLLIVANDERS Not frightening in any respect.

THE TALES OF BEEDLE THE BARD Some preschoolers may be scared of the large Death puppet used in "The Tale of the Three Brothers."

WORLD EXPO

FEAR FACTOR LIVE An intense stunt show featuring people wearing and/or eating live insects. Explosive ending may startle preschoolers; may nauseate guests of any age.

KANG & KODOS' TWIRL 'N' HURL Dumbo-style midway ride. A favorite of many young children.

MEN IN BLACK ALIEN ATTACK Dark ride with spinning cars and comical aliens may frighten some preschoolers.

Universal Studios Florida (Continued)

THE SIMPSONS RIDE Extremely intense visually, with USF's strongest simulated motion. May frighten many adults as well as kids.

WOODY WOODPECKER'S KIDZONE

ANIMAL ACTORS ON LOCATION! Not frightening in any respect, unless you have an animal phobia.

CURIOUS GEORGE GOES TO TOWN Not frightening in any respect, but your kid may get soaked.

A DAY IN THE PARK WITH BARNEY Not frightening in any respect, unless you have a purple-dinosaur phobia.

E.T. ADVENTURE Dark ride with simulated flight and psychedelic creatures. A little intense for a few preschoolers, but the end is all happiness and harmony.

FIEVEL'S PLAYLAND Not frightening in any respect, except for the big slide that may scare some preschoolers.

WOODY WOODPECKER'S NUTHOUSE COASTER A beginner's roller coaster; safe for all but the most timid tykes.

HOLLYWOOD

LUCY—A TRIBUTE Not frightening in any respect.

TERMINATOR 2: 3-D Very loud and intense with live gunfire, thick fog, and killer robots that startle viewers of all ages. Stationary seating is available to avoid a sudden seat drop.

UNIVERSAL ORLANDO'S HORROR MAKE-UP SHOW Gory props and film clips, presented educationally and humorously, may wig out wee ones, but most kids seem to handle it disturbingly well. Interestingly, very few families report problems with this or *Beetlejuice Graveyard Revue*.

Islands of Adventure

MARVEL SUPER HERO ISLAND

THE AMAZING ADVENTURES OF SPIDER-MAN Immersive 3-D effects and spinning simulator movement may frighten younger kids, but most take the comic book mayhem in stride. Technically similar to Transformers at USF but significantly less intense.

DOCTOR DOOM'S FEARFALL Visually intimidating to all guests, with an intense launch and brief weightlessness. The actual plummeting is less protracted than on WDW's Tower of Terror.

THE INCREDIBLE HULK COASTER Very intense looping coaster with a high-speed launch; a scary roller coaster by any standard.

STORM FORCE ACCELATRON Teacups-type midway ride can induce motion sickness in all ages, though most kids seem to love it.

TOON LAGOON

DUDLEY DO-RIGHT'S RIPSAW FALLS Visually intimidating from outside, with several intense, potentially drenching plunges. A toss-up, to be considered only if your kids like water-flume rides.

ME SHIP, *THE OLIVE* Not frightening in any respect.

POPEYE & BLUTO'S BILGE-RAT BARGES Potentially frightening and certainly soaking for guests of all ages, but most younger children handle it well.

JURASSIC PARK

CAMP JURASSIC Some preschoolers may be spooked by the dark caves and dinosaur sounds; guests who are afraid of heights should avoid the net climb.

JURASSIC PARK DISCOVERY CENTER Not frightening in any respect.

Islands of Adventure (Continued)

JURASSIC PARK (Continued)

JURASSIC PARK RIVER ADVENTURE Visually intimidating boat ride with life-size dinosaurs and an intense flume finale. May frighten and dampen guests of any age.

PTERANODON FLYERS A short, slow suspended roller coaster. Frightens some children who are scared of heights, and bores most adults who ride with them.

THE WIZARDING WORLD OF HARRY POTTER–HOGSMEADE

DRAGON CHALLENGE Very intense suspended looping roller coasters. May frighten guests of any age.

FLIGHT OF THE HIPPOGRIFF Another beginner coaster, barely bigger than Woody Woodpecker's Nuthouse Coaster at USF.

FROG CHOIR/TRIWIZARD SPIRIT RALLY Not frightening in any respect.

HARRY POTTER AND THE FORBIDDEN JOURNEY Extremely intense special effects and macabre visuals with wild simulated movement that may frighten and discombobulate guests of any age.

HOGWARTS EXPRESS: HOGSMEADE STATION Not frightening in any respect.

THE LOST CONTINENT

THE EIGHTH VOYAGE OF SINDBAD STUNT SHOW Slapstick violence, bad puns, and explosions; includes startling special effects, but kids tolerate it well.

THE MYSTIC FOUNTAIN Not frightening in any respect, but kids may get wet.

POSEIDON'S FURY Loud explosions, water effects, and brief periods of pitch darkness may scare younger kids. You must remain standing through the entire attraction.

SEUSS LANDING

CARO-SEUSS-EL Not frightening in any respect.

THE CAT IN THE HAT Mild spinning motion and modest visual effects may frighten a small percentage of preschoolers.

THE HIGH IN THE SKY SEUSS TROLLEY TRAIN RIDE! May scare children who are afraid of heights; otherwise, not frightening in any respect.

IF I RAN THE ZOO Not frightening in any respect.

OH! THE STORIES YOU'LL HEAR! Not frightening in any respect.

ONE FISH, TWO FISH, RED FISH, BLUE FISH A tame midway ride that is a great favorite of most young children, though they will likely get wet.

Continued from page 169

Universal Studios Florida's attractions prominently feature the family-friendly films *Despicable Me, Shrek,* and *E.T.* (which should already be on your kids' required viewing list), along with *Men In Black, Twister, Transformers, The Mummy,* and *The Terminator* (only bother with the first two movies) if they are old enough for PG-13 entertainment. *The Simpsons* are in perpetual reruns, so refreshing your memory of Homer and family shouldn't be hard. For extra credit, screen *Jaws* and *Back to the Future,* and then hunt for hidden tributes to their extinct attractions.

Islands of Adventure was inspired by literature, so start by reading the classics before bedtime—Dr. Seuss, Stan Lee's superheroes, ancient mythology, and the Sunday funnies. For Jurassic Park, you can cheat and watch the original Spielberg film. Of course, you'll want to be well-versed in all seven volumes of Harry Potter's academic career (along with the associated films, short stories, and spin-offs) to fully appreciate both Wizarding Worlds; if that's too much work, at a minimum you must watch the first movie before visiting Hogsmeade, and the last one before delving into Diagon Alley.

A more direct approach is to watch videos that show the attractions. Online, you'll find good point of view videos of most Universal attractions from TouringPlans, *Attractions Magazine,* Inside the Magic, and other bloggers. Videos of dark indoor rides—especially those that use 3-D glasses—never do the attractions justice, but they usually show enough for you to judge whether your child can comfortably handle the real thing. A Lexington, Kentucky, mom reports:

> *My timid 7-year-old daughter and I watched rides and shows on YouTube, and we cut out all the ones that looked too scary.*

ATTRACTIONS THAT EAT ADULTS

YOU MAY SPEND SO MUCH ENERGY worrying about Junior that you forget to take care of yourself. The attractions below can cause motion sickness or other problems for older kids and adults:

Potentially Problematic Attractions for Grown-Ups
UNIVERSAL STUDIOS FLORIDA
PRODUCTION CENTRAL   Hollywood Rip Ride Rockit | Transformers: The Ride 3-D
NEW YORK   Revenge of the Mummy
THE WIZARDING WORLD OF HARRY POTTER–DIAGON ALLEY   Harry Potter and the Escape from Gringotts
WORLD EXPO   The Simpsons Ride
ISLANDS OF ADVENTURE
MARVEL SUPER HERO ISLAND   Doctor Doom's Fearfall | The Incredible Hulk Coaster
TOON LAGOON   Dudley Do-Right's Ripsaw Falls
THE WIZARDING WORLD OF HARRY POTTER–HOGSMEADE   Dragon Challenge | Harry Potter and the Forbidden Journey

A WORD ABOUT HEIGHT REQUIREMENTS

ALL ATTRACTIONS AT UNIVERSAL ORLANDO require children to be at least 48 inches tall to ride without a supervising companion, also known as an older family member or guardian. Most moving attractions at Universal Orlando require children to meet additional minimum height requirements. If you have children too short to ride, instead of skipping the ride or splitting up, consider using the child swap (see below). For more information, see the table on page 174.

Child Swap (also known as Rider Swap, Baby Swap, or Switching Off)

Most Universal Orlando attractions have minimum height requirements. Some couples with children too small or too young forgo these

Attraction Height Requirements

UNIVERSAL STUDIOS FLORIDA	
Despicable Me Minion Mayhem	40" minimum height
E. T. Adventure	34" minimum height
Harry Potter and the Escape from Gringotts	42" minimum height
Hollywood Rip Ride Rockit	51" minimum height; 79" maximum height
Men in Black Alien Attack	42" minimum height
Revenge of the Mummy	48" minimum height
The Simpsons Ride	40" minimum height
Transformers: The Ride 3-D	40" minimum height
Woody Woodpecker's Nuthouse Coaster	36" minimum height
ISLANDS OF ADVENTURE	
The Amazing Adventures of Spider-Man	40" minimum height
The Cat in the Hat	36" minimum height
Doctor Doom's Fearfall	52" minimum height
Dragon Challenge	54" minimum height
Dudley Do-Right's Ripsaw Falls	44" minimum height
Flight of the Hippogriff	36" minimum height
Harry Potter and the Forbidden Journey	48" minimum height
The High in the Sky Seuss Trolley Train Ride!	40" minimum height
The Incredible Hulk Coaster	54" minimum height
Jurassic Park River Adventure	42" minimum height
Popeye & Bluto's Bilge-Rat Barges	42" minimum height
Pteranodon Flyers (Guests taller than 56" must be accompanied by a guest 36"–56".)	36" minimum height; 56" maximum height
Skull Island: Reign of Kong	34" minimum height

attractions, while others take turns riding. Missing some of Universal's best rides is an unnecessary sacrifice, and waiting in line twice for the same ride is a tremendous waste of time.

Instead, take advantage of child swap, also known as baby swap, rider swap, or switching off. To child swap, there must be at least two adults. Adults and children wait in line together. When you reach a team member at the entrance of an attraction, say you want to child swap. The employee will allow everyone, including young children, to enter the attraction. When you reach the loading area, one adult rides while the other waits in a special child swap holding area with the kids. Then the riding adult disembarks and takes charge of the children while the other adult rides. A third member of the party, either an adult or an older child, can ride twice, once with each switching-off adult, so that the switching-off adults don't have to ride alone.

Child swap at Universal is similar to Disney's version but superior in several respects. Instead of one adult waiting at the exit with the children and returning after through the FastPass+ queue, at Universal the entire family goes through the whole line together before being split into riding and nonriding groups near the loading platform. The nonriding parent and child(ren) wait in a designated room, usually with some sort of entertainment (for example, Harry Potter and the Forbidden Journey at IOA shows the first 20 minutes of *Harry Potter and the Sorcerer's Stone* on a loop), a place to sit down, and sometimes restrooms with changing tables. And nearly every attraction at Universal offers child swap, which can even be used if you don't have children; it works equally well for skittish or infirm adults who don't like thrill rides, or for designated baggage handlers in families who hate to use lockers.

Attractions where switching off is practiced are oriented to more mature guests. Sometimes it takes a lot of courage for a child just to move through the queue holding Dad's hand. In the boarding area, many children suddenly fear abandonment when one parent leaves to ride. Prepare your children for switching off, or you might have an emotional crisis on your hands.

A mom from Edison, New Jersey, writes:

> Once my son came to understand that the switch-off would not leave him abandoned, he did not seem to mind. I would recommend to your readers that they practice the switch-off on some dry runs at home, so that their child is not concerned that he will be left behind. At the very least, the procedure could be explained in advance so that the little ones know what to expect.

An Ada, Michigan, mother discovered that the child-swap procedure varies among attractions. She says:

> Parents need to tell the very first attendant they come to that they would like to switch-off. Each attraction has a different procedure for this. Tell every other attendant too because they forget quickly.

As at any theme park, the best tip we can give is to ask the greeter in front of the attraction what you're supposed to do.

UNIVERSAL CHARACTERS

FAMILIES VISITING WALT DISNEY WORLD once were content to meet a Disney character occasionally. They now pursue them relentlessly, armed with autograph books and cameras. Because some characters are rarely seen, character watching has become character collecting, and to cash in on character collecting, Disney sells autograph books throughout the World. Universal Orlando also has a stable of characters to call their own and will sell you a notebook to store your signatures in as well, but the interest in oversize cartoon vermin isn't anywhere near as intense; you'll occasionally see a Minion getting mobbed, or a couple dozen families queued to meet Sponge-Bob, but never anything like the four-hour waits that the *Frozen* sisters draw at the Magic Kingdom.

PREPARING YOUR CHILDREN TO MEET THE CHARACTERS

ALMOST ALL CHARACTERS ARE QUITE large, and several, like Sideshow Bob, are huge! Small children don't expect this, and preschoolers especially can be intimidated.

Discuss the characters with your children before you go. On first encounter, don't thrust your child at the character. Allow the little one to deal with this big thing from whatever distance feels safe. If two adults are present, one should stay near the youngster while the other approaches the character and demonstrates that it's safe and friendly. Some kids warm to the characters immediately; some never do. Most take a little time and several encounters.

unofficial **TIP**
Don't underestimate your child's excitement at meeting the Universal characters—but also be aware that very small children may find the large costumed characters a little frightening.

There are two kinds of characters: animated, or those whose costumes include face-covering headpieces (including animal characters and humanlike cartoon characters such as the Simpsons), and celebrities or face characters, those for whom no mask or headpiece is necessary. These include Marilyn Monroe, Lucille Ball, Doc Brown, and the Knight Bus and Hogwarts Express conductors, among others.

Only face characters speak. Because team members couldn't possibly imitate the animated characters' distinctive cinema voices, Universal has determined that it's more effective to keep such characters silent. Lack of speech notwithstanding, headpiece characters are warm and responsive, and they communicate effectively with gestures. Tell children in advance that these characters don't talk. Exciting exceptions are character encounters such as the Shrek meet-and-greet with Donkey and the Transformers photo op, where hidden actors or prerecorded audio clips are employed to allow interaction between costumed characters and guests.

Some character costumes are cumbersome and give performers very poor visibility. (Eyeholes frequently are in the mouth of the costume or even on the neck or chest.) Children who approach the character from the back or side may not be noticed, even if the child touches the character. It's possible in this situation for the character to accidentally step on the child or knock him down. A child should approach a character from the front, but occasionally not even this works. If a character appears to be ignoring your child, the character's handler will get its attention. Finally, some characters can't sign autographs because of their costumes.

It's OK for your child to touch, pat, or hug the character. Understanding the unpredictability of children, the character will keep his feet still, particularly refraining from moving backward or sideways. Most characters will pose for pictures or sign autographs. Costumes make it difficult for characters to wield a normal pen. If your child collects autographs, carry a pen the width of a Magic Marker.

UNIVERSAL CHARACTER-GREETING LOCATIONS

SOME UNIVERSAL ORLANDO CHARACTERS ARE confined to a specific location and visit with guests on a schedule that is printed on the park map. Characters who appear in the Superstar Parade also make daily Character Party Zone appearances in Hollywood, which include a mini-show and meet-and-greet. Other characters appear at random times in a few regular areas. Most mornings you'll find a rotating collection of characters near the entrance of the park. Not every character will appear every day; the busier the season, the more likely lesser-known characters will come out.

See page 178 for a guide to the places you're likely to find famous friends in Universal's parks.

CHARACTER DINING

CHARACTER DINING IS INCREDIBLY POPULAR, and profitable, over at Walt Disney World, which regularly books up its most sought-after princess repasts six months in advance. Universal Orlando also offers character meals at both its theme parks and hotels, but unlike Cinderella's Royal Table, you have a reasonable shot of supping with Dora and SpongeBob on short notice.

Character-Greeting Locations

UNIVERSAL STUDIOS FLORIDA

CELEBRITIES (FACE CHARACTERS)

Doc Brown from *Back to the Future* Hollywood; at the DeLorean outside Fast Food Boulevard

Knight Bus Conductor & Talking Head London Waterfront outside Diagon Alley

Lucille Ball Hollywood

Marilyn Monroe Hollywood

The Men in Black Hollywood; World Expo outside Men in Black Alien Attack

ANIMATED (COSTUMED CHARACTERS)

Barney the Dinosaur, B.J., & Baby Bop Woody Woodpecker's KidZone at *A Day in the Park with Barney* postshow

Curious George & the Man in the Yellow Hat Hollywood; Woody Woodpecker's KidZone

***Despicable Me* Minions** Hollywood; exit of Despicable Me Minion Mayhem ride

Dora the Explorer & Diego Hollywood

E.B. from *Hop* Hollywood

Gru, Agnes, Edith, Margo, and Vector from *Despicable Me* Hollywood

Homer, Marge, Bart, & Lisa Simpson Hollywood; World Expo outside Kwik-E-Mart

Optimus Prime, Bumblebee, & Megatron from *Transformers* Eighth Avenue between the *Shrek 4-D* exit & Mel's Drive-In

Scooby-Doo, Shaggy, and the Mystery Van Hollywood; Woody Woodpecker's KidZone

Shrek, Donkey, & Princess Fiona Eighth Avenue across from the *Shrek 4-D* exit

Sideshow Bob & Krusty the Clown World Expo outside Kwik-E-Mart

SpongeBob SquarePants, Squidward, & Patrick Hollywood; Woody Woodpecker's KidZone inside SpongeBob StorePants

Woody Woodpecker Front Lot

ISLANDS OF ADVENTURE

CELEBRITIES (FACE CHARACTERS)

Betty Boop Toon Lagoon outside The Betty Boop Store

Captain America Marvel Super Hero Island outside Captain America Diner

Dinosaur Keeper with Baby Triceratops Jurassic Park

The Grinch (live-action version) Seuss Landing inside All The Books You Can Read store (seasonally)

Hogwarts Express Conductor Hogsmeade across from Honeydukes

Popeye & Olive Oyl Toon Lagoon outside Comic Strip Cafe

Rogue & Storm Marvel Super Hero Island outside Marvel Alterniverse Store

Spider-Man Marvel Super Hero Island inside Marvel Alterniverse Store

Wolverine & Cyclops Marvel Super Hero Island outside Marvel Alterniverse Store

ANIMATED (COSTUMED CHARACTERS)

Beetle Bailey Toon Lagoon outside Comic Strip Cafe

Cat in the Hat, Thing 1, & Thing 2 Seuss Landing at *Oh! The Stories You'll Hear!*

Green Goblin & Doctor Doom Marvel Super Hero Island outside Doctor Doom's Fearfall

The Grinch (cartoon version) Seuss Landing at *Oh! The Stories You'll Hear!*

The Lorax & Sam I Am Seuss Landing at *Oh! The Stories You'll Hear!*

Woody Woodpecker Port of Entry

Velociraptor Jurassic Park outside the Discovery Center

Universal's Superstar Character Breakfast is held in USF on select mornings year-round and features Nickelodeon favorites along with the Minions. During the holiday season, the Grinch hosts a breakfast at IOA. Character meals are also scheduled at the luxury on-site hotels on a regular basis. For further details, see page 183.

BABYSITTING

CHILD-CARE CENTERS

CHILD CARE ISN'T AVAILABLE INSIDE the theme parks, but the three luxury Loews hotels each offer on-site kids' clubs that operate in the evenings to allow Mom and Dad a night out alone at CityWalk. Only on-site hotel guests may use the service, but they can register their kids at another hotel's club in case the seasonal operation schedule has one closed. Camp Portofino at Portofino Bay, Camp Lil'Rock at Hard Rock Hotel, and The Mariner's Club at Royal Pacific all feature story time, arts and crafts, computer games, and a movie room. There is one counselor for every 8–10 children; participants must be toilet-trained and between ages 4–14. Sitting costs $15 per hour, per child, and an additional $15 per meal if they stay through dinnertime. The clubs operate 5–11:30 p.m., Sunday–Thursday, and 5 p.m.–midnight, Friday–Saturday; hours vary seasonally and are subject to change. Call ☎ 407-503-1200 for information and reservations.

IN-ROOM BABYSITTING

A COUPLE OF COMPANIES PROVIDE in-room sitting in Universal Orlando and surrounding areas, but **Kid's Nite Out** (☎ 800-696-8105; **kidsniteout.com**) is the resort's preferred provider, and who the concierge will call if you ask for a babysitter; it also staffs the hotels' child-care centers. Kid's Nite Out also serves hotels in the greater Orlando area, including downtown. It provides sitters older than age 18 who are insured, bonded, screened, reference-checked, police-checked, and trained in CPR; bilingual sitters are also available. In addition to caring for your kids in your room, the sitters will, if you direct (and pay), take your children to the theme parks or other venues. Kid's Nite Out cares for children as young as six weeks old and can care for kids with special needs as well; rates start at $18 per hour for one child, up to $26 per hour for four children.

PART SIX

DINING *and* SHOPPING *at* UNIVERSAL ORLANDO

WHEN ASKED TO NAME GREAT GOURMET VACATION spots around the world—New York, Paris, Singapore—Orlando probably doesn't immediately pop to the top of most foodies' wish lists. But believe it or not, central Florida has developed a substantial culinary culture, from the prototype concepts tested by Darden and other major chains along Sand Lake Road's Restaurant Row and lauded gastropubs that have sprouted around downtown, to the explosive local growth of upscale food trucks.

Even so, while adventurous eaters have always known there's plenty to explore in the greater Orlando area, and even tourist-phobic locals have long been lured to WDW property by its lengthy list of restaurants, Universal has often been left out of the conversation. Thanks to the uniform mediocrity of Universal Studios Florida's counter-service food during the resort's formative years, the conventional wisdom was that Universal Orlando's food options simply weren't as delicious or as diverse as those at Disney.

The good news is that, today, food in Universal is almost always on par with, or a step ahead of, what you can find at Walt Disney World and other parks. Thanks largely to the efforts of the resort's award-winning executive chef Steven Jayson, more variety, better preparations, and more current trends are generally the rule at Universal. And best of all, a first-class meal at Universal will almost always leave less of a dent in your credit card than the equivalent repast would at Mickey's table.

Quick-service (or counter-service, as it is called at Disney) offerings are largely comparable to Disney, both in quality and cost, with the newest additions—Harry Potter's **Leaky Cauldron** and **Three Broomsticks,** and The Simpsons' **Fast Food Boulevard**—setting a new bar for theme park fast food.

USF's two full-service restaurants are **Finnegan's Bar and Grill** in New York and **Lombard's Seafood Grille** in San Francisco. Finnegan's serves typical bar food—burgers and wings—as well as fresh fish-and-chips and other takes on Irish cuisine. Lombard's is the better restaurant, but it's not in the same stratosphere as Disney's Hollywood Brown Derby (in quality or price).

IOA has two sit-down restaurants: **Confisco Grille** in Port of Entry and **Mythos Restaurant** in The Lost Continent. Confisco is fine for pizza and drinks. Despite its Hellenic-sounding name, Mythos isn't a Greek restaurant; rather it serves something-for-everyone fusion fare, including Italian risotto, Asian noodles, and Mexican fish tacos, plus steaks and burgers. Diners with dietary restrictions will be happy to see that Mythos has more options for vegetarian, vegan, and gluten-free diners than almost any other in-park Universal restaurant.

For even better eating options, exit the parks into **CityWalk,** Universal's dining, shopping, and entertainment district (think a more-compact counterpart to Disney Springs). CityWalk saw some welcome upgrades to its restaurant lineup in 2014 with the addition of **Vivo Italian Kitchen** and **Antojitos Authentic Mexican Food,** along with **The Cowfish's** much-better-than-it-sounds burger/sushi bar. The best choice for a white-linen experience at CityWalk is **Emeril's Restaurant Orlando.** We also like **Bob Marley** and **Pat O'Brien's** for drinks and music.

Many of the older CityWalk restaurants' menus are similar to Applebee's or Chili's. Given the average entrée from **Hard Rock Cafe** or **Jimmy Buffett's Margaritaville,** it would be difficult for a blindfolded diner to be certain from which restaurant it came. That blindfolded diner would probably guess that any plate with shrimp on it had a decent chance of coming from the **Bubba Gump Shrimp Co.,** but there's little else of note on its menu.

Some of Universal's best sit-down restaurants are found at the resort hotels. **The Palm Restaurant,** an upscale steak house in the Hard Rock Hotel, serves Grade A meat at prices to match. If you're in the mood for Italian, try **Bice** (expensive) or **Mama Della's Ristorante** (moderate), both at the Portofino. Asian food is the specialty at Universal's Royal Pacific, where **Emeril Lagasse's Tchoup Chop** is the top destination. Probably because they handle a lot of convention traffic, menu prices at Universal's deluxe resorts tend to be higher than you might expect, though they are still easier to swallow than the bill at Disney's top tables.

RESERVATIONS

ONE OF THE BIGGEST DIFFERENCES BETWEEN Walt Disney World and Universal Orlando is the ease with which you can secure dining reservations at the latter resort. If you're used to frantically booking your Disney Advance Dining Reservations 180 days before your vacation, you can relax. During much of the year, you can walk up and get a table at most Universal Orlando eateries with only a modest wait; guests staying at an on-site deluxe hotel can flash their key card to get seated even sooner.

While reservations are often not needed at Universal, you can use **opentable.com** or the OpenTable smartphone app to search for a seating at most of the sit-down hotel restaurants and some in City-Walk. The newer CityWalk locations and all the in-park table-service restaurants now use NexTable, which has no app nor customer-facing website for reservations; visit **universalorlando.com,** and select the restaurant for which you wish to make a reservation. Click the "Reserve Now" button to make your reservation. Unlike at Disney, no deposit is necessary to book a Universal restaurant reservation, so there's no penalty when your dinner plans inevitably change. The in-park restaurants only take reservations 30 days in advance, but most of the CityWalk and hotel restaurants accept bookings 90 days out, and a couple (Emeril's and The Palm) will let you reserve for next year. If you are visiting at a peak time of the year (such as Thanksgiving or late December) or during a major convention, we suggest making table-service reservations a couple of weeks to a month in advance.

DRESS

DRESS IS INFORMAL AT ALL THEME PARK restaurants and in CityWalk's restaurants. At upscale resort restaurants such as Hard Rock's Palm Restaurant or Emeril's Tchoup Chop, men are not permitted to wear sleeveless shirts, and resort casual wear is appropriate (but not required) for dinner: khakis, dress slacks, jeans, or dress shorts with a collared shirt for men and Capris, skirts, dresses, jeans, or dress shorts for women.

FOOD ALLERGIES AND SPECIAL REQUESTS

FOR SIT-DOWN MEALS, if you have food allergies or observe a specific diet such as eating kosher or gluten-free, make your needs known when you make your dining reservation and again when your waiter introduces himself at your table. The waitstaff or chef will be able to tell you the kinds of accommodations the kitchen is prepared to make for your meal.

Accommodating dietary needs is more difficult at fast-food places because the staff may not be as familiar with the menu's ingredients or preparation. Ask to see the allergen information book, which should be kept behind the counter at every quick-service location; it lists the menu items that can be made or modified for various diets. When our vegetarians and vegans have doubts about menu descriptions, their strategy is usually to default to the simplest, most-likely-to-be-acceptable item.

See page 151 in Part Four for additional dietary details.

CHARACTER MEALS

UNIVERSAL OFFERS ONE YEAR-ROUND in-park character breakfast, held 9–11 a.m., Thursday–Saturday, at **Cafe La Bamba** inside Universal Studios Florida. During the **Superstar Character Breakfast,** guests dine with characters from *Despicable Me, SpongeBob SquarePants, Hop,* and *Dora the Explorer.* Cost is $27.50 for adults and $14 for kids; park admission is required and not included. A plated meal with your choice of breakfast favorites (scrambled eggs, pancakes, fruit, and yogurt) is served, and attendees also get reserved viewing for that afternoon's character parade. Days and times are subject to change; call ☎ 407-224-3663 for reservations, or book at **universalorlando.com/restaurants/universal-studios-florida/superstar-character-breakfast.aspx.**

During the holiday season, Universal offers a breakfast in Islands of Adventure's **Seuss Landing** with the Grinch, played by an extremely interactive actor in film-quality prosthetic makeup. This meal is held only on select mornings in December, and pricing and reservations info is the same as the Superstar breakfast.

There's also a weekly character breakfast every Sunday, 8 a.m.–noon, at **Jake's** in the Royal Pacific Resort. Gru and his Minions from *Despicable Me* are the guests of honor, and E.B. and the Pink Beret bunnies from *Hop* also appear. The cost is $29 for adults, $16 for kids and includes both a Continental buffet (featuring a make-your-own-pancake machine) and a plated entrée—the Tahitian French toast and Yukon potato hash get high marks. Reserve by calling ☎ 407-503-3463.

In the evenings, Universal characters show up for dinner at the resort hotels on select nights each week. The cast of characters changes frequently, and it's possible to see the same characters in different restaurants during the same week. It's common to see Scooby-Doo and Shaggy from the *Scooby-Doo* cartoons, Shrek, Woody Woodpecker, or characters from *The Simpsons* at these evening meals.

You'll find characters at **Trattoria del Porto** in the Portofino Bay Hotel on Friday nights, 6:30–9:30 p.m. Characters also make appearances at **The Kitchen** at Hard Rock Hotel on Wednesdays and Saturdays, 6–9 p.m., and at the **Islands Dining Room** at the Royal Pacific Resort on Monday, Wednesday, and Thursday, 6:30–9:30 p.m.

Casting? There's been a mistake. We were supposed to get the Assorted Character Package with one SpongeBob, one Dora, one Gru . . .

UNIVERSAL ORLANDO DINING PLANS

UNIVERSAL HAS REPLACED ITS FORMER all-you-care-to-eat fast-food Meal Deals with a **Quick Service Universal Dining Plan** that provides one quick-service meal (including an entrée platter and soft drink), another soft drink, and one snack. The cost is $20 (plus tax) for adults, and $13 (plus tax) for kids age 9 and younger. It's valid at most quick-service eateries in both parks (including Three Broomsticks at The Wizarding World of Harry Potter–Hogsmeade, the Leaky Cauldron in Diagon Alley, and Fast Food Boulevard in Springfield U.S.A.) and a smattering at Universal CityWalk but not at any hotel eateries.

Virtually every entrée at participating venues can be purchased with a quick-service meal credit, even combo platters that include a side salad or milk shake. A few of the most expensive items, such as whole pizzas, aren't covered. For your nonalcoholic beverages, you can choose from a regular-size fountain soda; bottled water, juice, or sports drink; or coffee, cocoa, or tea (including tall Starbucks brews). Eligible snacks include *churros*, pretzels, popcorn, ice cream (regular-size cup or cone, or novelty bar), funnel cakes, cookies, and pastries. Some larger items from snack vendors, such as turkey legs and hot dogs, count as a quick-service meal. Credits can even be used inside The Wizarding Worlds, though the Universal Dining eligibility logo doesn't appear on Potter menus for thematic reasons. However, signature beverages such as Butterbeer will count as a snack, not a drink.

If two sodas a day isn't enough for you, a souvenir Coca-Cola Freestyle cup can be added to any quick-service dining plan for an additional $6, which includes unlimited refills from the Freestyle machines found around the parks (see page 191).

Universal claims that the plan can save you up to 30%, but unless you use all your credits and order carefully, you'll probably do as well or better buying à la carte with an annual pass or AAA discount (which cannot be applied to purchasing the plan). We're also not big fans in principal of prepaying for meals, but thankfully Universal doesn't tie you down by forcing you to book it for every day of your vacation, or every member of your party. It is possible to purchase the quick-service dining plan in advance when reserving your vacation, but there's really no need to.

Instead, take advantage of your ability to buy into the plan on a day-by-day basis at any participating restaurant *after* you've already made your menu selection. If your entrée and drink add up to at least $15 before tax, and you aren't eligible for any discounts, it's probably in your best interest to ask the cashier to sell you a quick-service plan. The extra few dollars will net another beverage (worth about $3) and snack (worth $3–$6) for the afternoon, saving you on balance between $1 and $4. Order a ribs platter and soda with a dining plan, and your second drink and snack are essentially free. On the other hand, if you order an $8 cheese pizza and a $3 bag of chips, you'll lose about $3 on the deal. The dining-plan cards aren't tied to a particular person, so they can be traded among family members, and they don't expire at the end of the day—unused credits hold their value as long as you hold onto the card.

A **Table Service Universal Dining Plan** is also offered to on-site hotel guests buying vacation packages, but it's an even worse bargain. The full-service plan costs $52 per adult per day ($18 for kids) and includes everything the quick-service plan does, plus one table-service meal (entrée, soft drink, and select dessert; gratuity not included) per day. Unfortunately, there are fewer than a dozen participating restaurants on property, none of which are in the resort hotels—which is strange because the only way to buy the table-service dining plan is as part of a Universal Orlando Vacations hotel package. The table-service plan probably wouldn't be a great deal even if Universal gave it away "free," as Disney does with its dining plan; at full price, you're basically throwing money away.

FAST FOOD *in* UNIVERSAL ORLANDO'S THEME PARKS

FAST FOOD IS AVAILABLE THROUGHOUT Universal Studios Florida and Islands of Adventure. The food compares in quality to McDonald's, Arby's, or Taco Bell but is more expensive, though often served in larger portions. Quick-service prices are fairly consistent from park to park. Expect to pay about the same for your coffee or hot dog at USF or IOA as at WDW.

QUICK-SERVICE RECOMMENDATIONS AT UNIVERSAL STUDIOS FLORIDA

MUCH OF THE QUICK SERVICE at Universal Studios Florida is utterly unremarkable: burgers, pizza, pasta, chicken fingers, sandwiches, and salads. The mediocre food is matched by the predictable theming in the park's original fast-food joints: American diner? Check. New York Italian? Got it. We're a little surprised that there's not a Chinese-takeout place next to a laundry in the San Francisco section.

The expansion in 2013 of the **Springfield U.S.A.** themed area revitalized USF's quick-service scene by bringing a number of wacky *Simpsons*-inspired eateries to life along **Fast Food Boulevard,** including **Krusty Burger, The Frying Dutchman** for seafood, **Cletus' Chicken Shack, Luigi's Pizza, Lard Lad Donuts, Lisa's Teahouse of Horror, Bumblebee Man's Taco Truck, Duff Brewery,** and **Moe's Tavern.** Serving sizes are large, and the food quality is an improvement over your run-of-the-mill theme park fare, with dozens of menu items (including tater tots and curly fries) that aren't available in any other quick-service location.

The best quick-service food in USF can currently be found at the **Leaky Cauldron.** Diagon Alley's flagship restaurant serves authentically hearty British pub fare such as bangers and mash, cottage pie, toad-in-the-hole, Guinness stew, and a ploughman's platter for two of Scotch eggs and imported cheeses. When you're done, head over to **Florean Fortescue's Ice-Cream Parlour** for some delicious Butterbeer ice cream.

QUICK-SERVICE RECOMMENDATIONS AT ISLANDS OF ADVENTURE

OF ISLANDS OF ADVENTURE'S QUICK-SERVICE OFFERINGS, we like the **Three Broomsticks,** the counter-service restaurant in The Wizarding World of Harry Potter–Hogsmeade, which serves Boston Market–style rotisserie chicken, plus fish-and-chips, shepherd's pie, and barbecue ribs. The **Hog's Head** pub, attached to Three Broomsticks, serves beer, wine, mixed drinks, and the obligatory Butterbeer (see the next page).

We're also fond of the gyros at **Fire Eater's Grill,** the kebabs at **"Doc" Sugrue's Desert Kebab House,** and especially the ribs and roasted corn at **Thunder Falls Terrace.** Almost all of the other IOA counter-service places serve some variation of burgers, chicken, pizza, or pasta, and while your superhero-loving kids are going to be drawn toward Marvel Island's **Café 4** and **Captain America Diner** as if the Pied Piper himself was leading them there, avoid both, as there are much better places to eat.

Finally, we'd be remiss in our duties if we didn't warn you to avoid eating the green eggs and ham sandwich at the **Green Eggs and Ham Cafe.** It makes a much better photo opportunity than meal.

QUICK-SERVICE COURTESY

GETTING YOUR ACT TOGETHER IN REGARD to quick-service restaurants in the parks is more a matter of courtesy than necessity. Rude guests rank fifth among reader complaints. A mother from Fort Wayne, Indiana, points out that indecision can be as maddening as out-right discourtesy, especially when you're hungry:

> *Every fast-food restaurant has menu signs the size of billboards, but do you think anybody reads them? People waiting in line spend enough time in front of these signs to memorize them and still don't have a clue what they want when they finally get to the counter. If, by some miracle, they've managed to choose between the hot dog and the hamburger, they then fiddle around another 10 minutes deciding what size Coke to order. Folks, PULEEEZ get your orders together ahead of time!*

On that note, it's also courteous to have your form of payment (cash, credit, hotel key, or dining-plan card) in hand by the time you approach the cashier.

THE WIZARDING WORLD OF BEVERAGES: BUTTERBEER AND BEYOND

The Butterbeer Craze

The first question you are likely to hear from friends upon returning home from a Universal Orlando vacation isn't, "How were the rides?" or, "Did you like the hotel?" but, "What does Butterbeer taste like?" In the fictional Wizarding World, **Butterbeer** is a mildly intoxicating treat favored by Harry Potter and other Hogwarts students. It made its first appearance in the book *Harry Potter and the Prisoner of Azkaban,* and ever since has made fans' mouths water with dreams of the taste, enticingly described as "a little bit like less-sickly butterscotch."

In the real world, the Butterbeer served at Universal Orlando is a nonalcoholic beverage served from a tap, with a butterscotch-y marshmallow foam head that's added after the drink is poured; it's guaranteed to leave you with a selfie-worthy mustache. Whereas in the books, Butterbeer can be bought cold in bottles or hot in "foaming tankards," at Universal there are four varieties, none of which are packaged for taking home. All were invented by chef Steven Jayson for The Wizarding World and had to meet J. K. Rowling's stringent specifications, which, among other things, required natural sugar (don't ask for Butterbeer Lite). We didn't expect to like it but were pleasantly surprised: It's tasty and refreshing, albeit really sweet.

First, there is the basic **Cold Butterbeer,** which is a vanilla cream soda-style liquid with the foam topping. There's also a **Frozen Butterbeer** that's sort of like a slushy made from the same cream soda base, again topped with foam. Frozen is the only variety that comes with a straw; beware of putting a straw in the cold kind because stirring the liquid can cause an embarrassing eruption.

After the success of the first two temperatures, Universal tested **Hot Butterbeer** during the 2014 Celebration of Harry Potter fan event and brought it back full-time at the start of that year's holiday season. The hot variety eschews the soda base for a rich, creamy beverage that resembles a vanilla chai latte, light on the chai. The signature foam stays on top, natch.

Sixteen ounces of the cold version in a plastic cup goes for $5, while the same size frozen is $6. The same drink in a Harry Potter souvenir cup sells for an additional $8, but there is no discount on Butterbeer refills. The hot version is sold in a 12-ounce paper cup for $5.

Note that while Butterbeer is gluten-free, and the base of Cold and Frozen Butterbeer has no dairy products, the "nondairy" foam topping contains whey, a protein derived from milk. For licensing reasons, they refuse to serve the drinks without the topping, even if you are vegan or lactose intolerant.

Finally, Diagon Alley introduced the world to soft-serve Butterbeer ice cream, which tastes almost exactly like the drinks. You can get it at Florean Fortescue's in a cup ($5), waffle cone ($6), or plastic souvenir sundae glass for $11. If you want only a cup of Butterbeer ice cream without toppings, the soft-serve is also served off menu at The Hopping Pot and The Fountain of Fair Fortune, where you'll find a shorter wait.

If forced to choose among the different types of Butterbeer, Seth's hands-down favorite is the frozen version; the ice crystals seem to dull the overpowering sweetness. That is, unless it's cold out or early in the morning, in which case Hot Butterbeer is the clear winner. Of course, for the ultimate indulgence, you have to order a Cold Butterbeer and a cup of Butterbeer ice cream. Mix the two together for a life-changing Butterbeer float; at the very least, it may send you into a sugar coma. Lastly, while it's officially forbidden to adulterate your Butterbeer, if you want to order a cup of the cold stuff at the Hog's Head alongside a shot of, say, Irish cream . . . we won't tell if you pour it in while the barkeep's back is turned.

It seems that everyone in the parks is dead set on trying Butterbeer, as confirmed by Universal's sale of its 5 millionth cup in December 2012. Unfortunately, in Islands of Adventure's Hogsmeade, the ambrosial liquid is sold only at **Three Broomsticks,** at the **Hog's Head** pub, and by two street vendors. That can mean long waits, as many guests buy from the outside carts, waiting 30 minutes or more in line to be served. The outdoor vendors also charge a few pennies more and don't honor annual pass discounts. We recommend that you try your luck at the Hog's Head; the wait here is generally 10 minutes or less, and often there's nobody in line, even when the outdoor carts have lines 30 people deep only 20 feet away. Once served, you can relax with your drink at a table in the pub or out on the rear patio.

Universal learned its lesson and installed more Butterbeer taps around USF's Diagon Alley, where it flows freely in the **Leaky Cauldron,**

The Hopping Pot, and **Fountain of Fair Fortune.** Unfortunately, it forgot to install enough seating to enjoy your drink. Once the picnic tables in Carkitt Market are full, your best bet is to squat on the "stairs to nowhere" next to Harry Potter and the Escape from Gringotts.

Beyond Butterbeer

Though Butterbeer gets most of the press, Hogsmeade has had a handful of other signature Harry Potter drinks since its inception, and Diagon Alley debuted many more. You might as well try one because you aren't going to find any Coca-Cola products whatsoever inside the Wizarding World.

Foremost at both parks is **Pumpkin Juice** ($4), which has a slightly pulpy texture and tastes like Thanksgiving dessert. It is available in a cup or plastic bottle, or in a sparkling **Pumpkin Fizz** version on tap only. Refreshing nonalcoholic **Cider** is also on draft in apple or pear flavors. Diagon Alley has expanded the list of exclusive drinks to include:

TONGUE TYING LEMON SQUASH ($4.79) A tart squeezed-to-order lemonade.

OTTER'S FIZZY ORANGE JUICE ($4.79) Lightly carbonated orange drink with a lip-smacking crust of cinnamon-sugar on the cup's rim; our favorite of the new drinks.

FISHY GREEN ALE ($5) Green cinnamon-mint boba tea with blueberry "fish eggs" that burst blueberry in your mouth when sucked through a straw. A must-try for the novelty factor but not necessarily a must-finish.

PEACHTREE FIZZING TEA ($4.79) Lightly carbonated sweetened iced tea with peach and ginger flavors.

GILLYWATER ($4) A small plastic bottle of filtered water with a Harry Potter label. Seriously! For only $8.25 you can get it paired with a vial of flavored "magical elixir" available in four varieties—**Fire Protection** (watermelon, peach, and strawberry), **Babbling Beverage** (fruit punch), **Draught of Peace** (blueberry, blackberry, cherry), and **Euphoria** (pineapple and mint)—to enhance your water. The most magical thing about the elixirs is how much money Universal has made disappear from Muggles' wallets with fancy Kool-Aid.

Finally, adults who imbibe shouldn't feel left out of the fun; Universal contracted Florida Brewing Company to come up with a trio of exclusive beers served only inside The Wizarding World. In Hogsmeade, the Three Broomsticks and Hog's Head pub serve **Hog's Head Brew,** a hoppy Scottish ale. Diagon Alley's Leaky Cauldron, The Hopping Pot, and Fountain of Fair Fortune pour **Wizard's Brew,** a heavy dark porter with chocolate notes, and **Dragon Scale,** a Vienna-style amber lager. All are served in 20-ounce cups and are poured from creative custom-carved taps. Ask your bartender about secret off-menu concoctions, such as the Triple (or Deathly Hallows), made from layers of Strongbow, Hog's Head ale, and Guinness. Cart vendors in the streets and queues around Diagon Alley also sell cans of "domestic" brews such as Guinness and Strongbow.

For an added kick, in 2015 Universal introduced **Bishen's Fire Whisky,** a 70-proof cinnamon-flavored liquor distilled exclusively for the parks by TerrePURE Spirits of South Carolina. The flavor is warm but wonderfully smooth, and much more drinkable than the superficially similar Fireball whiskey currently in vogue. Fire Whisky is available at the Leaky Cauldron and Hopping Pot in USF, and at the Hog's Head in IOA. It is served neat or on the rocks as single ($8) or double ($11.75) shots, or can be mixed in nonalcoholic apple or pear cider for the same price. A pint of Strongbow with a Fire shot is $10 and tastes like apple pie. While Fire Whisky can't officially be served in Butterbeer, we can vouch for a shot snuck into a cup of Hot Butterbeer as a breakfast eye-opener.

REFILLABLE DRINKS AND POPCORN

ONE SMART WAY TO CUT snacking costs—if not calories—around Universal Orlando is by investing in refillable souvenir containers. Souvenir cups never expire and can be brought back to the park months or years in the future.

Universal sells two different types of refillable soft drink cups. The standard **collectible souvenir cup** costs $9, including your first fill-up, and can be refilled at almost any soda fountain in the parks or City-Walk for 99¢. It can only be refilled for that price with regular fountain flavors—Coke, Diet Coke, Sprite, root beer, Hi-C—and not with any specialty drinks. However, you do get a modest discount when using a souvenir cup to purchase an ICEE, lemon slush, and some other specialty drinks. Pricier character cups (shaped like Transformers or Minions) and specialty souvenir cups (like Butterbeer mugs) can also be refilled with sodas for the same price, but you only get as much as those sometimes skimpy cups can contain.

In addition to the standard souvenir soda cups, Universal also sells **Coca-Cola Freestyle souvenir cups** at dining locations with Freestyle soda machines. These massive red marvels can mix dozens of different drink brands and additional flavorings together to dispense more than 100 soft drink combinations; you haven't lived until you've had an Orange Coke. The self-service Freestyle fountains can only be activated by the RFID computer chip on the base of the cup. The cup is valid for unlimited refills (with a 10-minute pause in between pours) for the entire day. Freestyle cups cost $12 ($6 if purchased with a quick-service dining plan at participating in-park locations) and can be reactivated for an additional $6 per day; rinse and repeat for as many days as you like. Freestyle cups cannot be refilled at regular soda fountains, and Freestyle machines aren't yet ubiquitous, with only seven or eight dispensers in each park. Even if you don't pay to activate a cup, you can still dispense free ice and water from any Freestyle machine; it's

Top Six Snacks Outside the Wizarding World

FINE DINING IS ALL WELL AND GOOD, but many park visitors consume the majority of their calories enjoying the kind of pushcart sweets and midway treats that make it possible to walk 10 miles a day during your Orlando vacation and *still* gain weight. With that in mind, we turned to Universal Orlando eating expert Derek Burgan—author of the popular "Saturday Six" series on TouringPlans.com—for the best snacks to be found at USF and IOA, beyond the aforementioned Wizarding World exclusives:

6. **CHURRO (both parks)** The omnipresent churro, a cinnamon-sugar stick of fried dough, remains one of the tastiest treats in the theme park world, along with being the easiest to traverse the parks with.

5. **CHEESECAKE (USF)** Not just any cheesecake, Beverly Hills Boulangerie cheesecake. These massive slices will set your heart aflutter (both literally and figuratively).

4. **LARD LAD'S BIG PINK DONUT (USF)** Big enough to share, this doughnut from Springfield U.S.A. is guaranteed to put a smile on your face (if not send you straight into a diabetic coma).

3. **GOURMET APPLE (both parks)** Candy apples at Universal are becoming works of art. One worth going out of your way to try is the Rocky Road Gourmet Apple. Covered with caramel, chocolate, pecans, and marshmallows, this apple is almost the size of a human head but much more delicious (no offense to our cannibal readers).

2. **BROOKIE (both parks)** The best thing since chocolate met peanut butter, the Brookie fuses a brownie with a chocolate-chip cookie, and it's just as good as it sounds.

1. **Brain Freezin D'oh-nut Sundae (USF)** The combination of soft-serve ice cream sandwiched between halves of a warm doughnut turns out to be one of mankind's greatest creations. A culinary delight.

Before we go, let's also mention the *worst* snack outside The Wizarding World: **candy filled with insects** (both parks). You will be shocked at how many stores on property carry lollipops or other pieces of candy with actual insects (such as ants and scorpions) encased inside them. It's the closest we here in America can come to re-creating the dinner scene from *Indiana Jones and the Temple of Doom*.

chilled and filtered and tastes much better than the sulfurous lukewarm liquid flowing from the parks' drinking fountains.

A related program is the **Sonic Fill Drink Package** souvenir cup sold exclusively at Cabana Bay Beach Resort. This cup costs $9 for one day of use, $12 for two days, $15 for three days, or $18 for the entire length of your stay at Cabana Bay. A day is considered a calendar day and ends at midnight. Sonic Fill mugs can be refilled at the regular soda stations in the Bayliner Diner seating area, as well as the Coke Freestyle machines located in the diner and at Galaxy Bowl upstairs. The cup is only compatible with the Freestyle machines at Cabana Bay and can't be used inside the parks; nor can the parks' Freestyle cups be used at Cabana Bay.

Lastly, street-cart vendors in Universal's parks sell fresh popcorn in either $3.49 single servings, or $6 **souvenir popcorn buckets** that can be refilled as often as your sodium level can stand for only $1.29. Flavored varieties such as caramel or cheese can be refilled for $3, and (like the soda cups) buckets can be brought back on future trips.

CUTTING YOUR DINING TIME AT THE THEME PARKS

EVEN IF YOU CONFINE YOUR MEALS to vendor and quick-service fast food, you lose a lot of time getting food in the theme parks. Here are some ways to minimize the time you spend hunting and gathering:

1. Eat breakfast before you arrive. Restaurants outside the parks offer some outstanding breakfast specials. Plus, some hotels furnish small refrigerators in their guest rooms, or you can rent a fridge or bring a cooler. If you can get by on cold cereal, rolls, fruit, and juice, this will save a ton of time.

2. After a good breakfast, buy snacks from vendors in the parks as you tour, or stuff some snacks in a fanny pack.

3. All theme park restaurants are busiest between 11:30 a.m. and 2:15 p.m. for lunch and 6 and 9 p.m. for dinner. For shorter lines and faster service, don't eat during these hours, especially 12:30–1:30 p.m.

4. Many quick-service restaurants sell cold sandwiches. Buy a cold lunch minus drinks before 11:30 a.m., and carry it in small plastic bags until you're ready to eat (within an hour or so of purchase). Ditto for dinner. Buy drinks at the appropriate time from any convenient vendor.

5. Most fast-food eateries have more than one service window. Regardless of the time of day, check the lines at all windows before queuing. Sometimes a window that's staffed but out of the way will have a much shorter line or none at all. Note, however, that some windows may offer only certain items.

6. If you're short on time and the park closes early, stay until closing and eat dinner outside the park before returning to your hotel. If the park stays open late, eat dinner about 4 or 4:30 p.m. at the restaurant of your choice. You should sneak in just ahead of the dinner crowd.

Beyond Quick-Service: Tips for Saving Money on Food

Though buying food from quick-service restaurants and vendors will save time and money (compared with full-service dining), additional strategies can bolster your budget and maintain your waistline.

Our readers offer the following suggestions for stretching food dollars.

A Missouri mom writes:

We arrived with our steel Coleman cooler well stocked with milk and sandwich fixings. I froze a block of ice in a milk bottle, and we replenished it daily with ice from the resort ice machine. I also froze small packages of deli-type meats for later in the week. We ate cereal, milk, and fruit each morning, with boxed juices. I also had a hot pot to boil water for instant coffee, oatmeal, and soup. Each child had a belt bag of his own, which he filled from a special box of goodies each day. Some things were actual food, such as packages of crackers and cheese, peanuts, and raisins. Some were worthless junk, such as candy and gum. Each child also had a small, rectangular plastic water bottle that could hang on the belt. We filled these at water fountains before getting into lines. We left the park before noon; ate sandwiches, chips, and soda in the room; and napped. We purchased our evening meal in the park at a quick-service eatery. We budgeted for both morning and evening snacks from a vendor but often didn't need them.

A Whiteland, Indiana, mom suggests:

One must-take item if you're traveling with younger kids is a supply of small paper or plastic cups to split drinks, which are both huge and expensive.

UNIVERSAL ORLANDO QUICK-SERVICE RESTAURANT MINI-PROFILES

TO HELP YOU FIND FLAVORFUL FAST FOOD while staying fleet of foot, we've developed mini-profiles of Universal Orlando's quick-service restaurants. The restaurants are listed alphabetically by location. Detailed profiles of all Universal Orlando full-service restaurants begin on page 209.

The restaurants profiled in the following pages are rated for quality and portion size as well as value. The value rating ranges from A to F as follows:

A	Exceptional value; a real bargain	**D**	Somewhat overpriced
B	Good value	**F**	Extremely overpriced
C	Fair value; you get exactly what you pay for		

Note: Because of special or unusual offerings, the following quick-service restaurants are profiled in full and are listed with the full-service restaurants:

Leaky Cauldron (Universal Studios Florida)
Three Broomsticks (Islands of Adventure)
Red Oven Pizza Bakery (CityWalk)

UNIVERSAL STUDIOS FLORIDA
Ben & Jerry's

LOCATION	New York	QUALITY	Good	VALUE	C+	Portion	Medium

Selections A large selection of ice cream, frozen yogurt, milk shakes, and smoothies. Adventurous families can try the Mini Vermonster (four scoops of ice cream topped with a freshly baked brownie, chocolate-chip cookie, banana, hot fudge or caramel, whipped cream, and two spoonfuls of your four favorite toppings).

Comments Located in the New York section of the park, the facade for Ben & Jerry's is the famous Hudson Street Home for Girls, the very orphanage in which Little Orphan Annie lived. While several places serve Ben & Jerry's soft-serve, this is the only place in the parks with a wide selection of hard-packed flavors, including Cherry Garcia and Stephen Colbert's AmeriCone Dream.

Beverly Hills Boulangerie

LOCATION	Hollywood	QUALITY	Fair-Good	VALUE	B-	Portion	Medium-Large

Selections Hot breakfast sandwiches; soups; fresh panini; veggie, turkey, roast beef, tuna, or ham-and-Swiss sandwiches; cookies, cakes, and pastries; espresso, cappuccino, and coffee.

Comments The pastries and coffee make an acceptable breakfast. Because it's at the front of the park, it's usually not as crowded as other restaurants for lunch. Most of the sandwiches are premade and cold, but you can get a hot pressed Italian melt on ciabatta or rosemary bread. The Boulangerie has the largest selection of muffins, cookies, and cheesecakes in the park.

Bumblebee Man's Taco Truck

LOCATION	World Expo	QUALITY	Good	VALUE	B-	Portion	Medium

Selections Chicken, fish, and beef soft-shell tacos served with tortilla chips. Coca-Cola fountain products, Buzz Cola, and Duff, Duff Lite, and Duff Dry beers.

Comments Capitalizing on the popular trend of food trucks, Bumblebee Man's Taco Truck is the first eatery guests encounter walking into Springfield U.S.A. from the main gates. The truck is adorned with a huge taco on the front bumper and an even bigger Bumblebee Man head coming out of the roof. The theming continues inside the truck as team members are dressed up in cute little bee costumes, complete with antennas on their hats. Each of the selections is well done. While the guacamole and salsa seemed to be off-the-shelf varieties, every other element tasted great. The quality is very competitive with the food at Moe's Southwest Grill in CityWalk. Our favorite picks are the carne asada and the Korean beef.

Cafe La Bamba *(open seasonally)*

LOCATION	Hollywood	QUALITY	Good	VALUE	B+	Portion	Medium-Large

Selections Standard American-style breakfast. Southwestern barbecue, tacos, and burritos for lunch/dinner.

Comments Modeled after the legendary Hollywood Hotel, home to many silent movie stars and captains of the film industry in the early 20th century, this is a lovely place to dine—if you can get inside. On select mornings, it's the scene of the Superstar Character Breakfast, which includes a plated breakfast and costumed cartoon friends. (See page 183 for details.) During peak seasons, Cafe La

Bamba also offers a lunch and dinner counter-service selection that is far from the norm of your average theme park food. Mojo roasted chicken, chipotle barbecue ribs, and chimichurri skirt steak are served, along with burritos, tacos, and tostado salads. The meat can be a bit dry, especially the steak, but it is surprisingly well seasoned, and the dishes are from a culinary culture that is otherwise underrepresented inside Universal's parks.

Chez Alcatraz

LOCATION San Francisco **QUALITY** Fair–Good **VALUE** B **Portion** Medium–Large

Selections Mixed drinks, beer, soda, and appetizers.

Comments With usually little to no wait, Chez Alcatraz can be a great place to relax and unwind with an adult beverage and a quick snack (we recommend the seasoned house-made chips with chipotle ketchup). With plenty of seating, it's a great place to take a break from touring the park, and you just happen to be next to one of the best photo ops in USF (Bruce the shark, from *Jaws*).

Duff Brewery

LOCATION World Expo **QUALITY** Fair–Good **VALUE** C **Portion** Medium

Selections Hot dogs and assorted snacks. Beverages include Coke products, Buzz Cola, Duff beer, and other Simpson-related drinks. In *The Simpsons* TV show, Duff, Duff Lite, and Duff Dry are all the exact same beer, but the Duff beers at Duff Brewery are completely different from each other. Duff beer is most equivalent to Yuengling, Duff Lite is closer to your standard light beer (like Miller Lite), and Duff Dry is a stout dark beer that can be compared to Guinness but has a strong coffee taste.

Comments A wonderful addition to the Universal waterfront, Duff Brewery is an outdoor bar area with plenty of seating nearby to relax. It is part of the larger Duff Gardens, which, in *The Simpsons* TV show, is a theme park run by a beer-brewing company. The character of Duffman is available for photo ops, and there are hilarious topiaries of the "7 Duffs." The 7 Duffs (Tipsy, Queasy, Surly, Sleazy, Edgy, Dizzy, and Remorseful), a parody of Disney's Seven Dwarfs, are the mascots of Duff Gardens. Duff beers are brewed exclusively for Universal by the Florida Brewing Company, which also brews beers for The Wizarding World of Harry Potter. Because Duff Brewery is out in the open and in view of every guest, it can often attract a big crowd, especially on a hot day. There is plenty of seating at the bar and the surrounding area, which also is a fine place to enjoy *Universal's Cinematic Spectacular* at night. At one time, the waterfront-viewing terrace was restricted during *CineSpec* showings, but now it is open to all. Order a drink here (the banana Squishee is especially tasty), but in the name of all that is good and holy, don't eat the hot dogs: They've been on those rollers longer than the ones in Apu's Kwik-E-Mart.

Fast Food Boulevard

LOCATION World Expo **QUALITY** Good–Excellent **VALUE** A– **Portion** Large

Selections Burgers, chicken, pizza, seafood, sandwiches, and salads. With different eateries pulled straight from *The Simpsons* TV series, guests dine on cleverly named selections from Krusty Burger, The Frying Dutchman, Flaming Moe's, Cletus' Chicken Shack, Luigi's Pizza, Lard Lad Donuts, and Lisa's Teahouse of Horror.

Comments Formerly the International Food and Film Festival, Fast Food Boulevard transformed quite possibly the worst food court in any Orlando theme park into one of the most fun. Besides the hilarious menus themselves (taste-tested by writers of *The Simpsons* TV show), Fast Food Boulevard contains items you can't get anywhere else in the park, including a pulled-pork sandwich, tater tots, and seasoned curly fries instead of the normal fries served everywhere else. Our favorites are the gloriously messy Clogger Burger, the tender fried calamari, and the chicken-and-waffle sandwich (with extra maple mayo on the side). And thanks in large part to Lisa's Teahouse of Horror, Fast Food Boulevard also has several options, outside of the ever-present salad, for the vegetarians and vegans in your party. Note that this is a very popular spot for lunch, and a long line can develop. Guests queue inside and are released to the serving stations in small groups. Once you order and receive your food, pay at the cashier, and an employee will find an empty table for you. The process can take a while on busy days, and the televisions broadcast a loop of classic *Simpsons* clips that is maddeningly brief. An Ambler, Pennsylvania, couple sampled the offerings:

> The doughnuts at Lard Lad were fresh, flavorful, and surprisingly delicious. (Mmm . . . doughnuts.) The Flaming Moe is an overpriced glass of orange soda with dry ice on the bottom—for $8, it should have some alcohol in it or be larger. The queuing for Krusty Burger was frustrating during the lunch rush—they let only a few guests up to the food court at a time—but once you go through the line and pay, an employee shows you to a table. Lunch for the four of us cost $88 with two beers and that one overpriced Flaming Moe. Duff beer was essentially a less-delicious Heineken. My husband's Krusty Burger was pretty good; my chicken-and-waffle sandwich was excellent but had too much sauce on it.

Florean Fortescue's Ice-Cream Parlour

LOCATION Diagon Alley QUALITY Excellent VALUE B PORTION Medium-Large

Selections Ice cream. Ice cream is served in cups, waffle cones, and plastic souvenir sundae glasses. A single order can contain two different flavors, and you can add unusual toppings such as shortbread crumbles and meringue pieces for under a dollar.

Comments Readers of the Harry Potter books will remember Florean Fortescue's Ice-Cream Parlour for its prominent appearance in *Harry Potter and the Prisoner of Azkaban.* When Harry spent several weeks staying in a room above the Leaky Cauldron, he would spend time at the ice cream parlor, and Florean Fortescue himself gave Harry free ice cream sundaes every half hour. Now Muggles can have their own sundaes in this very establishment, with some very "magical" flavors, including the first ever Butterbeer-flavored ice cream. Our favorites are the salted caramel blondie and chocolate chili—but be warned, it has a bite!

Fountain of Fair Fortune

LOCATION Diagon Alley QUALITY Good-Excellent VALUE B PORTION Medium

Selections Potter-themed drinks, both soft and hard.

Comments Named after a short story in *Tales of Beedle the Bard,* this pub sells Fishy Green Ale, Gillywater, Wizard's Brew, and Dragon Scale—and features an exclusive

Butterbeer souvenir mug not found in Hogsmeade Village. You can also get a cup of Butterbeer soft-serve here, usually with a much shorter wait than at the ice cream shop next door.

The Hopping Pot

LOCATION Diagon Alley QUALITY Good–Excellent VALUE B PORTION Medium

Selections Potter-themed drinks, including all four varieties of Butterbeer: cold, frozen, hot, or soft-serve. If you're peckish, snack portions of meat pasties and bags of British potato crisps are also available.

Comments Outdoor bar with eight different brews—including Wizard's Brew (a heavy porter) and Dragon Scale (a hoppy amber)—on draft, each with its own customized tap handle, along with the area's most complete selection of signature non-alcoholic drinks. Much better food is available elsewhere in Diagon Alley. Seating is at a limited number of picnic tables, within sight of the Carkitt Market stage.

KidZone Pizza Company

LOCATION Woody Woodpecker's KidZone QUALITY Fair VALUE C PORTION Medium

Selections Pizzas, chicken tenders, chef salad, and funnel cake.

Comments Located at the front of Woody Woodpecker's KidZone and directly next to the impressive SpongeBob StorePants, KidZone Pizza is going to be very enticing to your kids. There's no indoor seating, and even the few seats outdoors can fill up quickly during the busier times. The limited menu is missing the wow factor, as you can get better pizza at several other locations in the park. Unless your kids are absolutely famished, your best bet is to walk over to Fast Food Boulevard.

London Taxi Hut

LOCATION Outside Diagon Alley QUALITY Fair–Good VALUE C PORTION Medium

Selections You can get a jacket potato (baked potato to Americans) smothered with baked beans and cheese, broccoli and cheese, or the salty stuffing from a shepherd's pie. Bags of crisps (British potato chips), hot dogs, and canned European beers fill out the brief menu.

Comments Outside the gorgeous London Waterfront facades in front of Diagon Alley are two "cabman shelter" kiosks. One sells London-themed merchandise such as T-shirts, and this one sells quick-service food and drink items. The signature item is an extra-long hot dog in an odd tubelike bun; shape aside, it tastes about the same.

Louie's Italian Restaurant

LOCATION New York QUALITY Fair–Good VALUE C PORTION Medium

Selections Spaghetti with meatballs; fettuccine Alfredo; cheese, pepperoni, or veggie pizza; Caesar salad; soup; cookies; cake; fruit cups; gelato; Italian ices; turkey legs; beer.

Comments One of the largest indoor restaurants in the Studios and a good choice to get out of the hot sun. The name of the restaurant is an homage to the movie *The Godfather,* which had a very famous scene set at Louie's Restaurant. The food is nothing special, and the whole pies are outrageously overpriced at more than $30 apiece, but it's hard to screw up pizza and pasta. Guido's, a small counter in the corner, offers a limited selection of frozen Italian desserts. Be warned: It can be very crowded throughout the afternoon.

Mel's Drive-In

LOCATION Hollywood	QUALITY Fair	VALUE C	PORTION Medium-Large

Selections Hamburgers, cheeseburgers, chicken fingers, grilled chicken sandwich, grilled chicken salad, fries, onion rings, and ice cream floats.

Comments Based on the diner from the George Lucas movie *American Graffiti,* Mel's has several vintage automobiles in the parking lot that are always available for photo ops. Check out the license plates for some fun references. During Halloween Horror Nights, the neon lights in the Mel's Drive-in sign are creatively changed to Mel's Die-in.

More than half the menu lists some combination of hamburger patty, cheese, and bacon, with fries. The food is as bland as the selection. Root beer floats are available, but we wouldn't make a special trip here for anything.

Moe's Tavern

LOCATION World Expo	QUALITY Good	VALUE C+	PORTION Medium

Selections Duff beer and Flaming Moe.

Comments Grab a Duff beer (regular or Duff Lite on draft or bottle; Duff Dry in a bottle only) or a Flaming Moe from this replica of Homer and Barney's haunt from *The Simpsons* TV series. Filled with nods to the TV show, there's a large photo op with Barney along with a working Love Tester. If you're lucky and sitting by the red phone on the bar top, you just may happen to take a prank phone call. The Flaming Moe is the first signature drink "experience" we have seen to date. Pricey at about $8 each, a Flaming Moe comes in a souvenir glass that does a good job of hiding dry ice via a separate compartment. The orange soda–tasting drink bubbles up with smoke billowing out, giving a really good representation of being on fire. The nonalcoholic Flaming Moe is sure to be a hit with the younger set when they see it for the first time.

Richter's Burger Co.

LOCATION San Francisco	QUALITY Fair	VALUE C	PORTION Medium-Large

Selections Burgers, chicken sandwiches, salads, and milk shakes.

Comments Located near the *Disaster!* attraction, Richter's Burger Co. has a theme tied to the 1906 San Francisco earthquake. All of the menu items have earthquake-related names, and the decor around the surprisingly large seating areas includes photos from that era (including some wonderful ads for products that are just hilarious to read with 20/20 hindsight), as well as seismologist props. One of the more impressive elements in the restaurant is the faithful re-creation of the Louis Agassiz statue that fell off a Stanford University building during the 1906 earthquake. The statue lodged itself firmly into the concrete, head first, and Universal has re-created the striking image within Richter's. The food here is nothing to start quaking over, but there is a toppings bar for customizing your burger.

San Francisco Pastry Co.

LOCATION San Francisco	QUALITY Fair	VALUE C	PORTION Medium-Large

Selections Soups; veggie, turkey, roast beef, tuna, or ham-and-Swiss sandwiches; fruit plates; salads; cookies, cakes, pies, and pastries; espresso, cappuccino, and coffee; beer.

Comments Selection is similar to the Beverly Hills Boulangerie at the front of the park. The pastries and coffee make a good pick-me-up if you're in the area during the afternoon, but the sandwiches are premade and cold.

Schwab's Pharmacy

LOCATION	Hollywood	QUALITY	Good	VALUE	C+	PORTION	Medium

Selections Ice cream sundaes and milk shakes.

Comments Schwab's Pharmacy, modeled after the legendary drugstore counter where Lana Turner was supposedly discovered, serves frozen treats made with Ben & Jerry's ice cream. The selection is more limited here than at the other Ben & Jerry's location in New York. The medicines here are for display only; if you need a nostrum, head to First Aid.

Universal Studios' Classic Monsters Cafe

LOCATION	Production Central	QUALITY	Fair	VALUE	C	PORTION	Medium

Selections Rotisserie chicken with roasted potatoes; lasagna; cheeseburgers; hot dogs; ribs; cheese or pepperoni pizza; fries; cupcakes and cookies; beer.

Comments With a lot of indoor seating, Universal Studios' Classic Monsters Cafe can be a good place for a meal and to get out of the hot sun. The restaurant is filled with movie props from various monster films, including *The Creature from the Black Lagoon* and *The Mummy,* but also has references from *The Munsters* TV show. Since the home-style meat loaf was yanked from the menu, there's nothing served here that you can't get better somewhere else. The burgers and Nathan's chili cheese dogs are exactly as you'd expect, and the chicken and ribs are often dry or oversalted. The pizza slices are huge (and they better be for the monstrous price of $7.49 each) and are much better than your average theme park pizza.

ISLANDS OF ADVENTURE

Blondie's

LOCATION	Toon Lagoon	QUALITY	Fair	VALUE	C-	PORTION	Large

Selections Dagwood deli sandwiches; made-to-order roast beef, turkey, tuna, and ham sandwiches; Nathan's hot dogs; soup and chili.

Comments Avoid the signature sandwich—the Dagwood—which is premade and refrigerated until needed. It also has more bread than necessary, making it dry. If you're really in the mood for a sandwich, order one of the made-to-order turkey or ham subs; the roast beef is invariably too dry. Blondie's has three freshly baked bread options: multigrain, French baguette, and whole wheat. If you like Nathan's hot dogs, Blondie's serves the most styles in the parks: chili, Chicago, Reuben, and slaw.

The Burger Digs

LOCATION	Jurassic Park	QUALITY	Fair	VALUE	C	PORTION	Medium-Large

Selections Double cheeseburger, chicken sandwich, garden burger, and milk shakes.

Comments Burger Digs has indoor seating. The burgers and chicken sandwiches are nothing special, though they come on kaiser rolls, and a cold toppings bar allows for customization. The specialty burger is topped with sautéed mushrooms and onion rings. If you're looking for better food, try Thunder Falls Terrace a little farther along in Jurassic Park.

Cafe 4

LOCATION Marvel Super Hero Island **QUALITY** Fair **VALUE** C **PORTION** Medium

Selections Personal pizzas, pasta, meatball subs, Caesar salads, and breadsticks.

Comments The food is generic and fairly flavorless, but it is served rather speedily. However, Dr. Doom seems to think that an average price of $8 for a personal pie (which replaced the insanely expensive full pies) is reasonable in a theme park setting. This is not Via Napoli by any "stretch" of the imagination (that one is for the Mr. Fantastic fans), but the cafe does make specialties such as barbecue chicken pizza and spinach-Feta calzones. The exact same salads, meatball subs, basic pastas and sauces that are served at Louie's in USF round out the not-so-Fantastic menu.

Captain America Diner

LOCATION Marvel Super Hero Island **QUALITY** Fair **VALUE** C **PORTION** Medium–Large

Selections Cheeseburgers, chicken sandwiches, chicken fingers, chicken salad, milk shakes, and onion rings.

Comments The meat is entirely average but comes served on a sesame-seed bun. While it's titled Captain America Diner, the air-conditioned inside is themed to the Marvel Comics version of *The Avengers,* including references to C-level characters in the group such as the Black Knight and Wonder Man, and even the flooring is themed. Inside seating features a gorgeous look outside into the lagoon (and with a great view of Mythos and Hogwarts Castle).

Circus McGurkus Cafe Stoo-pendous

LOCATION Seuss Landing **QUALITY** Fair–Good **VALUE** C+ **PORTION** Medium–Large

Selections Fried chicken, pasta, pizza, cheeseburgers, and Caesar salads.

Comments This is certainly one of the more interesting counter-service venues. The High in the Sky Trolley Train Ride! passes overhead, and during inclement weather the *Oh! The Stories You'll Hear!* show takes place within the restaurant. The fried chicken is actually pretty good; it comes in two- or three-piece combos with corn on the cob and mashed potatoes with home-style gravy. Everything else on the menu is just average.

Comic Strip Cafe

LOCATION Toon Lagoon **QUALITY** Poor–Fair **VALUE** C– **PORTION** Medium–Large

Selections Asian barbecue chicken, stir-fry, chicken fingers, fish-and-chips, personal pizza, pasta, salads, cheeseburgers, and hot dogs.

Comments Formerly notorious for serving the worst fast food in IOA, Comic Strip Cafe has upgraded its recipes to be almost as average as every other quick-service restaurant. Even so, the "Chinese" dishes are pretty dire. Better fish-and-chips can still be found at Three Broomsticks, and better pizza is at Pizza Predattoria.

Croissant Moon Bakery

LOCATION Port of Entry **QUALITY** Fair–Good **VALUE** C+ **PORTION** Large

Selections Deli sandwiches, panini, freshly baked pastries, funnel cakes, and Lavazza coffee.

Comments Tucked into the right side of Port of Entry's main walkway as you enter the park, Croissant Moon Bakery is a good place to get a quick breakfast (its "on the run" Continental combo is a great deal) or a pastry and coffee pick-me-up between meals. Prices for fancy flavored lattes are lower here than at the Starbucks across the street. The cold sandwiches tend to be premade and refrigerated, so this isn't the best choice for subs, but you can get a hot pressed panino. You can also get a freshly fried funnel cake. The service is fast and friendly, and there's plenty of shaded seating outdoors, where you can people-watch.

"Doc" Sugrue's Desert Kebab House
(also known as Oasis Coolers)

LOCATION The Lost Continent	QUALITY Good	VALUE B	PORTION Medium

Selections Meat and vegetarian kebabs, hummus, snacks, and beverages.

Comments Though marked as Oasis Coolers on park maps, the signage on this food stand, next to The Mystic Fountain, says it's called "Doc" Sugrue's Desert Kebab House. Whatever the name, the stand offers nicely seasoned beef and chicken kebabs, while also being very vegetarian and vegan friendly, with hummus, fruit cups, Greek yogurt, and pretzels. This location also has several Coke Freestyle machines. A unique place to get a snack before entering *The Eighth Voyage of Sindbad Stunt Show,* "Doc" Sugrue's is in the unfortunate position of being between the popular eatery Mythos and The Wizarding World of Harry Potter. With many hungry guests making a beeline toward the Potter-themed food in Hogsmeade or the award-winning Mythos, both "Doc" Sugrue's and Fire Eater's Grill in Lost Continent see little to no waits on most days.

Fire Eater's Grill

LOCATION The Lost Continent	QUALITY Fair–Good	VALUE C	PORTION Medium

Selections Gyros, chicken tenders, hot dogs, and salads.

Comments The lamb gyro sandwich with salad is the best combination here, and also the most popular. You have to admire Universal's ability to combine the various entrées to make more meal options. One is a plain chicken tenders platter. Add hot sauce, and it becomes the Chicken Stingers platter. Omit the sauce and add lettuce, and it's the Crispy Chicken Salad. We're hoping for an entrée named Lamb Dog with Cheesy Chicken Stingers.

Green Eggs and Ham Cafe *(open seasonally)*

LOCATION Seuss Landing	QUALITY Fair	VALUE C	PORTION Medium

Selections Green eggs and ham sandwiches, cheeseburgers, chicken fingers, chicken sandwich, and fudge brownies.

Comments The cafe is only open seasonally, which is OK because it makes a better photo op than a restaurant. The signature eggs get their hue from diced parsley and other green herbs, not food coloring. If your group is really serious about eating the green eggs and ham, order one entrée to share with everyone. Few people decide to eat the whole thing.

Hog's Head

LOCATION Hogsmeade	QUALITY Good	VALUE B-	PORTION Medium

Selections Butterbeer, Pumpkin Juice, beer, wine, and mixed drinks.

Comments Wonderfully themed pub attached to the Three Broomsticks restaurant that offers both alcoholic and alcohol-free drinks. If you want a Butterbeer, the line is often shorter here than at either of the outdoor carts. A full liquor selection is kept behind the bar, but there are no sodas to mix with (only juice), nor are they allowed to add alcohol to nonalcoholic Potter drinks. The animatronic hog hanging behind the bar is known to snort and snarl if you slide the barkeep a tip.

Hop On Pop Ice Cream Shop

LOCATION	Seuss Landing	QUALITY	Fair	VALUE	C	PORTION	Medium

Selections Ice cream, waffle cones, root beer floats, and Dippin' Dots.

Comments A small ice cream stand in Seuss Landing with no indoor seating. The Sundae on a Stick, a vanilla ice cream bar dipped in chocolate and sprinkles, is exceptionally messy on warm summer days.

Moose Juice, Goose Juice

LOCATION	Seuss Landing	QUALITY	Good	VALUE	C	PORTION	Small–Medium

Selections Pretzels, cookies, and *churros*; frozen orange, apple, watermelon, or grape juice.

Comments Cartoon animal rights activists rest easy: No geese nor meese were harmed in the making of these drinks. Moose Juice is actually an orange tangerine-flavored frozen slush, and Goose Juice is a green sour apple-flavored slush. Both can hit the spot on a hot Florida day.

Pizza Predattoria

LOCATION	Jurassic Park	QUALITY	Fair–Good	VALUE	C+	PORTION	Medium

Selections Personal pizzas, meatball subs, Caesar salads, and brookies.

Comments The meat-lovers pizza is decent, as far as theme park pizza goes. Stick to that or the salads. The brookie—a cookie/brownie hybrid—is a brilliant development in the history of desserts.

Thunder Falls Terrace

LOCATION	Jurassic Park	QUALITY	Excellent	VALUE	A–	PORTION	Large

Selections Rotisserie chicken, ribs, smoked turkey legs, soups, and salads.

Comments A nice change from the usual theme park hamburgers and pizza served all over Islands of Adventure. The roasted corn on the cob and seasoned rice with beans are excellent. Thunder Falls is quite possibly the best bet for a meal in the park. Not being as busy as Three Broomsticks, with food almost as good, makes this location a winner.

The Watering Hole

LOCATION	Jurassic Park	QUALITY	Good	VALUE	B–	PORTION	Medium

Selections Nathan's hot dogs, nachos, *churros*, frozen beverages, beer, and liquor.

Comments A small takeaway food and drink stand in Jurassic Park. A few tables, some with umbrellas for shade, are nearby. The food is just a fig leaf; you're here for the libations. The bartenders are some of the friendliest on property, and they offer a daily happy hour for annual-pass holders with discounted draft beers and single-liquor well cocktails 3–5 p.m.

Wimpy's (open seasonally)

LOCATION	Toon Lagoon	QUALITY	Fair	VALUE	C	PORTION	Medium-Large

Selections Double cheeseburgers, chicken fingers, chicken wraps, chili dogs, and fries.

Comments This outdoor-only burger stand, themed to Popeye's perpetually indebted pal, serves entirely unremarkable American standards on the handful of days each year when it is open. Seriously, this "seasonal" restaurant is seen operating so infrequently that it's become the white whale of Universal dining. If you happen to spy it open during your visit, snap a photo and send it to our dining consigliere Derek Burgan (he'll burn with envy), and then continue on to a better eatery.

CITYWALK
Auntie Anne's

LOCATION	Waterfront	QUALITY	Good	VALUE	C	PORTION	Medium

Selections Pretzels, pretzel nuggets, pretzel dogs, and soft drinks.

Comments The familiar twisted-dough franchise has come to CityWalk, with prices only slightly more exorbitant than what you'll pay at the mall. Pretzels are made in original or cinnamon-and-sugar varieties, and dipping sauces (cheese, caramel, or sweet glaze) are extra.

BK Whopper Bar

LOCATION	Upper Level	QUALITY	Fair	VALUE	C	PORTION	Large

Selections A Burger King location with Whoppers of all kinds; fried chicken sandwich or strips; salads; fries; onion rings; shakes; sundae pie.

Comments Because the menu is so familiar, long lines can develop here during lunchtime. Prices are markedly higher than your local drive-thru, and there's no value menu, but you are getting a double Whopper with unique toppings (such as bleu cheese or angry onions), and the "small" fries and drink are the size of a medium elsewhere.

Bread Box Handcrafted Sandwiches

LOCATION	Upper Level	QUALITY	Good	VALUE	C-	PORTION	Small-Medium

Selections Hot and cold deli sandwiches, grilled cheese, house-made potato chips, soups, salads, milk shakes, beer, and wine.

Comments Bread Box is located in the former home of Cigarz. Bread Box obviously aims to fill the sandwich void in CityWalk, similar to how Earl of Sandwich has become destination dining at Disney Springs. The Bread Box claims that guests will be "transported back to your childhood kitchen or your favorite street corner deli" through its use of high-quality meats, vegetables, fresh bread, and simple preparation. Sounds good, and the menu indeed has a wide selection of grilled cheeses (stuffed with everything from bacon to pastrami to smoked brisket), along with house-made soups and various sandwiches made fresh to order. And you can't complain about Twinkies and Nutella milk shakes for dessert. The problem is that, while everything we've tasted at Bread Box has been yummy, you can't ignore how outrageously overpriced it is, especially compared to its noble competition; $8 will barely buy you half a foot-long here, and the potato chips (which are freshly cooked and wonderful) aren't even included. If you want a high-quality, creative snack and can stomach the price, give one of the grilled cheese creations a go, but save some money for another meal later.

Cinnabon

| LOCATION | Lower Level | QUALITY | Good | VALUE | B- | PORTION | Large |

Selections Original Cinnabon plus Pecanbons, Minibons, Seattle's Best Coffee, and soft-serve ice cream.

Comments The same cinnamon-sugar goodness sold inside IOA can also be found in CityWalk on the way to and from the parks. This location, along with the Starbucks across the street, is usually the first thing to open each morning for breakfasting early birds.

Cold Stone Creamery

| LOCATION | Lower Level | QUALITY | Good | VALUE | B- | PORTION | Medium |

Selections Hard-packed ice cream with mix-in toppings, waffle cones, and milk shakes.

Comments Using only the highest-quality ingredients, Cold Stone Creamery has made its name by preparing your ice cream creation in front of your eyes on a frozen granite slab. With a large selection of ice creams—and even larger choices of mix-ins—the possibilities seem almost endless. Cold Stone has a unique way of describing sizes with "Mine" (16 oz.), "Ours" (32 oz.), and "Everybody's" (480 oz.). This location is very popular with exiting guests and often sees a long line when the parks close.

Dockside and Shoreline

| LOCATION | Waterfront | QUALITY | Good | VALUE | C+ | PORTION | Medium |

Selections Craft beer, mixed drinks, snacks, and pizza delivery.

Comments Dockside and Shoreline are sibling outdoor bar areas with al fresco seating, allowing guests to take a break and enjoy a cool drink while touring the CityWalk waterfront. Dockside has a great view of Hollywood Rip Ride Rockit, where you can sit back with a Classic Long Island Tea and listen to the screaming of thrilled riders. With outdoor seating and the largest selection of craft beers in the Universal Orlando Resort outside of a sit-down restaurant, Shoreline is a great place to relax with a cold brew while overlooking the lagoon. Red Oven Pizza Bakery is available for delivery as well.

Fat Tuesday

| LOCATION | Upper Level | QUALITY | Good | VALUE | C | PORTION | Medium-Large |

Selections Premium frozen daiquiris.

Comments Fat Tuesday began on Bourbon Street in New Orleans more than 20 years ago and brings the Mardi Gras party atmosphere—and its world-famous frozen drinks—to CityWalk. Located between Pat O'Brien's and The Groove, Fat Tuesday is a to-go window with decent-size drinks for a good price. Be careful, because adding floaters to the daiquiris can catch up to you fast. Some of the more popular drink combinations include Peaches & Cream (Bellini and piña colada), Superman (Eye Candy and Cat 5 Hurricane), and Mochalada (mudslide and piña colada). Fat Tuesday is open daily, 4 p.m.–2 a.m.

Fusion Bistro Sushi & Sake Bar

| LOCATION | Upper Level | QUALITY | Good | VALUE | C | PORTION | Small-Medium |

Selections Raw and cooked sushi *nigiri* and maki, sake and Japanese beer, miso soup, edamame, hot appetizers, salads, and bento boxes.

Comments Opened in 2010, this restaurant is operated by Sushi House, with other locations in Atlanta and Orlando's Florida Mall. Fusion Bistro's unusual sushi preparations mix traditional Japanese with tastes and ingredients from throughout Eastern Asia and the Pacific Rim, all made in a glassed-in kitchen that you can observe from outside. The sushi here ain't cheap, but it's quicker and less expensive than The Cowfish, and because of extended hours, you can get your fix until the wee hours. Quality is a cut above your local supermarket, but because everything is made from fairly pedestrian fish—tuna, salmon, tilapia, escolar, shrimp, and eel—sushi snobs will want to eat elsewhere. The spicy tuna rolls are acceptable, and the $5 bento box deal adds miso soup, salad, seaweed, rice, and a mochi cake to any item.

Hot Dog Hall of Fame

LOCATION	Lower Level	QUALITY	Good	VALUE	C+	PORTION	Medium

Selections Vienna, Nathan's, Kayem, Farmer John's, Sabrett, Koegel, and bratwurst sausages with a variety of toppings; chicken sausage; fries; potato chips; beer and soda.

Comments Developed by Steve Schussler, the creative force behind Rainforest Cafe and T-REX, Hot Dog Hall of Fame is a tribute to the iconic baseball-park food. From the mustard bar curated by the National Mustard Museum in Wisconsin, to famous dogs from ballparks across the nation (such as the Dixie Dog and the Dirty Water Dog), Hot Dog Hall of Fame will resonate with baseball enthusiasts and foodies alike. The venue features large-screen televisions and bleacher-type seating (from actual MLB ballparks) for those interested in catching a game. It also sells fun extras such as "paint your wiener" (a blank vinyl wiener dog that guests can put their own designs on) and an electronic yodeling pickle. The sausages, buns, and toppings are all authentic and perfectly prepared, but because the dogs all cost the same, the value will vary with the variety; $7 for a New York Sabrett with kraut sounds pretty steep, but the Kansas City (pulled pork and coleslaw) and Milwaukee (bratwurst and grilled onions) dogs deliver a good bang for the buck. There's even a 2-foot dog for just under twice the price, if you want to share. The posted price is for the pup alone; shoestring fries or house-made chips cost extra, as do the peanuts and Cracker Jacks (natch) for dessert.

Lone Palm Airport

LOCATION	Waterfront	QUALITY	Good	VALUE	B-	PORTION	Medium

Selections Breakfast selections in morning. Wings, nachos, shrimp, quesadillas, pretzel sticks, beer, and specialty drinks for lunch/dinner.

Comments Across from Margaritaville lies the Lone Palm Airport tiki bar. A great place to grab your food and snacks on the go, the Lone Palm Airport is also home to Jimmy Buffett's seaplane, the *Hemisphere Dancer*. Outdoor seating makes the Lone Palm a great place to sit back with a nice cool drink and enjoy the atmosphere of Parakeet Beach (not to mention people-watch on CityWalk).

Menchie's Frozen Yogurt

LOCATION	Upper Level	QUALITY	Good	VALUE	C+	PORTION	Varies

Selections Self-service frozen yogurt with toppings and bottled soft drinks.

Comments Menchie's is a build-your-own yogurt chain that offers guests the ability to put themselves into a diabetic coma with an overwhelming amount of available toppings. Yes, there is fresh fruit for those who want to stay healthy, but for the rest of us there are sprinkles, Cinnamon Toast Crunch, Kit Kats, gummy bears, Cap'n Crunch, Twix, chocolate rocks, and more (MUCH more) to load on top of your yogurt. Just as Via Napoli imports its water from Pennsylvania, Menchie's brings its milk in from California. Why? We're not exactly sure, but this cartoon says it is better for you. Science, schmience—you put enough Oreo cookies in the yogurt, and the milk might as well be from Mars. Perhaps most important, one of the flavors in Menchie's regular rotation is Dole pineapple, otherwise known to Disney fans as the Dole Whip. This is one of the few places where the cult favorite flavor can be found outside Adventureland, and the only one where it can be topped with pink frosted animal crackers and marshmallow sauce. Menchie's is located between the first and second levels of CityWalk, next to Bread Box, in the former home of Katie's Candy Co. The price? Grab a cup (or a waffle bowl), and everything is $0.59 an ounce, so you can pay as much—or as little—as you'd like.

Moe's Southwest Grill

LOCATION	Upper	Level	QUALITY	Good	VALUE	B	PORTION	Large

Selections Tacos, burritos, quesadillas, nachos, fajitas, and taco salads made with steak, ground beef, chicken, tofu, or vegetarian; chips and salsa; cookies; beer.

Comments The Mexican-food equivalent of a Subway sandwich shop. You place your order (for example, steak tacos) at the front of a long assembly line, and then follow your plate down the line as it's passed from worker to worker, each of whom adds whatever garnishes, sides, and sauces you want. We like Moe's quite a bit. The menu is filled with references to TV shows and movies, such as the Art Vandalay (from *Seinfeld*), Billy Barou (from *Caddyshack*), and John Coctostan (from *Fletch*).

Panda Express Gourmet Chinese Food

LOCATION	Upper	Level	QUALITY	Fair	VALUE	C	PORTION	Medium–Large

Selections Chinese food including entrées of sweet-and-sour chicken; orange chicken; kung pao chicken; beef and broccoli; beef with mushrooms and asparagus; honey walnut shrimp; eggplant tofu; mixed veggies; chow mein; white or fried rice.

Comments The kung pao chicken has a darker, smoky flavor than most we've tried, and the sauces are heavier than our local Chinese takeouts. Still, Panda Express is a hit with the kids in our group, who want to eat here every time they see it. Panda Express usually has the longest line of the three fast-food joints on City-Walk's upper level.

Starbucks Coffee

LOCATION	Lower	Level	QUALITY	Good	VALUE	C	PORTION	Medium

Selections Coffees and teas in many blends and flavors; espresso, cappuccino, frozen coffees, and smoothies; pastries; cookies; and sodas.

Comments While the Starbucks locations in Islands of Adventure, Universal Studios Florida, and Cabana Bay Beach Resort feature the chain's full sandwich menu, this particular Starbucks offers a more limited selection of pastries but does offer a large amount of seating (with free Wi-Fi and accessible power ports) both inside and out. Though this handsomely designed coffee shop has much more barista capacity than the average franchise, its ground-central location leads to long lines around park opening. *Note:* Starbucks loyalty stars can be earned at Universal locations, but rewards may not be redeemed here. Universal annual-pass discounts and Starbucks gift cards are honored here.

RESORT HOTELS

Bayliner Diner

LOCATION Universal's Cabana Bay Beach Resort	QUALITY Excellent	VALUE B+
PORTION Medium–Large		

Selections Cheeseburgers, veggie burgers, chicken sandwich, hot dogs, beef churrasco, beef stew, roasted chicken, tofu stir-fry, ginger salmon, pizza, pasta, flatbread, panini, wraps, salad, and frozen yogurt bars.

Comments Much like the Landscape of Flavors food court at Disney's Art of Animation, Cabana Bay's Bayliner Diner has several different stations offering a wide range of food options. The preparations are a cut above the counter service found inside the parks, and they pay homage to home-cooking classics like tuna noodle casserole and beef stew. The churrasco-style flat iron with creamy chimichurri sauce is surprisingly tender and tasty for counter-service steak. For breakfast, the diner serves up all the usual suspects. Get waffles or French toast, or wait for a made-to-order omelet, but avoid the precooked eggs on the combo platter and croissant sandwich. Bayliner Diner offers the first Universal on-site hotel refillable mug program (Sonic Fill), which works exactly like Disney's Rapid Fill program. The Sonic Fill mugs have RFID chips on the bottom that are programmed with how many days a guest has paid for. See details under "Refillable Drinks and Popcorn" on page 191. The seating area, filled with booths and tables, is large. Similar to the Sci-Fi Dine-In at Disney's Hollywood Studios, large screens play retro commercials to evoke a feeling of nostalgia. One thing noticeable is the amount of usable outlets to charge your phones and tablets, including one outside of every booth.

Emack & Bolio's Marketplace

LOCATION Hard Rock Hotel	QUALITY Good	VALUE C	PORTION Medium

Selections Ice cream, sorbet, frozen yogurt, sundaes, Starbucks coffee, sandwiches, candy, pizza, snacks, soft drinks, cereal, and pastries.

Comments Boston-based Emack & Bolio's has a long history of associating with rock stars (check out the memorabilia on the walls) and naming ice cream flavors after their songs. Here you can have a cone or sundae made from Jumping Jack Grasshopper Pie, Bye Bye Miss American Mud Pie, or Deep Purple Cow. This location also has a grab-and-go selection of snacks, cold breakfast foods, and Starbucks drinks to speed you through your morning, plus a small selection of sandwiches and takeout pizzas (in 10- or 16-inch pies) after noon.

Sal's Market Deli

LOCATION Portofino Bay Hotel	QUALITY Good–Excellent	VALUE C+
PORTION Medium–Large		

Selections Pizza, deli sandwiches, salads, wine, and beer.

Comments This casual counter-service deli and pizzeria is practically the only affordable option on Portofino Bay property. For breakfast (6–11 a.m.), it serves coffee, egg sandwiches, and Krispy Kreme doughnuts. At lunch and dinner, the pizza is the best in Universal outside of Red Oven and can be made with gluten-free dough. Around the corner, a full-service Starbucks with an attached *gelateria* and bakery serves breakfast and desserts. Food can be packaged and taken back to your room, undercutting the expensive room service.

UNIVERSAL ORLANDO FULL-SERVICE RESTAURANT PROFILES

TO HELP YOU MAKE CHOICES FOR SIT-DOWN meals at breakfast, lunch, or dinner, we've provided full profiles of Universal's full-service places, most of which are located in the CityWalk complex. Each profile lets you quickly check the restaurant's cuisine, location, star rating, cost range, quality rating, and value rating. Profiles are listed alphabetically by restaurant. In addition to all full-service restaurants, we also list and profile a few quick-service eateries around the resort that transcend basic burgers, hot dogs, and pizza.

STAR RATING

THE STAR RATING REPRESENTS THE ENTIRE dining experience: style, service, and ambience, in addition to taste, presentation, and food quality. Five stars, the highest rating, indicates that the restaurant offers the best of everything. Four-star restaurants are above average, and three-star restaurants offer good, though not necessarily memorable, meals. Two-star restaurants serve mediocre fare, and one-star restaurants are below par. Our star ratings don't correspond to ratings awarded by AAA, Mobil, Zagat, or other restaurant reviewers.

COST RANGE

THE NEXT RATING TELLS HOW MUCH a complete meal (a main dish with vegetable or side dish and a choice of soup or salad) will cost. Appetizers, desserts, drinks, and tips aren't included. We've rated the cost as inexpensive, moderate, or expensive.

Inexpensive	$15 or less per person
Moderate	$15–$28 per person
Expensive	More than $28 per person

QUALITY RATING

THE FOOD QUALITY IS RATED ON A SCALE of one to five stars, five being the best. The quality rating is based on the taste, freshness of ingredients, preparation, presentation, and creativity of food. There is no consideration of price. If you want the best food available and cost is no issue, look no further than the quality ratings.

VALUE RATING

IF, ON THE OTHER HAND, YOU ARE looking for both quality and value, check the value rating, also expressed as stars:

★★★★★	Exceptional value; a real bargain
★★★★	Good value
★★★	Fair value; you get exactly what you pay for
★★	Somewhat overpriced
★	Extremely overpriced

PAYMENT

ALL UNIVERSAL ORLANDO RESTAURANTS accept American Express, MasterCard, Visa, Discover, Diners Club, and Universal resort hotel-room charges.

Antojitos Authentic Mexican Food   ★★★½

MEXICAN	Moderate	QUALITY	★★★½	VALUE	★★★½

CityWalk ☎ 407-224-3663

Customers Locals and tourists. **Reservations** Accepted via NexTable. **When to go** Lunch or dinner. **Entrée range** $14–$27. **Service rating** ★★★. **Friendliness rating** ★★★★. **Parking** Universal Orlando garage. **Bar** Full service. **Wine selection** Good. **Dress** Casual; *luchador* masks and sombreros optional. **Disabled access** Good. **Hours** Sunday–Thursday, 11 a.m.–11 p.m.; Friday–Saturday, 11 a.m.–midnight.

SETTING AND ATMOSPHERE This festive postmodern tribute to Mexican street culture features a large open kitchen framed by graffiti graphics and eye-catching neon, with the central bar and surrounding booths fashioned from reclaimed wood and metal. The downstairs can get very noisy, so if you want a quieter meal, ask for one of the private rooms upstairs. Or grab a seat on the patio or balcony to watch the CityWalk crowds go by.

HOUSE SPECIALTIES Guacamole prepared table-side, empanadas, roasted corn *esquites*, quesadillas, enchiladas, tacos, fajitas, pan-roasted mahi, seafood stew, roast pork loin, churrasco steak, and *cajeta de leche* cake with sour cream ice cream.

ENTERTAINMENT AND AMENITIES A modern mariachi ensemble plays outside and inside the restaurant.

SUMMARY AND COMMENTS The colorful Antojitos sits in the former home of The Latin Quarter, next to Jimmy Buffett's Margaritaville. A Universal Studios concept, Antojitos offers unique and crave-able tapas-style Mexican food, featuring hand-crafted tortillas, made-while-you-watch guacamole, and fresh sauces for a taste of Mexico City without the high crime rate.

For starters, you'll probably want a drink, and Antojitos has Orlando's best tequila selection this side of Epcot's La Cava. Order from the four-sided bar on the ground floor or from the converted Volkswagen bus outside the entrance. If you don't do straight shots, try a signature drink such as the Handsome George (made with George Clooney's own brand) or The Horse You Rode In On (garnished with an expensive Amarena black cherry).

When it comes to the food, while it's pricier than your local taco joint, Antojitos prepares familiar plates with exceptionally fresh ingredients. The table-side guacamole is a must-have that will convert the most hardened avocado-hater, and the *esquites asados* (roasted corn with *queso fresco* and jalapeño mayo) is almost a meal in itself. The portion sizes of the enchiladas and tacos aren't enormous, but you'll probably be full after the free chips (served hot with house-made salsa) and the excellent rice and black beans accompanying most entrées. The *comidas de la casa* include some holdovers from the short-lived upscale menu briefly served on the second floor; the churrasco steak and pork loin are wonderfully seasoned, though the pork can be a bit dry. Leave room for dessert because the sour cream ice cream served with the molten *cajeta de leche* cake will make you shout, "Ay, caramba!"

Bice ★★★★½

Italian	Expensive	QUALITY	★★★★½	VALUE	★★★★

Portofino Bay Hotel ☎ 407-503-1415

Customers Locals and tourists. **Reservations** Recommended via Open Table. **When to go** Dinner. **Entrée range** $19–$49. **Service rating** ★★★★★. **Friendliness rating** ★★★★. **Parking** $5 valet or free self-parking at hotel with validation. **Bar** Full service. **Wine selection** Very good. **Dress** Resort dressy. **Disabled access** Good. **Hours** Daily, 5:30–10 p.m.

SETTING AND ATMOSPHERE Cedarwood and marble floors, crisp white linens, opulent flower arrangements, and waiters in black suits give Bice ("beach-ay") the feeling of a formal restaurant, but there is nothing stiff or fussy about the space or the staff. It is immaculately clean, beautifully lit, and relatively quiet even when it's crowded. Outdoor seating overlooking the bay is available and is lovely during spring and fall evenings.

HOUSE SPECIALTIES Menu changes seasonally; selections may include prosciutto with fresh melon and baby greens; homemade braised beef spareribs ravioli with spinach in mushroom-Marsala sauce; veal Milanese with a Roma tomato and Kalamata olive Tuscan salad; or risotto of the day.

ENTERTAINMENT AND AMENITIES Piano in bar.

SUMMARY AND COMMENTS This is part of a chain of very upscale and quite impressive restaurants found in New York, Tokyo, Las Vegas, and other international locales. The food is incredibly fresh, well prepared, and elegant, and the service is top-notch. But be prepared: Even a modest meal will put a dent in your wallet, and even though the food and service are definitely worth it, it may be too expensive for many vacationers. If you want to try a variety of things on the menu, split a salad, appetizer, or pasta dish between two people for a starter; portions are large enough for sharing, and the staff is more than happy to accommodate.

Our favorite appetizers are the mussels with lemon butter sauce, and the Mediterranean seafood salad, which is served inside a large, scooped-out tomato. The other appetizers, mostly salads and antipasti of meats and cheeses, aren't bad, but you've probably had something similar already.

The best entrée is the roasted duck breast, topped with a truffle-oil glaze and accompanied by a small cheese soufflé. Also good is the breaded veal, pounded so thin that it takes up almost the entire plate. It's served with a small salad on top, and the salad's dressing serves to keep the veal juicy. The penne *all' arrabbiatta* is even spicier than advertised.

We rate Bice as one of the best restaurants in all of Universal Resort, and it compares favorably to any of the similar restaurants at Walt Disney World. Because the Portofino gets a lot of business-convention traffic, it's probably easier to get a reservation at 5:30 p.m. than 7:30 p.m. As for reservations, you can make them in person, over the phone, or online at **opentable.com.**

Bob Marley—A Tribute to Freedom ★★½

Jamaican/Caribbean	Moderate	QUALITY	★★★	VALUE	★★★

CityWalk ☎ 407-224-3663

Customers Locals and tourists. **Reservations** Accepted via NexTable. **When to go** Early evening. **Entrée range** $9–$17. **Service rating** ★★. **Friendliness rating** ★★★. **Parking** Universal Orlando garage. **Bar** Full service. **Wine selection** Poor. **Dress** Casual; dreadlocks if you have them. **Disabled access** Good. **Hours** Sunday–Thursday, 4–10 p.m.; Friday–Saturday, 4–11 p.m.

SETTING AND ATMOSPHERE Set in a replica of reggae singer Bob Marley's Jamaican home, the building is filled with memorabilia and photos showcasing his career and life. Lots of lions, the colors of the Jamaican flag, and other Rastafarian influences pay tribute to the musician's career. Most of the area is open to the elements, and there's no air-conditioning, though there are shelters from the occasional rainstorm.

HOUSE SPECIALTIES Jerk-marinated chicken breast; smoky white-Cheddar cheese fondue; Jamaican vegetable patties; beef patties; yucca fries; oxtail stew.

ENTERTAINMENT AND AMENITIES Live reggae band and DJ in courtyard nightly; cover charge after 9 p.m.

SUMMARY AND COMMENTS None of the food is spectacular or particularly adventurous, but it's worth it for the laid-back atmosphere. Sure, you're allowed to get up and dance.

The Bubba Gump Shrimp Co. Restaurant & Market ★★½

Southern/Seafood	Moderate	QUALITY	★★★	VALUE	★★

CityWalk ☎ 407-903-0044

Customers Tourists. **Reservations** Not accepted. **When to go** Anytime. **Entrée range** $10–$23. **Service rating** ★★★. **Friendliness rating** ★★★★. **Parking** Universal Orlando garage. **Bar** Full service. **Wine selection** Minimal. **Dress** Casual. **Disabled access** Good. **Hours** Daily, 11 a.m.–midnight.

SETTING AND ATMOSPHERE The movie that inspired the chain, *Forrest Gump,* plays on TVs throughout, but without sound, just subtitles. Movie memorabilia decorates the wooden walls of this seafood shanty. License plates that say RUN FORREST RUN on one side and STOP FORREST STOP on another help signal a waiter when you need service, and the waiters will ask you trivia questions from the movie.

HOUSE SPECIALTIES Fried, stuffed, or grilled shrimp (and shrimp cooked almost every other way); burgers; salads; grilled salmon; fried chicken; baby back ribs. A gluten-free menu is also offered.

SUMMARY AND COMMENTS The theme may seem a little cheesy, but this is a fun and festive atmosphere to bring the kids. The food is no worse than your average seafood chain (think Red Lobster without the cheese biscuits) and is not too spicy.

Confisco Grille ★★★

American	Moderate	QUALITY	★★★	VALUE	★★★

Islands of Adventure/Port of Entry ☎ 407-224-4012

Customers Park guests. **Reservations** Accepted via NexTable. **When to go** Anytime. **Entrée range** $9–$17. **Service rating** ★★★. **Friendliness rating** ★★★★. **Parking**

Universal Orlando garage. **Bar** Full service. **Wine selection** Moderate. **Dress** Casual. **Disabled access** Good. **Hours** 11 a.m.–park closing.

SETTING AND ATMOSPHERE A way station on the road to Morocco, perhaps? Actually, it's meant to look like a customs house. Look for "smuggled goods," representing the park's various islands, decorating the lobby's upper level. You'll see giant dinosaur skeletons from Jurassic Park, golden urns from Lost Continent, and even a wand from The Wizarding World of Harry Potter if you look hard enough.

HOUSE SPECIALTIES Wood-grilled pizzas; hummus served with a puffy lavash bread larger than most human heads; selection of salads; beef and chicken fajitas; grilled sandwiches and burgers; pad Thai.

SUMMARY AND COMMENTS Confisco isn't fine dining, but it does fine when you just can't stand in another line. Because of its varied menu of Mediterranean, Italian, Mexican, and Asian dishes, most people should find something to please them at Confisco Grille. Wood-grilled pizzas have a pleasing crust—check with your server to find out the daily special pies. Several options on the menu can be made vegetarian and vegan friendly. The adjoining Backwater Bar has happy hour 4–7 p.m. daily, with $3.75 draft Buds and red sangria and $4.25 well cocktails.

The Cowfish ★★★★

American/Sushi	Moderate	QUALITY	★★★★	VALUE	★★★½

CityWalk ☎ 407-224-2275

Customers Locals and park guests. **Reservations** Not accepted. **When to go** Early afternoon or late evening. **Entrée range** $12–$27. **Service rating** ★★½. **Friendliness rating** ★★★★. **Parking** Universal Orlando garage. **Bar** Full service. **Wine selection** Good. **Dress** Resort casual. **Disabled access** Good. **Hours** Sunday–Thursday, 11 a.m.–11 p.m.; Friday–Saturday, 11 a.m.–midnight.

SETTING AND ATMOSPHERE A photo op of this restaurant's mascot—a giant bug-eyed fish with a riding saddle on its back—should clue you in that this isn't the spot for stuffy food snobs. The Cowfish takes irreverent postmodernism and cranks it up to 11 with colorful Pop Art, larger-than-life displays (including Universal icon King Kong and a noodle-filled fishbowl), and silly signage—be sure to check out the restrooms. Guests can enter though the small lobby on the ground floor or the patio bar on the upper level; all seating—both indoors and outdoors—is on the second and third floor, offering spectacular views over CityWalk.

Aside from table seating, there are multiple bars at Cowfish. Another great thing Cowfish has going for it—especially if you dine with young children in your party—are the distractions throughout the restaurant. These include touch screen games and a make-your-own-fish app, which you can then watch swim in a virtual aquarium.

HOUSE SPECIALTIES Crab Rangoon dip, blackened tuna nachos, half-pound burgers, sushi and sashimi combos, fusion and "burgushi" rolls and bento boxes, handspun milk shakes, specialty cocktails, and spiked shakes.

SUMMARY AND COMMENTS The Cowfish was the final piece of Universal CityWalk's 2014 renovation that brought eight new dining venues to the resort. A one-of-a-kind dining concept that melds pan-Asian cuisine with the good ol' American burger, Cowfish was bringing something completely unique to the table. We were initially nervous about the fusion of a burger joint and a sushi place because it just seemed too out there. But it turns out that the folks behind this tiny North Carolina–based chain are really on to something: Like peanut butter and chocolate, The Cowfish's burgers and sushi both taste great, and taste great together.

The voluminous menu starts with familiar-sounding appetizers, such as Parmesan truffle fries and tuna nachos, expertly prepared and presented in generous portions (a recurring theme). Next comes an extensive list of half-pound hormone-free hamburgers, with names such as the Jalapeño Popper Show-Stopper, Big Squeal, and Rise & Swine. Veggie and turkey burgers are also available, and all are served with seasoned fries, which can be substituted with seaweed salad, bacon coleslaw, or edamame. The Boursin Bacon Burger, with garlic-herb cheese and sautéed mushrooms, is a standout. Traditional sushi selections range from chef combos of sashimi and *nigiri*, classic makimono rolls, and fusion specialties stuffed with tuna, coconut shrimp, shiitake mushrooms, or crabmeat; the premium tuna and salmon on Jen's Fresh Find roll was particularly flavorful.

Finally, we arrive at the creative center of Cowfish's menu: the burgushi. You can try a sushi roll made with lobster and filet mignon (The Prime Time), bison and fried green tomatoes (BuffalOOOO-shi), or pulled pork and barbecue sauce (High Class Hillbilly). On the flip side, "pick-ups" feature steak and pastrami or rare tuna, sandwiched between spring roll wrapper "buns" filled with sushi rice and *kani* (fake crab). Despite the bizarro pairing, all the ones we've sampled have been as delicious as they are odd, which is saying something; Doug's Filet roll (with ginger dipping sauce for the steak) is a safe bet. If you are still apprehensive, try a bento box, which brings a slider mini-burger, sushi roll, and several side dishes together on a Japanese TV-dinner tray.

If you still can't stomach The Cowfish's burgushi concept, you can still take comfort in its extensive craft cocktail list, including a bourbon and candied bacon concoction, and old-fashioned "mules" made with ginger beer. Hand-spun milk shakes (nonalcoholic or spiked) headline the dessert menu, which also features sushi-shaped pastries exclusive to the Orlando location.

The Cowfish has quickly become one of our favorite dining venues in Orlando. The menu is creative, the flavors are fantastic, and the drinks are worth going out of your way to try. We love the overall atmosphere, but the time that it takes for a meal to come out can be inexplicably long. Currently, the restaurant doesn't take reservations, and the wait can be long on a busy weekend, but the host will take your cell phone number when you check in, allowing them to text you when your table is ready. In addition, a free app for Apple and Android phones will let you join the wait list from anywhere within a half-mile of the restaurant; use it to check in while exiting a ride, but be sure to check in once you arrive because the app isn't prompt at letting you know your table is ready.

Emeril's Restaurant Orlando ★★★★

Southern	Expensive	QUALITY	★★★★	VALUE	★★★½

CityWalk ☎ 407-224-2424

Customers Locals and park guests. **Reservations** Required via Open Table. **When to go** Lunch; early or late evening. **Entrée range** $21–$45. **Service rating** ★★★★. **Friendliness rating** ★★★★. **Parking** Universal Orlando garage; check with restaurant about validation for valet during lunch. **Bar** Full service. **Wine selection** Very good. **Dress** Casual to dressy. **Disabled access** Good. **Hours** Sunday–Thursday, 11:30 a.m.–3 p.m. and 5–10 p.m.; Friday–Saturday, 11:30 a.m.–3 p.m. and 5–10:30 p.m.

SETTING AND ATMOSPHERE Not to be confused with Emeril's Asian-inspired Tchoup Chop at the nearby Royal Pacific Resort, Emeril's Orlando, the Florida outpost of Emeril Lagasse's New Orleans restaurant, has probably the best food and best wine list within CityWalk. The food is Louisiana-style with creative flair. The main dining room is two stories high and features hardwood floors, wooden beams, and stone walls, all of which act as sounding boards for the noisy dining room. Sliding glass doors lead to the kitchen, where Emeril probably won't be cooking. Part of the kitchen is open, and there are eight seats at a food bar—some of the best seats in the house.

HOUSE SPECIALTIES The menu changes frequently. The smoked wild and exotic mushroom appetizer is one of the menu highlights. The banana cream pie will renew your faith in humanity. Items that might be available include gumbo, slow-braised lamb shank, and andouille-crusted redfish.

SUMMARY AND COMMENTS Owner Emeril Lagasse gained popularity from his show on Food Network, and his restaurants were instant hits. But the food proves he's more than a flash in the proverbial pan. Lagasse also has restaurants in New Orleans and Las Vegas, so it's unlikely that he'll be on the premises, though he does visit sometimes. But even when he's not there, you're in for some good eating.

If you want a taste of Emeril's "bam" without the big bill, the lunch menu offers entrées such as shrimp and grits or mussels and *frites* for a more digestible $14–$19. Specials frequently offer a free appetizer or dessert with any entrée purchase for valid park-admission holders (including annual-pass holders), and a daily happy hour at the bar 4–8 p.m., with half-priced drinks and affordable small plates, can also soften the sting.

Note: Last-minute reservations may be hard to come by during peak season or major conventions. To get a table on the same day as your visit, check Open Table or call the restaurant at 3:15 p.m. and inquire about cancellations.

Emeril's Tchoup Chop ★★★★

Pan-Asian	Expensive	QUALITY	★★★★	VALUE	★★★★

Royal Pacific Resort ☎ 407-224-2467

Customers Locals and hotel guests. **Reservations** Required via Open Table. **When to go** Lunch or dinner. **Entrée range** $24–$34. **Service rating** ★★★★. **Friendliness rating** ★★★★. **Parking** Free valet parking available at Royal Pacific's convention entrance (don't pull up to the front lobby). **Bar** Full service. **Wine selection** Very good. **Dress** Smart casual to dressy. No sleeveless men's shirts. **Disabled access** Good. **Hours** Sunday–Thursday, 11:30 a.m.–2:30 p.m. and 5–10 p.m.; Friday–Saturday, 11:30 a.m.–2:30 p.m. and 5–10 p.m.

SETTING AND ATMOSPHERE A cavernous space on the bottom floor of the Royal Pacific, with painted concrete floors and tall ceilings. Tchoup Chop features an open kitchen with seating where you can watch your food being made. A glass and wood partition separates the bar from the main dining room, and there's an outdoor bar just a few feet from Tchoup Chop's entrance too.

HOUSE SPECIALTIES The menu changes frequently. Lunch offerings include rice and noodle bowls, large salads, and sandwiches. Dinner features *robata*-grilled vegetables, sushi (*nigiri* and maki), Korean fried chicken, smoked duck, and blackened fish.

SUMMARY AND COMMENTS Long a dark horse favorite among local foodies, Tchoup Chop's new chef de cuisine Ryan Vargas reinvigorated the restaurant in 2014, renovating its kitchen with an expanded sushi bar—rolling creatively over-stuffed maki such as the Red Dragon (tuna, panko shrimp, and habanero mayo) or Surf & Turf (blue crab, hibachi steak, and truffle oil)—and one of central

Florida's only *robata* grills, capable of searing small morsels (such as pork belly *tocino* or randomly spicy *shishito* peppers) at a scorching 1,000°F.

The best appetizer is still the deliciously messy kiawe-smoked baby back ribs, which are often discounted during the bar's daily (5–8 p.m.) happy hour and are Royal Pacific's best-kept culinary secret.

The beef and duck entrées stand out more than the seafood or vegetarian dishes, which is a bit surprising for a restaurant that bills itself as Asian/Polynesian fusion. The roasted duck breast was the hit of the meal. If you have your heart set on seafood, the cedar-wrapped salmon or sesame tuna is your best bet.

The bartenders seem to have a slightly better grasp of the wine list than some of the waitstaff. Don't be shy about asking one of the bar staff for a wine recommendation.

Finnegan's Bar & Grill   ★★½

Irish	Moderate	QUALITY	★★★	VALUE	★★½

Universal Studios/New York ☎ 407-363-8757

Customers Park guests. **Reservations** Accepted via NexTable. **When to go** Anytime. **Entrée range** $11–$22. **Service rating** ★★★. **Friendliness rating** ★★★★. **Parking** Universal Orlando garage. **Bar** Full service. **Wine selection** Limited. Ireland is not really known for its wines; good beer selection, though. **Dress** Casual. **Disabled access** Good. **Hours** Daily, 11 a.m.–park closing.

SETTING AND ATMOSPHERE Fashioned after an Irish bar in New York City, albeit one built as a movie set. Along with the requisite publike accoutrements—such as the tin ceiling and belt-driven paddle fans—are movie lights and half walls that suggest the back of scenery flats. Obligatory references to Guinness beer and New York City abound. The bar area is a popular gathering spot for locals and gets insanely busy during special events like Halloween.

HOUSE SPECIALTIES Shepherd's pie; fish-and-chips; Guinness beef stew; bangers and mash; Dingle seafood pie; Irish coffee.

ENTERTAINMENT AND AMENITIES Singer/guitarist in the bar.

SUMMARY AND COMMENTS The food is modest, but the entertainment is fun and the beer is cold; brew fans can happily explore a five-sample flight of international ales as they rest from the park. Add to that the fact that this is one of only two full-service spots in Universal Studios Florida, and the average pub fare starts to look a bit more attractive.

The fish-and-chips, which come wrapped in "newspaper," are about the same as those served in The Wizarding World. The Scotch egg was a dry disappointment, and the shepherd's pie was bland, but the potato-leek soup is good, and the fried potato/onion "web" is addictive. For entrées, burgers, sandwiches, salads, and Guinness stew are safe choices.

Galaxy Bowl   ★★

American	Inexpensive	QUALITY	★★½	VALUE	★★½

Cabana Bay Beach Resort ☎ 407-503-4000

Customers Park guests. **Reservations** Accepted via Open Table. **When to go** Early afternoon or late evening. **Entrée range** $6–$10. **Service rating** ★★. **Friendliness rating** ★★★. **Parking** $20 for self-parking at hotel. **Bar** Full service. **Wine selection** Limited. **Dress** Casual. **Disabled access** Good. **Hours** Daily, 11 a.m.–10 p.m.

SETTING AND ATMOSPHERE Galaxy Bowl, located on the second floor of the main Cabana Bay building directly above Starbucks, is the only full-service dining option inside the hotel. The 10-lane bowling alley is inspired by the Hollywood Star Lanes bowling alley, made famous in the film *The Big Lebowski*. The lanes are illuminated in trippy colors at night, and large projection screens broadcast sporting events.

HOUSE SPECIALTIES Chicken quesadillas, chicken wings, salads, sandwiches, hot dogs, burgers, and pizza.

ENTERTAINMENT AND AMENITIES Bowling costs $15 for adults, $9 for kids age 12 and under. Parties of one to three people get one hour of lane time; four to eight people get 90 minutes.

SUMMARY AND COMMENTS Some people enjoy the athleticism of basketball, while others admire the grace and skill of soccer, but we at the Unofficials favor bowling as our preferred sport, as it is the only one in which you can participate while eating chili cheese fries. Galaxy Bowl has several tables where you can enjoy a meal, but you can also order snacks and drinks while taking in a game of bowling. When the wait for a lane grows long (as it often does on rainy days), ask for a table, and order drinks and appetizers until your turn arrives.

The limited menu offers fast-food selections similar to items served downstairs in the Bayliner Diner, and quality is about on par for greasy bowling-alley grub. Draft beer is served in pitchers, and the list of specialty drinks is nearly as long as the food menu. The 300, a 32-ounce mega-margarita made with blood oranges, probably won't help your score much, but it will numb the embarrassment of those gutter balls. There are two Coke Freestyle machines at Galaxy Bowl for your Sonic Fill mugs.

Hard Rock Cafe ★★★

American	Moderate	QUALITY	★★★	VALUE	★★★

CityWalk ☎ 407-351-7625

Customers Tourists. **Reservations** Priority seating. **When to go** Afternoon or evening. **Entrée range** $10–$35. **Service rating** ★★★. **Friendliness rating** ★★. **Parking** Universal Orlando garage. **Bar** Full service. **Wine selection** Moderate. **Dress** Casual. **Disabled access** Good. **Hours** Daily, 11 a.m.–midnight.

SETTING AND ATMOSPHERE This is the biggest Hard Rock Cafe in the world (or in the Universe, as they like to say in this part of town). Shaped like the Coliseum, the two-story dining room is a massive museum of rock art memorabilia. The circular center bar features a full-size pink 1959 Cadillac spinning overhead. If you need to be told that this is a noisy restaurant, you've never been to a Hard Rock Cafe before. Everyone, however, should visit a Hard Rock at least once.

HOUSE SPECIALTIES Barbecue pork sandwich, charbroiled burgers, barbecued ribs, grilled fajitas, New York strip steak, hot fudge brownie, and milk shakes.

ENTERTAINMENT AND AMENITIES Rock-and-roll records and memorabilia, the biggest such collection on display anywhere in the Hard Rock chain. Ask at the check-in podium about free guided tours of the restaurant; if you're lucky, you may get a glimpse of the VIP-only John Lennon room upstairs.

SUMMARY AND COMMENTS The best meals we've had here are when we order only appetizers or only desserts, and drinks. The entrées are average, and you'd be hard-pressed to differentiate them from anything you'd get at, say, Margaritaville.

Hard Rock Cafe offers a 15% discount on food for Preferred and Premier Annual Pass holders before 5 p.m.; AAA and military discounts apply all day. You can sign up for a Hard Rock Rewards membership to get additional offers and earn points on purchases (including alcohol). Be aware that admission to the adjoining Hard Rock Live concert hall is completely separate from the restaurant, though you can sometimes order food from the venue's bar.

Islands Dining Room ★★★

Pan-Asian	Moderate	QUALITY	★★★½	VALUE	★★★

Royal Pacific Resort ☎ 407-503-DINE (3463)

Customers Hotel guests. **Reservations** Suggested for character dining and during holidays via Open Table. **When to go** Breakfast or character dinners. **Entrée range Breakfast**, $12–$17; **dinner**, $16–$30. **Service rating ★★★. Friendliness rating ★★★. Parking** Free self-parking at hotel with validation. **Bar** Full service. **Wine selection** Average. **Dress** Casual. **Disabled access** Good. **Hours** Monday–Friday, 7–11 a.m. and 5–10 p.m.; Saturday–Sunday, 7 a.m.–noon and 5–10 p.m.

SETTING AND ATMOSPHERE Pretty standard hotel dining room; big and open, and always spotless.

HOUSE SPECIALTIES Breakfast features waffles with mixed berries, Tahitian French toast à l'orange, and Hawaiian pancakes. Dinner options include family-style stir-fry, chicken wonton soup, seafood noodle pot, and Asian spice–rubbed rib eye.

ENTERTAINMENT AND AMENITIES Character dining is available on Monday, Wednesday, and Thursday nights 6:30–9:30 p.m.

SUMMARY AND COMMENTS Breakfast here is a treat—the specialties are all tasty and (surprisingly) moderately priced. Dinner is good too, but with all the other restaurants around, especially if you're spending the day in the parks, we suggest having a hearty breakfast here and an evening meal elsewhere. The exception is if you have kids who want to dine with the characters, who appear here three nights a week at no extra charge; children also get their own special dining area with downsized tables and a finger food buffet.

Jake's American Bar ★★★

American	Moderate	QUALITY	★★★	VALUE	★★½

Royal Pacific Resort ☎ 407-503-3200

Customers Hotel guests. **Reservations** Accepted via Open Table. **When to go** Early or late evening. **Entrée range** $13–$35. **Service rating ★★★. Friendliness rating ★★★. Parking** Free self-parking at hotel with validation. **Bar** Full service. **Wine selection** Average. **Dress** Resort casual. **Disabled access** Good. **Hours** Daily, 11 a.m.–1:30 a.m.

SETTING AND ATMOSPHERE Run-of-the-mill hotel bar and restaurant with a vaguely 1930s "Rick's Cafe" feel. The menu explains the backstory of Captain Jake McNalley and his association with Royal Pacific Airways, continuing the overall theme of the resort, which centers on the golden age of travel.

HOUSE SPECIALTIES Homemade pretzel rods, charcuterie, kale salad, flatbreads, pork osso buco, rib eye and *frites,* grilled salmon, and grilled tomato-and-mozzarella sandwich.

ENTERTAINMENT AND AMENITIES Live music or karaoke Thursday–Sunday; character breakfast on Sundays.

SUMMARY AND COMMENTS This is a viable option if you're staying in the hotel, but as far as special meals go, this place doesn't deliver—and really isn't meant to. Jake's hosts the hotels' only weekly character breakfast every Sunday morning; see "Character Meals" on page 183 for details.

Beer lovers will want to check out the four-sample flights, as well as the four-course pairing parties held on select nights. Jake's serves a limited late-night menu 10 p.m.–1:30 a.m. and is usually the only restaurant at the resort serving hot food after midnight.

Jimmy Buffett's Margaritaville ★★★

Caribbean/American	Moderate	QUALITY	★★★	VALUE	★★★

CityWalk ☎ 407-224-2155

Customers Local and tourist Parrotheads. **Reservations** Accepted via Open Table. **When to go** Early evening. **Entrée range** $13–$24. **Service rating** ★★★. **Friendliness rating** ★★★★. **Parking** Universal Orlando garage. **Bar** Full service. **Wine selection** Minimal. **Dress** Flowered shirts and flip-flops. **Disabled access** Good. **Hours** Sunday–Thursday, 11 a.m.–1 a.m.; Friday–Saturday, 11 a.m.–2 a.m.

SETTING AND ATMOSPHERE A boisterous tribute to the chief Parrothead, this two-story dining space has many large-screen TVs playing Jimmy Buffett music videos and scenes from his live performances. The focal point is a volcano that erupts occasionally, spewing margarita mix instead of lava.

HOUSE SPECIALTIES Cheeseburgers and margaritas, of course; fish tacos; jambalaya; coconut shrimp; Key lime pie.

ENTERTAINMENT AND AMENITIES Live music on the porch early; band on inside stage late evening.

SUMMARY AND COMMENTS This is a relaxing, festive place, but it's not always worth the wait (especially if it's two hours, which it has been known to be). This place is wildly popular with Jimmy Buffett fans, who stand in line just to get a beeper, so they can stand in line some more and wait for a table. The atmosphere, though, is like a taste of the beach without having to travel to the coast.

The food is a mix of Floridian and Caribbean, so expect lots of seafood and Jamaican seasoning. The food is good, but not good enough for non-Buffett fans to make a special trip. If the line for a table is outrageous, see if you can sidle up to the bar for a margarita and appetizers, which is just as much—if not more—fun than actually having a full meal. None of the entrées, including the cheeseburger, will make you think that you're in paradise, but fans don't seem to care.

The Kitchen ★★★½

American	Moderate	QUALITY	★★★	VALUE	★★★

Hard Rock Hotel ☎ 407-503-DINE (3463)

Customers Tourists. **Reservations** Recommended via Open Table. **When to go** Breakfast or dinner. **Entrée range** $15–$37. **Service rating** ★★. **Friendliness rating** ★★★★. **Parking** $5 valet or free self-parking at hotel with validation. **Bar** Full service. **Wine selection** Good. **Dress** Casual. **Disabled access** Good. **Hours** Daily, 7 a.m.–11 p.m.

SETTING AND ATMOSPHERE With the appearance of a spacious kitchen in a rock megastar's mansion, The Kitchen's walls are adorned with culinary-themed memorabilia from the Hard Rock Hotel's many celebrity guests. A colorful "kids' crib" adorned with beanbag chairs and televisions allows the adults to eat in peace.

HOUSE SPECIALTIES Breakfast choices include eggs Benedict, spinach-and-sausage frittata, and custom omelets. The lunch menu has salads, burgers, flatbreads, three-cheese mac and cheese, and chicken pot pie. At dinner, seared ahi tuna, crab cakes, shrimp tacos, and boneless short ribs are served. A gluten-free menu is available.

ENTERTAINMENT AND AMENITIES Rock stars occasionally visit to cook their specialties; signed aprons and rock memorabilia hang on the walls. Character dining is offered Saturday, 6–9 p.m., and a magician performs table-side on Friday, 6–9 p.m. On Tuesday and Thursday, Kids Can Cook their own pizzas or quesadillas 5–7 p.m. For adults, Re-Wine on Monday and Wednesday offers $35 flights and discounted bottles.

SUMMARY AND COMMENTS Though we must admit that our expectations weren't too high for this Hard Rock venture, we were pleasantly surprised with the food and service here. Though expensive, the food is actually quite good, and the setting is pretty fun. The 10-ounce Angus beef Kitchen Burger will set you back about $18, but the regular version is just as tasty and less expensive. Brave and/or crazy souls can take part in the Kitchen Sink Challenge, which consists of eating The Kitchen burger, a side of fries, a fried pickle, and the humongous Kitchen Sink cake within a 30-minute time limit. Visiting rock stars often perform cooking demonstrations of their favorite dishes at the Chef's Table, so call ahead to see if any rock stars will be in the kitchen—you may find yourself having dinner with Joan Jett or Bob Seger. If dinner is a little out of your price range but you still want the experience, visit at lunchtime or go for the $19.50 breakfast buffet ($10 for kids), which includes a host of fresh, yummy selections and an omelet station; for $31.50, adults can upgrade to unlimited Bloody Marys and mimosas, always a smart choice before walking around a hot theme park all day.

Leaky Cauldron ★★★½

British	Inexpensive	QUALITY	★★★½	VALUE	★★★★

Universal Studios/The Wizarding World of Harry Potter–Diagon Alley
☎ 407-224-4012

Customers Park guests. **Reservations** Breakfast only. **When to go** Early or late. **Entrée range** $9–$20. **Service rating** ★★★. **Friendliness rating** ★★★★. **Parking** Universal Orlando garage. **Bar** Beer and wine only. **Wine selection** Limited. **Dress** Casual. **Disabled access** Good. **Hours** Daily, Park opening–10:30 a.m. and 11 a.m.–park closing.

SETTING AND ATMOSPHERE Modeled after the Leaky Cauldron in the Harry Potter books and films, this table-service restaurant is the flagship diner of Diagon Alley. A haunt of wizards, Leaky Cauldron was located outside The Wizarding World on Charing Cross Road in the novels and movies but is located inside Diagon Alley in the Universal Studios version. (You can find a non-opening replica of the pub door from the original film just outside Diagon Alley, tucked between the bookstore and record shop.) To get a sense of what the restaurant looks like, check out "Prisoner of Azkaban—The Leaky Cauldron" on **youtube.com.**

Meals are ordered and drinks received at a counter; then you are seated with a candle, which helps servers deliver food directly to your table.

HOUSE SPECIALTIES Breakfast specialties include English bacon, black pudding, baked beans, and grilled tomato; pancakes with bacon; and an egg, leek, and mushroom pasty with breakfast potatoes. Lunch and dinner selections feature bangers and mash, cottage pie, toad-in-the-hole, Guinness stew, fish-and-chips, shepherd's pie, and a ploughman's platter for two of Scotch eggs and imported cheeses.

SUMMARY AND COMMENTS Diagon Alley's flagship restaurant, the Leaky Cauldron serves hearty British pub fare similar to that of the Three Broomsticks but with even more authentically Anglo favorites. You can reserve breakfast by booking through your travel agent or the ticket desk at your Universal resort hotel; walk-ins for day guests are also usually available. The morning menu costs $16 for adults ($12.39 for kids) with a small drink and has a similar mix of American and British breakfast foods to Three Broomsticks. The breakfast is fair at best; the blood sausage and beans aren't bad if you have a taste for them, but the scrambled eggs are awful, and the oatmeal outrageously overpriced, making the quichelike mushroom pasty your best bet. Before you ask, yes, you can have hot or cold Butterbeer for breakfast. If you want to eat breakfast here, do it as late in the morning as possible; your early-entry time is better spent riding Harry Potter and the Escape from Gringotts.

The star of the lunch and dinner menu is the ploughman's platter for two, with an array of gloriously stinky imported cheeses. The bangers are also bang on, whether ordered with mash, in a sandwich, or (best of all) baked into a toad-in-the-hole with Yorkshire pudding. The fish-and-chips are the same as those served in Hogsmeade, as is the soup and salad (which isn't vegan). The fisherman's pie is extremely salty, as is the Guinness stew, which comes served in a nearly inedible bread bowl. Top off your meal with chocolate potted cream or sticky toffee pudding for dessert. Children's menu items include macaroni and cheese, fish-and-chips, and mini meat pies (for your budding *Sweeney Todd* enthusiast).

Leaky Cauldron can be overwhelmed by Diagon Alley crowds. To avoid long waits, eat early or late.

Lombard's Seafood Grille ★★★

Seafood	Moderate	QUALITY	★★★½	VALUE	★★★

Universal Studios/San Francisco ☎ 407-224-6401

Customers Park guests. **Reservations** Recommended via NexTable. **When to go** Anytime. **Entrée range** $13–$20. **Service rating** ★★★. **Friendliness rating** ★★★. **Parking** Universal Orlando garage. **Bar** Full service. **Wine selection** Good. **Dress** Casual. **Disabled access** Good. **Hours** Daily, 11:30 a.m.–2 hours before park closes or park closing, depending on park attendance. Call to verify hours, as there is no set schedule.

SETTING AND ATMOSPHERE Situated on the park's main lagoon, Lombard's looks like a converted wharf-side warehouse. The centerpiece of the brick-walled room is a huge aquarium with bubble glass windows. A fish-sculpture fountain greets guests, and private dining rooms upstairs have balconies that overlook the park.

HOUSE SPECIALTIES Stuffed portobello mushrooms, crab-cake sandwich, shrimp mac and cheese, lobster roll, fried shrimp, beef medallions, and fresh fish selections.

SUMMARY AND COMMENTS Universal Studios Florida's San Francisco–inspired seafood restaurant, where the emphasis is on deep-fried favorites and daily fresh fish specials. Originally an attempt at in-park fine dining, with whole live lobsters formerly on the menu, Lombard's Seafood Grille now has a more casual focus. Unfortunately, so does the kitchen. There are arguably better food options in the park, but as one of only two full-service restaurants inside USF, it's your best choice for a quiet meal off your feet.

On nights when *Universal's Cinematic Spectacular* is being shown (see page 276), prix fixe dinner packages are available at Lombard's for $45 adults, $13 kids (tax and gratuity included; park admission required). Diners choose an appetizer and entrée from a limited menu (no crab or lobster, but you can get mahimahi) and later attend a dessert reception on the deck behind the restaurant with an up close view of the *Cinematic Spectacular*—sometimes drenchingly so, depending on which way the wind blows). Dinner seating starts at 4 p.m., and the dessert party starts one hour prior to showtime. After you purchase your dinner package online at **universalorlando.com,** you must call ☎ 407-224-7554 at least 24 hours before arrival to confirm your reservation.

With two floors of seating, it's generally easy to get a table, even during the busier times.

Mama Della's ★★★★

Italian	Expensive	QUALITY	★★★★	VALUE	★★★½

Portofino Bay Hotel ☎ 407-503-DINE (3463)

Customers Hotel guests. **Reservations** Recommended via Open Table. **When to go** Dinner. **Entrée range** $21–$38. **Service rating** ★★★★. **Friendliness rating** ★★★★. **Parking** $5 valet or free self-parking at hotel with validation. **Bar** Full service. **Wine selection** Good. **Dress** Nice casual. **Disabled access** Good. **Hours** Daily, 5:30–10 p.m.

SETTING AND ATMOSPHERE Just like being in the dining room of a Tuscan home, with hardwood floors, provincial printed wallpaper, and wooden furniture. Check out the collection of chicken-themed tchotchkes adorning the walls.

HOUSE SPECIALTIES Veal saltimbocca, pan-seared sea bass, grilled lamb chops with rigatoni, and lasagna.

ENTERTAINMENT AND AMENITIES Strolling musicians perform Italian American standards on select nights.

SUMMARY AND COMMENTS This restaurant falls on the fancy scale somewhere between Bice and Trattoria del Porto. Traditional Italian food is served in a comfortable atmosphere conducive to a special meal but not quite as extravagant as its lavish neighbor, Bice. If you want food (almost) as tasty but for (a bit) less dough, Mama Della's is a great choice.

Mythos ★★★½

Steak/Seafood	Moderate	QUALITY	★★★½	VALUE	★★★★

Islands of Adventure/The Lost Continent ☎ 407-224-4012

Customers Park guests. **Reservations** Recommended via NexTable. **When to go** Early evening. **Entrée range** $11–$20. **Service rating** ★★★. **Friendliness rating** ★★★. **Parking** Universal Orlando garage. **Bar** Full service. **Wine selection** Good. **Dress** Casual. **Disabled access** Good. **Hours** Daily, 11:30 a.m.–3 p.m. or park closing; call ahead for closing time.

SETTING AND ATMOSPHERE A grottolike atmosphere suggests that you're eating in a cave. Large picture windows, framed by water cascading down from waterfalls on top of the restaurant, look out over the central lagoon to The Incredible Hulk Coaster. You can time your meal by coaster launchings.

HOUSE SPECIALTIES Tempura shrimp sushi, roast-beef panini, crab-cake sliders, blackened fish tacos, Mediterranean chicken-salad wrap, meat loaf, seared salmon or mahimahi, pad Thai, and risotto of the day.

SUMMARY AND COMMENTS Outside the restaurant is a sign proclaiming that Mythos was voted BEST THEME PARK RESTAURANT. Read the fine print and you'll notice that the voting happened more than five years ago and was done by visitors to a theme park–centric website. This was originally the park's one stab at fine dining, but few guests seemed to be looking for that sort of dining experience, especially after getting soaked on one of the water-based rides. Things are now more casual, much to the chagrin of those who remember the whole roasted lobster, chicken Oscar, and blueberry pork chop.

We've tried almost everything on the current menu, and nothing stands out as either great or terrible. The food is well above average for theme park eats, and the setting provides a pleasant retreat. Your best bets among the entrées are the mushroom meat loaf, seared mahimahi, or daily risotto. Our usual advice in a situation such as this is to stick to appetizers (the tempura sushi is a cult favorite) and drinks, a less expensive option than a full meal with entrée. Regarding price, Mythos is generally less expensive than most Disney theme park sit-down restaurants. Make your reservation early if you want to dine here on a busy day.

During the off-season, Mythos may close before dinnertime, as this reader discovered:

We were disappointed to find out that Mythos closed at 5 when the park closed at 7 p.m. Due to its popularity, only the HP area remained completely open until 7 p.m.

NBC Sports Grill & Brew

American	Not open at press time

CityWalk

Customers Sports fans. **Parking** Universal Orlando garage. **Bar** Full service; more than 100 beers. **Dress** Casual.

SETTING AND ATMOSPHERE NBC Sports Grill & Brew will open in the fall of 2015 on the site of the former NASCAR Sports Grille. The new venue features 90 big-screen high-definition TVs and more than 100 beers—including a special draft available only here. The open design echoes a luxury skybox in a sports stadium (only on an enormous scale), and the central show kitchen sports a signature open-flame kettle grill. The exterior is distinguished by supersize video screens that will broadcast games to all of CityWalk, as well as an outdoor beer garden in which to relax.

HOUSE SPECIALTIES Burgers, steaks, and crab Scotch eggs.

SUMMARY AND COMMENTS At press time, not much was known about NBC Sports Grill, but with the exception of the beer list, the restaurant will likely be similar to its predecessor, NASCAR Sports Grille, with a more modern feel and diverse focus.

Orchid Court Lounge & Sushi Bar ★★★

American/Sushi	Moderate	QUALITY	★★★	VALUE	★★

Royal Pacific Resort ☎ 407-503-3000

Customers Hotel guests. **Reservations** Not accepted. **When to go** Early or late evening. **Entrée range** $12–$57. **Service rating** ★★★. **Friendliness rating** ★★★. **Parking** Free self-parking at hotel with validation. **Bar** Full service. **Wine selection** Average, but an excellent sake selection. **Dress** Resort casual. **Disabled access** Good. **Hours** Monday–Friday, 6–11 a.m.; Saturday–Sunday, 6 a.m.–noon. Lounge: Daily, noon–midnight. Sushi: 5–11 p.m.

SETTING AND ATMOSPHERE Located on the lobby level of the Royal Pacific Resort with gorgeous views of the pool and central reflecting fountain, the Orchid Court Lounge is decorated with inviting hand-carved Balinese furniture and flowering orchids. At one end of the lounge, you'll find a bar with coffee and liquor; at the other end, a traditional sushi bar with see-through seafood cases. In between, clusters of couches and armchairs separated by wooden screens form intimate seating areas.

HOUSE SPECIALTIES For breakfast, Starbucks coffee, cinnamon buns, pastries, cereal, and yogurt. The lounge menu has burgers, Asian chicken salad, a tomato-mozzarella sandwich, spring rolls, Thai lettuce wraps, and tuna tartare. The sushi bar offers miso soup, seaweed salad, edamame, tuna *tataki, nigiri*, sashimi, maki rolls, and cold and warm sake.

SUMMARY AND COMMENTS The Orchid Court Lounge, which almost exclusively caters to guests staying at the Royal Pacific Resort, has a tripolar personality. In the morning, it's a quick-service stop for Starbucks coffee and Continental breakfast pastries. From noon to midnight, it's a bar and lounge with free Wi-Fi and a brief "bytes" menu that incongruously features bacon cheeseburgers and grilled mozzarella sandwiches alongside orange-ginger chicken and rice paper rolls. Finally, in the evenings, the sushi chefs arrive, preparing fishy fare that falls (in terms of quality and creativity) somewhere between The Cowfish and Fusion Bistro at CityWalk. Most of their rolls are adequate executions of Japanese American standards—California, spicy tuna, spider, and volcano—though a couple, such as the Tropical, use more unusual ingredients such as kiwi and mango. This is the only place on Universal property to order some expert items such as Uni (sea urchin), but be warned: They are formerly frozen and outrageously expensive. Ordering à la carte can quickly add up, but the combinations aren't cheap either: A 25-piece sashimi combo will set you back more than $50, and a Tahitian longboat for four is more than $100.

The Palm ★★★★

Steak	Very	Expensive	QUALITY	★★★★	VALUE	★★

Hard Rock Hotel ☎ 407-503-7256

Customers Tourists. **Reservations** Recommended via Open Table. **When to go** Dinner. **Entrée range** $22.50-$79. **Service rating** ★★★. **Friendliness rating** ★★★. **Parking** Free valet at hotel with validation. **Bar** Full service. **Wine selection** Very good. **Dress** Resort, business casual, smart casual. No sleeveless men's shirts. **Disabled access** Good. **Hours** Sunday-Monday, 5-9 p.m.; Tuesday-Saturday, 5-10 p.m.

SETTING AND ATMOSPHERE Despite the celebrity caricatures drawn on the wall, the restaurant exudes sophistication due to the dark woods and white tablecloths. The chain's flagship location is in New York, and the decor reflects this. Waiters wear long, white aprons.

HOUSE SPECIALTIES New York strip, porterhouse, veal parmigiana, whole live lobster, Chilean sea bass with corn relish, Atlantic salmon, and iceberg lettuce wedge salad.

SUMMARY AND COMMENTS The crowd here can get noisy, so The Palm may not be the best place for a romantic night out. However, if you're looking to celebrate with friends or family, this is a good, if very expensive, choice. Stick with the signature dishes: The steaks are done well, and the ginormous lobsters are impeccably prepared, while some of the other dishes could be better. The side dishes are meant for sharing, and the creamed spinach and Brussels sprouts are justly famous. If you want a taste of The Palm on a hamburger budget, drop by the bar during PrimeTime (Sunday-Friday, 5-7 p.m.) for half-priced appetizers like steak sliders and lobster tempura.

Pat O'Brien's Orlando ★★★

Cajun	Inexpensive	QUALITY	★★★½	VALUE	★★★½

CityWalk ☎ 407-224-2106

Customers Tourists. **Reservations** Accepted via NexTable. **When to go** Anytime. **Entrée range** $10–$18. **Service rating** ★★. **Friendliness rating** ★★★. **Parking** Universal Orlando garage. **Bar** Full service. **Wine selection** Modest. **Dress** Casual. **Disabled access** Good. **Hours** Sunday–Thursday, 3–10 p.m.; Friday–Saturday, 3–11 p.m.; bar open until 2 a.m. nightly.

SETTING AND ATMOSPHERE A fairly faithful rendition of the original Pat O'Brien's in New Orleans, from the redbrick facade to the fire-and-water fountain in the courtyard. The outdoor dining area is the most pleasant place to eat. Inside areas include a noisy "locals" bar and a dueling piano bar, featuring some of Orlando's most talented musicians 5 p.m.–2 a.m. nightly. A cover charge is levied after 9 p.m. because it's mostly a music venue that also serves food.

HOUSE SPECIALTIES Shrimp gumbo, jambalaya, muffuletta, and red beans and rice.

SUMMARY AND COMMENTS The food is surprisingly good and surprisingly affordable. Be careful about ordering a Hurricane, the restaurant's signature drink. Not only is it deceptively potent, but you are also automatically charged for the souvenir glass, and if you don't want it, you must turn it in at the bar for a refund.

Red Oven Pizza Bakery ★★★½

Italian	Inexpensive	QUALITY	★★★½	VALUE	★★★★½

CityWalk ☎ 407-224-4233

Customers Tourists. **Reservations** Not accepted. **When to go** Anytime. **Entrée range** $9–$14. **Service rating** ★★. **Friendliness rating** ★★★. **Parking** Universal Orlando garage. **Bar** Wine and beer only. **Wine selection** Limited. **Dress** Casual. **Disabled access** Good. **Hours** Daily, 11 a.m.–2 a.m.

SETTING AND ATMOSPHERE Hardwood beams, colorful tile, and gleaming countertops make Red Oven look unexpectedly upscale for an open-air pizza joint. You can pose for photos on the red scooter parked out front.

HOUSE SPECIALTIES White and red pizza with gourmet toppings, salads, and imported beer and wine.

SUMMARY AND COMMENTS Red Oven Pizza Bakery may be seen as Universal's answer to Via Napoli in Epcot, which brought high-quality pizza to the theme park world. Like at Via Napoli's main dining area, only whole pies, not slices, can be ordered at Red Oven. However, with a reasonable price of only $12–$14 per pizza, two people can eat very cheaply. The five white and five red Neapolitan-style artisan pies are made with San Marzano tomatoes, organic extra-virgin olive oil, buffalo mozzarella, fine-ground "00" flour, and filtered water, and then baked in a 900°F oven while you watch. Salads and a limited selection of beer and wine are available, with free refills on soda.

After placing your food order and receiving your drinks, a server will seat you and bring your order once it's ready. Plenty of covered outdoor seating is available, which is a welcome relief from the Florida sun (and rain). Because of its location in the main hub of CityWalk, Red Oven is a great place to get a bite to eat and people-watch. Red Oven Pizza can also be delivered to the freestanding bars along the CityWalk waterfront.

Three Broomsticks ★★★

British	Moderate	QUALITY	★★★½	VALUE	★★★

Islands of Adventure/The Wizarding World of Harry Potter–Hogsmeade
☎ 407-224-4012

Customers Park guests. **Reservations** Breakfast only. **When to go** Early or late. **Entrée range** $8–$14. **Service rating** ★★★. **Friendliness rating** ★★★. **Parking** Universal Orlando garage. **Bar** Beer and wine only. **Wine selection** Limited. **Dress** Casual. **Disabled access** Good. **Hours** Park opening–10:30 a.m. and 11 a.m.–park closing.

SETTING AND ATMOSPHERE Modeled after the Three Broomsticks inn in the Harry Potter books and films, this buffeteria is the most visually interesting eatery at Islands of Adventure. Open beams, dark furniture, and the contiguous Hog's Head pub make the Three Broomsticks a place to linger and savor. The detail inside is amazing, and it's one of the best-themed restaurants we've seen. The amazing thing about the decor, aside from the vaulted ceiling, is that Universal's architects managed to hide virtually every modern convenience, such as air-conditioning vents, behind 18th-century facades. Al fresco dining is behind the restaurant.

HOUSE SPECIALTIES Breakfast items include English bacon, black pudding, baked beans, and grilled tomato; pancakes with bacon; and porridge with fruit. Lunch and dinner offerings are fish-and-chips, rotisserie chicken, smoked spareribs, shepherd's pie, Cornish pasty, turkey legs, and nonalcoholic Butterbeer. Children's menu items include chicken, macaroni and cheese, fish-and-chips, and chicken fingers.

SUMMARY AND COMMENTS Because it was converted from a larger restaurant during The Wizarding World development, quite a number of seats were sacrificed to achieve the desired look. The menu is very similar to Thunder Falls Terrace in Jurassic Park, with which it shares the title of best counter-service restaurant in IOA. The ribs or chicken, or the combo plate, are your best bets, though the tartar sauce is a tasty side to the fish-and-chips (made from fresh cod). As the only dining option in Hogsmeade, the Three Broomsticks stays busy all day. Like the Leaky Cauldron, you can reserve breakfast at Three Broomsticks by booking through your travel agent or the ticket desk at your Universal resort hotel, and walk-ins for day guests are also usually available, but there are probably better uses of your morning touring time.

Trattoria del Porto ★★★

Italian	Moderate	QUALITY	★★★	VALUE	★★

Portofino Bay Hotel ☎ 407-503-DINE (3463)

Customers Hotel guests. **Reservations** Suggested for dinner via Open Table. **When to go** Breakfast or dinner. **Entrée range Breakfast,** $12–$17; **dinner,** $18–$34. **Service rating** ★★★. **Friendliness rating** ★★★. **Parking** $5 valet or free self-parking at hotel with validation. **Bar** Full service. **Wine selection** Average. **Dress** Resort casual. **Disabled access** Good. **Hours** Tuesday–Wednesday, 7–11 a.m.; Thursday–Monday, 7–11 a.m. and 5:30–10:30 p.m.

SETTING AND ATMOSPHERE Like a boisterous down-home Italian kitchen. A play area lets kids watch cartoons while the grown-ups eat.

HOUSE SPECIALTIES Charred calamari, a 12-ounce New York strip, 10-ounce churrasco, shrimp and clam scampi, bone-in salmon steak, and pancetta-wrapped meat loaf.

ENTERTAINMENT AND AMENITIES Character dining is on Friday, 6:30–9:30 p.m.; face painter and balloon artists entertain on Thursday and Saturday, 6:30–9:30 p.m.

SUMMARY AND COMMENTS Where Mama Della's succeeds in not feeling like a hotel restaurant, Trattoria del Porto does not. The food is perfectly fine and moderately priced (relatively speaking). Fridays and Saturdays are interactive Pasta Cucina nights, where you can create your own entrée from a variety of noodles and sauces ($26 adults, $12 kids). Omelets at breakfast can set you back more than $14, so opt instead for the buffet offered most mornings.

Vivo Italian Kitchen ★★★★

Italian	Moderate	QUALITY	★★★★	VALUE	★★★★½

CityWalk ☎ 407-224-2318

Customers Locals and tourists. **Reservations** Accepted via NexTable. **When to go** Lunch or dinner. **Entrée range** $10–$27. **Service rating** ★★★. **Friendliness rating** ★★★. **Parking** Universal Orlando garage. **Bar** Full service. **Wine selection** Good. **Dress** Casual. **Disabled access** Good. **Hours** Daily, 11 a.m.–11 p.m.

SETTING AND ATMOSPHERE Sleek and contemporary without being stuffy, Vivo brings a touch of casual class to CityWalk's central crossroads. There are outdoor tables (with embedded chessboards) and a well-lit bar, along with plush semicircular booths surrounded by sinuous steel cages. But the real action is around the open kitchen; see if you can snag a seat at the food bar in front of the "tree" where fresh pasta is hung.

HOUSE SPECIALTIES Freshly made pasta, homemade mozzarella, pizza, salads, lasagna, chicken Marsala, and risotto.

SUMMARY AND COMMENTS Vivo, in the former home of Pastamore on the main level of CityWalk, replaced an average Olive Garden wannabe with Universal's best Italian food outside Portofino Bay, instantly making it one of the shining stars of CityWalk's 2014 renovation. The menu is filled with comfortingly familiar dishes—such as chicken piccata, veal parmigiana, spinach cannelloni, and linguine and clams—presented without unnecessary postmodern flourishes, just classic recipes prepared à la minute with the freshest ingredients. Best of all, you can dine here for half the price of Bice, Mama Della's, or one of Disney's Signature restaurants.

Start by ordering an enormous house-made meatball, hand-pulled mozzarella, or beet-and-Gorgonzola salad. Standout entrées include linguine (when razor clams are in season), black squid ink pasta with seafood, risotto with short ribs, and pear-stuffed *fiocchetti* in brown butter. Save room for warm orange-walnut cake; the recipe came directly from chef Steven Jayson's grandmother. On a cost/quality basis, this may be the best table-service meal you'll have on Universal property.

Wantilan Luau ★★★½

Hawaiian	Moderate	QUALITY	★★★	VALUE	★★★

Royal Pacific Resort ☎ 407-503-DINE (3463)

Customers Tourists. **Reservations** Required via Open Table. **When to go** Dinner only. **Entrée range Buffet:** $63 **adults,** $35 **children ages** 3–11. (Prices include gratuity for everyone, and mai tais, wine, and beer for guests age 21 and older.) **Service rating** ★★★. **Friendliness rating** ★★★★. **Parking** Free valet or free self-parking at hotel with validation. **Bar** Mai tais, wine, and beer available. **Wine selection** Limited. **Dress** Flowered shirts,

Universal Orlando Restaurants by Cuisine

CUISINE	LOCATION	OVERALL RATING	COST	QUALITY RATING	VALUE RATING
AMERICAN					
CONFISCO GRILLE	Islands of Adventure	★★★	Mod	★★★	★★★
THE COWFISH	CityWalk	★★★★	Exp	★★★★	★★★½
GALAXY BOWL	Cabana Bay Beach Resort	★★	Inexp	★★½	★★½
HARD ROCK CAFE	CityWalk	★★★	Mod	★★★	★★★
JAKE'S AMERICAN BAR	Royal Pacific Resort	★★★	Mod	★★★	★★½
JIMMY BUFFETT'S MARGARITAVILLE	CityWalk	★★★	Mod	★★★	★★★
THE KITCHEN	Hard Rock Hotel	★★★½	Mod	★★★	★★★
ORCHID COURT LOUNGE & SUSHI BAR	Royal Pacific Resort	★★★	Mod	★★★	★★★
ASIAN					
EMERIL'S TCHOUP CHOP	Royal Pacific Resort	★★★★	Exp	★★★★	★★★★
ORCHID COURT LOUNGE & SUSHI BAR	Royal Pacific Resort	★★★	Mod	★★★	★★
THE COWFISH	CityWalk	★★★★	Mod	★★★★	★★★½
ISLANDS DINING ROOM	Royal Pacific Resort	★★★	Mod	★★★½	★★★
WANTILAN LUAU	Royal Pacific Resort	★★★½	Mod	★★★	★★★
BRITISH AND IRISH					
THE LEAKY CAULDRON	Universal Studios Florida	★★★½	Inexp	★★★½	★★★★
THREE BROOMSTICKS	Islands of Adventure	★★★	Mod	★★★½	★★★
FINNEGAN'S BAR AND GRILL	Universal Studios Florida	★★½	Mod	★★★	★★½
CAJUN					
PAT O'BRIEN'S ORLANDO	CityWalk	★★★	Inexp	★★½	★★★½
CARIBBEAN/JAMAICAN					
BOB MARLEY—A TRIBUTE	CityWalk	★★½	Mod	★★★	★★★

beachy casual. **Disabled access** Average. **Hours** Saturday night, year-round; Tuesday night, seasonally; seating begins at 6 p.m., with registration starting 30 minutes before.

SETTING AND ATMOSPHERE Typical luau setting with tiki torches and wooden tables.

HOUSE SPECIALTIES Buffet includes pit-roasted suckling pig with spiced rum-soaked pineapple puree; Pacific catch of the day; Hawaiian chicken teriyaki; fire-grilled beef with mushrooms; and chicken fingers, mac and cheese, PB&J, and pizza for kids. Dessert buffet has johnnycakes and pineapple upside-down cake.

JIMMY BUFFETT'S MARGARITAVILLE	CityWalk	★★★	Mod	★★★	★★★
ITALIAN					
BICE	Portofino Bay Hotel	★★★★½	Exp	★★★★½	★★★★
MAMA DELLA'S	Portofino Bay Hotel	★★★★	Exp	★★★★	★★★½
RED OVEN PIZZA BAKERY	CityWalk	★★★½	Inexp	★★★½	★★★★½
TRATTORIA DEL PORTO	Portofino Bay Hotel	★★★	Mod	★★★	★★
VIVO ITALIAN KITCHEN	CityWalk	★★★★	Mod	★★★★	★★★★½
MEXICAN					
ANTOJITOS AUTHENTIC MEXICAN FOOD	CityWalk	★★★½	Mod	★★★½	★★★½
SEAFOOD					
EMERIL'S TCHOUP CHOP	Royal Pacific Resort	★★★★	Exp	★★★★	★★★★
THE BUBBA GUMP SHRIMP CO. RESTAURANT & MARKET	CityWalk	★★½	Mod	★★★	★★
THE COWFISH	CityWalk	★★★★	Mod	★★★★	★★★½
LOMBARD'S SEAFOOD GRILLE	Universal Studios Florida	★★★	Mod	★★★½	★★★
MYTHOS	Islands of Adventure	★★★½	Mod	★★★½	★★★★
ORCHID COURT LOUNGE & SUSHI BAR	Royal Pacific Resort	★★★	Mod	★★★	★★
SOUTHERN					
THE BUBBA GUMP SHRIMP CO. RESTAURANT & MARKET	CityWalk	★★½	Mod	★★★	★★
EMERIL'S RESTAURANT ORLANDO	CityWalk	★★★★	Mod	★★★★	★★★½
STEAK					
MYTHOS	Islands of Adventure	★★★½	Mod	★★★½	★★★★
THE PALM	Hard Rock Hotel	★★★★	Exp	★★★★	★★

ENTERTAINMENT AND AMENITIES Polynesian dancing, storytelling, hula dancers, and live music.

SUMMARY AND COMMENTS This is a fun diversion and a change of scenery from the other restaurants on Universal property. Though dinner is a bit expensive, it's the best food of any luau show in the area, and the entertainment is more energetic than *Disney's Spirit of Aloha Dinner Show*. Priority Seating reserves you a table near the front for an extra $7 per adult ($5 per kid), but either way the check-in process can take a while.

DINING *near*
UNIVERSAL ORLANDO

AS WE'VE MENTIONED PREVIOUSLY, guests staying at Universal Orlando's on-site resorts may find their dining options a bit limited and expensive compared to the restaurants found at some Walt Disney World hotels. The flip side is that, while Disney's resorts are largely isolated from the outside world, Universal hotel guests have an array of off-property eateries only a few minutes' drive—or even walk—away.

The closest off-site restaurants to Universal Orlando are found between the hotels along Major Boulevard, just east of the resort entrance on Kirkman Road. **Miller's Ale House** (5573 S. Kirkman Road; ☎ 407-248-0000; **millersalehouse.com**) is a popular after-hours hangout for Universal employees and serves the largest chicken nachos you'll ever see. Chefs at **Kobe Japanese Steakhouse & Sushi Bar** (5605 S. Kirkman Rd.; ☎ 407-248-1978; **kobesteakhouse .com**) perform at teppanyaki tables; ask about early bird and late-night specials. On the opposite side of Major Boulevard, you'll find a run-of-the-mill **T.G.I. Friday's** and **Tabla Bar and Grill** (5827 Caravan Ct.; ☎ 407-248-9400; **tablabar.com**), an upscale Indian restaurant tucked into the back of a Days Inn. A **Wendy's** and **Burger King** round out the block; more fast-food franchises and a **Carrabba's Italian** are located across the street on the north side of Vineland Road. Continue a few lights farther north, and you'll find a strip mall at the corner of Kirkman and Conroy Roads, housing a **Bubbalou's Bodacious Bar-B-Que** (5818 Conroy Road; ☎ 407-295-1212; **kirkman .bubbalous.com)** and **Sloppy Taco Palace** (4892 S. Kirkman Road; ☎ 407-574-6474; **stporlando.com**), which lives up to its name.

Slightly farther afield, international treasures near Universal Boulevard along International Drive include **Aashirwad Indian Cuisine** (5748 International Dr.; ☎ 407-370-9830; **aashirwadrestaurant.com**) and **Nile Ethiopian Restaurant** (7040 International Dr.; ☎ 407-354-0026; **nile07.com**). If you take Universal Boulevard south past I-Drive and Sand Lake Road, you can access rear entrances for I-Drive restaurants without the traffic, ending up at the **Pointe Orlando** shopping and dining complex. Finally, take Turkey Lake Road south from Universal to Sand Lake Road, and turn right toward Restaurant Row for a plethora of upscale chain restaurants, including **Seasons 52, Roy's, Bonefish Grill, Ocean Prime,** and many more.

Finally, if you want to take a drive to downtown Orlando or beyond in search of a fine meal, we can vouch for **The Ravenous Pig** (1234 N. Orange Ave.; ☎ 407-628-2333; **theravenouspig.com**), **Cask & Larder** (565 W. Fairbanks Ave.; ☎ 321-280-4200; **caskandlarder .com**), and **Kabooki Sushi** (3122 E. Colonial Dr.; ☎ 407-228-3839; **kabookisushi.com**).

SHOPPING *at* UNIVERSAL ORLANDO

WITHOUT THE INTERNATIONAL BAZAARS around Epcot's World Showcase, nor the expansive retail square footage of Disney Springs (formerly known as Downtown Disney), shopping opportunities at Universal Orlando are somewhat more restrained than at Walt Disney World. But fear not—you'll still have plenty of opportunities to take home overpriced dust magnets (oops, we meant to say priceless mementos) from your stay. And if you are staying on-site, you can charge them to your room using your hotel key card; just be prepared for the reckoning upon checkout.

If you return home and realize that you forgot something, or you just want to get a feel for prices before your trip, a selection of Universal Orlando merchandise can be ordered online at **universalorlando.com /merchandise/merchandisehome.aspx.**

SHOPPING AT UNIVERSAL STUDIOS FLORIDA

AS KANG AND KODOS OBSERVE at the end of The Simpsons Ride, it's apparently a state law that every Universal attraction must end in (or near) a gift shop. Most of these have the typical T-shirts and toys tied to the experience you just exited, though a few have offerings of note.

The Universal Studios Store sits near the park's entrance, serving as USF's answer to Main Street U.S.A.'s Emporium: If you forgot to get a gift elsewhere in the park, you can probably find it here. And if you forget to stop at the Studios Store, **It's A Wrap** straddles the exit, selling last season's souvenirs at discount prices, as well as serving as the park's package pickup point. If you prepurchased a Photo Connect package, stop in **On Location** to activate it or pick up prints.

In **Production Central, Super Silly Stuff** at Despicable Me Minion Mayhem is decorated like the candy-colored amusement park from the film. You can access the Minion photo op at the attraction's postshow from the shop if the ride's queue is too long. There's a magic mirror and some other fun decor in **Shrek's Ye Olde Souvenir Shoppe.** Transformers' **Supply Vault** has pricey collectibles, as well as toy versions of the attraction's cybertronic stars, including an exclusive model of the EVAC ride vehicle. Directly across from the Transformers entrance sits **The Film Vault,** a movie nerd's nirvana with new products tied to vintage Universal films, from *Psycho* and *Scarface* to *Back to the Future* and *The Big Lebowski.* Nearby, the **Park Plaza Holiday Shop** sells hand-painted Universal ornaments, be it October or August. Beware the self-service bulk candies at **Studio Sweets**; they are priced per quarter-pound, and small bags can add up very quickly.

New York's post-ride shops are fairly pedestrian, though you'll find cow apparel in *Twister*'s **Aftermath,** and faux-Egyptian jewelry in Revenge of the Mummy's **Sahara Traders. Rosie's Irish Imports** has everything Emerald Isle expats (or just admirers) need, from coat of arms key chains to football club sweatshirts.

The Wizarding World of Harry Potter–Diagon Alley is groaning with great shopping opportunities, including **Weasleys' Wizard Wheezes** (toys and candy), **Borgin and Burkes** (spooky stuff), **Madam Malkin's Robes for All Occasions** (clothing), **Magical Menagerie** (stuffed animals), and of course **Ollivanders** (wands). See page 261 in the Universal Studios Florida chapter for further Diagon Alley shopping details.

Over in **World Expo**, the **Kwik-E-Mart** has a great selection of *Simpsons* collectibles; it's worth stopping in to read the satirical signage, and be sure to answer the ringing pay phone outside. **MIB Gear** has a trippy room full of glow-in-the-dark toys, but a chronic mildew issue makes it the smelliest store in the resort.

KidZone is home to **SpongeBob StorePants,** where the big yellow guy himself holds court daily; adults will appreciate the snarky signs inside. **E.T. Toy Closet** has toys from that Spielberg classic and others, plus two adorable photo ops (one on a flying bicycle and the other in a closet full of toys) that are included with Photo Connect Star Card packages. The most notable thing about **The Barney Store,** aside from the world's largest collection of purple-dinosaur videos, is the character meet-and-greet in the adjoining playground.

Back in **Hollywood, Cyber Image** serves as *Terminator 2: 3-D*'s exit and stocks both Marvel and DC superhero swag; props from the attraction are on display, though there's hardly any "Ahhnold" merchandise. **Silver Screen Collectibles,** which adjoins the Lucille Ball tribute, has a small selection of Lucy books and videos, along with a bunch of Betty Boop products, including nightgowns. **Studio Styles** stocks sunglasses, watches, and apparel from upmarket brands such as Oakley, Prada, and Gucci. Note that in Universal's Hollywood, the **Brown Derby** is a hat shop, not a restaurant. The "free show" incessantly advertised outside **Theatre Magic** near Mel's Drive-In is actually a sales pitch to purchase tricks, but the performers are still pretty good; the 12-minute shows start every 30 minutes on the hour and half hour.

Finally, **The Hollywood Boulevard Preview Center,** located inside the former Darkroom one-hour photo developer (kids, ask your parents what those were), is like a shop in reverse. Instead of spending money, you can volunteer to watch a video—often from a potential NBC TV series—and answer a survey, in exchange for a gift card or modest amount of cash. It isn't always available, and you may have to meet certain demographic qualifications, but you can make up to $20 in less than an hour. For guests on a tight schedule, this is a poor use of park time, but if you are a local or are spending several days at Universal, it can be an interesting experience.

SHOPPING AT ISLANDS OF ADVENTURE

LIKE USF, IOA PLACES ITS BIGGEST RETAIL venue right near the entrance; **Islands of Adventure Trading Company** in **Port of Entry** has selections from every area of the park, especially The Wizarding World.

Next to it sits the open-air **Ocean Trader Market,** which sells exotic clothing and crafts while serving as the park's package pickup location. For Grinch fans, the **Port of Entry Christmas Shoppe** celebrates the holiday season 365 days a year. **DeFoto's Expedition Photography** is this park's Photo Connect headquarters, and **Port Provisions** is the last-chance gift discounter at the exit turnstiles.

The **Marvel Alterniverse Store** on **Marvel Super Hero Island** stocks life-size statues of the Avengers (does anyone really put these in their home?) and lets you pose for photos with Spidey himself, while the **Comic Book Shop** has a good selection of current releases and trade paperback classics, along with custom-painted guitars (seriously).

The main drag of **Toon Lagoon** is made up of two stores: the **Betty Boop Store** and **Toon Extra**—selling toys and apparel tied to characters no one under age 40 has heard of. **WossaMotta-U** sadly sells some of the tackiest Orlando T-shirts outside of I-Drive.

Jurassic Park's post-splashdown shop **Jurassic Outfitters** specializes in beach towels (small wonder), and the Discovery Center's **Dinostore** sells semiprecious gems and semieducational toys.

Before Diagon Alley opened, **The Wizarding World of Harry Potter–Hogsmeade** set the bar for theme park shopping. **Honeydukes** candy shop, **Dervish and Banges** toys and apparel, **Ollivanders** wands, and **Filch's Emporium of Confiscated Goods** at the *Forbidden Journey* exit will sap your wallet as surely as a Dementor sucks souls. See page 309 in the Islands of Adventure chapter for details.

The diminished **Lost Continent** still has a few curiosities in its Arabian bazaar, such as **The Coin Mint,** where you can watch money being made, and a heraldry shop with heavy armor. The most eclectic award goes to **Treasures of Poseidon,** where you can pick up a polo shirt, a potted plant, and a $16 pearl that's still inside a live oyster.

If you want a set of the Thing 1 and Thing 2 T-shirts you'll spot around Universal, **Cats, Hats and Things** at The Cat in the Hat ride exit in **Seuss Landing** is the spot. **Mulberry Street** has a small entrance door just for kids, but its limited edition prints and sculptures will appeal to adults. If your Theodor Geisel collection has any gaps, **All The Books You Can Read** can help fill it. And be warned: Upon exiting the High in the Sky Seuss Trolley Train Ride!, you may be forced to pass through **Snookers & Snookers Sweet Candy Cookers,** which is known to cause weight gain simply from staring at its case of fudge and candy apples.

SHOPPING AT UNIVERSAL CITYWALK

WHILE DISNEY SPRINGS IS 120 ACRES (with a strolling area equivalent to about 10 city blocks), CityWalk (**citywalk.com**) comprises 30 acres in a relatively compact area between the two Universal theme parks. CityWalk's shopping is most comparable to the West Side at Disney Springs—fun for browsing and impulse buys.

Our favorites include **Fresh Produce,** featuring swimwear and loungewear for women, kids, and infants; bags and accessories; and more. **Quiet Flight Surf Shop** sells merchandise from beachy brands such as

Billabong, Element, Hurley, Nixon, Oakley, Quicksilver, Reef, Rip Curl, Roxy, Volcom, and Von Zipper. And **The Island Clothing Company** features upscale resort wear from designers such as Lacoste, Lilly Pulitzer, and Tommy Bahama. Quiet Flight sports an iconic surfboard photo op outside, and its inside connects with Island Clothing, forming a handy shortcut between the parking garage and Universal Studios Florida.

Up for some ink? CityWalk also has a branch of **Hart & Huntington Tattoo Shop.** Get a gnarly deck to go with your new tats at the eco-friendly **Element** skateboard shop. For jewelry, **Fossil** has a notable collection of watches, as well as sunglasses and leather goods. **P!Q** (pronounced "pick") sells an oddball assortment of Pylones housewares, gag gifts, and novelty toys; think of it as Spencer's Gifts without the smut. **The Universal Studios Store,** renovated in 2014, offers one-stop shopping for all theme park merchandise, including the best selection of Harry Potter products outside the parks. Finally, many of the restaurants—including Bubba Gump, Margaritaville, Hard Rock Cafe, Bob Marley, Pat O'Brien's, and Emeril's—have merchandise shops, in case you want memories of your meal to live on forever in your closet.

SHOPPING AT UNIVERSAL ORLANDO RESORT HOTELS

THOUGH THE LOEWS HOTELS HAVE EVERY amenity you'll want during your Universal Orlando stay, there isn't much to get excited about in terms of resort shopping. Each of the on-site hotels has a main store near the central lobby carrying sundries, souvenirs, and branded apparel.

Hard Rock Hotel's Rock Shop carries hip brands such as Harajuku and English Laundry, sells the bed and bath linens used in guest rooms, and even has a touch screen video wall with info on the hotel's rock memorabilia collection. At **Portofino Bay Hotel,** you'll find resort-specific items in **Le Memories de Portofino** and a full array of Universal merch in the harbor promenade's **Universal Store,** along with **Alta Moda** resort wear and swim clothes, an art gallery, and a family photography studio. **Toko Gifts** and **Mas** are twin gift shops framing the **Royal Pacific Resort**'s entrance that cover all the essentials, while **Treasures of Bali** by the pool carries beach gear and island wear. Cabana Bay Beach Resort, the cheapest hotel, actually has one of the best stores, with retro clothes, custom candy, and even Jack LaLanne gear in the **Universal Gift Shop.**

SHOPPING *near* UNIVERSAL ORLANDO

IF YOU'VE EXHAUSTED UNIVERSAL ORLANDO'S SHOPPING venues and want to venture off property, central Florida's premier shopping experience is found only a couple exits east along I-4 at **The Mall at Millenia** (☎ 407-363-3555; **mallatmillenia.com**), anchored by

Bloomingdale's, Macy's, and **Neiman Marcus.** Other stores include **Anthropologie, Burberry, Cartier, Coach, Crate & Barrel, Gucci, Guess, J. Crew, Kate Spade, Louis Vuitton, Lululemon Athletica, Tiffany & Co., Tory Burch, Urban Outfitters,** and **Versace.** Hours are Monday–Saturday, 10 a.m.–9 p.m.; Sunday, 11 a.m.–7 p.m.

A few minutes south of Millenia, on the north end of International Drive, is **Artegon Marketplace** (5250 International Dr.; ☎ 407-351-7718; **artegonorlando.com**; open Monday–Saturday, 10 a.m.–9 p.m.; Sunday, 11 a.m.–7 p.m.), where the failed Festival Bay mall has been resurrected as an artsy bazaar à la Faneuil Hall or Chelsea Market; there's also some midrange restaurants and a nice movie theater attached.

On the south end of International Drive is **Pointe Orlando** (9101 International Dr.; ☎ 407-248-2838; **pointeorlando.com**), with a handful of stores. This complex gets a lot of its business from the convention center, less than a mile away, rather than from locals. Hours are October–May, Monday–Saturday, noon–10 p.m. and Sunday, noon–8 p.m.; June–September, Sunday–Thursday, noon–8 p.m. and Friday–Saturday, noon–9 p.m. (Bars and restaurants stay open later.) I-Drive is the heart of Orlando's tourist district, jammed with hotels, discount stores, and endless traffic; locals generally avoid the area or use Universal Boulevard (on the south end) and Grand National Drive (on the north end) to dodge the worst of the congestion.

OUTLETS NEAR UNIVERSAL ORLANDO

LIKE EVERY MAJOR TOURIST DESTINATION in the United States, central Florida has hundreds of factory-outlet stores, most of them situated near major attractions. Having spent many hours checking prices and merchandise, we generally conclude that at most stores you'll save about 20% on desirable merchandise and up to 75% on last-season (or older) stock. Some stores in the outlet malls are full retail or sell a few brands at a 20% discount and the rest at full price.

Orlando Premium Outlets–International Drive (4951 International Dr.; ☎ 407-352-9600; **premiumoutlets.com/orlando;** open Monday–Saturday, 10 a.m.–11 p.m.; Sunday, 10 a.m.–9 p.m.), on the north end of I-Drive, features 180 of the world's hottest designers and brand names, among them **BCBG Max Azria, Hugo Boss Factory Store, Kenneth Cole, Michael Kors, Saks Fifth Avenue OFF 5TH, Sean John, St. John, Tommy Hilfiger, Under Armour, Victoria's Secret,** and the only **Neiman Marcus Last Call** in central Florida. There's even a **Disney's Character Warehouse,** where unsold Walt Disney World souvenirs go to die. You can reach the outlets by car, taxi, or I-Ride Trolley (it's stop #1).

PART SEVEN

UNIVERSAL STUDIOS FLORIDA

WHEN UNIVERSAL STUDIOS BEGAN developing its first Orlando park, the park was originally envisioned along the lines of the Hollywood Studio Tour, with the majority of the guest experiences occurring during an extensive tram tour of the limited-access back lot, along with a handful of rides and shows in the front of the park. When Disney aped that exact game plan for WDW's Hollywood Studios park (which opened in 1989 as Disney/MGM Studios), Universal did a dramatic 180 with its designs, breaking out the tram tour's iconic encounters—King Kong, Earthquake, and Jaws—into their own headliner attractions, each of which easily exceeded its Disney contemporaries in technology and thrill (if not reliability) upon **Universal Studios Florida**'s (USF's) 1990 debut.

Despite that difference, during their first decade, the competing parks were roughly equivalent in many guests' minds. Both parks offered movie- and TV-themed rides and shows, while other attractions provided an educational, behind-the-scenes introduction to the cinematic arts. And both had working film- and TV-production facilities.

Since the turn of the millennium, the two parks have gone in different directions. Whereas Disney's Hollywood Studios (DHS) essentially abandoned its production facilities long ago, USF test-markets TV pilots to guests and has limited actual filming, some of which visitors can attend. More important, Universal has updated, upgraded, or entirely replaced nearly every attraction that opened in the 1990s, replacing Kong with Revenge of the Mummy, Back to the Future with The Simpsons Ride, and Jaws with Harry Potter's Diagon Alley. With each renovation came groundbreaking advancements in ride hardware and special effects. In contrast, only one truly innovative attraction has opened at DHS in the past decade: 2008's Toy Story Midway Mania! While work is now underway to revitalize DHS, at the moment it offers only 5 real rides, versus USF's 10 major moving attractions.

Watching Universal Studios Florida's constant evolution has been thrilling, but it can also be disconcerting. If the last time you visited Universal was in the early 2000s, you literally won't recognize the majority of the park. USF celebrates its 25th anniversary in 2015, but precious little early history is left intact in the park for longtime visitors who loved long-gone opening-day attractions such as *Alfred Hitchcock: The Art of Making Movies,* The Funtastic World of Hanna-Barbera, and *Ghostbusters Spooktacular.* Even so, there are no signs that Comcast is slowing down in its extreme makeover of USF: Look for the Woody Woodpecker's KidZone and San Francisco areas to receive major remodelings in the coming years.

NOT TO BE MISSED AT UNIVERSAL STUDIOS FLORIDA		
PRODUCTION CENTRAL • Hollywood Rip Ride Rockit • Transformers: The Ride 3-D		
HOLLYWOOD • *Terminator 2: 3-D* • *Universal Orlando's Horror-Make-Up Show*		
NEW YORK • Revenge of the Mummy		
WORLD EXPO • Men in Black Alien Attack • The Simpsons Ride		
THE WIZARDING WORLD OF HARRY POTTER–DIAGON ALLEY • Harry Potter and the Escape From Gringotts • Hogwarts Express • Ollivanders		

GETTING ORIENTED *at* UNIVERSAL STUDIOS FLORIDA

USF IS LAID OUT IN A P CONFIGURATION, with the rounded part of the P sticking out disproportionately from the stem. Beyond the main entrance plaza (known as the **Front Lot**), a wide boulevard stretches past several shows and rides to the park's New York area. Branching off this pedestrian thoroughfare to the right are four streets that access other areas of the park and intersect a promenade circling a large, oval man-made lake, where the majority of the shows and attractions are located. The area of USF open to visitors is a bit smaller than Epcot.

Beginning at the park entrance and going clockwise, the first area you'll encounter is **Production Central,** which includes Despicable Me Minion Mayhem, Hollywood Rip Ride Rockit, Transformers: The Ride 3-D, and *Shrek 4-D* attractions. At the top of the P is the **New York** area, including *Twister* and Revenge of the Mummy. Next is **San Francisco,** with *Beetlejuice Graveyard Revue* and *Disaster!*; **The Wizarding World of Harry Potter—Diagon Alley,** with Hogwarts Express—King's Cross Station and Harry Potter and the Escape from Gringotts; **World Expo,** with Men in Black Alien Attack and The Simpsons Ride; and **Woody Woodpecker's KidZone,** containing E.T. Adventure, *A Day in the Park with Barney,* a small roller coaster, and several play areas. The last themed area, back near the front of the park, is **Hollywood,** featuring *Universal Orlando's Horror Make-Up Show, Terminator 2: 3-D,* and *Lucy—A Tribute.*

In most of USF, the line where one themed area begins and another ends is blurry because much of the architecture consists of boring box-like soundstages barely concealed behind false fronts. No matter; guests orient themselves by the major rides, sets, and landmarks and refer, for instance, to "the waterfront," "over by E.T.," or "by Mel's Drive-In." In diametric contrast, the new **Wizarding World of Harry Potter—Diagon**

Alley (and, to a much lesser extent, the Springfield U.S.A. area around The Simpsons Ride) is an immersive themed area whose scope and scale exceed those of any current Walt Disney World land.

Almost all guest services are found in the **Front Lot,** just inside the main entrance. Services and amenities include stroller and wheelchair rentals to the left as you enter; lockers, Lost and Found, and First Aid are to the right. You'll also find the **Studio Audience Center,** where you can sign up to be an audience member at any live TV productions that may be recording that day. Past series taped at USF have included game shows, talk shows, cooking shows, Telemundo's *La Voz Kids,* and TNA's *IMPACT Wresting.* Call ☎ 407-363-8400 and select option 5 to find out what's scheduled during your visit.

A "secret" secondary entrance to USF is tucked under the Hollywood Rip Ride Rockit track, between Despicable Me Minion Mayhem and the Universal Studios Store. It doesn't open until late morning (usually around 10:30 a.m.), but it can save you a few minutes entering on a busy afternoon; follow the signs from CityWalk for the Blue Man Group theater to find it. It also makes an excellent egress when you want to exit toward Islands of Adventure.

UNIVERSAL STUDIOS FLORIDA ATTRACTIONS

PRODUCTION CENTRAL

PRODUCTION CENTRAL SITS AT THE FRONT of Universal Studios Florida and is the first land guests see upon entering the park and passing through the Front Lot. It's a shame, therefore, that this is one of the most meh main streets of any theme park, with bland beige buildings broken up only by the incongruously colossal coaster tracks. Its underwhelming aesthetics don't seem to hurt the area's attractiveness to guests because Production Central holds three of the park's most popular attractions outside of Diagon Alley.

In addition to the rides, show, and counter-service restaurant, Production Central is home to Music Plaza Stage, a Hollywood Bowl–inspired amphitheater with an Astroturf viewing lawn (where you'll often find unconscious tourists sprawled on sunny days) that's used during Mardi Gras concerts and similar special events. There is also access (when applicable) from here to the soundstages used for TV production and Halloween haunted houses.

Despicable Me Minion Mayhem *(Universal Express)*
★★★★

| APPEAL BY AGE | PRESCHOOL ★★★★ | GRADE SCHOOL ★★★★ | TEENS ★★★★ |
| YOUNG ADULTS ★★★★ | OVER 30 ★★★★ | SENIORS ★★★★ | |

Continued on page 242

Universal Studios Florida

1. *Animal Actors on Location*
2. *Beetlejuice Graveyard Revue*
3. *The Blues Brothers Show*
4. Curious George Goes to Town
5. *A Day in the Park with Barney*
6. Despicable Me Minion Mayhem
7. *Disaster!*
8. E.T. Adventure
9. *Fear Factor Live*
10. Fievel's Playland
11. Harry Potter and the Escape from Gringotts
12. Hogwarts Express
13. Hollywood Rip Ride Rockit
14. Kang & Kodos' Twirl 'n' Hurl
15. *Lucy—A Tribute*
16. Men in Black Alien Attack

17. Ollivanders
18. Revenge of the Mummy
19. *Shrek 4-D*
20. The Simpsons Ride
21. *Terminator 2: 3-D*
22. Transformers: The Ride 3-D
23. *TWISTER . . . Ride It Out*
24. *Universal's Cinematic
    Spectacular* (seasonal)
25. *Universal Orlando's
    Horror Make-Up Show*
26. Woody Woodpecker's
    Nuthouse Coaster

Parade Route: • • • • • • • • • • • •

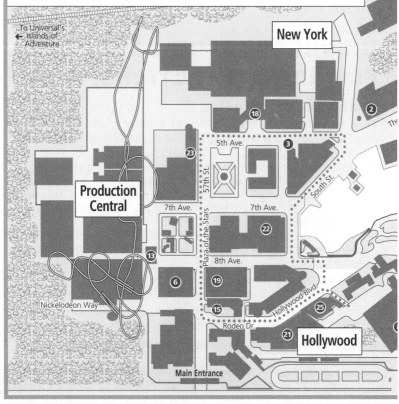

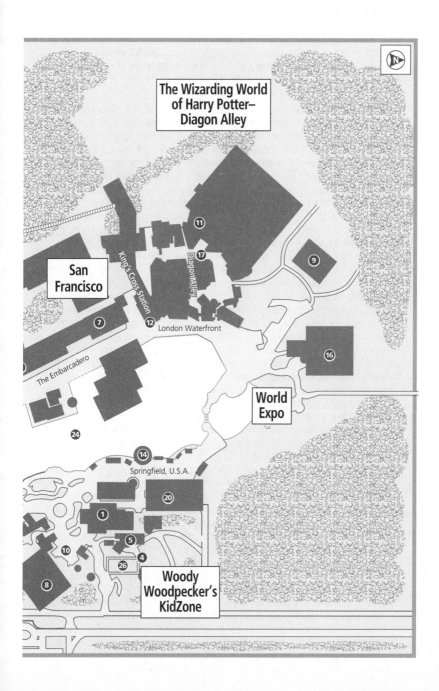

Continued from page 239

What it is Motion-simulator 3-D ride. **Scope and scale** Major attraction. **When to go** Immediately after park opening or just before closing. **Special comments** Expect *long* waits in line. **Authors' rating** Great fun; ★★★★. **Duration of ride** 5 minutes. **Average wait in line per 100 people ahead of you** 7 minutes; assumes all simulators in use. **Loading speed** Moderate–slow.

DESCRIPTION AND COMMENTS Despicable Me Minion Mayhem is a 3-D

Motion Sickness
motion-simulator ride similar to Universal's The Simpsons Ride and Star Tours at Disney's Hollywood Studios. You're seated in a ride vehicle that faces a large video screen, onto which the attraction's story is projected. When the story calls for you to drop down the side of a building, your ride vehicle tilts forward as if you were falling; when you need to swerve left or right, your ride vehicle tilts the same way. This particular motion-simulator system premiered as The Funtastic World of Hanna-Barbera when the park opened in 1990; was used again in Jimmy Neutron's Nicktoon Blast, which replaced the former in 2003; and was refurbished for the attraction's third incarnation as Despicable Me Minion Mayhem, which opened in summer 2012.

As with its former incarnations, the main difference between Minion Mayhem and other simulators is that most other simulators usually provide one video screen per ride vehicle, while Minion Mayhem arranges all of its eight-person vehicles in front of one large IMAX-size video screen. The ride vehicles are set on raised platforms that get slightly higher toward the back of the theater, affording good views for all guests in the rear. Though the simulators have been updated, the most significant upgrade is incorporated in the projection system, which employs high-definition 3-D digital technology.

The ride's story serves as a mini-sequel to the original animated movie *Despicable Me,* starring Gru, the archvillain, along with his adopted daughters and his diminutive yellow Minions. The preshow area is inside Dr. Gru's house, where you see his unique family tree and other artifacts. Our favorite is the mounted lion's head (in the lion's mouth is a dog, in the dog's mouth is a cat, and in the cat's mouth is a mouse). The premise of the ride is that you are being turned into one of Dr. Gru's Minions. Once converted you must navigate the Minion Training Grounds, where your "speed, strength, and ability not to die" are tested. Something soon goes amiss, though, and your training turns into a frenetic rescue operation. The events of this ride take place exactly one year after the *Despicable Me* film; a subplot of the ride involves Gru's daughters (Edith, Agnes, and Margo) celebrating the anniversary of their adoption. In a brilliant marketing tie-in, the adorable gift that Agnes gives to Gru can be purchased in the Super Silly Stuff gift shop on your way out.

The ride itself (which lasts about 5 minutes) is a fast-paced series of dives, climbs, and tight turns through Gru's Rube Goldberg–esque machines. Like The Simpsons Ride, there are more sight gags and interesting things to see here than anyone possibly could in a single ride; luckily, it's Universal's least intense motion simulator, so re-rides are less likely to make you lose your lunch. Guests exit the ride into a disco party with interactive video screens and a photo op where they can boogie down with a Minion.

TOURING TIPS Despicable Me Minion Mayhem is unfortunately situated at the very front of the park, within a few yards of the entrance turnstiles. As a result, and because it's one of the park's newest attractions, long lines develop as soon as the park opens. If you're among the first to enter and the wait is 20 minutes or less, get in line for Despicable Me, and then ride Hollywood Rip Ride Rockit. However, if the line for Despicable Me exceeds 20 minutes, try late afternoon or the hour before the park closes. Note that the posted standby time is just the wait to enter the building; you'll be watching preshows for an additional 10 minutes before you actually ride.

The 3-D perspective from simulators on the sides can be skewed, and the vehicles up front are a bit too close; for the best view, you want to be in the middle of one of the center rows. Stationary seating is available for those prone to motion sickness and for children less than 40 inches tall; ask an attendant for directions.

Hollywood Rip Ride Rockit *(Universal Express)*
★★★★

APPEAL BY AGE	PRESCHOOL —	GRADE SCHOOL ★★★★	TEENS ★★★★½
YOUNG ADULTS ★★★★½	OVER 30 ★★★★½	SENIORS ★★★½	

What it is High-tech roller coaster. **Scope and scale** Headliner. **When to go** The first hour after park opening or after 5 p.m. **Special comments** 51″ minimum height requirement; expect long waits in line. **Authors' rating** Woo-hoo! (and ouch!); not to be missed; ★★★★. **Duration of ride** 2½ minutes. **Average wait in line per 100 people ahead of you** 6–8 minutes. **Loading speed** Moderate.

Motion Sickness

DESCRIPTION AND COMMENTS Opened in the summer of 2009, Hollywood Rip Ride Rockit is USF's candidate for the most technologically advanced coaster in the world. Well, that distinction didn't last very long, but for sure this ride has some features we've never seen before. Let's start with the basics: Rip Ride Rockit is a sit-down X-Car coaster that runs on a 3,800-foot steel track, with a maximum height of 167 feet and a top speed of 65 miles an hour. Manufactured by German coaster maker Maurer Söhne, X-Car vehicles are more maneuverable than most other kinds and use less restrictive restraints, making for an exhilarating ride.

You ascend—vertically—at 11 feet per second to crest the 17-story-tall first hill, the highest point reached by any roller coaster in Orlando, until Mako in SeaWorld opens in 2016. The drop is almost vertical too, launching you into Double Take, a loop inversion in which you begin on the inside of the loop, twist to the outside at the top (so you're upright), and then twist back inside the loop for the descent. Double Take stands 136 feet tall, and its loop is 103 feet in diameter at its widest point. You next hurl (no, not that kind of hurl!) into a stretch of track shaped like a musical treble clef. As on Double Take, the track configuration on Treble Clef is a first. Another innovation is Jump Cut, a spiraling negative-gravity maneuver. Usually on coasters, you experience negative gravity on long, steep vertical drops; with Jump Cut you feel like you're in a corkscrew inversion, but you never actually go upside down. Other high points include a 95-degree turn, a downhill into an "underground chasm" (gotta love those Universal PR wordsmiths!), and a final incline loop banked at 150 degrees.

The ride starts in the Production Central area; weaves into the New York area near *Twister . . . Ride It Out,* popping out over the heads of guests in the square below; and then storms out and over the lagoon separating Universal Studios Florida from Islands of Adventure.

Each train consists of two cars, with riders arranged two across in three rows per car. Each row is outfitted with color-changing LEDs and high-end audio and video technology for each seat. Like Rock 'n' Roller Coaster at Disney's Hollywood Studios, the "Triple R" features a musical sound track, but in this case you can choose the genre of music you want to hear as you ride: classic rock, country, disco, pop, or rap.

When it's over, Universal flogs a digital-video rip of your ride, complete with the sound track you chose, that you can upload to YouTube, Facebook, and the like. The video intercuts stock footage of the coaster with clips recorded by your seat-mounted camera but is not a continuous point of view of your ride. It costs about $50 and is not included with the Photo Connect Star Card, though still images can be manually transferred to your account for free; ask the photo counter attendant to print your code number.

From a Whalton, England, mom:

A fabulous, gut-wrenching coaster that thrilled the socks off my 8- and 9-year-olds. (Mum found it a bit too brutal to repeat.)

A perhaps-jaded Easton, Connecticut, coaster aficionado offers this:

The loud music blasting in our ears canceled out the sound of the coaster. If only they had a "None of the Above: Silence" selection. The singles line hint was a real time-saver.

When Hollywood Rip Ride Rockit premiered in 2009, it was pretty smooth. Alas, the wheels on the cars haven't held up well in the hot Florida sun, and though some of the cars have been overhauled to make the ride more comfortable, none of the fixes have helped much long-term. While perfectly safe, Rip Ride Rockit now subjects you to a lot of side-to-side jarring. To crib a phrase from Tina Turner, some folks like it easy . . . and some folks like it *rough.*

TOURING TIPS Rip Ride Rockit can put more trains on the tracks simultaneously than any other coaster in Florida, which means, on paper, that it should be able to handle about 1,850 riders per hour. In practice, you'll wait about 6–8 minutes for every 100 people in the queue ahead of you, indicating an hourly capacity of 1,500 riders. Because the ride is so close to the USF entrance, it's a crowd magnet, creating bottlenecks from park opening on. Your only chance to ride without a long wait is to be one of the first to enter the park when it opens.

Shrek 4-D *(Universal Express)*   ★★★½

APPEAL BY AGE PRESCHOOL ★★★★ **GRADE SCHOOL** ★★★★★ **TEENS** ★★★★★
YOUNG ADULTS ★★★★★ **OVER 30** ★★★★★ **SENIORS** ★★★★★

What it is 3-D movie. **Scope and scale** Headliner. **When to go** Anytime after experiencing the rides. **Authors' rating** The snarkiest 3-D show in town; ★★★½. **Duration of presentation** 20 minutes. **Probable waiting time** 16 minutes.

DESCRIPTION AND COMMENTS An indoor 3-D film, with moving theater seating, set between the franchise's first two films, *Shrek 4-D* follows the adventures of Shrek, Donkey, and Dragon as they attempt to rescue Fiona after she's kidnapped by Lord Farquaad. The preshow holding area is themed as Lord Farquaad's dungeon, where the Three Little Pigs and the Gingerbread Man warn riders about the pains and tortures in store for everyone, until the diminutive despot appears to deliver a monologue about his evil plan to reclaim his lost bride. The plan is posthumous because Lord Farquaad ostensibly died in the movie, and it's his ghost making the plans, but never mind.

Guests then move into the main theater, don their 3-D glasses, and recline in seats equipped with "tactile transducers" and "pneumatic air propulsion and water spray nodules capable of both vertical and horizontal motion." In English, that means the seats move, bump, and vibrate along with the action, like the D-BOX seats now found in local cinemas. The film's 3-D effects aren't bad, and the 3-D glasses you'll wear do a good job even if you're putting them over prescription glasses, but it relies on older polarized 3-D projection instead of the newer dichroic system used by Despicable Me. As far as the phrase *4-D* goes, physicists may point out that the Earth's fourth dimension is time, but as far as theme parks go, the fourth dimension is water. Expect to get a mild spritz or three during the show. Guests are also subjected to leg ticklers and smells relevant to the on-screen action (oh, boy).

Technicalities aside, *Shrek 4-D* is a mixed bag. It's frantic, laugh-out-loud funny, and iconoclastic. Concerning the last, the film takes a good poke at Disney, with Pinocchio, the Three Little Pigs, and Tinker Bell (among others) all sucked into the mayhem. But the video quality and 3-D effects are dated by today's ultra-HD standards, the story line is incoherently disconnected from the clever preshow, and the franchise's relevance has faded since the lackluster fourth film. On the upside, in contrast to Disney's *It's Tough to Be a Bug!*, *Shrek 4-D* doesn't generally freak out kids under age 7.

TOURING TIPS Universal claims that it can move about 2,400 guests per hour through *Shrek 4-D*, but the show's location at the front of the park and directly across from Despicable Me Minion Mayhem translates to heavy traffic in the morning. If you see lines longer than 20 minutes, try visiting during mealtimes or in the last two hours the park is open. There's not much in the film or preshow to scare small children. Stationary seating is available on request.

Transformers: The Ride—3-D ★★★★★

APPEAL BY AGE PRESCHOOL ★★★ GRADE SCHOOL ★★★★★ TEENS ★★★★★
YOUNG ADULTS ★★★★★ OVER 30 ★★★★★ SENIORS ★★★★

What it is Multisensory 3-D dark ride. **Scope and scale** Super-headliner. **When to go** First 30 minutes the park is open or after 4 p.m. **Special comments** Must be 40" tall to ride; single-rider line available. **Authors' rating** A breathtaking, deafening blur; not to be missed; ★★★★★. **Duration of ride** 4½ minutes. **Average wait in line per 100 people ahead of you** 5 minutes **Loading speed** Moderate–fast.

DESCRIPTION AND COMMENTS Transformers—those toy robots from the 1980s that you turned and twisted into trucks and planes—have been around long enough to go from commercial to kitsch to cool and back again. Thanks to director Michael Bay's recent movie trilogy, "Robots in Disguise" are again a blockbuster global franchise, and in 2013 Transformers fans finally received a USF attraction (cloned from earlier rides in Singapore and Hollywood) befitting their pop-culture idols. Recruits to this cybertronic war enlist by entering the N.E.S.T. Base (headquarters of the heroic Autobots and their human allies) beneath a 28-foot-tall statue of Optimus Prime. Inside an extensive, elaborately detailed queue, video monitors catch you up on the backstory. Basically, the Decepticon baddies are after the Allspark, source of cybernetic sentience. We're supposed to safeguard the shard by hitching a ride aboard our friendly Autobot ride vehicle EVAC, presumably without getting smooshed like a Lincoln in a souvenir penny press every time he shifts into android form. Needless to say, Megatron and his pals Starscream and Devastator won't make things easy, but you'll have Sideswipe and Bumblebee (in his modern Camaro form; look for an old-school Volkswagen Beetle in the final scene) backing you up. For the ride's 4.5 minutes, you play human Ping-Pong ball in an epic battle between these Made in Japan behemoths.

To do justice to this Bay-splosion-packed war of good versus evil, Transformers harnesses the same traveling simulator system behind Islands of Adventure's Amazing Adventures of Spider-Man ride, and it ups the ante with photo-realistic high-definition imagery, boosted by dichroic 3-D glasses that produce remarkably sharp, vivid visuals. The plot amounts to little more than a giant game of keep-away, and the uninitiated will likely be unable to tell one meteoric mass of metal from another, but you'll be too dazzled by the debris whizzing by to notice. Fanboys will squeal with delight at hearing original cartoon actors Peter Cullen and Frank Welker voicing the pugilistic protagonists, and then spill into the post-ride gift shop to purchase armloads of exclusive merchandise, while the rest of us might need a bench on which to take a breather afterward. We'll admit slight disappointment at not getting to see an actual four-story-tall animatronic transform, but the ride's mix of detailed (though largely static) set pieces and video projections was likely a much more maintenance-friendly solution for bringing these colossi to life. Either way, this is one of the most intense, immersive thrill rides found in any theme park.

TOURING TIPS This ride draws crowds. Your only solace is that The Wizarding World of Harry Potter–Diagon Alley draws even larger throngs. Follow our touring plan to minimize waits. The single-rider line will get you on board faster, but as singles lines go, this is one of the slower ones and will be closed off if it becomes backed up. Finally, it's hard to focus on the fast-moving imagery from the front row; center seats in the second and third rows provide the best perspective.

NEW YORK

NEW YORK'S CITY STREETS are re-created in the New York section of Universal Studios Florida. Along with London and Hollywood, New York represents some of the best theming found in the park. Make sure to explore the crooked alleyways behind *The Blue Brothers* stage for some authentic-looking urban backdrops. Trivia note: The statue near the border with San Francisco has the body of Abraham Lincoln and the head of late MCA/Universal mogul Lew Wasserman.

New York has two attractions, one sit-down restaurant, one counter-service restaurant, an arcade, and a Starbucks coffee cafe. *The Blues Brothers Show* is also performed here. First Aid station is located in the alley between Louie's Italian Restaurant and *Beetlejuice Grave-yard Revue*.

The Blues Brothers Show   ★★★½

APPEAL BY AGE PRESCHOOL ★★★ **GRADE SCHOOL** ★★★½ **TEENS** ★★★½
YOUNG ADULTS ★★★½ **OVER 30** ★★★★ **SENIORS** ★★★★

What it is Rhythm and blues concert. **Scope and scale** Diversion. **When to go** Scheduled showtimes. **Special comments** A party in the street. **Authors' rating** Energetic; ★★★½. **Duration of presentation** 12 minutes. **Probable waiting time** None.

DESCRIPTION AND COMMENTS Held on the corner of the New York area, across from the lagoon, *The Blues Brothers Show* features Jake and Elwood performing a few of the hit songs from the classic 1980 movie musical, including "Soul Man" and "Sweet Home Chicago." The brothers are joined on stage by Jazz the saxophone player and Mabel the waitress, who belts an Aretha Franklin cover to start the show.

Blues Brothers is one of the better musical performances in the Studios. The singers have captured many of the movie's dance moves and vocal styles, and the music's tempo keeps everyone's toes tapping. The concert is a great pick-me-up, and the short running time keeps the energy high.

During the holiday season, a special *Blues Brothers Holiday Show* is performed, featuring songs such as "Blue Christmas" and "Run Rudolph Run," sung around a festive tree festooned with beer cans and cigarette packs. It's even better than the regular show.

TOURING TIPS Check the daily entertainment schedule for showtimes. The audience stands on the street during the 12-minute show, without cover or shade. If you arrive early, you might be able to find a seat on a stoop across the street, but why would you want to sit?

Revenge of the Mummy *(Universal Express)*   ★★★★½

APPEAL BY AGE PRESCHOOL ★★ **GRADE SCHOOL** ★★★★ **TEENS** ★★★★★
YOUNG ADULTS ★★★★½ **OVER 30** ★★★★ **SENIORS** ★★★½

What it is Combination dark ride and roller coaster. **Scope and scale** Super-headliner. **When to go** The first 2 hours the park is open or after 4 p.m. **Special comments** 48" minimum height requirement; child swap available (see page 173). **Authors' rating** Killer! Not to be missed; ★★★★½. **Duration of ride** 3 minutes. **Average wait in line per 100 people ahead of you** 7 minutes. **Loading speed** Moderate.

DESCRIPTION AND COMMENTS It's hard to wrap your mind around this attraction, but trust us when we say that you're in for a very strange experience. Here, quoting Universal, are some of the things you can look forward to: "authentic Egyptian catacombs"; "high-velocity show-immersion system" (Huh? quickie baptism?); "magnet-propulsion launch wave system"; "a 'Brain Fire' [!] that hovers [over guests] with temperatures soaring to 2,000°F"; and "canopic jars containing grisly remains."

When you read between the lines, Revenge of the Mummy is a high-tech hybrid indoor roller coaster/dark ride based on the *Mummy* flicks starring Brendan Fraser. The ride's premise is that a movie production crew has taken over New York's Museum of Antiquities to film a sequel titled *Revenge of the Mummy*. The queuing area serves to establish the story line: You're in a group touring a set from the *Mummy* films when you enter a tomb where the fantasy world of film gives way to the real thing. You'll notice lots of interactive details built into the queue, including hints that the movie filming isn't going according to plan. By the time you board your clunky, jeep-like ride vehicle, you've learned that the movie's villain, Imhotep, is trying to use the film crew's souls to become immortal. Only the mystical Medjai symbol can save you from certain doom (cue dramatic music).

The ride begins as a slow, very elaborate dark ride, passing through various chambers, including one where flesh-eating scarab beetles descend on you. Suddenly your vehicle stops and then drops backward and rotates. Here's where you're shot at high speed up the first hill of the roller coaster part of the ride. We won't give away any of Mummy's secrets, but here's what you need to know: It's mostly in the dark and there are no loops, inversions, or any kind of upside-downness; there are plenty of tight turns and high-speed drops and a maximum speed of around 45 miles per hour (roughly in the middle between Disney's Space Mountain and Expedition Everest coasters). Though it's a wild ride by anyone's definition, the emphasis remains as much on the visuals, robotics, and special effects as on the ride itself. As far as those special effects go, they're pretty good: video effects, animatronics, lighting, and enough fire-spewing gas vents to rotisserie a chicken. The endings (yes, plural) are pretty clever.

TOURING TIPS Diagon Alley, Hollywood Rip Ride Rockit, and Despicable Me Minion Mayhem have diminished the Mummy's early-morning crowds. Nevertheless, try to ride during the first two hours the park is open. If lines are long, one fallback is to use the singles line, which can cut your wait to a third of the posted wait time. If you must wait on a hot day, the consolation is that Mummy's air-conditioning system is one of the best in the park.

The front left seat gets the best view of the animatronic effects, while the back corner seats offers the most air time in the coaster sections. Request row three for extra legroom if you found the test seat outside the attraction entrance to be a tight fit. Concerning motion sickness, if you can ride Space Mountain without ill effect, you should be fine on Revenge of the Mummy. Finally, note that the Mummy's queue contains enough scary stuff to frighten little kids all on its own. While most grade-schoolers we surveyed who were plucky enough to ride the Mummy gave it high marks, one father feels our rating for that age group is inappropriate:

> *This ride should NOT be recommended for grade-schoolers, for which you rated the ride a 4. My second-grader (who wasn't scared at all on Space Mountain) was terrified during this ride and cried afterward. I am really upset I encouraged her to ride it and worried she'll have nightmares. Even I thought it was quite scary, and other adults on our ride echoed the same. I think you should really consider a lower rating for grade-schoolers, in addition to a warning about the VERY frightening aspects of this ride.*

Twister . . . Ride It Out *(Universal Express)* ★★★½

APPEAL BY AGE	PRESCHOOL ★★	GRADE SCHOOL ★★★★	TEENS ★★★★
YOUNG ADULTS ★★★★	OVER 30 ★★★★	SENIORS ★★★	

What it is Theater presentation featuring special effects from the movie *Twister*. **Scope and scale** Major attraction. **When to go** Anytime after experiencing all rides. **Special**

comments High potential for frightening young children. **Authors' rating** Gusty;
★★★½. **Duration of presentation** 15 minutes. **Probable waiting time** 10 minutes.

DESCRIPTION AND COMMENTS *Twister* is a walk-through special effects show
based on the 1996 film that starred Helen Hunt and Bill Paxton as storm
chasers, driving around the Midwestern United States trying to measure
the intensity of tornadoes as they appear. The preshow includes many
clips from the film's action sequences, interviews with Hunt and Paxton,
and real-life footage showing the devastating aftermath that follows a
tornado. (Hidden Mickey alert! Look for a Mouseketeer hat stuck to the
crashed car's tire in the second preshow.)

The main presentation replicates a scene from that movie involving a
tornado ripping through a drive-in theater. Guests stand on the far edge of
a soundstage, between a gas station and a restaurant, with the movie
screen off in the distance. The tranquil calm of a summer evening is dis-
turbed when storm clouds appear in the distance. The storm gathers
strength as it gets larger and heads toward the audience. Wind and rain
soon surround everyone, and the town has to ride through the full impact
of the tornado that eventually appears at the middle of the soundstage.
The climax combines a five-story-tall simulated tornado (created by circu-
lating more than 2 million cubic feet of air per minute) with enormous
explosions and a short but dramatic floor drop.

We like *Twister* quite a bit, especially when the strong wind and air-
conditioning provide a few minutes of shelter from Florida's own brutal
summer weather. Though the attraction is well into its second decade, most
guests are still impressed when an actual floor-to-ceiling mini-tornado is
created inside the soundstage. It's one of our favorite effects too. Our favorite effect, though, is Bill Paxton's almost entirely monotone delivery of his
script in the preshow. By the time he says his big line—"Hold on for your
life"—in a robotlike drone, you'll be repeating every line as flatly as you can.

TOURING TIPS The wind, pounding rain, and freight-train sound of the tornado are deafening, and the entire presentation is exceptionally intense.
Schoolchildren are mightily impressed, while younger children are terri-
fied and overwhelmed. Unless you want the kids hopping in your bed
whenever they hear thunder, try this attraction yourself first. Stationary
standing areas are available to avoid the drop.

It's exceptionally rare to have to wait more than one show cycle (about
15 minutes) for *Twister.* The best view of the finale is from the front and center of any level; guests in the back get the most water sprayed on them. If
you are interested in effects, ask to stay and watch the set reset; you may
even be invited into the booth to see how it all works.

Catch *Twister* while you can because Project 727 demolition permits
have already been filed to transform the soundstage into 30 Rockefeller
Center, where *The Tonight Show*'s Jimmy Fallon will reportedly take guests
on an aerial tour of New York.

SAN FRANCISCO

UNIVERSAL'S TRIBUTE TO BAGHDAD by the Bay is a bit too abbre-
viated to leave your heart in, but the designers did manage to squeeze
two attractions, along with a number of eateries and shops, into only a

couple of blocks of brick and boardwalk. Be on the lookout for Bruce the shark; this trophy formerly stood in front of the Jaws ride and was transplanted to the Frisco wharf once that attraction sailed away. The entire area has been rumored for years to be high on the list for potential renovation or even replacement.

Beetlejuice Graveyard Revue (Universal Express) ★★★

APPEAL BY AGE	PRESCHOOL ★★★★	GRADE SCHOOL ★★★★	TEENS ★★★★
YOUNG ADULTS ★★★½	OVER 30 ★★★½	SENIORS ★★★	

What it is Rock-and-roll stage show. **Scope and scale** Major attraction. **When to go** Try to catch the first scheduled showtime. **Authors' rating** Capable of waking the dead; ★★★. **Duration of presentation** 18 minutes. **Probable waiting time** None.

DESCRIPTION AND COMMENTS *Beetlejuice Graveyard Revue* features Dracula, the Wolfman, and Frankenstein and his bride singing mash-ups of pop music from the 1980s and '90s, such as Michael Jackson, Cyndi Lauper, and Mötley Crüe hits, with a few recent pop songs thrown in for the kids. Beetlejuice, the title character from the 1988 film of the same name, serves as the show's emcee, adding monster jokes, groan-worthy puns, and pop-culture references between songs. New characters—including Cleopatra, a female mummy; Phantasia, a female Phantom of the Opera; and a quartet of ghoulish backup dancers—were added when the show was updated in 2014.

This is not Orlando's best theme park show, but the new version is an improvement over the last. The performers don't play any instruments, so the show seems a little like a Halloween-themed karaoke party, minus the booze. But the cast gives their all in executing the energetic, nonstop choreography, and several of the actors have stellar vocal chops.

In response to concerns from parents, *Beetlejuice*'s bawdy banter has been toned down since the show's original incarnation, but he still does a bit of off-color improv with the audience before the show. Also, keep an eye on BJ in the background during songs for some risqué sight gags.

While the show runs around 20 minutes, there is almost no break between any of the songs (or mash-ups), so sitting through a set can be something of an ordeal. The pyrotechnics are less percussive but more frequent than before, and the sound track is still cranked to 11, making for an audio assault on the audience.

TOURING TIPS The show is staged in a covered theater and participates in Universal Express. Check the daily entertainment schedule for showtimes. Its proximity to Diagon Alley makes the crowds larger than in the past. The most comfortable viewing is from the bleachers near the sound booth, or sit down front on the aisle if you want to interact with the performers.

Disaster! (Universal Express) ★★★½

APPEAL BY AGE	PRESCHOOL ★★★	GRADE SCHOOL ★★★★	TEENS ★★★★
YOUNG ADULTS ★★★★	OVER 30 ★★★★	SENIORS ★★★★	

What it is Combination theater presentation and adventure ride. **Scope and scale** Major attraction. **When to go** In the late morning or afternoon. **Special comments** May frighten young children. **Authors' rating** Shaken, not stirred; ★★★½. **Duration of presentation** 20 minutes. **Loading speed** Moderate. **Probable waiting time** 18 minutes.

DESCRIPTION AND COMMENTS An upgraded version of Universal's opening-day *Earthquake* attraction, *Disaster!* (subtitled *A Major Motion Picture Ride . . . Starring YOU!*) serves as both an entertaining introduction into movie-making special effects and a parody of low-budget action flicks, bad acting, and Hollywood egos. In the first part of the attraction, guests are recruited for roles in a film called *Mutha Nature,* directed by the overbearing and conceited Frank Kincaid (Christopher Walken) and starring an unnamed actor you'll recognize as Dwayne "The Rock" Johnson.

After the volunteers are selected, the crowd gets a standing-room-only audience with Kincaid, who appear as a full-size hologram, seemingly interacting with a live performer on stage. The effect is accomplished with a Musion Eyeliner screen, which is also employed inside the Harry Potter attractions. The audience is then seated in a soundstage, where a number of seemingly random scenes are filmed starring the guests-cum-volunteers. Each volunteer is placed in front of a green screen and given some unremarkable task to perform, possibly while being pelted with foam debris from whatever disaster will later be overlaid onto the film. The humor comes from the volunteer's slightly delayed reaction to whatever is going on around him or her, the emcee's running commentary of his or her acting ability, and Walken's deadpan delivery of his director's lines.

Finally, guests board a faux city subway to shoot the final scene, which sees the train subjected to earthquakes, explosions, and onrushing water. The finale's effects are a bit dated (when and if they are working), but the pyrotechnics still impress most first-time riders. Following the quake, while the subway returns to the station, the audience gets to see the finished "film," which pieces together the green screen performances from earlier with the subway ride.

TOURING TIPS Not usually crowded. We recommend seeing *Disaster!* in the late morning or afternoon, after tackling the park's other major rides. If you're unsure about all the shaking, you can enjoy the preshows and skip the ride portion.

THE WIZARDING WORLD OF HARRY POTTER-DIAGON ALLEY

WHEN UNIVERSAL OPENED The Wizarding World of Harry Potter at Islands of Adventure, it created a paradigm shift in the Disney–Universal theme park rivalry. Not only did Universal trot out some groundbreaking ride technology, but it also demonstrated that it could trump Disney's most distinctive competence: the creation of infinitely detailed and totally immersive themed areas. To say that The Wizarding World was a game changer is an understatement of the first order.

It was immediately obvious that Universal would build on its Potter franchise success—but how and where? Universal's not sitting on 27,000-plus acres like Disney, so real estate was at a premium. If Potterville was going to grow, something else had to go. Conventional wisdom suggested that The Wizarding World expansion would gobble up The Lost Continent section of Islands of Adventure, and that may happen yet. But looking at the ledger, it was clear that the older Universal Studios Florida theme park could use a boost.

It just so happened that a substantial chunk of turf at USF was occupied by the aging Jaws ride and its contiguous Amity themed area. The space would allow for substantial development; plus, its isolated location—in the most remote corner of the park—was conducive to creating a totally self-contained area where Potter themes could be executed absent any distraction from neighboring attractions. In short, it was perfect.

So how would the new Potter area tie in to the original at IOA? And what Harry Potter literary icons could be exploited? It was pretty clear that a new suburb of Hogsmeade wasn't going to cut it. The answer was virtually shouting from the pages of the Harry Potter novels, which observe a clear dichotomy of place—plots originate in London and then unfold at distant Hogwarts.

Two London sites that figure prominently in the Potter saga brim with attraction possibilities: Diagon Alley, a secret part of London that is a sort of sorcerers' shopping mall; and the King's Cross railroad station, where wizarding students embark for the train trip to Hogwarts.

Following much deliberation and consultation with Warner Bros. and author J. K. Rowling, the final design called for a London Waterfront street scene flanking Universal Studios Lagoon. The detailed facades, anchored by the **King's Cross** railroad station on the left and including **Grimmauld Place** and **Wyndham's Theatre,** recall West London scenes from the books and movies. **Diagon Alley,** secreted behind the London street scene, is accessed through a secluded entrance in the middle of the facade. Like Hogsmeade at IOA, Diagon Alley features shops and restaurants in addition to three attractions and live entertainment.

Diagon Alley covers 20 acres—about the same area as the Hogsmeade original—but offers about two-and-a-half times the pedestrian space because it doesn't have space- (and people-) eating outdoor roller coasters. With only one high-capacity ride (**Harry Potter and the Escape from Gringotts**), along with an enlarged version of the **Ollivanders** wand-shop experience in Hogsmeade and the **Hogwarts Express** train connecting the two Wizarding Worlds, the new area's increased elbow room is somewhat offset by a relatively reduced hourly attraction capacity, making Diagon Alley's maximum capacity approximately 8,000 persons, about double Hogsmeade's occupancy limit.

In the attraction department, Universal once again came out swinging for the fences. As before with Harry Potter and the Forbidden Journey, the headliner attraction for the expansion is high-tech and cutting-edge—and once again a dark ride, but this time of the roller coaster genre. The labyrinthine passages and caverns of Gringotts Wizarding Bank, the financial institution of choice for the wizarding set, are the setting of this plot-driven 3-D dark ride–coaster.

Though the Gringotts attraction is Diagon Alley's headliner, the most creative element in the two-park Potter domain is Hogwarts Express, which re-creates the train trip from London to Hogwarts and vice versa. Serving as both an attraction and transportation between USF and IOA, the Express unifies the two disparately located Wizarding Worlds.

Diagon Alley in Detail

Diagon Alley and its London Waterfront are sandwiched between the San Francisco and World Expo areas of the park, about as far from Universal Studios Florida's main entrance as you can get. From the park entrance, turn right on Rodeo Drive to Mel's Drive-In; from here, circumnavigate the lagoon counterclockwise, keeping it to your left until you reach the entrance to the London Waterfront, where wrought iron fencing surrounds a parklike promenade. Here you can access London through the gateway closest to the *Fear Factor Live* stadium. You can also access the London Waterfront from the San Francisco area by walking clockwise around the lagoon; usually you can enter from either end, but on the busiest days, you'll have to take a shoreline bypass along the embankment to the World Expo side of the Potter-themed area. Note that if you take Hogwarts Express from Islands of Adventure, you'll debark into San Francisco just outside of the London Waterfront.

WIZARDING WORLD WHISPERS WITH JIM HILL

KEEP YOUR TIME TURNER HANDY Which Harry Potter films are celebrated in The Wizarding World? Depends on where you are. According to art director Alan Gilmore, The Wizarding World exists as a "moment frozen in time" outside of the Potter time line, in which events from different books can coexist. Hogsmeade appears in the middle of *Harry Potter and the Goblet of Fire,* just before Harry attempts the first task. Forbidden Journey occurs sometime after the discovery of the Room of Requirement in *Harry Potter and the Order of the Phoenix.* If you're entering Diagon Alley through the back wall of the Leaky Cauldron, the setting is *Harry Potter and the Sorcerer's Stone,* where Harry and Hagrid first enter the Wizarding Center of London. The queue for Harry Potter and the Escape from Gringotts recalls the part of *Harry Potter and the Deathly Hallows* in which Harry, Ron, Hermione, and Griphook break in to the Lestrange family vault to retrieve the Horcrux. And if you stop to shop at Weasleys' Wizard Wheezes at Diagon Alley, you're in one of the settings of *Harry Potter and the Half-Blood Prince.*

Having arrived at the London area, take a moment to spot Kreacher (the house elf regularly peers from a second-story window above 12 Grimmauld Place); listen to the receiver in the red phone booth for a message from the Ministry of Magic; poke your head in the back door of the triple-decker purple Knight Bus; and chat with the Knight Bus conductor and his Caribbean-accented shrunken head. For some Easter eggs from the attraction designers—including the first of several tributes to Jaws, the original occupant of this area—inspect the record albums in the music store window. You'll also find a couple "cabman's shelters" selling snacks (jacket potatoes, British crisps, and hot dogs in cylindrical buns) and London souvenirs, along with an exacting replica of the towering Shaftesbury Memorial Fountain from Piccadilly Circus.

Now enter Diagon Alley next to the Leicester Square marquee in the approximate center of the building facades. As in the books and films, the unmarked portal is concealed within a magical brick wall that is ordinarily reserved for wizards and the like. (Unfortunately, the wall doesn't actually move, due to safety concerns.) However, the endless parade of Muggles (also known as plain old humans) in shorts and flip-flops will leave little doubt where that entryway is, and just in case you're completely clueless, Universal positions attendants outside to obtrusively point the way.

Once admitted, look down the alley to the rounded facade of **Gringotts Wizarding Bank,** where a 40-foot fire-breathing Ukrainian Ironbelly dragon (as seen in *Harry Potter and the Deathly Hallows: Part 2*) perches atop the dome. The dragon doesn't move, but about every 10 minutes (weather permitting), he unleashes a jet of flame; get your camera ready when you hear him growl. To your left is the **Leaky Cauldron,** the area's flagship restaurant, serving authentically hearty British pub fare.

Intersecting Diagon Alley near the Leaky Cauldron is **Knockturn Alley,** a labyrinth of twisting passageways where the Harry Potter bad guys hang out. A covered walk-through area with a projected sky creating perpetual night, it features spooky special effects in the faux shop windows—don't miss the creeping tattoos and crawling spiders! Finally, to the right of Gringotts is **Carkitt Market,** a canopy-covered plaza where short live shows are staged every half hour or so. All the sections of Diagon Alley are crammed with elaborate signage, animated window displays, and endless hidden details to discover.

Discover is an important word in Diagon Alley because this overwhelmingly intricate area actually feels like a place you can explore and get lost in, much like, say, Epcot's Morocco Pavilion or Disneyland's New Orleans Square. We can't overstate how seamlessly Diagon's designers have rendered the illusion of a living world, topping even Disney California Adventure's Cars Land. *Immersion* is an often-overworked buzzword in themed entertainment, but the new Wizarding World exemplifies it, enveloping fans in Potter's world to a degree that far exceeds Hogsmeade's high standards. And even if you aren't a follower of the franchise, you may find yourself falling for the fictional universal after experiencing Universal's incarnation.

Diagon Alley Attractions

Harry Potter and the Escape from Gringotts ★★★★★

APPEAL BY AGE PRESCHOOL ★★ GRADE SCHOOL ★★★★ TEENS ★★★★★
YOUNG ADULTS ★★★★★ OVER 30 ★★★★★ SENIORS ★★★★

What it is Super-high-tech 3-D dark ride with roller coaster elements. **Scope and scale** Super-headliner. **When to go** First thing during early entry or during late afternoon. **Special comments** Expect *looong* waits in line; 42" minimum height requirement. **Authors' rating** The ultimate realization of "Ride the Movies"; not to be missed; ★★★★★. **Duration of ride** 4½ minutes. **Probable waiting time per 100 people ahead of you** 4 minutes. **Loading speed** Moderate–fast.

DESCRIPTION AND COMMENTS Owned and operated by goblins, Gringotts is the Federal Reserve of the wizarding economy, as well as the scene of memorable sequences from the first and final Potter installments. It's known for its toppling column facade, chandelier-adorned lobby, and bottomless caverns (and the heart-stopping rail carts running through them). The theme park adaptation is the centerpiece of Diagon Alley and is the ultimate expression of the virtual reality rides that Universal has been refining since IOA opened.

Like Forbidden Journey at IOA, Harry Potter and the Escape from Gringotts incorporates a substantial part of the overall experience into its elaborate queue, which (like Hogwarts Castle) even non-riders should experience. You enter through the bank's lobby, where you're critically appraised by glowering animatronic goblins. Your path takes you to a "security checkpoint," where your photo will be taken (to be purchased afterward as an identity lanyard in the gift shop, natch), and past animated newspapers and office windows where the scenario is set up.

Unlike Forbidden Journey, Gringotts doesn't rush you through its queue but rather allows you to experience two full preshows before approaching the ride vehicles. In the first, goblin banker Blordak and Bill Weasley (Ron's curse-breaking big brother) prepare you for an introductory tour of the underground vaults. Then you're off for a convincing simulated 9-mile plunge into the earth aboard an "elevator" with a bouncing floor and ceiling projections. All this is before you pick up your 3-D glasses (identical to those at Transformers: The Ride—3-D) and ascend a spiral staircase into the stalactite-festooned boarding cave where your vault cart awaits.

Also unlike Forbidden Journey, and indeed all the rest of The Wizarding World, Gringotts is not set in a nebulous "moment frozen in time," where incidents from various stories simultaneously coexist. Instead, visitors enter the bank at the exact moment that Harry, Ron, Hermione, and Griphook have arrived to liberate the Hufflepuff's Cup Horcrux from Bellatrix Lestrange's vault. Only in this retelling of *Harry Potter and the Deathly Hallows: Part 2*'s iconic action scene, you (as Muggles opening new bank accounts) are ingeniously integrated into the action. Familiar film moments featuring the vaults' guardian dragon play out in the ride's background as Bellatrix and Voldemort appear to menace you with snakes and sinister spells, whereupon the heroic trio pauses its quest to save your hapless posteriors. The storytelling, which is much more coherent than Forbidden Journey's hodgepodge approach, may disorient scholars of the Potter canon, but it's an intelligent way to allow fans to relive a favorite adventure without merely rehashing the plot.

Gringotts's ornately industrial ride vehicles consist of two-car trains, each holding 24 people in rows of four. The ride merges Revenge of the Mummy's indoor coaster aspects with The Amazing Adventures of Spider-Man's seamless integration of high-resolution 3-D film (the finale dome completely surrounds your car) and massive sculptural sets (some of the rockwork inside is six stories tall), while adding a few new tricks such as independently rotating cars and motion-simulator bases built into the track.

The result is a ride that, though it doesn't break completely new ground as Forbidden Journey and Spider-Man did, combines favorite innovations from its predecessors in an exhilarating new way. It isn't quite the perfect attraction some might be anticipating. The visuals are sometimes murky and the dialogue difficult to discern. And it's slightly disappointing that no animatronic figures, moving set pieces, or actual pyrotechnics appear in the ride, though you will get spritzed with water, blasted with warm air, and sprayed with fog—this is Universal, after all. Finally, though Helena Bonham Carter and Ralph Fiennes reprised their screen roles, Daniel Radcliffe and Emma Watson did not. Harry and pals' computer-generated image stand-ins look OK, as they're never seen up close, but Hermione's voice double is dreadful.

Nitpicks aside, whether Escape from Gringotts is *the* greatest themed thrill ride of all time or merely *one* of the greatest can be happily debated by park fans until the next great leap forward comes along.

TOURING TIPS Gringotts is the pot of gold at the end of Universal's rainbow that a kazillion crazed guests are racing toward. Though the interior line is gorgeous and air-conditioned, the mostly unshaded outdoor extended queue holds 4,000 guests—you don't want to be at the end of it. If you're a Universal resort guest and you qualify for early entry, use it. During off-season when USF doesn't offer Early Park Admission, day guests who arrive before official opening may be allowed to queue for Gringotts before it begins running. Otherwise, try the attraction around lunchtime or in the late afternoon; wait times usually peak after opening but become reasonable later in the day. Just be aware that the queue may shutter to new arrivals before the park closes if the posted wait time exceeds the remaining operating hours by more than 60 minutes, or even earlier if the ride breaks down. Be warned that, as with any ride this advanced, Gringotts can be expected to experience some downtime almost daily. Most operational interruptions are brief and resolved within 10 or 15 minutes.

As far as physical thrills go, Gringotts falls somewhere between Disney's Seven Dwarfs Mine Train and Space Mountain, with only one short (albeit unique) drop and no upside-down flips. It was designed to be less intense (read: less nauseating) than Forbidden Journey and therefore more appealing to families, with fewer height, weight, and size restrictions. The restraints are similar to Revenge of the Mummy's, with bars across your lap and shins, but slightly more restrictive. Use the test seat to the left of the front entrance if you're unsure, and request the third or sixth row for additional legroom.

The ride feels noticeably different depending on the row you're seated in. The front is closest to the action and has the scariest view of the drop; 3-D effects look better farther back. The sixth row gets the most coaster action, especially from the initial fall, but the screens are slightly distorted. The far right seat in row 4 is the sweet spot.

As is the case with most of Universal's thrill rides, you must leave your bags in a free locker. Luckily, unlike at Hogwarts Express, the lockers are separated from the attraction entrance, greatly improving guest flow. Universal Express is *not* currently accepted at this attraction. If you don't have bags and don't mind breaking up your group, the singles line will cut your wait to about a third of the posted standby time, but you'll skip all the pre-shows past the lobby; we don't advise this option until after your first ride.

Hogwarts Express ★★★★½

APPEAL BY AGE PRESCHOOL ★★★★ GRADE SCHOOL ★★★★★ TEENS ★★★★
YOUNG ADULTS ★★★★½ OVER 30 ★★★★½ SENIORS ★★★★½

What it is Transportation attraction. **Scope and scale** Headliner. **When to go** Late morning or just before park closing. **Special comments** Requires a park-to-park ticket. **Authors' rating** A moving experience; not to be missed; ★★★★½. **Duration of ride** 4 minutes. **Probable waiting time per 100 people ahead of you** 7 minutes. **Loading speed** Moderate.

DESCRIPTION AND COMMENTS Part of the genius of creating Diagon Alley at USF is that it's connected to Hogsmeade at Islands of Adventure (see Part Eight) by Hogwarts Express, just as in the novels and films. The counterpart to Hogsmeade Station in IOA is Universal Studios's King's Cross Station, a landmark London train depot that has been re-created a few doors down from Diagon Alley's hidden entrance. (It's important to note that King's Cross has a separate entrance and exit from Diagon Alley: You can't go directly between them without crossing through the London Waterfront.)

The passage to Platform 9¾, from which Hogwarts students depart on their way to school, is concealed from Muggles by a seemingly solid brick wall, which you'll witness guests ahead of you dematerializing through. (Spoiler: The Pepper's Ghost effect creates a clever but congestion-prone photo op, but you experience only a dark corridor with whooshing sound effects when crossing over yourself.)

Once on the platform, you'll pass a pile of luggage (including an owl cage with an animatronic Hedwig) before being assigned to one of the three train cars' seven compartments. The train itself looks exactingly authentic to the nth degree, from the billowing steam to the brass fixtures and upholstery in your eight-passenger private cabin. Along your one-way Hogwarts Express journey, you'll see moving images projected beyond the windows of the car rather than the park's backstage areas, with the streets of London and the Scottish countryside rolling past outside your window. The screen isn't 3-D, but it's slightly curved to conceal the edges and create a convincing illusion of depth. Even more impressive are the frosted-glass doors you enter through, which turn out to be amazing screens that make it seem as if someone is standing on the other side. You experience a different presentation coming and going, and in addition to pastoral scenery, there are surprise appearances by secondary characters (Fred and George Weasley, Hagrid) and threats en route (bone-chilling Dementors, licorice spiders), augmented by vibration and sound effects in the cars.

Hogwarts Express isn't an adrenaline rush in the same way that Escape from Gringotts is, but for those invested in Potter lore, it may be even more emotionally thrilling. And unlike most Potter attractions, it can be experienced by the whole family, regardless of size.

TOURING TIPS There's a capacity-versus-authenticity issue front and center with Hogwarts Express—and if you know J. K. Rowling's reputation for perfectionism where adaptations of her books are concerned, you know the sticky wicket this presented for Universal. The train cars from the films and novels are divided into private compartments that seat eight, but replicating those compartments means fewer seats and longer loading times (and longer queues too). As a result, its carrying capacity is relatively small because the track can accommodate only two trains, each moving in a different direction and passing one another in the middle of the journey. This leaves Universal with a few crowd-mitigating options:

First, because using the train for a one-way trip involves park-hopping, one-way passengers will need a valid park-to-park ticket. Disembarking passengers must enter the second park and, if desired, queue again for their return trip. You'll be allowed (nay, encouraged) to upgrade your one-park Base Ticket at the station entrance.

Second, Universal Express is (ironically) unavailable for Hogwarts Express, at least for the time being.

Third, if the line becomes too long, Universal could limit you to only one one-way ride per day. If you wish to take a same-day return trip, you could be relegated to a secondary queue that promises to be exponentially slower than the already glacial standby queue. (Thankfully, this has only been enforced a couple of times.)

Despite all these challenges, Hogwarts Express managed to move 1 million riders in its first month of operation, surprising everyone with its operational efficiency. As a result, lines rarely exceed 15 minutes in the morning and evening, though the queue may swell to an hour in midafternoon. The walk from one train station to the other is just under a mile and takes 20 minutes at a moderate pace. If the posted wait is 15 minutes or less, it is typically quicker to take the train than to walk to the other Wizarding World.

Guests exiting in Hogsmeade have a chance to take a photo with the locomotive before it backs out for its next run. Guests departing from Hogsmeade should pose with the static train outside the station before they queue up.

Ollivanders ★★★★

APPEAL BY AGE PRESCHOOL ★★★★ GRADE SCHOOL ★★★★★ TEENS ★★★★ YOUNG ADULTS ★★★★ OVER 30 ★★★½ SENIORS ★★★½

What it is Combination wizarding demonstration and shopping op. **Scope and scale** Major attraction. **When to go** After riding Harry Potter and the Escape from Gringotts. **Special comments** Audience stands. **Authors' rating** Enchanting; ★★★★. **Duration of presentation** 6 minutes. **Probable waiting time per 100 people ahead of you** 12 minutes.

DESCRIPTION AND COMMENTS Ollivanders, located in Diagon Alley in the books and films, somehow sprouted a branch location in Hogsmeade at IOA (see page 320). Potter purists pointed out this misplacement, but the wand shop stayed put with J. K. Rowling's blessing and became one of the more popular features of The Wizarding World. It also became a horrendous bottleneck, with long lines where guests roasted in an unshaded queue. In the Diagon Alley version, Ollivanders assumes its rightful place, and with much larger digs. At IOA, only 24 guests at a time can experience the little drama where wands choose a wizard (rather than the other way around). At USF, the shop has three separate choosing chambers, changing it from a popular curiosity into an actual attraction. As for the IOA location, it continues to operate.

The actual show inside is identical to IOA's original outpost in script and special effects. Every few minutes, following a script from the Potter books, a wand-selection show takes place where a random customer (often a child dressed in Potter regalia) is selected to take part in a wand-choosing ceremony. Usually just one person in each group gets to be chosen by a wand, though occasionally siblings are selected together. This is one of the most truly imaginative elements of The Wizarding World: A Wandkeeper sizes you up and presents a wand, inviting you to try it out; your attempted spells produce unintended, unwanted, and highly amusing consequences. Ultimately, a wand chooses you, with all the attendant special effects.

The Celtic zodiac-inspired wands ($45) presented in the ceremony are now the new, more detailed interactive models that interact with shop windows throughout The Wizarding World (see below). After the presentation, guests exit into a greatly enlarged gift shop, where interactive wands are available for purchase, along with noninteractive "famous wizard" replica wands ($37) for a vast variety of characters and toy "learner" wands ($25) for li'l wizards.

TOURING TIPS Check out the self-sweeping broom (shades of *Fantasia*?) while waiting for the show. To increase your odds of being picked, be a cute kid, stand up front, and make eye contact. If your young 'un is selected to test-drive a wand, be forewarned that you'll have to buy it if you want to take it home.

Interactive Wands and Spell-Casting Locations in Diagon Alley

With the opening of Diagon Alley, Universal also introduced interactive wands ($45) to the parks, supplementing the nonfunctional replica wands ($37) that continue to be sold at both **Ollivanders** outposts and in the smaller selection at **Wands by Gregorovitch** in Diagon Alley. Interactive wands are available in 13 Ollivanders Original styles inspired by the Celtic calendar; interactive wands modeled after those wielded by a variety of characters (including Harry, Hermione, Dumbledore, Sirius Black, and Luna Lovegood) are also available. The widest selection of wands is found in the two Ollivanders shops. Stores outside of The Wizarding World at the entrance of each park, as well as CityWalk's Universal Studios Store and gift shops at each hotel, carry a limited variety of interactive and noninteractive wands. Wands can also be ordered from Universal Orlando's merchandise website.

Medallions embedded in the ground designate a couple dozen locations split between the two Wizarding Worlds, where hidden cameras in storefront windows can detect the waving of these special wands and respond to the correct motions with special effects both projected and practical. You might use the swish and flick of Wingardium Leviosa to levitate one object or the figure-four Locomotor spell to animate another.

It's a much more thematically satisfying form of interactivity than the gimmicky games found at the Magic Kingdom, but it can take some practice to get the hang of spell casting. Wizards wander around the area to assist novices and demonstrate spells (though they may not loan their wands), but queues to trigger certain effects can grow to a dozen deep at peak times. A map provided with each wand purchase details the location and movement for most effects, but there are some secret ones to uncover on your own. (Hint: One is in Scribbulus's window, and two more are in the Slug & Jiggers storefront.) Look at your map under the ultraviolet lights in Knockturn Alley for another surprise.

Note that the price of the interactive wands includes unlimited activations of the hidden effects; you don't have to pay to recharge your wand on subsequent visits, or even replace a battery. If you encounter a spell-casting location with a sign saying it CURRENTLY HAS AN ANTI-JINX IN PLACE, just move along to the next one; that's Potter-speak for "it's broken."

We've received positive feedback so far on the interactive wands, like this praise from a New York, New York, family:

> We took our interactive wand and map . . . and explored all the many interactive surprises for well over an hour and had a fantastic time. An interactive wand is highly recommended. Our girls are 12 and 14, and they found every spot where something happened and had a blast making the wand motions and watching the windows come to life.

Entertainment in Diagon Alley

An elevated area in Carkitt Market, between The Hopping Pot and the Gringotts money exchange, comes to life with short shows inspired by Rowling's stories. Though modest in scope, these are some of the best performances found at Universal, and well worth working into your touring plan if you have more than one day at the resort. Showtimes aren't listed in the park map, but performances usually start every 30 minutes on the hour and half hour.

Celestina Warbeck and the Banshees (★★★★) is a live musical show showcasing the Ella Fitzgerald–esque Singing Sorceress with her comely backup crew, swinging to jazzy tunes with a 1940s big band feel. With song titles created by Harry Potter author J. K. Rowling ("You Stole My Cauldron But You Can't Have My Heart," "A Cauldron Full of Hot Strong Love," and "You Charmed the Heart Right Out of Me"), Celestina and her three Banshees perform a lively show that also uses audience participation. (Shy Muggles need not worry: The guest performers are asked ahead of time.) While the songs contain a plethora of references to the Potter books and movies that fans will love, guests who don't know (or care) about the Harry Potter universe will still enjoy the elaborate choreography, fantastic singing, and witty music and lyrics courtesy of Weiner and Alan Zachary, the duo behind Disney Cruise Line's *Twice Charmed: An Original Twist on the Cinderella Story*. The show runs about 12–13 minutes.

Tales of Beedle the Bard (★★★½) recounts one of two wizard fables—"The Three Brothers" from *Harry Potter and the Deathly Hallows*, or "The Fountain of Fair Fortune"—using puppets crafted by Michael Curry (Broadway's *The Lion King, Finding Nemo—The Musical*). The story is chosen "randomly" at the start of each performance. The puppets are gorgeous in a creepy kind of way, and the way the actors perform while maneuvering them is quite clever, though some of the dialogue can get difficult to understand, especially during the "Fountain" tale. The show runs 10–12 minutes.

Shopping in Diagon Alley

Shopping is a major component of Diagon Alley in Potter lore; while Hogsmeade visitors went wild for the few wizardy shops there, Diagon Alley is the planet's wackiest mall, with a vastly expanded array of enchanted tchotchkes to declare bankruptcy over. Shops include:

WEASLEYS' WIZARD WHEEZES, a joke shop with many of the toys previously found in Hogsmeade's Zonko's, plus new gags such as Skiving Snackboxes and Decoy Detonators. Look up through the three-story store's glass ceiling for fireworks.

WISEACRE'S WIZARDING EQUIPMENT, at the exit of Harry Potter and the Escape from Gringotts, sells crystal balls, compasses, and hourglasses.

MADAM MALKIN'S ROBES FOR ALL OCCASIONS stocks school uniforms, Scottish wool sweaters, and dress robes for wizards and witches. The talking mirror will critique your ensemble if you stand in front of it.

MAGICAL MENAGERIE is where you can adopt a plush cat, rat, owl, or hippogriff; the adorable animatronic kneazle is unfortunately not for sale.

SHUTTERBUTTON'S will film your family in front of a green screen and insert you into a DVD of Potter scenes ($70 in a souvenir case or $50 with a Photo Connect Star Card package).

QUALITY QUIDDITCH SUPPLIES sells golden snitches and jerseys for your favorite teams, including all Hogwarts houses and the Holyhead Harpies.

SCRIBBULUS carries quills, notebooks, and similar school supplies.

BORGIN AND BURKES in Knockturn Alley stocks objects from the dark side of magic (watch out for the mummified hand!).

You can pay for all this loot in **Gringotts bank notes,** which you can purchase inside the **Gringotts Money Exchange** overseen by an imperious interactive animatronic goblin, and then spend it anywhere within Universal Orlando (think Disney Dollars); see page 136 in Bare Necessities for details. In general, Diagon Alley's stores are larger and more plentiful than the tiny shops over in Hogsmeade, with carefully planned external and internal queues to corral waiting customers.

Diagon Alley Touring Strategy

The Wizarding World of Harry Potter–Diagon Alley is the queen of the hop in the theme park world in 2015 and beyond. Because of the crowds, experiencing Diagon Alley without interminable waits is a challenge—if you visited The Wizarding World of Harry Potter–Hogsmeade during its first three years at IOA, you know of what we speak. Hogsmeade opened with three rides and Ollivanders; now it has four rides plus the wand shop. As discussed earlier, Diagon Alley has another Ollivanders and only two rides, one of which (Hogwarts Express) it shares with Hogsmeade in IOA. Because only half of each day's total train passengers can board at the USF station, Diagon Alley in essence has only one-and-a-half rides, plus Ollivanders and the various shops, to entertain the expected masses. In other words, it's crazy, y'all.

When Early Park Admission is offered, USF admits eligible on-site resort guests one hour before the general public, with the turnstiles opening up to 90 minutes before the official opening time. Early entry is a tremendous perk if you're staying on-property, but you'll still be competing with thousands of other resort guests, so arrive at least 30 minutes before early entry starts; during peak season, showing up on the very first boat or bus from your hotel is recommended. If you're a day guest visiting on an Early Park Admission day, Diagon Alley will already be packed when you arrive. Even when Universal Studios Florida doesn't offer Early Park Admission, all guests may enter Diagon Alley from the front gates up to 30 minutes before park opening, and hotel guests in Islands of Adventure will arrive via Hogwarts Express a little after that, though Harry Potter and the Escape from Gringotts doesn't begin operating until close to official opening time.

Universal has multiple operational options for allowing guests into USF's Wizarding World. On low to moderate attendance days, you'll be able to stroll in and out of Diagon Alley without restriction. On days of heavy attendance, barricades may limit access to the London Waterfront, forcing guests to queue near *Fear Factor Live* and enter Diagon Alley at a controlled pace, exiting only toward San Francisco. If the park is so busy that Diagon Alley reaches maximum capacity, free timed-entry return tickets specifying when you can visit will be distributed from touch screen kiosks located between Men in Black Alien Attack and *Fear Factor Live*. Guests are given a selection of one-hour return windows, assuming any are still available. Once your time comes, report to the gates at the end of London near *Fear Factor Live*. On the busiest days, standby queues may snake from *Fear Factor Live* behind Men in Black Alien Attack toward The Simpsons Ride, but waiting in these is strongly discouraged. By late afternoon you should almost always be able to waltz right into Diagon Alley without a wait. (Gringotts itself is, of course, another story.)

When the park opens for early entry, eligible guests will be walked around the lake clockwise to Diagon Alley. At rope drop for regular operations, day guests are led counterclockwise to the London Waterfront through World Expo. When crowd-control measures are in place during busy days, hustling to the waterfront counterclockwise through the Simpsons area is the most direct path to the ticket kiosks and standby entrance.

On the upside, the rush to Diagon Alley diminishes crowds and waits at other attractions. The downside to that upside: Those who can't enter Diagon Alley right away spread to nearby attractions, particularly *Disaster!*, Men in Black Alien Attack, and to a lesser extent The Simpsons Ride and Revenge of the Mummy. Diagon Alley spill-over affects wait times at these attractions all day, so experience them as early as possible.

WORLD EXPO

WORLD EXPO, WHICH STRETCHES around Universal Studios's central lagoon from Diagon Alley to the *Animal Actors on Location* theater, somewhat clumsily incorporates several competing aesthetics. The World Expo name, as well as the theming of Men in Black (MIB) Alien Attack in the area's center, is derived from the 1964 World's Fair's New York State Pavilion. Butting up against the MIB's modernist architecture is **Springfield U.S.A.,** the setting of the long-running animated sitcom *The Simpsons.* What started as just The Simpsons Ride and Kwik-E-Mart store was hugely expanded in 2013, with a fabulous re-creation of Moe's Tavern, the Jebediah Springfield statue (emblazoned with A NOBLE SPIRIT EMBIGGENS THE SMALLEST MAN.), and other cartoon landmarks. Springfield is a de facto land unto itself but is still officially wedded to World Expo on park maps. Finally, you have the *Fear Factor Live* stadium, whose theme appears to be "ugly warehouse."

Fear Factor Live (Universal Express) ★★½

APPEAL BY AGE	PRESCHOOL ★	GRADE SCHOOL ★★	TEENS ★★★★
YOUNG ADULTS ★★★	OVER 30 ★★★	SENIORS ★★	

What it is Live version of the gross-out stunt TV show. **Scope and scale** Headliner. **When to go** 3–5 shows daily; crowds are smallest at the first and second-to-last shows. **Authors' rating** Ewwww; ★★½. **Duration of presentation** 30 minutes.

DESCRIPTION AND COMMENTS *Fear Factor Live* is a stage version of the uniquely stomach-turning reality show that ran on NBC from 2001 to 2006 and again from 2011 to 2012. In the theme park iteration, six volunteers compete for one prize; this varies but is always a package that contains Universal goodies ranging from park tickets to T-shirts. Contestants must be 18 years or older (with a photo ID to prove it) and weigh at least 110 pounds. Those demented enough to volunteer should arrive at least 75 minutes before showtime to sign papers and complete some obligatory training for the specific competitive events. Anyone who doesn't wish to compete in the stage show itself can sign up for the Critter Challenge or the Food Challenge. With an adult's permission, volunteers as young as age 16 can compete in the latter.

The stage show is performed in a covered theater and consists of three different challenges. In the first, all six contestants are suspended two-and-a-half stories in the air and try to hang on to a bar as long as possible. The difficulty is compounded by heavy-duty fans blasting the contestants' faces (as you can imagine, this stunt requires exceptional upper-body strength). Only four people go on to the next round, and the person who hangs on to the bar the longest gets to choose his or her partner for the next event.

Once the first two contestants are eliminated, it's time for a brief intermission called the Desert Hat Ordeal. This involves a brave audience member–lunatic who has signed up for the Critter Challenge. Prepared with eye goggles and a mouthpiece, the volunteer is put in a chair with a glass case over his or her head. A wheel is spun to determine what will be crawling over the volunteer's head; the creepy-crawly choices include spiders, snakes, roaches, and scorpions. The only incentive to participate is a free photo of the ordeal for contestants to take to their therapists.

Back at the main competition, the four remaining contestants are split into two teams to compete in the Eel Tank Relay. This consists of one team member grabbing beanbags out of a tank full of eels and throwing them to his or her partner to catch in a bucket. Audience members drench the contestants with high-powered water guns, further spicing up the event. The duo who buckets the most beanbags wins, going on to compete against each other in the final round for the prize package.

As the stage is prepared for the finale, the folks who volunteered for the Food Challenge are split into two teams and invited to drink a mixture of curdled milk, mystery meat, and various live bugs that are all blended together on stage. The team that drinks the most of the mixture within the time limit wins a glamorous plastic mug that says, "I Ate a Bug," a convenient euphemism for "I have the brain of a nematode."

The last event has the two remaining contestants scramble up a wall to retrieve flags, jump into a car that is lifted in the air, and then jump out of the car to retrieve more flags. When the required climbing, jumping, and flag-grabbing are accomplished, the first player to remove a rocket launcher from the backseat of the car and hit a target on the stage wall wins.

The above description may make the show sound more entertaining than it is. It's our duty to confess that this is one of our least favorite shows in any theme park, anywhere, ever. You have been warned.

TOURING TIPS If you've ever wanted a chance to test your mettle (sanity?), *Fear Factor Live* may be your big chance. Participants for the physical stunts are chosen early in the morning and between performances outside the theater, so head there first thing if you want to be a contestant. The contestants for the skeevier stunts, such as the bug-smoothie drinking, are chosen directly from the audience. Sit close to the front and wave your hands like crazy when it comes time for selection. Finally (and seriously), this show is too intense and gross for kids age 8 and under.

An extremely relevant query from two University of Iowa students:

> *We're thinking about volunteering to drink the bug smoothie and want to know if it's better to chew the bugs or just chug the smoothie and hope they die after crawling around for a while in your stomach. Also, do you recommend holding your nose?*

We recommend practicing both options at home, preferably while heavily medicated and under the supervision of a psychiatrist.

Kang & Kodos' Twirl 'n' Hurl ★★★

APPEAL BY AGE	PRESCHOOL ★★★★	GRADE SCHOOL ★★★	TEENS ★★★
YOUNG	ADULTS ★★★	OVER 30 ★★★	SENIORS ★★

What it is Spinning ride. **Scope and scale** Minor attraction. **When to go** After The Simpsons Ride. **Special comments** Rarely has a long wait. **Authors' rating** The world's wittiest spinner; ★★★. **Duration of ride** 1½ minutes. **Probable waiting time per 100 people ahead of you** 21 minutes. **Loading speed** Slow.

DESCRIPTION AND COMMENTS The Twirl 'n' Hurl is primarily eye candy for Springfield U.S.A., USF's new *Simpsons*-themed area. Think of it as Dumbo with Bart's sense of humor: Guests ride around in little flying saucers while the alien narrators, Kang and Kodos, hold pictures of *Simpson* characters; make the characters speak and spin by steering your craft to the proper altitude. All the while, Kang exhorts you (loudly) to destroy Springfield and makes insulting comments about humans. Preschoolers enjoy the ride, while older kids and *Simpsons* fans crack up over the gags.

TOURING TIPS   Twirl 'n' Hurl rarely attracts the long lines that similar spinners at Disney do, but (like all rides in this style) it can be very slow loading. If you want to enjoy the jokes without the wait, you can easily hear them all from the sidelines. If you have folks who are hot to ride, get them on whenever there are 50 or fewer guests in line. Try before 11 a.m. It should take awhile for most guests to arrive in Springfield, U.S.A., especially with Diagon Alley, Transformers, and Despicable Me keeping guests busy elsewhere.

Twirl 'n' Hurl may stop running early on nights when *Cinematic Spectacular* starts before park closing, so as not to distract from the show.

Men in Black Alien Attack *(Universal Express)*   ★★★★½

APPEAL BY AGE	PRESCHOOL ★★	GRADE SCHOOL ★★★★★	TEENS ★★★★★
YOUNG ADULTS ★★★★★	OVER 30 ★★★★★	SENIORS ★★★★	

What it is Interactive dark thrill ride. **Scope and scale** Headliner. **When to go** During the first 2 hours the park is open. **Special comments** May induce motion sickness; 42″ minimum height requirement; child swap available (see page 173). **Authors' rating** Buzz Lightyear's Space Ranger Spin on steroids; not to be missed; ★★★★½. **Duration of ride** 4½ minutes. **Average wait in line per 100 people ahead of you** 5 minutes. **Loading speed** Moderate–fast.

DESCRIPTION AND COMMENTS   Men in Black Alien Attack brings together Will Smith and Rip Torn (as Agent J and Men in Black [MIB] director Zed) for an interactive sequel to the hit sci-fi franchise. You'll notice that the ride's building pays homage to the architecture from the 1964 World's Fair, including the observation towers from the New York State Pavilion that featured in the 1997 film's finale. That theme is carried over to the attraction's preshow, which perfectly parodies the style of *Walt Disney's Carousel of Progress* before taking a surprise turn. The story line has you recruited as an MIB trainee. After an introduction warning that aliens "live among us" and articulating MIB's mission to round them up, Zed expounds on the finer points of alien spotting and familiarizes you with your training vehicle and your weapon, an alien zapper.

You then load up in a six-passenger spinning ride vehicle and are dispatched into an innocuous training room, which is a shooting gallery full of plywood targets shaped like aliens. Your training is cut short when it is revealed that a real alien spaceship has landed in New York and you must save the city. The meat of the ride consists of careening around Manhattan in your MIB vehicle and shooting aliens. There are more targets than anyone could possibly shoot, and they're presented at a fast pace. Each ride vehicle is paired with another ride vehicle running on a parallel track, and both vehicles compete to see who can shoot the most aliens. At a certain point during the ride, you'll be able to shoot at the "fusion exhaust port" of the opposing ride vehicle, causing it to spin momentarily. This disorients the other riders and causes them to lose precious time splatting the aliens. Of course, the other riders (and some of the aliens!) can shoot at you too.

Men in Black is interactive in that your marksmanship and ability to blast yourself out of some tricky situations will determine how the story ends. You're awarded both a personal score (as at the Magic Kingdom's Buzz Lightyear's Space Ranger Spin) and a score for your car. There are about three dozen possible outcomes and literally thousands of different ride experiences determined by your pluck, performance, and, in the final challenge, your intestinal fortitude. Regardless of your score, all recruits are deemed not ready to join MIB, and everyone's memories of the game are wiped at the end of the ride.

TOURING TIPS Each alien figure has sensors that activate special effects and respond to your zapper. Aim for the eyes and keep shooting because you can score repeatedly on the same target. Your gun has auto-fire and unlimited ammo, so just keep the trigger depressed the whole ride; you'll even get a small number of points for missed shots. Targets above you score the most points: Look for aliens behind second-story windows. At the ride's climax, listen carefully for Zed to instruct you to "push the red button," and do so when he says the "b" in "button" to score a bonus 100,000 points. If you're good enough, you can max out with 999,999 points—trust us, it can be done.

The ride is packed with Universal in-jokes. Keep a sharp eye out for an alien seated on a park bench, hiding behind a newspaper. The head-on-a-stick that the alien uses as a disguise bears an uncanny resemblance to Steven Spielberg, executive producer of the *Men in Black* films.

Avoid a long wait and ride during the first two hours the park is open, or try the single-rider line if you don't mind splitting your group. However, the singles and Express queues skip the preshow, which is worth seeing at least once. You can re-ride by following the signs for the child swap at the top of the exit stairs.

If it isn't too busy, ask the attendant out front if you can have a free Immigration Tour. If you're lucky, they'll take you into the large preshow room below the queue, where you can take selfies sitting at an agent's desk and get a close-up look at the animatronic alien twins.

The Simpsons Ride *(Universal Express)* ★★★★

APPEAL BY AGE	PRESCHOOL	★★	GRADE SCHOOL	★★★★	TEENS	★★★★
YOUNG ADULTS	★★★★		OVER 30	★★★★	SENIORS	★★★½

What it is Mega-simulator ride. **Scope and scale** Super-headliner. **When to go** During the first 2 hours the park is open or after 4 p.m. **Special comments** 40" minimum height requirement; not recommended for pregnant women or people prone to motion sickness. **Authors' rating** Despicable Me Minion Mayhem with attitude; not to be missed; ★★★★. **Duration of ride** 4½ minutes, plus preshow. **Average wait in line per 100 people ahead of you** 5 minutes. **Loading speed** Moderate.

Motion Sickness

DESCRIPTION AND COMMENTS Another animated film coupled to a motion simulator, The Simpsons Ride is as much a satire of theme parks as it is a high-speed thrill ride through the Fox animated series that is now TV's longest-running sitcom. Featuring the voices of Dan Castellaneta (Homer), Julie Kavner (Marge), Nancy Cartwright (Bart), Yeardley Smith (Lisa), and other cast members, the attraction uses a visit to

Krustyland—the absurdly unsafe amusement park owned by the show's cantankerous Krusty the Clown—as an excuse to skewer Disney, Sea-World, and even Universal itself.

The queue area and preshows involve *Simpsons* video clips (both classic and newly created) that help define the characters for guests who are unfamiliar with the TV show, and mock virtually every classic Disney attraction from The Haunted Mansion (here as the Haunted Condo, with "999 unhappy teen employees") to *Hall of Presidents* (redone as *Hall of the Secretaries of the Interior*—wait time 0 minutes). Not even ride-safety videos are spared; The Simpsons's version is an outrageous gore-fest starring Itchy and Scratchy demonstrating how *not* to behave.

The attraction itself recycled the foundations of Universal's former Back to the Future ride; watch the queue video for a time-traveling cameo by Doc Brown. It is a simulator similar to Star Tours at DHS and Despicable Me Minion Mayhem (see page 239), but with a larger curved screen more like that of Soarin' at Epcot. The ride vehicles hold eight guests in two rows of four.

The story line has the conniving Sideshow Bob secretly arriving at Krustyland, the aforementioned amusement park, and plotting his revenge on Krusty and Bart for sending him to jail. Sideshow Bob gets even by making things go wrong with the attractions that the Simpsons (and you) are riding. While there are dozens of dips, turns, climbs, and drops during the ride, there are probably hundreds of one-liners and visual puns. Like the show on which it's based, The Simpsons Ride definitely has an edge and operates on several levels. There will be jokes and visuals that you'll get but will fly over your children's heads—and most assuredly vice versa.

TOURING TIPS Because the screen you sit in front of is a giant curved dome, anyone sitting outside the central sweet spot gets a distorted view, which may aggravate motion sickness. For the best experience, ask the attendant at the bottom of the ramps for Level 2, and then ask the next attendant you see for Room 6. Taller guests (6 feet or over) should sit in the front row to avoid bumping their heads.

As far as motion simulators go, The Simpsons Ride isn't as sickness-inducing as many. The wider screen seems to help, as this mom from Huntington, New York, said:

> I'm not a fan of wild motion simulators, but I was fine on this ride. The field of vision makes it very engrossing, like Soarin'. However, our family still rates Star Tours higher than The Simpsons Ride, as participating in the Star Tours simulation was most like actually being a character in the original Star Wars movie!

Though not as rough and jerky as its predecessor, The Simpsons Ride is a long way from being tame. Skip it if you're an expectant mom or prone to motion sickness. Some parents may find the humor too coarse for younger kids.

WOODY WOODPECKER'S KIDZONE

NAMED AFTER THE CLASSIC WALTER LANTZ cartoon character, Universal's answer to Disney's Storybook Circus is situated in a colorful cul-de-sac between Hollywood and World Expo. Woody Woodpecker's

KidZone holds most of the park's child-themed attractions, including a pint-size roller coaster and several elaborate playgrounds. In 2015, Universal announced a partnership to bring Nintendo video game characters (which include Super Mario and Donkey Kong) to its parks, and KidZone is rumored to be their initial destination. E.T. Adventure is supposedly safe, but the rest of KidZone could be looking at the wrecking ball before long.

Animal Actors on Location (Universal Express) ★★★½

| APPEAL BY AGE | PRESCHOOL ★★★★ | GRADE SCHOOL ★★★★ | TEENS ★★★ |
| YOUNG | ADULTS ★★★ | OVER 30 ★★★★ | SENIORS ★★★★ |

What it is Animal tricks and comedy show. **Scope and scale** Major attraction. **When to go** After you've experienced all rides. **Authors' rating** Cute li'l critters; ★★★½. **Duration of presentation** 25 minutes. **Probable waiting time** None.

DESCRIPTION AND COMMENTS *Animal Actors on Location* is a live show featuring performing dogs, birds, pigs, and a menagerie of other animals in a covered outdoor stadium. This show integrates video segments with live sketches, jokes, and animal tricks performed onstage. A human trainer acts as the show's host, explaining how the animals are conditioned to perform the tricks. Several of the animal thespians are veterans of TV and movies; many were rescued from shelters. Featured performers include Marley from *Marley & Me* and Frank the Pug from *Men In Black*; the orangutan who was the show's longtime star has retired. The show usually makes use of audience volunteers (mostly children) in a couple of segments. Sit in the center of the stadium about halfway up for the best chance to be selected.

If you've seen *Flights of Wonder* at Disney's Animal Kingdom, you'll recognize many of the bird routines in *Animal Actors*. What sets *Animal Actors* apart is the use of varied and unusual kinds of animals, as well as the opportunity to see the animals being trained onstage. Pet owners (and parents) will note that the animals are trained using only positive reinforcement—that is, rewarding the animal when it performs the correct behavior—and no negative reinforcement (punishing for incorrect behavior).

TOURING TIPS Check the daily entertainment schedule for showtimes. You shouldn't have any trouble getting into the next performance. The stadium is covered but not enclosed, meaning that it is still hot during summer and cold during winter. Come to the front of the stage at the conclusion to snap a photo with some of the furry stars.

Curious George Goes to Town ★★½

| APPEAL BY AGE | PRESCHOOL ★★★★ | GRADE SCHOOL ★★★½ | TEENS — |
| YOUNG | ADULTS — | OVER 30 — | SENIORS — |

What it is Interactive playground. **Scope and scale** Minor attraction. **When to go** Anytime. **Authors' rating** *The* place for rambunctious kids; ★★½.

DESCRIPTION AND COMMENTS Curious George Goes to Town, an interactive playground, exemplifies the Universal obsession with wet stuff; in addition to innumerable spigots, pipes, and spray guns, two giant roof-mounted buckets periodically dump a thousand gallons of water on unsuspecting visitors below. Kids who want to stay dry can mess around in the foam-ball playground, also equipped with chutes, tubes, and ball blasters.

TOURING TIPS Visit after you've experienced all the major attractions.

A Day in the Park with Barney (Universal Express) ★★★

APPEAL BY AGE PRESCHOOL ★★★★★ GRADE SCHOOL ★★★ TEENS ★★
YOUNG   ADULTS   ★★★   OVER   30   ★★★   SENIORS   ★★★

What it is Live-character stage show. **Scope and scale** Major children's attraction. **When to go** Scheduled showtimes. **Authors' rating** A great hit with preschoolers; ★★★. **Duration of presentation** 20 minutes, plus 5-minute preshow and character greeting after the show. **Probable waiting time** None.

DESCRIPTION AND COMMENTS Barney—the cuddly purple dinosaur of public-TV fame—leads his sidekicks Baby Bop and BJ in an audience sing-along of toddler classics, including "If You're Happy and You Know It," "If All The Raindrops," and "I Love You, You Love Me," the toddler set's "Freebird." A short preshow featuring a live actor playing Mr. Peek-a-boo gets the kids lathered up before they enter Barney's Park (the theater). The characters are supplemented with props—including cartoon cows, pigs, ducks, and skunks—during some of the songs. Interesting theatrical effects include wind, falling leaves, clouds and stars in the simulated sky, and faux snow.

The show is held indoors on a raised, Y-shaped stage placed in the middle of the theater. This clever arrangement allows most of the audience to be seated within a few rows of Barney no matter when they arrive, and affords a good view for anyone in the theater. To accommodate the attention spans of small children, one song follows another almost immediately during the show—we counted no more than 20–30 seconds of talk between numbers. As far as fright potential goes, there's one brief segment where most of the theater goes almost completely dark (to introduce a song about imagination), and there are a couple of seconds of thunder and lightning at the beginning of "If All The Raindrops." We didn't see any child or parent concerned about any of these, and most kids should be absolutely fine.

After some shows, Barney sometimes hangs out for a brief postshow dance party, where you can snap a selfie with the whole dino herd. On other days, Barney and a pal can be found posing for photos with parents and children in the indoor playground at the theater exit.

TOURING TIPS If your child likes Barney, this show is a must. There's also a great indoor play area nearby, designed especially for wee tykes. In the weeks around Christmas (dates vary year to year), this show becomes A Barney Holiday.

E.T. Adventure (Universal Express) ★★★½

APPEAL BY AGE PRESCHOOL ★★★★ GRADE SCHOOL ★★★★ TEENS ★★★
YOUNG   ADULTS   ★★★   OVER   30   ★★★★   SENIORS   ★★★★

What it is Indoor adventure ride based on the beloved movie. **Scope and scale** Major attraction. **When to go** Within 30 minutes of ride opening or late afternoon. **Special comments** 34″ minimum height requirement. **Authors' rating** A long, strange, happy trip; ★★★½. **Duration of ride** 4½ minutes. **Average wait in line per 100 people ahead of you** 5 minutes. **Loading speed** Moderate.

DESCRIPTION AND COMMENTS Inspired by Steven Spielberg's classic 1982 film (and the not-so-classic 1985 sequel novel *Book of the Green Planet*), this is the only ride at Universal that's remained essentially unchanged since opening day. Guests board bicycle-like ride vehicles (suspended from the ceiling, similar to Peter Pan's Flight at the Magic Kingdom) on an adventure returning everyone's favorite Extra-Terrestrial from Earth to his dying home planet.

After a brief video introduction from Mr. Spielberg himself, guests provide their first name to an attendant and receive a credit card–size interplanetary passport (more on this later) before wending their way through a dark forest of tall pine trees; this is one of the most evocative indoor ride queues in any park. As the ride itself starts, you're weaving through the woods, evading the moon-suited scientists and earthly law-enforcement officials trying to capture E.T. As in the film, you're airborne soon enough, flying your way over Los Angeles (a lovely tableau, Universal's answer to Peter Pan's London) and into a warp tunnel to E.T.'s home planet. You arrive just in time to allow E.T.'s healing touch to save everything, and the ride ends in a mash-up of colorful flowers, lighting, and aliens. Concerning the latter, where E.T. is reunited with family and friends, Len Testa likens it to *The Wizard of Oz*'s Technicolor transition, only restaged with a cave full of naked mole rats. (C'mon, Len, where's the love?)

Before you return home, E.T. bids each rider farewell by name, thanks to those passports you received earlier. The speech system was overhauled in 2014, allowing E.T. to say more than 20,000 names (many of which you can now actually understand). A Baton, North Carolina, reader with perhaps too much time on his hands got to wondering:

> *Why do the inhabitants of E.T.'s home planet, who presumably have never visited Earth, speak better English than he does?*

While the attraction's premise is good, its sophistication has lost some luster over its 25-year run. The human animatronics in the first half look laughably like dime-store dummies, and some of E.T.'s pals in the acid-soaked second act are downright disturbing with their out-of-synch facial animation. Even so, because E.T. is one of Universal's only family-friendly dark rides that relies on sets and robotics instead of screens—a type of attraction the resort could use more of—we hope it sticks around for a long time to come.

TOURING TIPS Most preschoolers and grade-school children love E.T. We think it's worth a 20- to 30-minute wait, but no longer than that. The ride often doesn't open until 10 a.m., and lines build quickly within 30 minutes of opening; waits can reach two hours on busy days. Ride in the morning or late afternoon. On peak days, a time-saving single-rider line is occasionally opened.

A mother from Columbus, Ohio, writes about horrendous lines at E.T.:

> *The line for E.T. took two hours! The rest of the family waiting outside thought that we had really gone to E.T.'s planet.*

Fievel's Playland ★★★

| APPEAL BY AGE | PRESCHOOL | ★★★★ | GRADE SCHOOL | ★★★★ | TEENS | — |
| YOUNG | ADULTS | — | OVER 30 | — | SENIORS | — |

What it is Children's play area with waterslide. **Scope and scale** Minor attraction. **When to go** Anytime. **Authors' rating** A much-needed attraction for preschoolers; ★★★. **Probable waiting time** 20–30 minutes for the waterslide; otherwise, none. **Loading speed** Slow for the waterslide.

DESCRIPTION AND COMMENTS A great place for the little ones to blow off some steam. The idea behind this whimsical playground in Woody Woodpecker's KidZone is that you've been shrunk to the size of *An American Tail*'s rodent protagonist, and let loose to explore the detritus in an Old West town. The playground features ordinary household items reproduced on a giant scale, as a mouse would experience them. Kids can climb nets, walk through a huge boot or 1,000-gallon cowboy hat, splash in a sardine-can fountain, sway along elevated wooden bridges, seesaw on huge spoons, and clamber onto a cow skull.

Most of the playground is reserved for preschoolers and grade-schoolers, but a combo waterslide and raft ride is open to all ages. The rafts of the three-story waterslide hold two people, so you should start faking that old war/football/child-bearing back injury to other adults in your group as soon as you get near the Playland. You will get wet.

TOURING TIPS Most of Fievel's Playland requires no waiting, so you can visit anytime and stay as long as you want. Younger children love the oversize items, and there's enough to keep teens and adults busy while little ones let off steam. Most of the play sets are designed for kids old enough to run, climb, and slide by themselves. If your kids aren't quite ready for Fievel, an interactive play area called Barney's Backyard is located next door for smaller kids.

The waterslide is extremely slow-loading and carries only 300 riders per hour. During warmer months, it's possible for the waterslide to develop a wait of 20–30 minutes. We don't think the 16-second ride is worth that kind of wait. If riding the slide is important to your child, try visiting right after lunch or dinner, when many other families are still eating.

Lack of shade is a major shortcoming of the entire attraction—the playground is scorching during the heat of the day.

Woody Woodpecker's Nuthouse Coaster ★★½

APPEAL BY AGE	PRESCHOOL ★★★★	GRADE SCHOOL ★★★★	TEENS ★★
YOUNG ADULTS ★★½	OVER 30 ★★½	SENIORS ★★½	

What it is Interactive playground and kids' roller coaster. **Scope and scale** Minor attraction. **When to go** Anytime. **Special comments** 36″ minimum height requirement; children 36″–48″ must be accompanied by a supervising companion. **Authors' rating** A suitable starter thrill ride; ★★½. **Average wait in line per 100 people ahead of you** 5 minutes. **Loading speed** For the coaster, *slooow*.

DESCRIPTION AND COMMENTS Woody Woodpecker's Nuthouse Coaster is a short, relatively low roller coaster designed to introduce small children to this kind of amusement park ride. In terms of theme, size, and scariness, Nuthouse Coaster is virtually identical to the Magic Kingdom's Barnstormer coaster. The Nuthouse Coaster is small enough for kids to enjoy but sturdy enough for adults, though its moderate speed might unnerve some smaller children (the minimum height to ride is 36 inches). The entire ride lasts about a minute, and at least 20 of those 60 seconds is spent cranking the train up the first (and only) lift hill. There are several tight turns, but the ride doesn't go upside down or even come close.

TOURING TIPS Visit after you've experienced all the major attractions. If your young child has never before experienced a roller coaster, this would be an appropriate first attempt. The entire attraction is visible from the walkway around it, so your child should be able to see exactly what the ride entails before boarding. It's worth spending a few minutes with your child watching the trains go by and observing the reactions of the kids coming off the ride.

HOLLYWOOD

THE HOLLYWOOD AREA RE-CREATES the glamour and energy of southern California from the 1930s through the 1950s. Several areas surrounding Hollywood, including Beverly Hills and the Hollywood Hills, are represented. The faux Garden of Allah villas (famed home of F. Scott Fitzgerald, Marlene Dietrich, and other Hollywood golden age legends), which were some of the best themed buildings in either park, were being converted at press time into an NBC Media Center.

Lucy—A Tribute ★★½

APPEAL BY AGE	PRESCHOOL ★	GRADE SCHOOL ★★	TEENS ★★
YOUNG ADULTS ★★★	OVER 30 ★★★	SENIORS ★★★	

What it is Walk-through exhibit about Lucille Ball. **Scope and scale** Diversion. **When to go** Anytime. **Authors' rating** A touching remembrance; ★★★. **Probable waiting time** None.

DESCRIPTION AND COMMENTS A walk-through tribute to the life and career of actress Lucille Ball, with emphasis on her role as Lucy Ricardo in *I Love Lucy. Lucy—A Tribute* contains photos, props, awards, correspondence, and film clips from the comedienne's 60-plus years in show business. Well designed and informative, the exhibit succeeds admirably in recalling the talent and temperament of the beloved redhead.

Adults of a certain age will remember seeing Lucy's comedy routines on CBS or in syndication. The peak of Lucille Ball's popularity, however, was more than 50 years ago. Sadly, it's unlikely that anyone under the age of 20 will have heard of these performers. Even sadder, the displays here have seen little maintenance in the last couple decades, leaving the rare stereoscopic photographs almost illegibly faded.

TOURING TIPS An indoor exhibit with air-conditioning. See *Lucy* during the hot, crowded midafternoon. *Lucy* may be shuttered by the time you read this and converted into an interactive Hello Kitty store.

Terminator 2: 3-D (Universal Express) ★★★★

APPEAL BY AGE PRESCHOOL ★★★	GRADE SCHOOL ★★★★	TEENS ★★★★
YOUNG ADULTS ★★★★★	OVER 30 ★★★★★	SENIORS ★★★★

What it is 3-D thriller mixed-media presentation. **Scope and scale** Headliner. **When to go** After noon. **Special comments** One of the nation's best theme park theater attractions; very intense for some preschoolers and grade-schoolers. **Authors' rating** Furiously paced and not to be missed; ★★★★. **Duration of presentation** 22 minutes, including 8-minute preshow. **Probable waiting time** 20–30 minutes.

DESCRIPTION AND COMMENTS When *Terminator 2: 3-D* (or *T2 3-D: Battle Across Time,* as it was originally billed) debuted in 1996, no one had ever before seen such a seamless blending of stereoscopic film, stunt actors, and special effects—and almost 20 years later, no one has done better. Oscar winners James Cameron and Stan Winston collaborated with designer Gary Goddard to create a multidimensional stage sequel to their blockbuster film that continues to draw audience applause, even though the franchise (most recently represented by 2015's *Terminator Genisys*) has long since left this show's story line behind.

In case you missed the original *Terminator* flicks, here's a refresher: At some point in the not-too-distant future, the military builds Skynet, an artificial intelligence computer system so smart that it quickly figures out that the biggest threat to world peace is humans themselves. Skynet embarks on a decades-long war against mankind, eradicating most of it. The humans left, led by John Connor, fight back and are about to win when Skynet plays the ace up its sleeve: Robots are sent back in time to kill Connor's mother (played by Linda Hamilton) before he was born, and later Connor himself as a tween (Edward Furlong), which would alter history and assure Skynet's victory.

In Universal's theme park adaptation, guests are getting a guided tour of Cyberdyne Systems, the cheerfully evil inventors of Skynet, when your perky host's amusingly dated "Imagine the Future" propaganda video is interrupted by John and Sarah Connor, who hack into the feed and warn civilians to evacuate before they blow up the building. Once you're seated in the 700-seat main auditorium, the Connors make a dramatic entrance, closely followed by the liquid-metal T-1000, sent from the future to kill them and menace the audience. Then a pre-gubernatorial Arnold Schwarzenegger, playing another homicidal robot assassin who has been helpfully reprogrammed to be good, pops up to save the boy. The bad robot chases the boy and the good robot through a time portal into the future, sucking guests along with them for the ride.

The attraction, like the films, is all exceptional special effects and nonstop action, so you really don't need to understand much. What's interesting is that the show uses 3-D film and a theater full of sophisticated technology to integrate the real with the imaginary. The action unfolds on three walls, and images seem to move in and out of the film, not only in the manner of traditional 3-D but also in reality: Remove your 3-D glasses a moment, and you'll see that the guy on the motorcycle is actually onstage. Some of the special effects and computer-generated animation are outdated, and the 3-D projectors could stand a Spider-Man-style 4K upgrade. But overall the show works because of the fast pace, the sheer size of the presentation, and timeless appeal of shiny robots. Even shiny robots of death.

TOURING TIPS The 700-seat theater changes audiences about every 20–30 minutes, or may operate on a posted schedule during slower times. The show has been eclipsed by newer attractions such as Harry Potter and the Escape from Gringotts, Hollywood Rip Ride Rockit, and Despicable Me Minion Mayhem. We suggest that you save *Terminator* and other theater presentations until you've experienced all the rides. Expect to wait less than 30 minutes.

Families with young children will be relieved to know that the violence characteristic of the movie series is largely absent from the attraction—there's suspense and action but not much blood and guts. Ask for stationary seating if you want to avoid a short but surprising seat drop during the finale.

Universal Orlando's Horror Make-Up Show (Universal Express) ★★★★½

APPEAL BY AGE PRESCHOOL ★★★ GRADE SCHOOL ★★★★ TEENS ★★★★
YOUNG ADULTS ★★★★★ OVER 30 ★★★★ SENIORS ★★★★

What it is Theater presentation on the art of makeup. **Scope and scale** Major attraction. **When to go** Scheduled showtimes; after you've experienced all rides. **Special comments** May frighten young children. **Authors' rating** A gory knee-slapper; not to be missed; ★★★★½. **Duration of presentation** 25 minutes. **Probable waiting time** None.

DESCRIPTION AND COMMENTS The *Horror Make-Up Show* is a brief but humorous look at how basic monster-movie special effects are done. The show includes onstage demonstrations of effects, such as blood-spurting fake knives and rubber limbs, plus how mechanical effects are combined with latex masks to transform human heads into wolf-shaped skulls. The hosts pay tribute to Universal makeup pioneers such as Lon Chaney, Jack Pierce, Tom Savini, and Rick Baker, while also poking fun at some of the studio's less successful spooks. Film clips are interspersed throughout the presentation, showing how computer-generated special effects are blended into live-action films. The finale involves an audience volunteer and a remote-controlled creature that isn't all he appears.

This may be Universal's most entertaining live show. While there's plenty of fake blood thrown around, the script is much more funny than scary funny. The hosts keep everything moving along at a fast pace (except when they start to improv and crack each other up like the old Carol Burnett show), and their running commentary about horror-filmmaking is interspersed with plenty of pop-culture jokes for the kids, along with some surprisingly subversive stabs at the hand that feeds them; after offering a dry towel to a damp volunteer, they'll demand cash, smiling, "Welcome to Orlando!"

TOURING TIPS The *Horror Make-Up Show* is the sleeper attraction at Universal, and one of the only theme park comedy shows we can watch over and over again. Its humor and tongue-in-cheek style transcend the gruesome effects, and most folks (including preschoolers) take the blood and guts in stride. But it's the exception that proves the rule, as this reader relates:

> My 7- and 9-year-olds had no problem with Terminator but were scared by the Horror Make-Up Show (despite my telling them that the guy was not really cutting anyone's arm off!). We ended up leaving before the show was over.

A good test is to take your child into the theater lobby between shows, where display cases filled with bloody props and monster masks act as a mini-museum of Universal horror history from *The Hunchback of Notre Dame* to *Hellboy*. If the static severed heads here send your kid into hysterics, the show itself may have you paying therapy bills for decades to come.

LIVE ENTERTAINMENT *at* UNIVERSAL STUDIOS FLORIDA

IN ADDITION TO THE SHOWS profiled previously, USF offers two major daily outdoor entertainments, along with a wide range of smaller street performances.

Costumed comic book and cartoon characters (Shrek and Donkey, SpongeBob SquarePants, Transformers) pose with guests at organized meet-and-greets that are marked on the park maps. Others, like Woody Woodpecker, along with look-alikes of movie stars (both living and deceased), roam the Hollywood and Front Lot areas for photo ops. See page 175 in Part Five for more character information.

The Studio Brass Band performs familiar TV and movie theme songs in a funky, high-energy style. You'll see them in the morning as you enter, set up on the corner near *Lucy—A Tribute*. Showtimes are listed in the map and usually end by early afternoon. The band may take five during slow seasons.

During peak seasons, you may find break-dancers demonstrating their skills in Hollywood or New York, a corps of trash can–beating drummers near Woody Woodpecker's KidZone, or a troupe of gymnasts in a random spot; it's impossible to say what kind of acts Universal will pull out when the parks get packed.

Universal's Superstar Parade ★★★½

APPEAL BY AGE	PRESCHOOL ★★★★	GRADE SCHOOL ★★★	TEENS ★★★
YOUNG ADULTS ★★★	OVER 30 ★★★		SENIORS ★★★

What it is Parade with animated characters. **Scope and scale** Major attraction. **When to go** Check daily entertainment schedule for parade and showtimes. **Authors' rating** Colorful but inconvenient; ★★★½. **Duration of presentation** 15–20 minutes. **Probable waiting time** None.

DESCRIPTION AND COMMENTS In 2012 USF introduced the Disney-like Universal's Superstar Parade, featuring dancers and performers, four large and elaborate floats inspired by cartoons, and a very mixed bag of street-prowling Universal characters. The featured franchises are Dora the Explorer (with acrobatic monkeys swinging from her float), SpongeBob SquarePants (accompanied by a phalanx of in-line skating fish), E.B. and the Pink Beret bunnies from *Hop* (a forgettable computer-generated imagery Easter fable), and Gru's whole Despicable Me crew, from his adopted daughters to the adorable yellow Minions. The parade is not very long, but it stops twice—once in New York near Revenge of the Mummy and again in Hollywood in front of *Terminator 2: 3-D*—for a highly choreographed ensemble number. Though impressive in its scope and coordination, the performance is well-nigh impossible to take in from any given viewing spot.

The parade, which is marked in the park map, begins at the Esoteric Pictures gate in Hollywood between *Universal Orlando's Horror Make-Up Show* and Cafe La Bamba. It turns right, then immediately makes a hard left around Mel's Drive-In, and follows the waterfront past Transformers toward San Francisco. From there it turns left at Louie's Pizza and proceeds along Fifth Avenue, past Revenge of the Mummy. At the end of Fifth Avenue, the parade takes a left onto 57th Avenue/Plaza of the Stars and heads toward the front of the park, where it makes another left onto Hollywood Boulevard, from whence it disappears backstage through the gate where it entered.

The same floats used in the parade are trotted out individually to the Character Party Zone (located in Hollywood at the corner near Mel's Drive-In) at scheduled times in the late morning and early afternoon for mini-shows and character meet-and-greets. These are a much better opportunity than the parade itself for your kids to get up close and personal with their favorite character.

TOURING TIPS The best viewing spots are along Fifth Avenue, on the front steps of faux buildings in New York. The reserved viewing area for character breakfast ticket holders, along with the wheelchair viewing area, is in front of the Macy's facade. If you miss part of the parade in the New York area, you can scoot along the waterfront to Mel's Drive-In and catch it as it comes down Hollywood Boulevard. If, after watching the parade on the New York streets, you plan to leave the park, you can use the same route to access Hollywood Boulevard and the park exit before the parade arrives.

Universal's Cinematic Spectacular: 100 Years of Movie Memories (seasonal) ★★★½

APPEAL BY AGE	PRESCHOOL ★★★	GRADE SCHOOL ★★★★	TEENS ★★★½
YOUNG ADULTS ★★★★	OVER 30 ★★★★	SENIORS ★★★★	

What it is Fireworks, dancing fountains, and movies. **Scope and scale** Major attraction. **When to go** 1 show a day, usually at park closing. **Authors' rating** Good effort; ★★★½. **Special comments** Movie trailers galore; seasonal, when park is open late. **Duration of presentation** 15–20 minutes. **Probable waiting time** None.

DESCRIPTION AND COMMENTS This is USF's big nighttime event, designed to cap your day at the park. Shown on the lagoon in the middle of the park, the presentation runs through film clips and music from the first 100 years of Universal's biggest movies. The scenes are projected onto three enormous "screens" made by raining a curtain of water from a frame into the lagoon (similar to *Fantasmic!* at Disney's Hollywood Studios, but much sharper). Fireworks, lasers, and colored lights are also used to good effect throughout the presentation, which is narrated by God himself (actually Morgan Freeman, but lots of people make that mistake). It's an enjoyable way to end your day at the park.

The show premiered in May 2012, with reviews generally either mixed or positive. This mother of two liked it:

> My family really enjoyed the show. It didn't have the same emotional impact as [Disney's] Wishes, but it was entertaining. There were so many great movies that we hadn't thought about in ages! I wouldn't make a special trip to see it, but it was nice to have a night

event to end the day. We'll definitely stay for the Cinematic Spectacular *on our next trip.*

If you've been experiencing USF attractions throughout the day, you've already been exposed to many of the characters and memorable scenes spotlighted in the nighttime show. Reliving them again so soon may seem redundant, though there are dozens of films referenced that aren't otherwise honored in the parks; sharp-eyed viewers will catch fleeting references to cult favorites such as *Mallrats* and *Army of Darkness.*

The main complaints we have with *Cinematic Spectacular,* and for that matter with Disney's *Fantasmic!* and *World of Color,* is that the "stirring movie montage" idea is now found in so many places that there's little difference between any studio's implementation. Every park's montage has the same predictable narrative arc: First show clips and witty dialog from your most memorable and recent movies. Transition to something sensitive to remind us that we're all human. Then introduce an action sequence that covers the whole "good versus evil" battle. Show the good guys win amid a bunch of pyrotechnics and roaring fountains. We're pretty sure that you could swap the film clips from Disney's Great Movie Ride with *Universal's Cinematic Spectacular,* and 90% of the audience wouldn't know or care.

TOURING TIPS The best viewing spot is in Central Park directly across the lagoon from Richter's Burger Co., where the sidewalk makes a small protrusion overlooking the water. Because acquiring a spot here can be difficult during peak season, we recommend arriving up to 45 minutes ahead of time; in slower seasons you can stroll up 5 or 10 minutes prior. Other good spots are in the seating area behind Duff Brewery in World Expo, the dock behind Richter's Burger Co. in San Francisco, and the waterfront embankment in front of Diagon Alley. Wherever you plant yourself, make certain that you have a straight-on view of at least one water screen; they can be seen equally well from either side. The Men in Black end of the lagoon is not recommended for viewing, but the terraced area near Mel's Drive-In at the opposite end affords a good look at the lasers and fireworks.

Before the show begins, realize that not all of the movie clips may be suitable for young viewers. The horror montage, for example, mixes excerpts from hoary black-and-white monster movies with potentially fright-inducing clips from films such as *The Birds, Halloween, Psycho, The Silence of the Lambs,* and *Tales from the Crypt.*

Finally, just as Disney does with *Fantasmic!,* Universal offers a dinner package for the *Cinematic Spectacular.* As of now, the only restaurant option is Lombard's Seafood Grille; the cost is $45 for adults and $13 for kids, including tax and tip. After the meal, you'll go to a special seating area to watch the show and enjoy a dessert buffet. It's a decent option if you're in the mood for seafood and you planned to see the show anyway. Reservations are required and can be made online (**tinyurl.com/cinematic spectaculardining**) or by phone (☎ 407-224-7554, Monday–Saturday, 7:30 a.m.–10 p.m. Eastern time; until 9 p.m. on Sunday); see the Lombard's review on page 221 for more information.

SPECIAL EVENTS *at* UNIVERSAL STUDIOS FLORIDA

BEYOND ITS YEAR-ROUND OFFERINGS, USF also hosts some of the best seasonal events in the theme park industry, and several of them are included with any regular admission (including annual passes). For those events that aren't—Rock the Universe and Halloween Horror Nights—you'll need to purchase a separate ticket, and daytime Universal Express Passes (including those included with hotel rooms) won't be honored.

A CELEBRATION OF HARRY POTTER *(late January)*

THIS WEEKEND-LONG EVENT, held in late January, brings Harry Potter fans together with the actors and artists who helped create the blockbuster franchise. Similar to sci-fi and comic book conventions held around the country, the celebration features panel discussions and question-and-answer sessions, where guests can see some of the series's stars in person and possibly get an autograph. Past participants have included Michael Gambon (Dumbledore), Tom Felton (Draco Malfoy), Evanna Lynch (Luna Lovegood), and James and Oliver Phelps (Fred and George Weasley). Paul Harris, the choreographer who created wand combat for *Harry Potter and the Order of the Phoenix,* leads popular master classes in wizard dueling, and the designers of The Wizarding World answer questions about their craft.

Most of the presentations are free for all park attendees and are held on the Music Plaza Stage in Production Central. There is also a Celebration of Harry Potter Expo in Soundstage 33 (accessible from New York near *Twister*), where fans can be selected for a Hogwarts house by the Sorting Hat, sign up for the Pottermore website, and purchase limited edition memorabilia. Other fan-oriented events include photo meet-ups organized by house, kids' dance and combat classes, and trivia contests. The celebration currently takes place over only three days, but based on the response to the first few editions, we can see Universal expanding its run, much like Disney's Star Wars Weekends.

Autograph sessions require tickets, which are distributed for free early each morning on a first-come, first-serve basis near the Blue Man Group theater. Autograph tickets are limited to one per person, per day, and you must be present to claim one; in 2015, they were all claimed hours before the park opened by fans who arrived before 5 a.m.

We generally advise against buying Universal Orlando vacation packages, but attending the Celebration of Harry Potter is one of the few times when it offers an advantage. A private after-hours party inside The Wizarding World is open only to those purchasing exclusive (and expensive) vacation packages, which go on sale in August and always swiftly sell out. (A limited number of packages are also made available to annual-pass holders.)

Potter packages also afford priority access to the expo and reserved viewing at the presentations, which can be a big boon. The expo can fill to capacity within an hour of opening; if you don't have a package, visit first thing to avoid long waits. To get an optimal viewing spot at Music Plaza Stage, plan to arrive a minimum of one hour before showtime.

If you are planning to visit the parks during the celebration but are not interested in the Potter events, fear not; while the parks will be crowded with robe-clad fans, their presence shouldn't substantially impact wait times for most attractions outside The Wizarding Worlds. For more information, visit **universalorlando.com/events /celebration-of-harry-potter.**

MARDI GRAS *(early February–mid-April)*

YOU ARE NO DOUBT FAMILIAR with the gigantic Mardi Gras celebration in New Orleans, Louisiana, or at least the idea of it. Well, Universal Studios has a yearly festival as well. Sure, it's not quite as bawdy as its French Quarter compatriot, but it is exceedingly fun and probably a better event to bring the kids along.

Mardi Gras originated in the religious observation of "Fat Tuesday" (the literal translation of the name), which is the day before Ash Wednesday on the Catholic calendar, and the start of Lent's 40 days of dietary restrictions. People would bid "farewell to flesh" with a "carnivale" where they would indulge in the meat and drink they were about to forswear. Mardi Gras is the New Orleans, Louisiana, variation on this tradition—which is echoed in other cities from Venice, Italy, to Rio de Janeiro, Brazil.

Over the centuries, the religious significance has been stripped away, and most Mardi Gras revelers attend for strictly secular reasons— namely, epic quantities of booze, beads, and bare breasts. About 20 years ago, Universal took a look at the festivities and said, "This will make a fine family-friendly event," and amazingly it is—minus the bare breasts, of course. But that doesn't mean that it's inauthentic; much as Universal partnered with Macy's for its holiday parade, Universal engages Blaine Kern Studios, the same company that's been building floats for the real deal since 1947, to create the park's parade platforms. And musicians and recipes imported from the Big Easy add to the French Quarter feel. Of course, the real Bourbon Street doesn't have concerts from big-name recording artists after each parade, much less a high-speed roller coaster cruising by in the background.

In addition to the parade and headliner concerts, Universal carves a miniature Bourbon Street out of its New York back lot. Chef Steve Jayson and his culinary team pride themselves on the authentic N'awlins flavors they bring to the French Quarter Courtyard, an area between Revenge of the Mummy and Transformers with temporary food and beverage booths that open at 4 p.m. each Mardi Gras event night. The jambalaya, andouille sausage, and beignets are all pretty good. You can eat to the beat and enjoy live blues and zydeco musicians from Louisiana on the French Quarter stage. Universal started this tradition a decade ago to support New Orleans artists in the wake of Hurricane Katrina.

The good times roll on select nights (usually every Saturday and a few Fridays and Sundays) from February through April, or even longer in some years. In 2015, the party ran February 7–April 18, but in 2014 it stretched all the way into June. Viewing of the parade and concerts are included with any valid admission, and all annual-pass holders are admitted in the evening, even on blackout dates. For more information, visit **universalorlando.com/events/mardi-gras.**

Mardi Gras Parade

Universal's version of a Mardi Gras parade includes the crazy characters of the New Orleans version but is much more compact. Floats are updated every year with new themes—the inspiration for 2014's additions was Jules Verne's classic adventure novel *Around the World in 80 Days*—but you can always count on the massive King Gator float and multistory Riverboat to roll down Universal's boulevards. The floats are each accompanied by dozens of strolling performers and stilt walkers, while costumed revelers ride upon them and toss colorful plastic beads to the crowds below.

The parade typically follows the same route as the daily Superstar Parade but in reverse, starting and ending at Hollywood's Esoteric Pictures gate near the *Horror Make-Up Show* and traveling clockwise around New York and the waterfront.

Viewing Tips: The parade takes about 15 minutes to pass by any one spot, and it lasts around 45 minutes. The parade generally begins around 7:15 p.m. before Daylight Saving begins, and 7:45 p.m. after the clocks spring forward. Times may vary with operating hours, so check the park map for details. You can find good viewing anywhere along the parade route, and unless you insist on standing right up front, there's no need to save your spot more than 10 or 15 minutes in advance.

Special reserved viewing areas are also available for annual-pass holders (near Mel's Drive-In), American Express card holders (near Finnegan's), guests with disabilities (near Macy's in New York), and young Little Jesters and their families (near *Terminator 2: 3-D*).

If you really want to get in on the action, it's possible to volunteer as a bead-tossing float rider. Annual-pass holders can sign up for themselves and a guest online; you must RSVP at least one week in advance. If space is available, additional riders may be recruited from park guests in the afternoon. All riders must be at least 18 years old (or accompanied by an adult) and 48 inches tall; space is limited and availability is not guaranteed.

Mardi Gras Live Concerts

Every Mardi Gras event night, after the parade concludes (approximately 45 minutes after it begins), a "big-name" concert kicks off on Music Plaza Stage underneath the Hollywood Rip Ride Rockit roller coaster. The concerts are a definite highlight of Universal's Mardi Gras celebration. With dozens of great musical acts entertaining the crowd at no extra cost, there is really no downside to these fantastic concerts, other than the extraordinary crowds that popular artists can draw. To get an idea of the quality of the acts, performers in recent years have included heavyweights from the past—Foreigner, Huey Lewis and the News, Olivia Newton-John, Styx, Heart, The B-52s—and present, such as Nelly, Weezer, Daughtry, Robin Thicke, All-American Rejects, and Trey Songz. In addition to the headliners, Universal also sets up a small stage near the French Quarter food stalls, where authentic New Orleans musicians play zydeco and blues before the big show.

Viewing Tips: There is no additional charge for Mardi Gras concerts; they are included with park admission. All concerts are standing-room only and first-come, first-serve; crowds can be enormous, and folks sometimes start lining up shortly after park opening for the hottest acts. There is no extra-cost VIP area available, but there is an ADA-accessible viewing section near the *Twister* restrooms. Large video screens broadcast the stage to those standing in the far back, so consider watching from the New York Battery Park area if you aren't an überfan of the artist.

ROCK THE UNIVERSE *(early September)*

UNIVERSAL ORLANDO BILLS ROCK the Universe, its annual weekend of fist-pumping praise rock-and-roller coasters, as "Florida's biggest Christian music festival." Ironically, it's always scheduled on the exact same two early September days as Disney's eerily similar Night of Joy event; that kind of cutthroat competition doesn't seem quite Christian to us, but what do we know? Only that this hard-ticket after-hours event attracts hordes of surprisingly rowdy church youth groups, who get access to the parks starting at 4 p.m. and keep boogieing for the Lord until 1 a.m.

Concerts take place across three stages inside Universal Studios Florida, and start after the park closes to day guests at 6 p.m. Past acts have included Kari Jobe, Third Day, Newsboys, Jeremy Camp, Switchfoot, tobyMac, and Lecrae. Most of the park's thrill rides (*except* Diagon Alley) operate during Rock the Universe, and Hollywood Rip Ride Rockit is reprogrammed with Christian rock songs. There's also a Saturday night candle-lighting ceremony and a Sunday morning worship service in the *Fear Factor Live* stadium (we always pray at that show).

In 2015, Rock the Universe takes place on the nights of September 11 and 12. Single-night tickets start around $62, with a weekend pass with daytime park-to-park access going for about $161. Attendees can buy discounted Rock Your Weekend tickets that combine both event nights with daytime park tickets. Universal Express Passes run an additional $20–$30 per night. Youth group leaders get a free ticket for every 10 their charges purchase, plus free access to Universal Express ride queues and lounges with free snacks. Learn more at **universalorlando.com/events/rock-the-universe/event-info.aspx.**

HALLOWEEN HORROR NIGHTS
(late September and October)

THE GODFATHER (OR IS THAT GOREFATHER?) of all Universal Orlando seasonal events, Universal Orlando's Halloween Horror Nights (or HHN, as it's known to its legions of bloodthirsty fans) is recognized as the nation's most popular and industry-awarded haunted theme park event. Originally a locals-friendly filler during a normally slow season, Universal Studios Florida's Halloween celebration started in 1991 as a single weekend of Fright Nights and proved popular enough to almost single-handedly save Universal's financial skin during the park's lean early years. Over the last quarter century, HHN has grown so famous that the seven-week-long scare-abration can provide a substantial percentage of USF's annual attendance statistics. Much like visiting any of Orlando's theme parks during a peak holiday season, an evening at HHN can be tremendous fun if you go in with a solid plan and sane expectations. Without those things . . . well, you might be better off eaten by zombies!

We've been attending HHN every year since 1996, and it has become one of our favorite after-dark activities in any park, but it isn't for everybody. Before attending, make sure Universal's brand of Halloween is right for you; this ain't Mickey's Not-So-Scary. Halloween Horror Nights is a gory, gruesome bacchanalia of simulated violence and tasteless satire, marinated with a liberal dose of alcohol and rock-and-roll. In other words, it's a heck of a party as long as you know what you're getting into. If the idea of copious blood, guts, and booze doesn't appeal to you, we advise staying far, far away. Needless to say, it is not appropriate for young children, though you will likely see many there.

The three basic elements of each year's event are haunted houses (or mazes), outdoor scare zones, and theater shows. Universal also makes many of its regular rides available during HHN, though admission to The Wizarding World of Harry Potter–Diagon Alley is *not* included in the event.

Planning for Halloween Horror Nights

Even more so than daytime touring, a successful HHN visit requires a careful date selection. In 2015, Halloween Horror Nights is held on 30 select nights between September 18 and November 1; visit **halloweenhorrornights.com/orlando/dates.html** for the operational calendar. In short, you want to avoid all Saturdays (especially the final three leading up to Halloween) like the plague. Fridays in October—particularly the last two before Halloween—aren't much better. Wednesday nights are usually the least crowded, followed by Thursdays (especially the first two) and Sundays (especially the first, but excluding the last). Halloween night itself and any nights after it are often extremely quiet. The price of Express Passes on a given night (as listed at **halloweenhorrornights.com/orlando/express-pass.html**) is your best guide to how busy it will be: The larger the cost, the larger the crowds.

If you walk up to the box office on the night of the event, you'll pay $102 plus tax—a frightening sum for a little as 5.5 hours in the park—and likely wait in a ridiculously long line for the privilege. Instead, study the myriad online ticket options in advance and purchase before you leave home.

Deep discounts (up to $52 off) are offered online to Florida residents with coupon codes from Coca-Cola cans. If you aren't eligible for those, consider getting an annual pass, which entitles you to even deeper price breaks and early event entry during pass-holder parties on select nights during the opening weekends.

Finally, if you are a hard-core haunt fan and spending more than a night in the area, you'll want a Frequent Fear (valid every Sunday–Thursday event night, with Fridays included in the Plus version for an extra fee) or Rush of Fear (valid every event night through the first Sunday in October) multiday pass.

unofficial **TIP**
You can buy a Rush of Fear ticket and upgrade it to a Frequent Fear ticket on or before its expiration date for maximum value.

Universal Orlando's paid line-skipping service is a welcome luxury during the day but an absolute lifesaver at night. On peak event nights, queues for the haunted houses will approach three hours, and even on the slowest nights, they will hit 60 minutes. HHN Express Passes reduce that wait to 25%–33% of what it would otherwise be, which can make the difference between experiencing two or three houses in a night or visiting seven or eight. The only catch is that Express starts at $70 per person and goes up to more than $120 depending on the night. Express is also available as an add-on for Rush of Fear or Frequent Fear multinight passes. Express Passes often sell out and may be more expensive or unavailable inside the park, so if you do want them, buy in advance. On off-peak nights it is possible to experience all eight houses and at least one show without Express, if you arrive early. On peak nights it is virtually impossible to do the same without Express Passes, and can be challenging even with them.

If you're feeling particularly flush and are fed up with any kind of queue, the RIP guided tour will whisk you to the head of every line for "only" $140 and up, admission not included. A private RIP tour for you and up to 10 of your friends starts at $1,399. When money is no object and you want to feel like theme park royalty, the RIP tours are highly recommended. Call ☎ 866-346-9350 or e-mail **vipexperience@ universalorlando.com** for pricing and reservations.

For the superfans with extra spending money, Universal offers a choice of in-depth HHN experiences. Join one of Universal's designers on daytime light-on trips through three houses on each of the two Unmasking the Horror behind-the-scenes tours ($65 and up for one tour, $120 for both). These tours can't be booked online; call ☎ 866-346-9350 or e-mail **vipexperience@universalorlando.com** for pricing and reservations.

Halloween Horror Nights Touring Tips

The event officially begins each evening at 6:30 p.m., but the front gates typically open as early as 6 p.m. If you have an HHN ticket but not daytime admission, you'll want to be outside the park gates, ticket in hand, by 5:45 p.m. at the latest on slow nights, and as early as 5 p.m. on peak nights. Be sure to leave ample time for I-4 traffic and parking, which is full price until 8 p.m. and $5 until 10 p.m. Valet parking is available, but remember that there is no free or discounted valet for annual-pass holders on event nights.

Your goal is to be among the first through the security check-points, which can slow entry down for latecomers. You will have your bags inspected, be asked to empty your pockets, and pass through a metal detector—basically the full TSA treatment, minus removing your shoes. If you travel light (highly recommended), look for a much swifter "no bags" security check, which may be available to the left of the entry arches.

On-site hotel guests also get their own exclusive entrance on the far right end of the USF arches. Note that the unlimited Express access included with some resort rooms is not valid during HHN.

Once through the checkpoint, secure a spot as close to the turn-stiles as possible; don't be shy about lining up at the temporary entry scanners at the center gate. Early arrivals also get a view of the gate-opening performance, which occurs on the balcony above the ticketing area closest to Guest Services. Don't worry if you miss this minor event; it's a nice touch but not essential.

Better yet, get a jump on the general public outside the gates by being inside the park before they open. The park closes to daytime guests at 5 p.m. on event nights, but anyone holding a ticket for that night's HHN is allowed to remain inside the park in designated holding areas. Universal no longer sells a specific Stay & Scream ticket for early entry; anyone can access this opportunity if they have any valid daytime park ticket, including annual-pass holders.

Note that the park is officially open for regular operations until 5 p.m., but you'll want to enter before 4:30 p.m. to avoid dealing with the evening security setup. Between the park's closing and reopening, guests remaining in the park are confined to one of the following Stay & Scream locations:

- The **Woody Woodpecker's KidZone** section near E.T. Adventure features priority access to the first two haunted houses that open each evening. Guests in this area can queue as early as 4 p.m. and are allowed into the two houses with entrances there between 5:30 and 5:45 p.m. Guests are released from the area at 6 p.m. and can be the first to queue for the house nearest to Men in Black Alien Attack. There is a limited selection of food and drink vendors available in this location. Note that on the first two weekends, this area is restricted to annual-pass holders who have registered online for an exclusive pass-holder event, during which three houses are opened as early as 5:15 p.m.

- The **New York** holding area includes Finnegan's Bar and Grill, which offers a full liquor bar and table-service food, though reservations are virtually impossible to secure between 4 and 7 p.m. Guests here are released around 5:45 p.m., giving them first crack at the soundstage houses.

- A small overflow holding area is located in **Hollywood** near *Lucy—A Tribute*. There is no food or beverage available here, but you do get early access to the soundstages.

- Finally, there is a holding area at **Diagon Alley,** and guests with both park-to-park daytime tickets and HHN admission may ride the Hogwarts Express train in from Islands of Adventure. Guests here are staged on the bridge leading to Springfield and reach the maze near Men in Black Alien Attack around the same time as those exiting KidZone do.

The haunted houses (expanded to nine for the 25th anniversary) are the signature attractions at HHN and quickly develop wait times ranging from moderate to absolutely ridiculous. Each year, due to theme or location, some houses seem to attract longer queues than others. In 2014, *Aliens vs. Predators, Halloween,* and *The Walking Dead* were the most popular, with *From Dusk Til Dawn* and *Roanoke* drawing shorter lines than average. For the 2015 silver anniversary, popular event icon Jack the Clown returns as ringmaster, with horror heavyweights such as Freddy Krueger, Jason Voorhees, Scream, and the American Werewolf in London headlining the haunted houses. Keep this in mind when deciding whether to bite the bullet and queue up for a particular maze.

Even the least popular houses, however, will have peak waits of 30 minutes or more, even on less busy nights. Your first hour at the event is therefore essential to making the most of the evening, and your initial plan of attack is determined by which location you start your night from:

- **Woody Woodpecker's KidZone Holding Area:** If you are among the first inside the KidZone Stay & Scream area, queue up for the parade building house (enter near E.T. Adventure) as soon as allowed. The exit of that maze leads directly to the entrance of the first sprung tent house (enter next to the KidZone stage), which is conveniently your second stop. Alternatively, if you are late entering the holding area, the queue for the first house may already be posted at an hour or more. In that case, do the tent house first, saving the parade building for later in the early-entry period (the wait should diminish rapidly) or late in the evening. Guests should be released from the KidZone area between 5:45 and 6 p.m. and can line up for the second tent house near MIB Gear, or cross the park to the open soundstage houses.

- **Finnegan's Bar and Grill Holding Area:** Enter the New York holding area between 4 and 5 p.m. (the earlier the better, especially if you want get food or drink), receive a wristband, and relax until released around 5:45 p.m. You will have a short head start on everyone else for the first of the soundstage houses to open. Once the general public is admitted through the front gates (as early as 6 p.m.), queues at the soundstage houses will swiftly build; see as many as you can until waits exceed 30 minutes, and then proceed to the houses in the back of the park.

- **General Admission:** If you are among the first folks through the gates when they open around 6 p.m., head straight to the open soundstage houses and jump in line if it is still 15 minutes or less. Otherwise, the majority of guests will mob the four houses located in the soundstages near the front of the park. You should avoid the horde by heading in the opposite direction, toward Woody Woodpecker's KidZone, which should have processed the majority of Stay & Scream guests by now. You can also continue around the London Waterfront to the house in the *Disaster!* queue.

*un**official* TIP

Don't waste time at the beginning of the evening queuing for a house that hasn't yet opened when you could be enjoying short waits at the mazes that are operating. Houses that don't open until after 6:30 will accumulate a large backlog of guests before they begin operating, so save them for the end of the night instead.

After the haunted houses, the *Bill & Ted's Excellent Halloween Adventure* show (staged inside the *Fear Factor Live* stadium) is the event's most popular element. Each year's skits skewer pop-culture celebrities and current events while pulling out the stops with pyrotechnics and barely clad dancers. The first and last showings are typically the only ones you can attend without lining up 45–60 minutes in advance. If you have already seen three or four houses by 7 p.m. (and are interested in a raunchy spoof), make your way to *Bill & Ted* about 30 minutes before the 7:30 p.m. first show. You'll be entertained by a parade of painful-looking YouTube clips while you wait for the show to start.

If you've only hit one or two houses so far, and posted wait times are still moderate (under 30 minutes), you can skip the first *Bill & Ted* and slide into the final showing 15 minutes before showtime, as there are sometimes empty seats for the last performance on off-peak nights. In addition to *Bill & Ted*, there is usually a bawdy rock musical or magic show in the *Beetlejuice Graveyard Revue* or *Animal Actors on Location* stage. You can usually catch any of the midevening shows by arriving 10–20 minutes in advance.

After the sun sets (around 7:30 p.m.) and the waits for the houses become unbearable, begin exploring the scare zones, which are like open-air haunted mazes minus the conga-line queues. Just as much fun as getting scared yourself is finding a vantage point to stand still and see others getting spooked; this is some of the best people-watching you'll ever find. Be on the lookout for staged scenes, in which actors attack planted "victims" within the crowd.

By the midpoint of the evening, standby waits for all the houses will be substantial, and lines for the rides will be astronomical on Saturdays, but experiencing several top attractions should still be manageable using single-rider queues. Men in Black Alien Attack, Revenge of the Mummy, and Transformers: The Ride–3-D all have fairly efficient single-rider operations. (Transformers' singles queue is closed when it hits about 30 minutes but usually reopens after 10 or 15 minutes, so hang around nearby without blocking the entrance.) Hollywood Rip Ride Rockit has a single-rider line, but it is often as long as the standby queue, and none of the other operating rides have one at all. On off-peak nights, you may find ride queues shockingly short: Transformers and Despicable Me Minion Mayhem have been as short as 10 minutes even on peak event nights.

Even on a slow night, Horror Nights crowds can drive you to drink, and many of your fellow guests will doubtlessly be imbibing. There are temporary bars serving expensive mixed drinks on seemingly every spare square foot of sidewalk, but for serious in-park boozing, we prefer Finnegan's Bar or Duff Brewery in Springfield U.S.A. Better yet, if the park is open past midnight, get out of Dodge for an hour or so and retreat to CityWalk. Most HHN passes include admission to CityWalk's clubs, or you can grab a drink at Antojitos without a cover charge.

As the evening's event approaches its final hour, wait times at the haunted mazes drop dramatically. If you are interested in *Bill & Ted's Excellent Halloween Adventure* and didn't catch the first showing, show up 20–30 minutes before the last performance on peak nights (or 15 minutes before showtime off-peak). Otherwise, use the final hours to catch up on the houses you missed earlier. Lines at the two KidZone houses should remain manageable for most of the evening, and the house in the *Disaster!* queue is best experienced after dark. The last 30–60 minutes before park closing is the best time to hit the most popular houses. If you didn't see the most popular mazes at the start of the night, step into line for one of them at the last possible minute; you'll be allowed to stay in the queue until you're through.

Unless you leave significantly before closing time, you're best off dawdling in the park or CityWalk on the way out. The parking garage exits will be at a standstill, so you might as well grab a seat outside and relax rather than breathing fumes in a traffic jam.

HOLIDAYS AT UNIVERSAL STUDIOS & MACY'S HOLIDAY PARADE *(early December–early January)*

UNIVERSAL ORLANDO CELEBRATES the holiday season every year from the first Friday of December through the Saturday after New Year's. While Mickey's Very Merry Christmas Party, the Osborne Family Spectacle of Lights, and other seasonal entertainment at Walt Disney World seem to get the lion's share of publicity this time of year, visitors to Orlando shouldn't overlook Universal Orlando's holiday offerings. Universal Orlando holidays might not have quite the nostalgic lure of Mickey's merrymaking, but its options are every bit as expertly produced and have the benefit of all being included with regular park admission (unlike the extra-cost hard-ticket nighttime parties at the Magic Kingdom).

Universal Studios Florida's holiday festivities feature seasonal decoration on the front archway and throughout the park, holiday songs broadcasting from speakers in the streets, and a giant tree that is ceremoniously lit every evening at dusk. Several park attractions, such as *The Blues Brothers Show* and *A Day in the Park with Barney,* get into the spirit with special versions tied to the season. But the star of the holidays at Universal Studios is undoubtedly the Macy's Holiday Parade.

USF has been bringing **Macy's Holiday Parade** down to Orlando for a post-Thanksgiving encore every December for more than a decade. While the largest balloons you've seen sailing through Manhattan on television can't make it down the narrower streets of Universal Studios, several of the smaller ones are paraded through both productions, and more of the classic king-size inflatables (such as Garfield and Grover) can be seen on stationary display around the park.

Since 2013, the newest star of the Macy's Holiday Parade is the Happy Purple Hippo (complete with pink toenails), a throwback to the 1940s that was re-created by Macy's parade design team at the express request of Universal show director Lora Wallace. The hippo is the centerpiece of a preshow dance routine that can be seen outside the Esoteric Pictures gate (near the *Horror Make-Up Show*) approximately 45 minutes before each parade.

The Macy's Holiday Parade begins each evening around 5 p.m. (subject to change; check the show schedule in your park map) near the *Horror Make-Up Show,* continues down Hollywood Boulevard toward the park entrance, travels past Despicable Me Minion Mayhem and *Shrek 4-D* toward New York, and then turns near Revenge of the Mummy and again past Transformers, exiting through the gate it originally entered.

You can get a good view of the parade from anywhere along the route, but ideal viewing spots are near Mel's Drive-In at the beginning of the route and near the large tree in New York toward the end. Reserved viewing areas are marked on the park map for guests with disabilities (in front of Macy's in New York), for annual-pass holders (near Mel's Drive-In), and for young Little Stars and their families (near *Terminator 2: 3-D*).

If you've always fantasized about guiding a giant inflatable animal down Fifth Avenue, you can volunteer to participate in the parade as a balloon handler for free. Volunteers must be 18 years or older, at least 48 inches tall and 125 pounds, English speaking, and able to walk the mile-long route for up to an hour. Sign-up is held daily two hours before the parade starts in Woody Woodpecker's KidZone near E.T. Adventure. A limited number of spots are available for guests each day, and you'll have to sign a waiver to participate.

After the parade on select nights, Universal Studios Florida's Music Plaza Stage hosts live concerts by **Mannheim Steamroller.** The electrified orchestra usually performs its amped-up holiday classics on the first two Saturdays and Sundays of the season. These shows can be popular, so arrive at least 45 minutes early if you want a close-up view.

UNIVERSAL STUDIOS
FLORIDA TOURING PLANS

BEGINNING ON PAGE 368, our step-by-step touring plans are field-tested for seeing *as much as possible* in one day with a minimum of time wasted in lines. They're designed to help you avoid crowds and bottlenecks on days of moderate to heavy attendance. Understand, however, that there's more to see at Universal Studios Florida than can be experienced in one day during peak season. If you are visiting on days of lighter attendance (see "Trying to Reason with the Tourist Season," page 28) or using Universal Express (see page 57), our plans will save you time but won't be as critical to successful touring as on busier days.

In general, most visitors find that they can be far more flexible with their touring plans at Universal than at Disney and still see everything they want to see. But if you are at the parks on a busy day, you're going to want to stick to the script, at least until you get the most popular attractions out of the way. Afternoon touring at USF is largely dependent on Universal's ever-shifting show schedule, so check showtimes on the park map as soon as you arrive and shuffle the steps accordingly.

Before using any of our Universal Orlando touring plans, first become familiar with Universal's park-opening procedures, as described on page 52 of Part One. Purchase your admission ahead of time, and call ☎ 407-363-8000 or check **universalorlando.com** the day before you go to verify official operating hours. If you are eligible for Early Park Admission (see page 54), arrive at Universal Studios Florida 90–120 minutes before the official park opening time. If you are not eligible for early entry, arrive at the park 30–45 minutes prior to opening time.

If you are using our Lines smartphone app, you can select any of the following premium touring plans, copy it to your list of personalized plans, and optimize the plan steps to your preferences. Once you arrive at the park, "select" the appropriate plan in the app to make it active, and track your progress during the day by marking each attraction as complete after exiting. Optimize the plan repeatedly during your day to refine it with the latest wait-time information. If you are following a two-park plan, a link to part two will appear at the top of the plan; switch to the second part when moving to the second park, and then return to part one when you return to the original park.

Once you're admitted into the park, move quickly from attraction to attraction, following your chosen touring plan exactly. If you're not interested in an attraction it lists, simply skip that attraction and proceed to the next. When you encounter a very long line at an attraction that the touring plan calls for, skip the attraction in question and go to the next step, returning later to retry. Don't worry that other people will be following the plans and render them useless. Fewer than 2 in every 100 people in the park will have been exposed to this info.

CHOOSING THE APPROPRIATE TOURING PLAN

WE PRESENT THREE UNIVERSAL STUDIOS Florida touring plans:

- Universal Studios Florida One-Day Touring Plan for Adults
- Universal Studios Florida One-Day Touring Plan for Parents with Small Children
- Universal Studios Florida One-Day Touring Plan for Seniors

In addition, we have three Universal Orlando touring plans that combine both Universal Studios Florida and Islands of Adventure, for guests with park-to-park admission:

- Universal Orlando Highlights One-Day/Two-Park Touring Plan
- Wizarding World One-Day/Two-Park Touring Plan
- Universal Orlando Comprehensive Two-Day/Two-Park Touring Plan

If you have two days at Universal Orlando, the Comprehensive Two-Day/Two-Park Plan is by far the most relaxed. The two-day plan takes advantage of early morning, when lines are short and the park hasn't filled with guests. This plan works well year-round and eliminates much of the extra walking required by the one-day plans. No matter when the park closes, our two-day plan guarantees the most efficient touring and the least time in lines. The plan is perfect for guests who wish to explore the attractions and the atmosphere of Universal Studios Florida and Islands of Adventure, with an emphasis on both Wizarding World areas.

If you have only one day to visit Universal Studios Florida and do not have park-to-park tickets, then use the One-Day Touring Plan for Adults. It's exhausting, but it packs in the maximum. If you have one-day park-to-park passes, the Universal Orlando Highlights Touring Plan will help you pack in all of the best thrill rides at USF and IOA, including The Wizarding World ones, at the expense of most shows and a lot of shoe leather. Alternatively, Harry Potter superfans who have one-day park-to-park passes, and zero interest in anything at Universal outside Hogsmeade and Diagon Alley (a mistake in our estimation, but it's your money), can follow The Wizarding World One-Day/Two-Park Touring Plan to maximize their magical immersion.

If you have young ones in tow, adopt the One-Day Touring Plan for Parents with Small Children. It's a compromise, blending the preferences of younger children with those of older siblings and adults. The plan includes many children's rides but omits roller coasters and other attractions that frighten young children or are off-limits because of height requirements greater than 40 inches. Or use the One-Day Touring Plan for Adults and take advantage of child swap, a technique whereby children accompany adults to the loading area of a ride with age and height requirements but don't board (see page 173).

If you have three days at Universal Orlando, use the Comprehensive Two-Day/Two-Park Touring Plan on the first two days, and use the Universal Orlando Highlights One-Day/Two-Park Touring Plan or Wizarding World Touring Plan on your last day. With four or more days, you can pretty much explore the parks at your leisure, using any of the plans as a general guideline.

UNIVERSAL STUDIOS FLORIDA ONE-DAY TOURING PLAN FOR ADULTS *(page 368)*

THIS PLAN IS FOR GUESTS without park-to-park tickets and includes every recommended attraction at USF. If a ride or show is listed that you don't want to experience, skip that step and proceed to the next. Move quickly from attraction to attraction, and if possible, hold off on lunch until after experiencing at least six rides.

UNIVERSAL STUDIOS FLORIDA ONE-DAY TOURING PLAN FOR PARENTS WITH SMALL CHILDREN *(page 369)*

THIS PLAN IS FOR GUESTS without park-to-park tickets and eliminates all rides with a minimum height requirement greater than 40 inches. The plan includes a midday break of at least two hours back at your hotel. It's debatable whether the kids will need the nap more than you, but you'll thank us later, we promise.

UNIVERSAL STUDIOS FLORIDA ONE-DAY TOURING PLAN FOR SENIORS *(page 370)*

THIS PLAN IS FOR GUESTS without park-to-park tickets and is specifically designed for seniors and grandparents, taking walking distances and attraction ratings from this group into account. This plan focuses on shows and family-friendly attractions and avoids thrill rides.

UNIVERSAL ORLANDO HIGHLIGHTS ONE-DAY/ TWO-PARK TOURING PLAN *(pages 374–375)*

THIS PLAN IS FOR GUESTS with one-day park-to-park tickets who wish to see the highlights of Universal Studios Florida and Islands of Adventure in a single day. The plan uses Hogwarts Express to get from one park to the other and then back again; you can walk back to the first park for the return leg if the line is too long. The plan includes a table-service lunch at Mythos (make reservations online a few days before your visit) and dinner at the Leaky Cauldron; during holiday periods, you may need to substitute a quick-service snack for one or both meals to fit in all of the plan's attractions.

WIZARDING WORLD ONE-DAY/TWO-PARK TOURING PLAN *(pages 376–377)*

THIS PLAN IS FOR GUESTS with one-day park-to-park tickets who wish to experience The Wizarding World of Harry Potter to the exclusion of everything else Universal has to offer. The plan uses Hogwarts Express to get from one park to the other and then back again; you can walk back to the first park for the return leg if the line is too long. The plan includes lunch at Three Broomsticks and dinner at the Leaky Cauldron; during holiday periods, you may need to substitute a quick-service snack for one or both meals to fit in all of the plan's attractions.

UNIVERSAL ORLANDO COMPREHENSIVE TWO-DAY/ TWO-PARK TOURING PLAN *(pages 378–381)*

THIS PLAN IS FOR GUESTS with multiday park-to-park tickets who wish to explore Universal Studios Florida and Islands of Adventure in-depth over two days. The plan includes one Hogwarts Express trip between parks per day. Incidentally, all the water rides are concentrated in the morning of the second day, so if bad weather is in the forecast, consider flipping the plan days.

PART EIGHT

UNIVERSAL'S ISLANDS *of* ADVENTURE

UNIVERSAL STUDIOS FLORIDA HAD BARELY opened before planning began on Project X, the second theme park that would provide Universal with enough critical mass to actually compete with Disney. Originally envisioned as Cartoon World, with areas devoted to DC Comics superheroes and Looney Tunes characters, the concept evolved into Islands of Adventure (IOA), a fully themed fantasy park inspired by family-friendly literature.

From its very inception, IOA was designed to directly compete with Disney's Magic Kingdom. (How direct a competitor is it? See page 296 for a comparison.) The park has more kid-friendly rides and cartoon characters (like Fantasyland), thrill rides in a sci-fi city (like Tomorrowland), and a jungle river with robot creatures (like Adventureland). Its layout—a central entry corridor leading to a ring of connected lands—even mimics the classic Disneyland model, with one major exception: Instead of a hub and castle in the center, Universal built a large lagoon, whose estuaries separate the park's thematically diverse "islands" (actually peninsulas).

Universal's Islands of Adventure debuted in 1999 as a state-of-the-art park competing with a Disney park decades older, but it didn't initially do gangbuster business, thanks partly to a botched marketing rollout and Universal's failure to add any major attractions during IOA's first decade. That all changed in 2010, which marked IOA's coming-out party. In one of the greatest seismic shifts in theme park history, Universal opened the first Harry Potter–themed area within the park. Harry P. is possibly the only fictional character extant capable of trumping Mickey Mouse, and Universal went all out, under J. K. Rowling's watchful and exacting eye, to create a setting and attractions designed to be the envy of the industry.

Continued on page 296

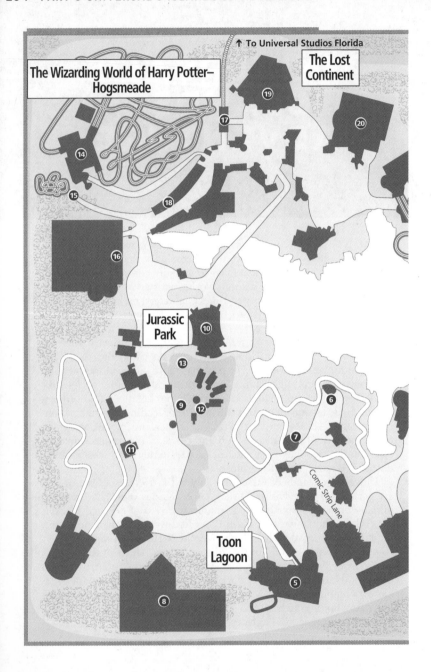

↑ To Universal Studios Florida

The Lost Continent

The Wizarding World of Harry Potter–Hogsmeade

Jurassic Park

Toon Lagoon

Comic Strip Lane

Marvel Super Hero Island

1. The Amazing Adventures of Spider-Man
2. Doctor Doom's Fearfall
3. The Incredible Hulk Coaster
4. Storm Force Accelatron

Toon Lagoon

5. Dudley Do-Right's Ripsaw Falls
6. Me Ship, *The Olive*
7. Popeye & Bluto's Bilge-Rat Barges

Skull Island

8. Skull Island: Reign of Kong (opens 2016)

Jurassic Park

9. Camp Jurassic
10. Jurassic Park Discovery Center
11. Jurassic Park River Adventure
12. Pteranodon Flyers
13. Raptor Encounter

The Wizarding World of Harry Potter–Hogsmeade

14. Dragon Challenge
15. Flight of the Hippogriff
16. Harry Potter and the Forbidden Journey
17. Hogwarts Express
18. Ollivanders

The Lost Continent

19. *The Eighth Voyage of Sindbad Stunt Show*
20. *Poseidon's Fury*

Seuss Landing

21. Caro-Seuss-el
22. The Cat in the Hat
23. The High in the Sky Seuss Trolley Train Ride!
24. If I Ran the Zoo
25. *Oh! The Stories You'll Hear!*
26. One Fish, Two Fish, Red Fish, Blue Fish

Seuss Landing

Port of Entry

Pharos Lighthouse

Marvel Super Hero Island

Continued from page 293

IOA AND THE MAGIC KINGDOM AT A GLANCE	
ISLANDS OF ADVENTURE	**MAGIC KINGDOM**
• Seven "islands" *(includes Port of Entry)*	• Six "lands" *(includes Main Street)*
• Two adult roller coaster attractions	• Two adult roller coaster attractions
• A Dumbo-type ride	• Dumbo the Flying Elephant
• One log flume ride	• One log flume ride
• Toon Lagoon character area	• Storybook Circus character area

NOT TO BE MISSED AT ISLANDS OF ADVENTURE
MARVEL SUPER HERO ISLAND • The Amazing Adventures of Spider-Man • The Incredible Hulk Coaster
TOON LAGOON • Popeye & Bluto's Bilge-Rat Barges
JURASSIC PARK • Jurassic Park River Adventure • Skull Island: Reign of Kong
THE WIZARDING WORLD OF HARRY POTTER–DIAGON ALLEY • Dragon Challenge • Harry Potter and the Forbidden Journey • Hogwarts Express

BEWARE OF THE WET AND WILD

THOUGH WE'VE DESCRIBED Universal's Islands of Adventure as a direct competitor to the Magic Kingdom, know this: Whereas most Magic Kingdom attractions are designed to be enjoyed by guests of any age, attractions at Islands of Adventure are created largely for an under-40 population. The roller coasters at Universal are serious with a capital *S*, making Space Mountain and Big Thunder Mountain look about as frightening as Dumbo. In fact, seven of the top nine attractions at IOA are thrill rides; of these, three will not only scare the crap out of you but will also drench you with water.

*un*official **TIP**
Roller coasters at Islands of Adventure are the real deal—not for the faint-hearted or for little ones.

For families, there are three interactive playgrounds as well as six rides that young children will enjoy. Of the thrill rides, only the two in Toon Lagoon (described later) are marginally appropriate for little kids, and even on these rides, your child needs to be fairly hardy.

GETTING ORIENTED *at* UNIVERSAL'S ISLANDS *of* ADVENTURE

ISLANDS OF ADVENTURE is laid out much like Epcot's World Show-case—arranged in a large circle surrounding a lagoon—but it evinces the same thematic continuity present in the Magic Kingdom. Each "land," or "island" in this case, is self-contained and visually consistent in its theme.

You first encounter **Port of Entry,** a mélange of Middle Eastern and Asian architecture where you'll find Guest Services, lockers, stroller and wheelchair rentals, ATM banking, Lost and Found, and shopping. From the Port of Entry, moving clockwise around the lagoon, you access **Marvel Super Hero Island, Toon Lagoon, Jurassic Park, The Wizarding World of Harry Potter–Hogsmeade, The Lost Continent,** and **Seuss Landing.** There is no in-park transportation to move you between lands.

As you enter Islands of Adventure, lockers and rentals are to your left, and First Aid and Guest Services are to your right. Before bolting through Port of Entry to your first adventure—or at least on your way out before leaving—take a few moments to appreciate the Disney-quality details that Universal lavished on this area, from the fountain made of giant leaves, to the sounds of gamblers from an upstairs casino, to the jail that's been broken and the fire station that burned down. Also listen for the original background music, which is synchronized throughout the park and changes as you move from island to island. Port of Entry doesn't have any attractions, but it does have dining (including a Starbucks) and shopping options.

UNIVERSAL'S ISLANDS *of* ADVENTURE ATTRACTIONS

MARVEL SUPER HERO ISLAND

THIS ISLAND, WITH ITS FUTURISTIC and retro-future design and comic book signage, offers shopping, dining, and two of Orlando's best thrill rides, all based on Marvel Comics characters. The architecture, which some fault as flat, seeks to re-create the Pop Art look of comic book backgrounds; some buildings have Chrome Illusion paint that changes colors depending on the angle of sunlight. Look for the meteor impact sculpture covered in hundreds of Marvel characters, as well as communication booths delivering messages from S.H.I.E.L.D.

Several times a day on a published schedule, Marvel heroes parade in on all-terrain vehicles and take over the streets greeting guests; the activity can make it tough to navigate through the area. Between the Hulk's roar and the bass beats surrounding the Spider-Man building, Super Hero Island is also one of the loudest sections of the park; seek refuge along the water behind Captain America Diner.

In case you were curious: Yes, Disney now owns Marvel Comics, but Universal locked up the theme park rights to certain character groups—the Avengers, Spider-Man, Fantastic Four, and X-Men—in perpetuity on the East Coast. You may see Iron Man and Captain America in Disneyland or Mickey's international parks, but they are exclusive to Islands of Adventure in Orlando (and Universal Studios Japan) for the indefinite future.

The Amazing Adventures of Spider-Man
(Universal Express) ★★★★★

APPEAL BY AGE	PRESCHOOL ★	GRADE SCHOOL ★★★★★	TEENS ★★★★★
YOUNG ADULTS ★★★★½	OVER 30 ★★★★½	SENIORS ★★★★★	

What it is Indoor adventure 3-D simulator ride. **Scope and scale** Super-headliner. **When to go** During the first 40 minutes the park is open. **Special comments** 40" minimum height requirement. **Authors' rating** One of the best attractions anywhere; not to be missed; ★★★★★. **Duration of ride** 4½ minutes. **Probable waiting time per 100 people ahead of you** 5 minutes. **Loading speed** Fast.

DESCRIPTION AND COMMENTS Widely regarded as one of the best theme park attractions in Orlando, and one of our favorite rides anywhere in the world, The Amazing Adventures of Spider-Man was enhanced in 2012 with a complete 4K high-definition digital upgrade, maintaining its position at the top of IOA's must-do list. The attraction moves a spinning, tilting ride vehicle through 13 scenes (covering 1.5 acres) of mayhem, which fuse 3-D digital projections almost seamlessly with actual sets and props, accompanied by special effects including fog, water, and fire. In many instances guests cannot tell until the action begins whether they're looking at a movie screen or an actual brick wall.

The total package is astonishing—frenetic yet fluid, and visually rich. The ride is wild yet very smooth. Though the attractions are not directly comparable, Spider-Man is technologically ahead of The Twilight Zone Tower of Terror at Disney's Hollywood Studios—which is to say it will leave you in awe.

The story line is that you're visiting the *Daily Bugle* newspaper (where Peter Parker, also known as Spider-Man, works as a mild-mannered photographer), when crime reports start coming in. The Sinister Syndicate—consisting of Spidey's archenemies Doctor Octopus, Hobgoblin, Electro, Hydro-Man, and Scream—have used an antigravity gun to steal (we promise we're not making this up) the Statue of Liberty. You're drafted on the spot by cantankerous editor J. Jonah Jameson to get the story. You board a 12-passenger SCOOP vehicle—a mobile open-top motion simulator identical to the cars used in USF's Transformers—and follow the "Spider Signal" straight into an epic battle between the web-slinger and his foes.

The Amazing Adventures of Spider-Man combines your ride vehicle's motion so smoothly with the film sequences that you quickly believe you're part of the action. Without giving away too much of the surprise, one part of the attraction has you raised high above the city skyline. After speeding around, you experience a 400-foot sensory drop from a skyscraper roof all the way to the pavement. The blending of 3-D film and pitching of the ride car is so convincing that, during our first ride, we were sure that we were being lifted inside the building; we had to ride a second time, with our glasses off, to see how the effect was done while keeping the car on the ground.

Even though Spidey's cybertronic sibling in USF has proven popular, the original 3-D dark ride has held its ground as the first and still favorite in its genre. It's less frantic and frenetic than Transformers and features more dialogue and humor. And despite using similar systems, some folks who get motion sick on Transformers find that they can tolerate this ride better.

TOURING TIPS If you were on hand at park opening, ride after experiencing Harry Potter and the Forbidden Journey, Dragon Challenge, and The Incredible Hulk Coaster. If you elect to bypass The Wizarding World congestion, ride after Hulk. If you arrived more than 15 minutes after park opening, skip Wizarding World attractions and ride Spider-Man after Hulk.

Seats in the first row are the most immersive, but we find that the 3-D effects focus better from a row or two back. The rear corners get the most movement, while the center of the second row is the most stable.

The standby and Express queues both wind through portions of the *Daily Bugle* newsroom, but only standby stops at a green screen photo op that puts you on the cover of the paper. The single-rider option, when available, can greatly cut your wait as long as the line doesn't reach the stroller parking area.

UNIVERSAL UNDERCOVER WITH JIM HILL

WHERE'S WALDO—UH, STAN? Marvel Comics founder Stan Lee angles for a cameo appearance in any film featuring the characters he helped create, so the Universal creative team decided to get in on the fun by folding him into the recently retooled Spider-Man ride. Lee appears in four scenes in the attraction: as the truck driver who swerves to miss your SCOOP vehicle early in the ride, in the crowd as Spidey and Doc Ock duke it out in New York City's Theater District, in the street after your vehicle falls to the ground, and finally with the cops as the stolen Statue of Liberty is being flown back into place. He also is the voice that bids you farewell before disembarking.

Doctor Doom's Fearfall *(Universal Express)*   ★★★

APPEAL BY AGE	PRESCHOOL ★	GRADE SCHOOL ★★★★½	TEENS ★★★★½
YOUNG	ADULTS ★★★★	OVER 30 ★★★½	SENIORS ★★

What it is Tower launch and free fall. **Scope and scale** Headliner. **When to go** First 40 minutes the park is open. **Special comments** 52″ minimum height requirement. **Authors' rating** More bark than bite; ★★★. **Duration of ride** 40 seconds. **Probable waiting time per 100 people ahead of you** 18 minutes. **Loading speed** Slow.

DESCRIPTION AND COMMENTS Here you are (again), strapped into a seat with your feet dangling and blasted 200 feet up in the air and then allowed to partially free-fall back down. Imagine the midway game wherein a macho guy swings a sledgehammer, propelling a metal sphere up a vertical shaft to ring a bell—on this ride, you're the metal sphere.

That prospect sounds worse than it actually is. The scariest part of the ride by far is the apprehension that builds as you sit, strapped in, waiting for the ride to launch. Blasting up and falling down are actually pleasant, with one exhilarating, fleeting moment of negative-g "air time" at the top. Riders in chambers 3 and 4 get a great view of the park, while those in 1 and 2 look out over I-4 and International Drive.

TOURING TIPS We've seen glaciers that move faster than the line for Doctor Doom's Fearfall, though the ominous queue and satirical propaganda films compensate slightly. If you want to ride without investing half a day, be one of the first to ride. If you're on hand at opening time, being among the first isn't too difficult (mainly because the nearby Wizarding World, Hulk, and Spider-Man attractions are bigger draws).

Fortunately, as this reader discovered, Doctor Doom also has a singles line that's nearly always open:

If you ask a staff member for the single-rider line, they'll send you through the exit in the arcade. Then just follow the signs.

The Incredible Hulk Coaster *(Universal Express)* ★★★★½

What it is Roller coaster. **Scope and scale** Super-headliner. **When to go** During the first 40 minutes the park is open. **Special comments** 54″ minimum height requirement. **Authors' rating** A coaster-lover's coaster; not to be missed; ★★★★½. **Duration of ride** 2¼ minutes. **Probable waiting time per 100 people ahead of you** 9 minutes. **Loading speed** Moderate.

DESCRIPTION AND COMMENTS Screams from The Incredible Hulk Coaster are

Motion Sickness

heard almost from the minute you enter IOA. Those shrieks dominate the auditory experience of anyone in the front half of the park, much the same way Hulk's giant green, curved steel track dominates the landscape, and the ride's distinctive roar (the track was intentionally designed without the normal dampening) is nearly deafening if you stand under the initial inversion as a car rushes past.

The coaster's backstory is that Dr. Bruce Banner is trying to reverse the effects of gamma ray radiation he previously suffered, which is responsible for periodically turning him into the colossal green monster with incredible strength known as the Hulk. Something goes wrong during the process, and you're swept along through the mayhem. The story falls apart almost as soon as the ride starts, but you'll be too scared to notice.

What you need to know about this attraction is simple. You'll be shot like a carrier-launched jet from 0 to 40 mph in two seconds, flung upside down into a zero-gravity barrel roll 100 feet off the ground (which will, of course, induce weightlessness), and then thrown immediately into a pair of cobra rolls and a vertical loop of more than 100 feet, into a belowground tunnel, no less! Two more rolls and another loop follow, for a total of seven upside-down experiences in a ride of a little more than 2 minutes. At the end of the ride, you may be just as green as the Hulk.

Seriously, the Hulk is a great roller coaster, one of the best in Florida, providing a ride comparable to that of Kumba or Montu (Busch Gardens) with the added thrill of an accelerated launch, instead of the more typical uphill crank. The Hulk's ride is no longer as remarkably smooth as in years past, but Hulk's steel track doesn't yet supply the side-to-side head shaking or uncomfortable jerkiness of Rip Ride Rockit next door. Luckily, a major refurbishment of the Hulk coaster—from track to launch mechanism to theming—is rumored for the near future. Yes, the experience is terrifying, but you'll be focused on the gut-wrenching drops and turns, not on having your head bumped around.

TOURING TIPS Our advice is to skip The Wizarding World attractions in the early morning and ride The Incredible Hulk Coaster first thing. Alternatively, if you insist on going to Hogsmeade at rope drop (or you are eligible for Early Park Admission), you should ride Hulk immediately after you've enjoyed Harry Potter and the Forbidden Journey, Flight of the Hippogriff, and Dragon Challenge.

Universal provides electronic lockers near the entrance of the Hulk to deposit any items that might depart your person during the ride. Use the lockers for anything—and we mean anything—that could be dislodged during your ride: hats, glasses, cell phones, camera bags, and toupees. The lockers are free for the duration of your wait, and use of these lockers is enforced; be prepared to pat down your pockets for loose change, or you'll be pulled aside for a TSA-style wanding after triggering the metal detectors.

When you reach the boarding area, note that the Hulk has a separate line for those who want to ride in the first row. Riders in the front row of Hulk get a spectacular, brief view of the park. If you get to Hulk early enough and the line is short enough, opt for the special front-row line near the boarding area. It's worth waiting an extra 5 or 10 minutes. The best seat is actually the back left, which gets the best zero-g effect from the opening inversion.

There's also a singles line, but it isn't always open. Even when it is, you may not notice it at first, as this reader attests:

> *The single-rider line is kind of hard to find—ask where it is. I stood in the standby line for 20 minutes before I realized my mistake.*

Storm Force Accelatron *(Universal Express)* ★★½

APPEAL BY AGE	PRESCHOOL ★★★★★	GRADE SCHOOL ★★★½	TEENS ★★★
YOUNG ADULTS ★★★½	OVER 30 ★★½		SENIORS—

What it is Covered spinning ride. **Scope and scale** Minor attraction. **Special comments** May induce motion sickness. **When to go** During the first hour the park is open. **Authors' rating** Spiffed-up teacups; ★★½. **Duration of ride** 1½ minutes. **Probable waiting time per 100 people ahead of you** 21 minutes. **Loading speed** Slow.

Motion Sickness

DESCRIPTION AND COMMENTS Storm Force Accelatron is a spiffed-up version of Disney's nausea-inducing Mad Tea Party. In Storm Force Accelatron, up to five people are seated in a round plastic ride vehicle that has a metal wheel mounted in the center. Turning the metal wheel causes the ride vehicle to spin on its central axis. While that's happening, each ride vehicle is part of a group of three similar vehicles, also spinning around a common axis. And the entire group of 12 ride vehicles is simultaneously spinning around the Accelatron's center.

In Universal's take on this carnival classic, you spin to the accompaniment of a simulated thunderstorm. Flashing lights and loud music either really enhance the experience or make it much, much worse, depending on your stomach. A story line involving the *X-Men* heroine Storm loosely ties this midway-type ride to the Marvel Super Hero Island area, but it's largely irrelevant and offers no advice on keeping your lunch down.

Young children, teens, and masochists like to lure the unsuspecting onto the ride, and then turn the wheel like maniacs. It's also effective for seeing if you've recently developed any kind of inner-ear disorder.

TOURING TIPS Ride early or late to avoid long lines. Crowds tend to find Storm Force Accelatron from late morning, after hitting the headliner attractions, through late afternoon. Try first thing after the park opens or save it until the last couple of hours the park is open. If you're prone to motion sickness, keep your distance.

TOON LAGOON

WHIMSICAL AND GAILY COLORED, with rounded and exaggerated lines, Toon Lagoon translates cartoon art into real buildings and settings. King's Row and Comic Strip Lane, the main drags of Toon

Lagoon, are the domains of such vintage Sunday-funnies favorites as Beetle Bailey, The Family Circus, and Blondie and Dagwood—in other words, intellectual property that Universal could get for cheap. Across a bridge lies Sweethaven, home to Popeye and Olive Oyl, and a mountain dedicated to Dudley Do-Right looms around the corner.

The island's King Features Syndicate and Jay Ward comic characters, though classic, are probably unrecognizable to anybody born after 1980, but that doesn't stop kids from enjoying the resort's two wettest water rides, both of which are found here. Entering Toon Lagoon from Marvel Super Hero Island, you'll have to pass a midway of unthemed carnival games and an enormous amphitheater that sits empty 99% of the time, making this transition the biggest eyesore in an otherwise exquisite park. There are some great photo ops here, especially the sideways sign where you can snap a gravity-defying shot with Marmaduke the Great Dane.

If your kids want to get wet but are too small for the water rides (or you don't want to wait in line), send them to the splash pads at either entrance to Toon Lagoon. A few minutes frolicking in fountains of sulfurous water should satisfy them.

Dudley Do-Right's Ripsaw Falls
(Universal Express) ★★★½

APPEAL BY AGE PRESCHOOL ★½ GRADE SCHOOL ★★★★½ TEENS ★★★★
YOUNG ADULTS ★★★★ OVER 30 ★★★★½ SENIORS ★★★★

What it is Flume ride. **Scope and scale** Major attraction. **When to go** Before 11 a.m. **Special comments** 44" minimum height requirement. **Authors' rating** A minimalist Splash Mountain; ★★★½. **Duration of ride** 5 minutes. **Probable waiting time per 100 people ahead of you** 9 minutes. **Loading speed** Moderate.

DESCRIPTION AND COMMENTS Dudley Do-Right's Ripsaw Falls features characters spun off from the old Rocky and Bullwinkle TV show. Dudley is a cheerfully incompetent Canadian Mountie who pursues Snidely Whiplash, his nemesis, throughout the Great White North. Snidely inevitably tries to kidnap Nell, the girl of Dudley's dreams, and Dudley (with trusted horse, Horse) rescues her, usually in spite of himself. The original cartoons parodied everything from the implausible plots of early silent movie melodramas to the "friendly Canadian" trope, complete with really bad Quebecois accents. Being fans of the show, we think this attraction may have been inspired by Dudley's "Saw Mill" cartoon circa 1970.

Story line aside, IOA's tribute to the cartoon is a flume ride similar to the Magic Kingdom's Splash Mountain. Riders sit single file in loglike boats and bob along a man-made river, floating past mostly static scenes telling the story of Snidely kidnapping Nell, with Dudley's eventual rescuing.

As far as log flume rides go, Ripsaw Falls is pretty good. There are several medium-size drops during the 5-minute ride, and a heart-stopping 75-foot one near the end. Universal claims that this is the first flume ride to "send riders plummeting 15 feet below the surface of the water"; you're just plummeting into a tunnel, but it's a nifty effect. The ride queue and loading area have some visual gags that would make the original show's writers proud, and the on-board ride audio is also good.

That being said, the theming and visuals of Ripsaw Falls aren't in the same league as Disney's Splash Mountain attraction, to which everyone inevitably compares it. Most of Ripsaw Falls' effects are nonmoving statues, whereas Splash Mountain is loaded with moving animatronics, water effects, and gorgeous scenery. Dudley's defects are partly intentional, in keeping with the cartoon's satirical spirit, like an exposed view of backstage following the "scenic overlook" that is cheekily labeled "overlooked scenery." But the flaws are mostly due to the ride's rushed completion (it opened a year earlier than originally scheduled), resulting in a potential classic that was never properly finished.

TOURING TIPS This ride will get you wet, but on average not as soaked as on Popeye & Bluto's Bilge-Rat Barges. If you want to stay dry, however, arrive prepared with a poncho. If you're going to ride both Ripsaw Falls and Bilge-Rat Barges, see them one after another during the morning (if it's sunny enough to dry you off) or at the end of the day before slogging back to your hotel. After riding, take a moment to gauge the timing of the water cannons that go off along the exit walk. This is where you can really get drenched. Ride this after experiencing all of the Marvel Super Hero rides.

This is one of the few single file log flumes that uses lap bar restraints, and it makes for a mighty tight fit. Make sure that you try the test seat outside the queue before waiting in line. If you don't want to ride, you can pump quarters into the water sprayers along the bridge leading to Jurassic Park, and amuse yourself by dousing guests who just survived the big drop.

Me Ship, *The Olive* ★★★

APPEAL BY AGE	PRESCHOOL ★★★★★	GRADE SCHOOL ★★★★½	TEENS ★★
YOUNG	ADULTS ★★	OVER 30 ★★½	SENIORS ★★

What it is Interactive playground. **Scope and scale** Minor attraction. **When to go** Anytime. **Authors' rating** Colorful and appealing for kids; ★★★.

DESCRIPTION AND COMMENTS *The Olive* is Popeye's beloved boat come to life as a three-floor interactive playground. *The Olive* offers a chance for kids to run around and expend some of the energy they've pent up in lines. Besides slides, stairs, and climbing platforms, kids can play with props, including the ship's wheel, bell, and throttle. Those who climb to the second floor will find water cannons that can reach riders on the nearby Bilge-Rat Barges. A separate play area, called Swee'Pea's Playpen, is available for smaller children.

TOURING TIPS Usually opens at 10 a.m., or an hour after the park opens. If you're into the big rides, save this for later in the day. Also, take a few minutes to explore the shoreline pathways behind the ship; you'll find some punny Popeye props, and a little peace and quiet.

Popeye & Bluto's Bilge-Rat Barges
(Universal Express) ★★★★

APPEAL BY AGE	PRESCHOOL ★½	GRADE SCHOOL ★★★★★	TEENS ★★★★½
YOUNG	ADULTS ★★★★	OVER 30 ★★★★	SENIORS ★★★★

What it is Whitewater rapids raft ride. **Scope and scale** Major attraction. **When to go** Before 11 a.m. **Special comments** 42" minimum height requirement. **Authors' rating**

Bring your own soap; not to be missed; ★★★★. **Duration of ride** 4½ minutes. **Probable waiting time per 100 people ahead of you** 5 minutes. **Loading speed** Moderate.

DESCRIPTION AND COMMENTS Hands down our favorite whitewater raft ride on the East Coast, Bilge-Rat Barges is only bested in its genre by Grizzly River Run at Disney California Adventure. Bilge-Rat Barges seats 10 riders at a time on a circular raft down a man-made canyon of gushing rapids, waterfalls, twists, turns, and dips. Some of the scenery is visually interesting, such as the 18-foot octopus crammed into a cave two sizes too small, but the minimally moving props along the side don't quite make for an immersive story line.

TOURING TIPS If you didn't drown on Dudley Do-Right, here's a second chance. You'll get a lot wetter from the knees down on this ride, so use your poncho or garbage bag and ride barefoot with your britches rolled up. Each raft has a covered center console into which you can place backpacks, socks, and shoes; lockers or zip-top bags are strongly suggested for anything electronic.

This ride usually opens an hour later than the rest of the park, typically 10 a.m. Experience the barges in the morning after the Marvel Super Hero attractions and Dudley Do-Right. Some people ride the Bilge-Rat Barges and Dudley Do-Right's Ripsaw Falls consecutively, right before leaving the park, to avoid sloshing around in wet clothes most of the day.

Some children may be frightened more by the way the rapids look, and by the screams coming from the ride as it passes through Toon Lagoon, than by the roughness of the ride itself. These are screams of laughter. If your child is apprehensive about riding, take them to any of the platforms overlooking the ride to see how much fun everyone is having.

SKULL ISLAND

Skull Island: Reign of Kong *(opens summer 2016)*

APPEAL BY AGE NOT YET RATED

What it is Indoor/outdoor truck safari with 3-D effects. **Scope and scale** Super-headliner. **When to go** Immediately after park opening or just before closing. **Special comments** 34" minimum height requirement. **Authors' rating** Not yet rated; not to be missed. **Duration of ride** More than 4½ minutes. **Probable waiting time per 100 people ahead of you** Not available at press time. **Loading speed** Not available at press time.

DESCRIPTION AND COMMENTS Brace yourself and hide the bananas because the greatest ape of them all is on his way back to Universal Orlando. Skull Island: Reign of Kong is both an attraction and an entire "island" unto itself, located on a former backstage area between Toon Lagoon's Dudley Do-Right's Ripsaw Falls and the Thunder Falls Terrace restaurant in Jurassic Park, which has relocated its entry archway to accommodate the new neighbor. Extinct attractions don't often get second acts in the theme park industry, but King Kong—star of Kongfrontation, which was one of Universal Studios Florida's signature attractions from opening day until it was replaced by Revenge of the Mummy in 2002—is still fondly remembered more than a decade after his departure, prompting Universal to resurrect him in a completely new ride.

This attraction isn't exactly based on the 2005 *King Kong* remake (though director Peter Jackson did consult on the design), nor is it directly tied to the *Kong: Skull Island* film scheduled for release in 2017. Rather, the ride is an original adventure set in the 1930s, which begins as you pass beneath a stone archway, shaped like a massive monkey skull, and start exploring the elaborate, immersive queue. Pathways wind through dense foliage and an ancient temple inhabited by a hostile indigenous tribe before leading you to your transportation: an oversize open-sided "expedition vehicle" that superficially resembles Animal Kingdom's Kilimanjaro Safari trucks.

Your ride starts with a short loop outside through the jungle (which may be bypassed in inclement weather), ending at the massive torch-framed doors in the center of Skull Island's imposing 72-foot-tall facade. The doors open, allowing you to enter a subterranean maze of corridors and caverns in which you'll be assaulted by all manner of prehistoric beasts and bugs. After barely surviving a series of multisensory near misses with various nasties, you come to an encounter with King Kong himself, brought to life through enormous 3-D screens, similar to the *King Kong 360 3-D* attraction on Universal Studios Hollywood's tram tour. Finally, just when you think it's all over, you'll have one last face-to-face with the "eighth wonder of the world," only this time in the fur-covered flesh.

TOURING TIPS Skull Island: Reign of Kong promises to be epic in every sense: from the monumental exterior, which compares with Disneyland's Cars Land for scale of sculpting, to the length of the experience, said to be one of the longest in the resort. It also promises to attract queues of equally epic proportions. On the plus side, Kong should draw some guests away from The Wizarding World of Harry Potter, helping rebalance the park. You'll want to visit Skull Island first thing in the morning, or immediately following the Hogsmeade attractions if you are using Early Park Admission.

Skull Island: Reign of Kong has a minimum height requirement of only 34 inches, one of the lowest in the resort, and is designed to be physically accessible to almost all members of the family. However, on a sensory and psychological level, it is extremely intense; if you or your little one has a fear of darkness, insects, or man-eating monsters, you may want to forgo the monkey.

JURASSIC PARK

JURASSIC PARK IS A STEVEN SPIELBERG film franchise about a theme park with real dinosaurs. Jurassic Park at Islands of Adventure is a real theme park (or at least a section of one) with fictitious dinosaurs. The iconic visitor center from the original film is one of the first things guests will see across the lagoon after walking through Port of Entry. The amount of space within Jurassic Park is deceptively large, and the entire area is completely immersive as you walk through it (except where Harry Potter's Hogwarts intrusively pokes above the trees).

There are two main entrances into this island, one coming from Toon Lagoon and another from The Wizarding World of Harry Potter. A third way in is the bridge between Lost Continent and Jurassic Park, which allows guests to bypass Hogsmeade on busy days.

Camp Jurassic ★★★½

What it is Interactive play area. **Scope and scale** Minor attraction. **When to go** Anytime. **Authors' rating** Creative playground, confusing layout; ★★★½.

DESCRIPTION AND COMMENTS Camp Jurassic is the most elaborate kid's play area at Universal, and one of the best theme park playgrounds you'll find anywhere. A sort of dinosaur-themed Tom Sawyer Island (minus the rafts), it allows kids to explore lava pits, caves, mines, and a rain forest. Explore and you'll find an echo cavern, bat caves, amber-bound bugs, and dilophosaurus heads that double as water blasters. The playground is big enough for many kids to spend a solid hour just running around. You may end up having to go into Camp Jurassic just to get the little nippers out, if you can find them.

TOURING TIPS Camp Jurassic will fire the imaginations of the under-13 set. If you don't impose a time limit on the exploration, you could be here awhile. The layout of the play area is confusing and intersects the queuing area for Pteranodon Flyers. It's easy for kids and parents to get disoriented. If you think your children may get lost, you may end up having to climb, crawl, and slide along with them. Your chiropractor will thank you.

Jurassic Park Discovery Center ★★½

What it is Interactive natural history exhibit. **Scope and scale** Minor attraction. **When to go** Anytime. **Authors' rating** Definitely worth checking out; ★★½.

DESCRIPTION AND COMMENTS This interactive educational exhibit mixes fiction from the movie *Jurassic Park*, such as using fossil DNA to bring dinosaurs to life, with skeletal remains and other paleontological displays. The best exhibit here lets guests watch an animatronic raptor being hatched, with a young witness getting to name the newborn. You never know quite when one will emerge, but ask an attendant if you should stick around. Other exhibits allow you to digitally "fuse" your DNA with a dinosaur's to see what the resultant creature would look like, play a cheesy game show with dino trivia, or "be a saurus" by seeing through the eyes of a life-size animatronic (if they happen to be working).

TOURING TIPS Usually opens later than the rest of the park and may close earlier as well; typical hours are 10 a.m.–5 p.m. Cycle back after experiencing all the rides or on a second day. Most folks can digest this exhibit in 10–15 minutes. Behind the Discovery Center is a gorgeous waterfront terrace where you can get away from the crowds—at least when it isn't being used for a special event or as a Hogsmeade holding area.

Jurassic Park River Adventure *(Universal Express)* ★★★★

What it is Indoor-outdoor river-raft adventure ride. **Scope and scale** Headliner. **When to go** Before 11 a.m. **Special comments** 42″ minimum height requirement. **Authors' rating** Aging but still exciting; not to be missed; ★★★★. **Duration of ride** 6½ minutes. **Probable waiting time per 100 people ahead of you** 5 minutes. **Loading speed** Fast.

DESCRIPTION AND COMMENTS One of IOA's original headliner attractions, Jurassic Park River Adventure is inspired by a scene in Michael Crichton's original *Jurassic Park* novel. Guests board tour boats for an aquatic ride through the grounds of Jurassic Park. Everything is tranquil as the tour begins, as the boat floats among large herbivorous dinosaurs such as ultrasaurus and stegosaurus, along with prehistoric-looking plants and the occasional geyser.

To no one's surprise, something goes horribly wrong, and your tour boat is nudged off course by a dinosaur at exactly the most inopportune time: just as you're floating past the vicious raptor enclosure, whose gates have been mysteriously unlocked and left open. Before you have time to ask what OSHA's inspectors really do during the day, your boat is climbing through the inside of the raptor facility amid the destruction and carnage wrought by the escaped animals. Your first face-to-face encounter with a T. Rex is also your last, as you find rescue by plunging 85 feet (the tallest such drop in Florida, and a world record when it was built) into the river below.

The drop is a doozy; the scenery, background music, and ride narration are all done well; and Jurassic Park River Adventure is overall one of the more immersive attractions in the entire resort. But the dinosaurs are fewer in number than at this ride's California cousin, and those it has look increasingly arthritic, despite a 2015 refurbishment of their faded rubber skins.

TOURING TIPS Riders don't get as wet on River Adventure as they do on Bilge-Rat Barges or Dudley Do-Right's Ripsaw Falls. Though the boats make a huge splash at the bottom of the 85-foot drop, you can stay relatively dry if you are sitting in an interior seat; sitting behind a larger person and keeping your arms down can help. Still, bring a poncho or plastic bag if you want to keep as dry as possible; paid lockers are located inside the queue. There's a viewing area to the left of the ride's final, big drop, where you can see how wet riders are getting, before you decide to ride.

A Honolulu reader thinks Jurassic Park doesn't pass the smell test:

> *The Jurassic Park ride is a lot of fun—so fun, in fact, that you won't realize how truly HEINOUS the water that drenches you during the climactic splashdown is until much later. We sat in the front row for the ride and got soaked. Three hours later, my girlfriend and I realized we reeked.*

Young children must endure a double whammy on this ride. First, they're stalked by giant, salivating (sometimes spitting) reptiles, and then sent catapulting over the falls. Unless your children are fairly hardy, wait a year or two before you spring the River Adventure on them.

Because the Jurassic Park section of IOA is situated next to The Wizarding World of Harry Potter–Hogsmeade, the boat will experience heavy crowds earlier in the day. Try to ride before 11 a.m.

Pteranodon Flyers   ★★

APPEAL BY AGE PRESCHOOL ★★★½ **GRADE SCHOOL** ★★★★ **TEENS** ★★★★
YOUNG ADULTS ★★★½ **OVER 30** ★★★ **SENIORS** ★★★★

What it is Kiddie suspended coaster. **Scope and scale** Minor attraction. **When to go** In the first or last 30 minutes of the day, or (better yet) not at all. **Special comments** Adults and older children must be accompanied by a child between 36" and 56" tall. **Authors' rating** All sizzle, no steak; ★★. **Duration of ride** 1¼ minutes. **Probable**

waiting time per 100 people ahead of you 28 minutes. **Loading speed** Slower than a hog in quicksand.

DESCRIPTION AND COMMENTS This is Islands of Adventure's biggest blunder. Engineered to accommodate only 170 persons per hour, the ride dangles you on a swing below a track that passes over a small part of Jurassic Park. We recommend skipping this one. Why? Because the next ice age will probably end before you reach the front of the line! And your reward for all that waiting? A 1-minute-and-15-second ride.

TOURING TIPS This attraction is designed for children 36–56 inches in height. An adult or older child over 56 inches in height must accompany a child meeting the 36- to 56-inch height requirement.

We're amazed that the ride still exists, given its low capacity and long lines. Rumors of its demise have run rampant for years, but none (unfortunately) have panned out yet. We don't think Pteranodon Flyers is worth the wait, and Universal Express isn't valid on the attraction. If your children insist on riding, and abject bribery fails, get in line as quickly as possible after opening, or just before the park closes.

Raptor Encounter ★★★½

APPEAL BY AGE	PRESCHOOL ★★	GRADE SCHOOL ★★★★	TEENS ★★★★
YOUNG ADULTS ★★★½	OVER 30 ★★★½	SENIORS ★★★	

What it is Photo op with lifelike dinosaur. **Scope and scale** Minor attraction. **When to go** Check park map or attraction for appearance times. **Author's rating** Clever girl! Sure to scare the spit out of small kids; ★★★½. Duration of encounter About a minute. **Probable waiting time per 100 people ahead of you** 30 minutes. **Loading speed** Very slow.

DESCRIPTION AND COMMENTS Just when everyone thinks that Disney has a lock on the meet-and-greet market, between its talking Mickeys and *Frozen* sisters, Universal does the impossible—breeds a live velociraptor and makes it pose for pictures! OK, it isn't actually a real dinosaur on display just outside the Jurassic Park Discovery Center, inside a portion of the long-closed Triceratops Encounter walk-through attraction. In fact, it's an amazingly realistic puppet, created by Michael Curry (who created designs for Disney's *Lion King and Finding Nemo* musicals, as well as Diagon Alley's *Tales of Beedle the Bard* show) and brought to life by talented performers.

Several times each hour, the blue siren lights around the sunken predator paddock signal the arrival of Lucy or Ethel, the park's new semi-tame stars. A game warden briefs one family at a time regarding proper safety procedures (convey calm assurance, move in slowly, and try not to smell like meat) before they step up for a photo. Don't peer too closely over the edge of the raptor enclosure; you'll spot the cleverly camouflaged legs of the puppeteer inside and spoil the illusion. A Photo Connect photographer will take your picture with his or her camera (included with Star Card packages) or your own, and selfies are also encouraged—just don't be surprised if the dino snaps when you say, "Smile!"

TOURING TIPS The Raptor Encounter has quickly become quite popular, and with limited capacity and little shade, this can become an unpleasant wait. If appearance times aren't printed on the park map, check with a team member outside the paddock entrance and arrive at least 15 minutes before a scheduled session; 20-minute appearances begin around 11 a.m. and occur about every half hour until 6 p.m. Don't try to touch the raptor, or you may come home minus a hand; surreptitiously feeding your offspring to the dinosaurs is also discouraged by management.

THE WIZARDING WORLD OF HARRY POTTER— HOGSMEADE

THE 20-ACRE WIZARDING WORLD is an amalgamation of landmarks, creatures, and themes that are faithful to the films and books. You access the area through an imposing gate that opens onto **Hogsmeade,** depicted in winter and covered in snow. This is The Wizarding World's primary shopping and dining venue. Exiting Hogsmeade, you first glimpse the towering castle housing **Hogwarts School of Witchcraft and Wizardry,** flanked by the **Forbidden Forest** and **Hagrid's Hut.** The grounds and interior of the castle contain part of the queue for the super-headliner **Harry Potter and the Forbidden Journey.**

Universal went all out on the castle, with the intention of creating an icon even more beloved and powerful than Cinderella Castle at Disney's Magic Kingdom, and very nearly succeeded—if only they'd added a bit more brick and rockwork to conceal the big honking soundstage that holds the land's groundbreaking ride.

Hogsmeade in Detail

THE WIZARDING WORLD OF HARRY POTTER–Hogsmeade is in the northwest corner of Islands of Adventure, between The Lost Continent and Jurassic Park. From the IOA entrance, the most direct route there is through Port of Entry and then right, through Seuss Landing (staying to the left of Green Eggs and Ham) and The Lost Continent, to the Hogsmeade main gate. The alternative route is to cross the bridge connecting The Lost Continent with Jurassic Park, and then turn right after entering the latter area. Note that the bridge is closed on slower days.

For the moment, though, let's begin our exploration at The Wizarding World's main entrance, on the Lost Continent side. Passing beneath a stone arch, you enter the village of **Hogsmeade.** The **Hogwarts Express** locomotive sits belching steam on your right. The village setting is rendered in exquisite detail: Stone cottages and shops have steeply pitched slate roofs, bowed multipaned windows, gables, and tall, crooked chimneys. Add cobblestone streets and gas streetlamps, and Hogsmeade is as reminiscent of Sherlock Holmes as of Harry Potter.

Your first taste—literally—of the Harry Potter universe comes courtesy of **Honeydukes.** Specializing in Potter-themed candy such as Acid Pops (no flashbacks, guaranteed), Tooth Splintering Strong Mints, and Fizzing Whizzbees, the sweet shop offers no shortage of snacks that administer an immediate sugar high. There's also a small bakery inside; while we highly recommend the Cauldron Cakes, the big draw is the elaborately boxed Chocolate Frogs. The chocolate inside isn't anything special, but the packaging looks as if it came straight from a Harry Potter film, complete with lenticular wizard trading card.

Next door to Honeydukes and set back from the main street is **Three Broomsticks,** a rustic tavern serving English staples such as fish-and-chips, shepherd's pie, Cornish pasties, and turkey legs; kids' fare includes the obligatory mac and cheese and chicken fingers. To the rear of the tavern is the Hog's Head pub, which serves a nice selection of beer as well as The Wizarding World's signature nonalcoholic brew, Butterbeer (see page 188). Three Broomsticks and the Hog's Head were carved out of The Lost Continent's popular Enchanted Oak Tavern, which was Potterfied pretty effectively in its reincarnation, though a good deal of seating capacity was sacrificed. To dine at Three Broomsticks anytime from its opening until roughly 8 p.m., you'll have to wait in a long queue during busier times of year, with waiting times exceeding 30 minutes on busy days.

Roughly across the street from the pub, you'll find benches in the shade at the **Owlery,** where animatronic owls (complete with lifelike poop) ruffle and hoot from the rafters. Next to the Owlery is the **Owl Post,** where your can have mail stamped with a Hogsmeade postmark before dropping it off for delivery (an Orlando postmark will also be applied by the real USPS). The Owl Post also sells stationery, toy owls, and magic wands. Here, once again, a nice selection of owls preens on the timbers overhead. You access the Owl Post in either of two ways: through an interior door following the wand-choosing demonstration at Ollivanders (see page 320), or through **Dervish and Banges,** a magic-supplies shop that's interconnected with the Owl Post. You can't enter through the Owl Post's front door on busy days, when it serves exclusively as an exit. Because it's so difficult to get into the Owl Post, IOA sometimes stations a team member outside to stamp your postcards with The Wizarding World postmark.

At the far end of the village, the massive **Hogwarts** castle comes into view, set atop a rock face and towering over Hogsmeade and the entire Wizarding World. Follow the path through the castle's massive gates to the entrance of Harry Potter and the Forbidden Journey. Below the castle and to the right, at the base of the cliff, are the **Forbidden Forest, Hagrid's Hut,** and the **Flight of the Hippogriff** children's roller coaster. In the village, near the gate to Hogwarts Castle, is **Filch's Emporium of Confiscated Goods,** which offers all manner of Potter-themed gear, including Quidditch clothing, magical-creature toys, film-inspired chess sets, and, of course, Death Eater masks (breath mints extra).

In keeping with the stores depicted in the Potter films, the shopping venues in The Wizarding World of Harry Potter–Hogsmeade are small and intimate—so intimate, in fact, that they feel congested when they're serving only 12–20 shoppers. With so many avid Potter fans, lines for the shops develop most days by 9:30 or 10 a.m., creating a phenomenon we've never seen in all our years of covering theme parks: The lines for the shops are frequently longer than the wait to ride the roller coasters. Filch's Emporium is the only shop in

The Wizarding World that you can enter during high season without waiting in line; problem is, it doubles as the exit for Forbidden Journey. As throngs of riders flow out continuously, trying to enter Filch's is not unlike swimming upstream to spawn; still, it's a whole lot better than standing in lines for the other shops. Because the stores are so jammed, IOA sells some Potter merchandise, including wands, through street vendors and in Port of Entry shops.

At the end of the village and to the left is the bridge to **Jurassic Park,** the themed area contiguous to The Wizarding World. This is the best vantage point to get your photo with Hogwarts Castle in the background, as the hordes of people posing in the middle of the walkway will attest.

Entertainment in Hogsmeade

Hogsmeade raised "retail theater" in theme parks to unprecedented levels, as nearly every shop space and storefront window sports some sort of animatronic or special effects surprise. At **Dervish and Banges,** the fearsome *Monster Book of Monsters* rattles and snarls at you as Nimbus 2001 brooms strain at their tethers overhead. At the **Hog's Head** pub, the titular porcine part, mounted behind the bar, similarly thrashes and growls when the barkeep receives a gratuity.

Two brief street entertainments are staged in a raised outdoor alcove at the Forbidden Journey end of Hogsmeade. Showtimes aren't listed in the park map, but performances usually start every 30 minutes on the hour and half hour.

The **Frog Choir** (★★★) is composed of four singers, two of whom are holding large amphibian puppets sitting on pillows. Inspired by a brief scene in *Harry Potter and the Prisoner of Azkaban,* the group sings three or four a cappella wizarding-related songs, including "Hedwig's Theme" and "Something Wicked This Way Comes." The 10-minute show is followed by a photo op. Though cute, the Frog Choir isn't much more than filler for IOA's attraction list, and probably not worth going out of your way for.

The **Triwizard Spirit Rally** (★★★½) showcases a group of three men performing martial arts–type moves including jumps, kicks, and simulated battle with sticks; and a group of four women performing simple rhythmic gymnastic moves with ribbons. The entire performance lasts about 6 minutes. After each show, the students of Beauxbatons Academy of Magic and the Durmstrang Institute are available for group photos. Though marginally more exciting than the Frog Choir, this is only a must-do for major Potter fans.

Hogsmeade Touring Strategy

While the opening of Diagon Alley has taken some pressure off Hogsmeade, crowds at IOA's Wizarding World are still large during the summer and holidays, and you'll encounter lines for the attractions even at slower times of year.

When IOA offers Early Park Admission, on-site hotel guests are allowed into Hogsmeade one hour before the general public (either via the front gate or Hogwarts Express). If you have early-entry privileges for the Wizarding World, use them, arriving as early during the early-entry period as possible. Otherwise, we suggest leaving The Wizarding World for late in the day, as the area will be occupied by hotel guests by the time the first day guests arrive.

Wizarding World crowd management has been a work in progress for Universal. Now, with six years of operation under its belt, Universal has settled on a flexible system of basic crowd-control options predicated on the expected level of attendance for any given day. (Similar procedures are in place at Diagon Alley; see page 261 in Part Seven.)

On most days of the year, from the slowest off-season through the busiest summer weeks, you can enter and depart The Wizarding World–Hogsmeade as you please. The waits for the rides will still be more than an hour at times, but gaining entry to the themed area itself is not an issue.

On days when the park is busiest, such as during spring break or between December 25 and January 1, access to Hogsmeade may be limited for part of the day. Barricades are placed at both entrances to The Wizarding World–Hogsmeade once the area reaches maximum occupancy. You can then go to touch screen ticket kiosks outside the Jurassic Park Discovery Center and obtain a free return ticket (not unlike the old paper FastPasses at Walt Disney World) to come back during your choice of designated time windows. You do not need your admission ticket to receive a timed-return ticket, and one person can retrieve a time for your entire party (up to nine people). At the specified time, return to The Lost Continent entrance and present your pass to the barricade crew to gain entry.

The return time on your pass depends on crowd conditions and how many Universal resort guests are in The Wizarding World–Hogsmeade before the park opens to the general public. Depending on demand, your possible return times may be many hours in the future, and it's possible (though extremely rare) for return tickets to run out entirely. Another factor that will affect your wait is how well Harry Potter and the Forbidden Journey is operating because this is what those in line are waiting for. If the ride comes up on schedule and runs trouble-free, everything runs smoothly. If Forbidden Journey experiences problems, though, especially first thing in the morning, it gums up the works for everyone.

On these peak days, a standby queue may also be erected in the waterfront landing behind the Jurassic Park Discovery Center; because more guests can enter only as others leave, this line can be painfully slow, so a return ticket is strongly suggested. It is common for the entrance barricades to be removed during the last hour or two the park is open, thus presenting the opportunity to come and go as you please.

Once admitted to The Wizarding World–Hogsmeade, you'll still have to wait for each ride, store, and concession, as well as for the area's one restaurant. Because Hogsmeade has less elbow room than Diagon Alley, it will reach maximum occupancy and require return tickets on days when Diagon does not, and feel more crowded once you finally get inside.

Note that guests arriving on the Hogwarts Express disembark outside of Hogsmeade and must still retrieve a ticket before entering. The timed-return tickets are neither needed nor accepted for Hogwarts Express itself.

Crowds finally dissipate about an hour or so before closing, even on the busiest days. A bonus of visiting late is enjoying the exquisite lighting and magical nighttime personality of The Wizarding World. Forbidden Journey will accommodate anyone already in line at park closing, and many of the Hogsmeade shops stay open awhile after closing.

However complicated, it's all doable, as a multigenerational Grosse Pointe, Michigan, family attests:

unofficial **TIP**

If you leave The Wizarding World while the entrance barriers are in place and you wish to return, you'll either have to wait in line to get another pass (provided they haven't all been distributed) or wait until late in the day, when the barricades come down as crowds disperse.

Convinced of your rectitude, we went without fear to Universal. We made it to Harry Potter by 8:05, were out of the Forbidden Journey and on the Hippogriff by 8:30, and had our Butterbeer by 9.

Dragon Challenge (Universal Express)   ★★★★

APPEAL BY AGE PRESCHOOL ★ **GRADE SCHOOL** ★★★★★ **TEENS** ★★★★½
YOUNG   ADULTS ★★★★★ **OVER 30** ★★★★½ **SENIORS** ★★★

What it is Twin suspended looping roller coasters. **Scope and scale** Headliner. **When to go** Immediately after Harry Potter and the Forbidden Journey. **Special comments** 54″ minimum height requirement. **Authors' rating** Almost as good as the Hulk Coaster; not to be missed; ★★★★. **Duration of ride** 2½ minutes. **Probable waiting time per 100 people ahead of you** 9 minutes. **Loading speed** Moderate.

DESCRIPTION AND COMMENTS Dragon Challenge, formerly Dueling Dragons and part of The Lost Continent, was renamed and incorporated into The Wizarding World in 2010. The story line is that you're preparing to compete in the Triwizard Tournament from *Harry Potter and the Goblet of Fire*. As you wind through the long, long queue, you pass through tournament tents and dark passages that are supposed to be under the stadium. You'll see the Goblet of Fire itself and dragon eggs on display, and hear the distant roar of the crowd in the supposed stadium above you.

Riders board one of two coasters—Chinese Fireball (red) or Hungarian Horntail (blue)—that are launched separately on tracks that are closely intertwined. The tracks are configured so that you get a different experience on each, and both include close encounters with the surroundings, including the Hogwarts Express train station. Originally, the coasters were designed to dispatch simultaneously and duel, with three near miss interactions during the ride. Ever since a few injuries were caused by flying objects, the dragon-shaped trains have dispatched sequentially instead of simultaneously, so it looks as if one train is chasing another, robbing the attraction of its most memorable gimmick.

Because this is an inverted coaster, your view of the action is limited unless you're sitting in the front row. Regardless of where you sit, there's plenty to keep you busy. Dragon Challenge is the highest coaster in the park and also claims the longest drop at 115 feet, plus five inversions. As on the Hulk, it's a smooth ride all the way.

Coaster fans argue about which seat on which train provides the wildest ride. We prefer the front row of Horntail for the visuals during the close call with the castle, and the last row of Fireball for added g-forces during the more intense inversions.

TOURING TIPS Use the restroom before getting in line. The queuing area for Dragon Challenge is the longest, most convoluted affair we've ever seen, winding endlessly through a maze of faux subterranean passages. After what feels like a comprehensive tour of Mammoth Cave, you finally emerge at the loading area, where you must choose between Chinese Fireball or Hungarian Horntail. Of course, at this critical juncture, you're as blind as a mole rat from being in the dark for so long. Our advice is to follow the person in front of you until your eyes adjust to the light.

Waits for Dragon Challenge, one of the best coasters in the country, rarely exceed 30 minutes before 11 a.m. Ride after experiencing Harry Potter and the Forbidden Journey. Even if there's no line to speak of, it takes 10–12 minutes just to navigate the passages and not much less time to exit after riding. There used to be a shortcut from the exit back into the queue for re-rides. But since Universal began enforcing the mandatory locker policy with metal detectors outside the castle, everyone must be inconveniently inspected before each trip. Finally, if you don't have time to ride both coasters, the Unofficial crew unanimously prefers Chinese Fireball.

Flight of the Hippogriff *(Universal Express)* ★★★

APPEAL BY AGE PRESCHOOL ★★★½ **GRADE SCHOOL** ★★★★ **TEENS** ★★★
YOUNG ADULTS ★★½ **OVER 30** ★★★½ **SENIORS** ★★★

What it is Kiddie roller coaster. **Scope and scale** Minor attraction. **When to go** First 90 minutes the park is open or after 4 p.m. **Special comments** 36" minimum height requirement. **Authors' rating** A good beginner coaster; ★★★. **Duration of ride** 1 minute. **Probable waiting time per 100 people ahead of you** 14 minutes. **Loading speed** Slow.

DESCRIPTION AND COMMENTS Below and to the right of Hogwarts Castle, next to Hagrid's Hut, the Hippogriff is short and sweet but not worth much of a wait. An outdoor, elevated coaster designed for children old enough to know about Harry Potter but not yet tall enough to ride Forbidden Journey, the ride affords excellent views of the area within Wizarding World and of Hogwarts. The theming is also very good, considering this isn't a major attraction. As a children's coaster only slightly taller and longer than Woody Woodpecker's in USF, there are no loops, inversions, or rolls: It's just one big hill and some mild turns, and almost half of the 1-minute ride time is spent going up the lift hill.

For fans of Harry Potter, there are two gorgeous items in this attraction that you will want to see. The first is a faithful re-creation of Hagrid's Hut in the queue (complete with the sound of Fang howling) while the second is an incredible animatronic of Buckbeak that you pass by while on the ride. Remember, that when Muggles encounter hippogriffs such as Buckbeak, proper etiquette must always be maintained to avoid any danger. Hippogriffs are extremely proud creatures and must be showed the proper respect by bowing to them, and waiting for them to bow in return.

TOURING TIPS Have your kids ride soon after the park opens while older siblings enjoy Forbidden Journey or Dragon Challenge.

Harry Potter and the Forbidden Journey ★★★★★

APPEAL BY AGE PRESCHOOL ★ GRADE SCHOOL ★★★★½ TEENS ★★★★★ YOUNG ADULTS ★★★★★ OVER 30 ★★★★★ SENIORS ★★★★★

What it is Motion-simulator dark ride. **Scope and scale** Super-headliner. **When to go** Immediately after park opening or just before closing. **Special comments** Expect *long* waits in line; 48″ minimum height requirement. **Authors' rating** Marvelous for Muggles; not to be missed; ★★★★★. **Duration of ride** 4¼ minutes. **Probable waiting time per 100 people ahead of you** 4 minutes. **Loading speed** Fast.

DESCRIPTION AND COMMENTS This ride provides the only opportunity at Uni-

Motion Sickness

versal Orlando to come close to Harry, Ron, Hermione, and Dumbledore as portrayed by the original actors. Half the attraction is a series of preshows, setting the stage for the main event, a thrilling dark ride. You can get on the ride in only 10–25 minutes using the singles line, but everyone should go through the main queue at least once. The characters are incorporated into the queue and serve as an important element of the overall experience, not merely something to keep you occupied while you wait for the main event.

From Hogsmeade you reach the attraction through the imposing Winged Boar gates and progress along a winding path. Entering the castle on a lower level, you walk through a sort of dungeon festooned with various icons and prop replicas from the Potter flicks, including the Mirror of Erised from *Harry Potter and the Sorcerer's Stone*. You later emerge back outside and into the Hogwarts greenhouses. The greenhouses compose the larger part of the Forbidden Journey's queuing area, and despite some strategically placed mandrakes, there isn't much here to amuse. If you're among the first in the park and in the queue, you'll move through this area pretty quickly. Otherwise . . . well, we hope you like plants. The greenhouses are not air-conditioned, but fans move the (hot) air around. Blessedly, there are water fountains but, alas, no restrooms.

Having finally escaped horticulture purgatory, you reenter the castle, moving along its halls and passageways. One chamber you'll probably remember from the films is a multistory gallery of portraits, many of whose subjects come alive when they take a notion. You'll see for the first time the four founders of Hogwarts: Helga Hufflepuff holding her famous cup, Godric Gryffindor and Rowena Ravenclaw nearby, and the tall, moving portrait of Salazar Slytherin straight ahead. The founders argue about Quidditch and Dumbledore's controversial decision to host an open house at

Hogwarts for Muggles (garden-variety mortals). Don't rush through the gallery—the effects are very cool, and the conversation is essential to understanding the rest of the attraction.

Next up, after you've navigated some more passages, is Dumbledore's office, where the wizard principal appears on a balcony and welcomes you to Hogwarts. The headmaster's appearance is your introduction to Musion Eyeliner technology—a high-definition video-projection system that produces breathtakingly realistic, three-dimensional, life-size moving holograms. The technology uses a special foil that reflects images from HD projectors, producing holographic images of variable sizes and incredible clarity. After his welcoming remarks, Dumbledore dispatches you to the Defence Against the Dark Arts classroom to hear a presentation on the history of Hogwarts.

As you gather to await the lecture, Harry, Ron, and Hermione pop out from beneath an invisibility cloak. They suggest you ditch the lecture in favor of joining them for a proper tour of Hogwarts, including a Quidditch match. After some repartee among the characters and a couple of special effects surprises, it's off to the Hogwarts Official Attraction Safety Briefing and Boarding Instructions Chamber—OK, it's actually the Gryffindor common room, but you get the picture. The briefing and instructions are presented by animated portraits, including an etiquette teacher. Later on, even the famed Sorting Hat gets into the act. All this leads to the Room of Requirement, where hundreds of candles float overhead as you board the ride.

After all the high-tech stuff in your queuing odyssey, you'll naturally expect to be wowed by your ride vehicle. Surely it's a Nimbus 3000 turbo-broom, a phoenix, a hippogriff, or at least the Weasleys' flying car. But no, what you'll ride on the most technologically advanced theme park attraction in America is . . . a *bench*? Yep, a bench.

A bit anticlimactic, perhaps, but as benches go, this one's a doozy, mounted on a Kuka robotic arm. When not engaged in Quidditch matches, a Kuka arm is a computer-controlled robotic arm similar to the kind used in heavy manufacturing. If you think about pictures you've seen of automotive assembly plants, Kuka arms are like those long metal appendages that come in to complete welds, move heavy stuff around, or fasten things. With the right programming, the arms can handle just about any repetitive industrial tasks thrown at them (see **kuka-robotics.com** for more info).

Bear with us for a moment; you know how we Unofficials like techno-geekery. When you put a Kuka arm on a ride platform, it provides six axes—six degrees of freedom, with synchronized motion that can be programmed to replicate all the sensations of flying, including broad swoops, steep dives, sharp turns, sudden stops, and fast acceleration. Here's where it gets really good: Up to now, when Kuka arms and similar robotic systems have been employed in theme park rides, the arm has been anchored to a stationary platform. In Forbidden Journey, the arm is mounted on a ride vehicle that moves you through a series of live sets and action scenes projected all around you. The movement of the arm is synchronized to create the motion that corresponds to what's happening in the film. When everything works right, it's mind-blowing.

When the ride was being designed, it was assumed that Kuka's robotic programming could easily produce the various movements called for in each scene. What nobody considered, however, is that the program was designed for maximum industrial efficiency. If, to correspond to the action in a given scene, the Kuka arm had to simulate 22 different motions, the software—not knowing a theme park ride from a diesel assembly line—would think, "OK, let's knock these 22 movements down to 13 and save half a minute." Because this would throw the timing of everything out of whack, Universal ended up having to create a program that would behave as it was told and not be so anal about efficiency. Luckily for us, Universal worked out the kinks, and Forbidden Journey is now remarkably reliable for such an advanced attraction.

High-tech hijinks aside, is the attraction itself ultimately worthy of the hype? In a word, *yes*! Your 4.25-minute adventure is a headlong sprint through the most thrilling moments from the first few Potter books: You'll soar over Hogwarts Castle, narrowly evade an attacking dragon, spar with the Whomping Willow, get tossed into a Quidditch match, and fight off Dementors inside the Chamber of Secrets. Scenes alternate between enormous physical sets (complete with animatronic creatures), elaborate lighting effects, and high-definition video-projection domes that surround your field of view, similar to Soarin' or The Simpsons Ride. Those Kuka-powered benches really do "levitate" in a manner that feels remarkably like free flight, and while you don't go upside down, the sensation of floating on your back or being slung from side to side is certainly unique.

un of ficial **TIP**
Even if your child meets the height requirement, consider carefully whether Forbidden Journey is an experience he or she can handle—because the seats on the benches are compartmentalized, kids can't see or touch Mom or Dad if they get frightened.

The seamless transitions between screens and sets, and the way the domes appear to remain stationary in front of you while actually moving (much like Dreamfinder's dirigible in the original Journey into Imagination at Epcot), serve to blur the boundary between actual and virtual better than any attraction before it. The greatest-hits montage plotline may be a bit muddled, but the ride is enormously effective at leaving you feeling as though you just survived the scariest scrapes from the early educational career of The Boy Who Lived.

Having experienced Forbidden Journey for ourselves, we have two primary bones to pick. First, Islands of Adventure team members rush you through the queue. To understand the story line and get the most out of the attraction, you really need to see and hear the entire presentation in each of the preshow rooms. This won't happen unless, contrary to the admonishments of the team members, you just park yourself and watch a full run-through of each preshow. Try to find a place to stop where you can let those behind you pass and where you're as far away from any staff as possible. As long as you're not creating a logjam, the team members will leave you alone as often as not.

Another alternative is to tell the greeter at the castle entrance that you want to take the **castle-only tour.** This self-guided experience lets guests who don't want to ride view the features of the castle via a different queue. You can pause as long as you desire in each of the various chambers and savor the preshows without being herded along. At the end, if you decide to ride, ask to be guided to the singles line—using this strategy, you'll maximize your enjoyment of the castle while minimizing your wait for the ride. Note that the castle-only tour is often unavailable on peak-attendance days.

Another gripe: The dialogue in the preshows is delivered in English accents of varying degrees of intelligibility, and at a very brisk pace. Add an echo effect owing to the cavernous nature of the preshow rooms, and it can be quite difficult for Yanks to decipher what's being said. This is especially evident in the staccato repartee between Harry, Ron, and Hermione in the Defence Against the Dark Arts classroom.

TOURING TIPS Harry Potter and the Forbidden Journey quickly became the most popular attraction at Islands of Adventure, and one of the most in-demand theme park attractions in America. While much of the attention has turned toward Gringotts at USF, the best way to ride Forbidden Journey with a reasonable wait is to be one of the first through the turnstiles in the morning or to visit in the final hours of the evening.

Upon approaching Forbidden Journey's front gates, those who have bags or loose items and therefore require a free locker may be directed into an extended outdoor queue. Our wait-time research has shown that in some cases, not needing a locker can save you as much as 30 minutes of standing in line. If you do need to stow your stuff, be aware that the Forbidden Journey locker area is small, crowded, and confusing. It may make more sense to stash your things in the lockers beside Dragon Challenge and pay the fee if you go over time. Alternatively, have one member of your party hold your bags for you in the child swap area.

Universal warns you to secure or leave behind loose objects, which most people interpret to mean eyeglasses, purses, ball caps, and the like. However, the ride makes a couple of moves that will empty your trousers faster than a master pickpocket—ditto and worse for shirt pockets. When these moves occur, your stuff will clatter around like quarters in a slot-machine tray. Much better to use the small compartment built into the seat back for keys, coins, phone, wallet, and pocket Bible. Be prepared, however: Team members don't give you much time to stow or retrieve your belongings.

The single-rider line is likewise unmarked, as relatively few guests use it. Whereas on most attractions the wait in the singles line is one-third the wait in the standby line, at Forbidden Journey it can be as much as one-tenth. Because the individual seating separates you from the other riders whether your party stays together or not, the singles line is a great option, as this wife from Edinburgh, Scotland, discovered:

> Trust me, sitting next to hubbie on Forbidden Journey, romantic though it may be, is not as awesome as having to wait only 15 minutes as a single rider.

To get there, enter the right (no-bags) line and keep left all the way into the castle. Past the locker area, take the first left into the singles line.

If you see a complete iteration of each preshow in the queue and then experience the ride, you'll invest 25–35 minutes even if you don't have to wait. If you elect to skip the preshows (the Gryffindor Common Room, where you receive safety and loading directions, is mandatory) and use the singles line, you can get on in about 10–25 minutes at any time of day. At a time when the posted wait in the regular line was two hours, we rode and were out the door in 15 minutes using the singles line.

Universal has toned down the Kuka programming and added fans to each seat that blow cool air on rider's foreheads in a somewhat successful effort to reduce motion sickness. We nonetheless recommend that you not ride with a full stomach. If you start getting queasy, fix your gaze on your feet and try to exclude as much from your peripheral vision as possible.

If you have a child who doesn't meet the minimum height requirement of 48 inches, a child-swapping option is provided at the loading area.

In response to many larger guests being denied rides when Forbidden Journey first opened, the end seats on each flying bench were redesigned to accommodate a wider variety of body shapes and sizes. Though these modified seats allow many more people to ride, it's still possible that guests of size can't fit in them. The best way to figure out whether you can fit in a regular seat or one of the modified ones is to sit in one of the test seats outside the queue or just inside the castle. After you sit down, pull down on the safety harness as far as you can. One of three safety lights will illuminate: A green light indicates you can fit into any seat, a yellow light means you should ask for one of the modified seats on the outside of the bench, and a red light means that the harness can't engage enough for you to ride safely.

In addition, IOA team members select guests of all sizes "at random" to plop in the test seats, but they're really looking for large people or those who have a certain body shape. Team members handle the situation as diplomatically as possible, but if they suspect you're not the right size, you'll be asked to sit down for a test. For you to be cleared to ride, the overhead restraint has to click three times; once again, it's body shape rather than weight (unless you're over 300 pounds) that's key. Most team members will let you try a second time if you don't achieve three clicks on the first go. Passing the test by inhaling sharply is not recommended unless you can also hold your breath for the entire 4-plus minutes of the ride.

With The Wizarding World and especially Forbidden Journey soaking up so many guests in IOA, waits for attractions in the other themed areas are minimal up to around 11 a.m.

Hogwarts Express ★★★★½

APPEAL BY AGE PRESCHOOL ★★★★ **GRADE SCHOOL** ★★★★★ **TEENS** ★★★★
YOUNG ADULTS ★★★★½ **OVER 30** ★★★★½ **SENIORS** ★★★★½

What it is Transportation attraction with special effects. **Scope and scale** Headliner. **When to go** Immediately after park opening. **Special comments** Requires park-to-park admission. **Authors' rating** A moving experience; not to be missed; ★★★★½. **Duration of ride** 4 minutes. **Probable waiting time per 100 people ahead of you** 7 minutes. **Loading speed** Moderate.

DESCRIPTION AND COMMENTS The counterpart to Universal Studios's King's Cross is Hogsmeade Station, which lies within the footprint of the Dragon Challenge roller coaster and provides pedestrian access to Hogsmeade and IOA's Lost Continent themed area. See Part Seven, page 256, for a full review of the Hogwarts Express experience.

TOURING TIPS Because the Hogsmeade Station doesn't include the cool Platform 9¾ effect found at the King's Cross end, you'd expect waits for the one-way trip to be shorter here. Surprisingly, lines can be longer here than at USF on slower days, though King's Cross is the busier end during peak periods. Lines are usually less than 20 minutes through the morning but can build later in the day. Hogsmeade Station also lacks other King's Cross amenities, such as air-conditioning and an in-queue snack stand, though there is a moving carriage (drawn by an invisible Thestral) at the exit.

On most days, disembarking guests will be allowed directly into Hogsmeade, less than a minute's walk away. On peak days when the area reaches capacity, they'll be directed to the bridge between The Lost Continent and Jurassic Park, where they'll have to either queue to enter Hogsmeade or obtain a free timed-entry ticket to visit The Wizarding World at a specified time.

If you wish to experience the train, do so before the queue builds in midafternoon. If the line grows very long, guests wishing to ride a second time in one day may be relegated to a slower re-ride queue.

Ollivanders ★★★★

APPEAL BY AGE PRESCHOOL ★★★★ GRADE SCHOOL ★★★★★ TEENS ★★★★	
YOUNG ADULTS ★★★★ OVER 30 ★★★½ SENIORS ★★★½	

What it is Combination wizarding demonstration and shopping op. **Scope and scale** Minor attraction. **When to go** In the first or last 30 minutes of the day. **Special comments** Audience stands; identical to USF version but with a much slower line. **Authors' rating** Enchanting, but inefficient; ★★★★. Duration of presentation 6 minutes. **Probable waiting time per 100 people ahead of you** 7 minutes.

DESCRIPTION AND COMMENTS Next to the Owl Post is Ollivanders, a musty little shop stacked to the ceiling with boxes of magic wands. Inside you'll find the same intimate wand-choosing ceremony found in the Diagon Alley attraction of the same name (see page 258). It's great fun, but the tiny shop can accommodate only about 24 guests at a time. After the show, the whole group is dispatched to the Owl Post and Dervish and Banges to make purchases. Wand prices range from $25 for a toy "learner wand" to $47 for an interactive model that triggers special effects hidden inside shop windows throughout Hogsmeade and Diagon Alley.

The wand experience is second in popularity only to Harry Potter and the Forbidden Journey. Lines build quickly after opening, and there's little to no shade. The average wait time during summer and other busy periods is 45–85 minutes between 9:30 a.m. and 7:30 p.m. If you're just looking to buy a wand without the interactive features, a cart is usually set up between Filch's Emporium of Confiscated Goods and the Flight of the Hippogriff exit, with little to no wait.

TOURING TIPS Due to its very low capacity (about 150 guests per hour), long lines for the show at Ollivanders form quickly upon park opening and last until just before the park closes. If you need to see this show, and you can't go to the USF branch, go first thing in the morning or as late as possible.

You do not need to see the wand-selection show to purchase a wand at Ollivanders—just enter the store directly rather than wait in the long outdoor queue. Also, noninteractive wands and other Harry Potter merchandise are available online and at other stores in the Wizarding World, as well as at Islands of Adventure Trading Company.

Interactive Wands and Spell-Casting Locations in Hogsmeade

Interactive wands sold in either park come with a map that shows Diagon Alley spell-casting locations on one side and Hogsmeade locations on the other. All of the spells in Hogsmeade are found in the central village, not near Hogwarts Castle or Hogwarts Express. Effects aren't as numerous or as elaborate in Hogsmeade as they are in Diagon Alley, and several are adaptations of older effects that previously ran automatically. There are also no hidden effects in Hogsmeade (as far as we know). On the other hand, there usually aren't quite as many kids trying to trigger effects here. If you are only visiting IOA, it probably isn't worthwhile to buy an interactive wand, but if you are visiting both parks, make sure to test out your purchase from USF's Ollivanders here.

THE LOST CONTINENT

THE LOST CONTINENT WAS ONCE AMONG ISLANDS of Adventure's largest areas, until its medieval Merlinwood section was repurposed into The Wizarding World of Harry Potter–Hogsmeade, leaving only the Arabian and Ancient Greek portions intact. What's left of Lost Continent is extremely well themed and features the park's only attractions that aren't tied to a licensed intellectual property. Lost Continent can be reached directly from Hogsmeade or Seuss Landing, or on busy days via a bypass bridge to Jurassic Park.

The best attraction in Lost Continent may be the **Mystic Fountain,** an interactive talking fountain in front of the entrance to *The Eighth Voyage of Sindbad Stunt Show.* A cast member behind the scenes controls the fountain and is able to talk to and hear from anyone who approaches. Many kids seem mesmerized by it. Parents can grab a quick snack or drink while the little ones are entertained by the fountain mere steps away. The park's second First Aid station is also located here, behind the coin vendor.

The Eighth Voyage of Sindbad Stunt Show
(Universal Express) ★★½

APPEAL BY AGE	PRESCHOOL	★★	GRADE SCHOOL	★★★½	TEENS	★★★
YOUNG	ADULTS	★★★	OVER 30	★★½	SENIORS	★★½

What it is Theater stunt show. **Scope and scale** Major attraction. **When to go** Any time on the daily entertainment schedule. **Authors' rating** Explosively awful; ★★½. **Duration of presentation** 17 minutes. **Probable waiting time 15 minutes**.

DESCRIPTION AND COMMENTS Held in a large, covered, open-air auditorium, this stunt show follows Sindbad the Sailor and his klutzy sidekick Kabob as they search for treasure in a mysterious cave. Sindbad and Kabob meet various monsters and an evil queen, braving water explosions, 10-foot-tall circles of flame, and various other eruptions and perturbations as they (of course) rescue a princess in distress. The show climaxes in an impressive fire-burn stunt where a flaming actor takes a high dive into the lagoon.

As far as Orlando's stunt shows go, *Sindbad* ranks near the bottom. The stunning set was built before the script was even written, and it shows. Not unlike an action movie that substitutes a mind-numbing succession of explosions, crashes, and special effects for plot and character development, the production is so vacuous and redundant (not to mention silly) that it's hard to get into the spirit of the thing. A 2015 refurbishment freshened up the fisticuffs and updated some pop-culture references, while adding an inane audience participation preshow. The "improvements" weren't enough to upgrade our opinion of the production. When our researchers went to review *Sindbad*, one team member passed, explaining that the show is like a colonoscopy: Once every 10 years is enough.

TOURING TIPS See *The Eighth Voyage* after you've experienced the rides and the better-rated shows. We'd only recommend this show if it was unbearably hot or grapefruit-size hail was falling from the sky. We'd take our chances going someplace else if it was just, you know, golf ball–size hail. Shows typically begin around noon, and it's rare for the theater to fill up. Thanks to the Grade Z dialogue, guests with limited or no English skills seem to enjoy this show more than native speakers.

Poseidon's Fury *(Universal Express)* ★★★½

APPEAL BY AGE PRESCHOOL ★★ GRADE SCHOOL ★★★½ TEENS ★★½ YOUNG ADULTS ★★★ OVER 30 ★★★ SENIORS ★★★

What it is High-tech theater attraction. **Scope and scale** Headliner. **When to go** After experiencing all the rides. **Special comments** Audience stands throughout. **Authors' rating** Dumb but dazzling, ★★★½. **Duration of presentation** 17 minutes, including preshow. **Probable waiting time** 25 minutes.

DESCRIPTION AND COMMENTS In the first incarnation of this story, the Greek gods Poseidon and Zeus duked it out, with Poseidon as the heavy. Poseidon fought with water, and Zeus fought with fire, though both sometimes resorted to laser beams and smoke machines. In the current incarnation, the rehabilitated Poseidon now tussles with an evil wizardish guy—named Lord Darkenon, of all things—and they fight with fire, water, lasers, and smoke machines.

As you might have inferred, the story is somewhat incoherent, but the special effects are still amazing, as is the theming of the preshow area. The plot unfolds in installments as you pass through a couple of antechambers and finally into the main theater. Though the production plods a bit at first, it wraps up with quite an impressive flourish. *Poseidon* is far and away the best of the Islands of Adventure theater attractions (its only competition is *Sindbad*).

TOURING TIPS Catch *Poseidon* after getting your fill of the rides. The attraction opens one or more hours after the rest of the park (usually at 10 a.m.) and closes 30 minutes or more before park closing. Check the daily entertainment schedule for showtimes.

If you're still wet from Dudley Do-Right's Ripsaw Falls, Popeye & Bluto's Bilge-Rat Barges, or the Jurassic Park River Adventure, you might be tempted to cheer the evil wizard's flame jets in hopes of finally drying out. Our money, however, is on Poseidon—it's legal in Florida for theme parks to get guests wet, but setting them on fire is frowned upon.

While most of the action takes place on movie screens, *Poseidon's Fury* can frighten many small children. The entire theater is thrown into total darkness many times during the show, and many of the special effects involve fire, loud noises, and flashing lights.

As impressive as the facade of *Poseidon's Fury* is, this Massachusetts mom of a family of four thinks the attraction itself is a letdown:

The one attraction we wished we'd skipped was Poseidon's Fury. *The posted wait time was 10 minutes. After waiting 30 minutes, we*

were ushered into a series of rooms with no chairs to watch a set
of poorly executed special effects. I'm 5 feet tall and saw none of it
because everyone was standing, and the floor was poorly slanted.
At the end, we were all tired and wanted to go home.

SEUSS LANDING

THIS 10-ACRE THEMED AREA IS BASED on Dr. Seuss's famous children's books. Buildings and attractions replicate a whimsical, brightly colored cartoon style with exaggerated features and rounded lines. The odd-shaped facades were carved from Styrofoam and sprayed with concrete, and the impossibly bent palm trees were salvaged from Hurricane Andrew, resulting in a land without a single straight line or right angle.

Look for a photo op with top-hatted dignitaries outside the Mulberry Street Store; the one with the beard and glasses is Dr. Theodor "Seuss" Geisel himself.

Caro-Seuss-el *(Universal Express)*   ★★★

APPEAL BY AGE	PRESCHOOL ★★★★★	GRADE SCHOOL ★★★★	TEENS ★★★
YOUNG	ADULTS ★★★	OVER 30 ★★★½	SENIORS ★★★★

What it is Merry-go-round. **Scope and scale** Minor attraction. **When to go** Anytime. **Special comments** Ride is outside but covered. **Authors' rating** Wonderfully whimsical; ★★★. **Duration of ride** 2 minutes. **Probable waiting time per 100 people ahead of you** 9 minutes. **Loading speed** Slow.

DESCRIPTION AND COMMENTS Totally outrageous, this full-scale, 56-mount merry-go-round is made up entirely of Dr. Seuss characters, each of which has an interactive effect (wagging tongues, blinking eyes) that the rider can control. While you turn, a Seussian orchestra of ridiculous instruments plays like a cacophonous calliope.

TOURING TIPS A gentle ride, even for the smallest children. If you are too old or don't want to ride, Caro-Seuss-el is still worth an inspection. If you do want to ride, waits are usually not too long, even in the middle of the day.

The Cat in the Hat *(Universal Express)*   ★★★½

APPEAL BY AGE	PRESCHOOL ★★★★½	GRADE SCHOOL ★★★★	TEENS ★★½
YOUNG	ADULTS ★★½	OVER 30 ★★½	SENIORS ★★★

What it is Indoor cartoon dark ride. **Scope and scale** Major attraction. **When to go** Before 11:30 a.m. or after 4 p.m. **Special comments** 36″ minimum height requirement. **Authors' rating** Dr. S. would be proud; ★★★½. **Duration of ride** 3½ minutes. **Probable waiting time per 100 people ahead of you** 5 minutes. **Loading speed** Moderate.

DESCRIPTION AND COMMENTS Universal's answer to Disney's vintage Fantasyland dark rides, this indoor, sit-down attraction recounts the entire *Cat in the Hat* story from beginning to end, in a little more than 4 minutes. Guests ride on "couches" through 18 different sets inhabited by animatronic Seuss characters. Of course, mayhem ensues when Cat brings Thing 1 and Thing 2 over to play, as the beleaguered goldfish tries to maintain order in the midst of bedlam, but the entire mess is cleaned up just before Mom gets home.

The audio narration is clear, and each scene is crammed with the kind of crazy furniture and bizarre housewares found in the book. The ride is straightforward enough, but we wish it had more sophisticated animatronics and better effects. Unfortunately, in 2014 the ride's energetic spinning was greatly dampened, and a new height minimum was imposed, reducing its appeal for both tykes and teens.

TOURING TIPS This is fun for all ages. Try to ride early, or ride late in the day after families with young children have started to depart.

Because the vehicles now barely rotate, we think there's almost nothing here to frighten small children beyond some loud noises. A father of three from Natick, Massachusetts, disagrees:

> The Cat in the Hat ride has quite the fright potential. My wife took my fairly advanced 3½-year-old daughter on the ride, and she was screaming her head off. Nearly two years later, she still reminds me of the scary Cat in the Hat ride (it hasn't affected her love for the books, though!).

The High in the Sky Seuss Trolley Train Ride!
(Universal Express) ★★★½

APPEAL BY AGE	PRESCHOOL ★★★★★	GRADE SCHOOL ★★★½	TEENS ★★★
YOUNG ADULTS ★★★	OVER 30 ★★★	SENIORS ★★★★	

What it is Elevated train. **Scope and scale** Major attraction. **When to go** Before 11:30 a.m. **Special comments** 40″ minimum height requirement. **Authors' rating** A relaxed look at the park; ★★★½. **Duration of ride** 3½ minutes. **Probable waiting time per 100 people ahead of you** 9 minutes. **Loading speed** Molasses.

DESCRIPTION AND COMMENTS An elevated train ride through and around the buildings in Seuss Landing, the Trolley Train is a shorter, distant cousin to the Magic Kingdom's PeopleMover in Tomorrowland. Trains putter along elevated tracks while a voice reads a Dr. Seuss story over the train's speakers. As each train makes its way through Seuss Landing, it passes a series of simple animatronic characters in scenes that are part of the story being told.

The slow ride around Seuss Landing is pleasant and affords great views of most of the park, including Marvel Super Hero Island. Little tunnels and a few mild turns make this a charming attraction, but a bizarrely high minimum height requirement (raised in recent years to 40″) means that many in the Trolley's target demographic will be banned from riding.

Note that you can choose from two different train tracks at the boarding station. As you face the platform, to your left is the Beech track, which is aquamarine; to your right is the Star track, which is purple. If you're riding with a large group, keep your group together if you all want the same experience because the track on each side offers different visuals and two randomly selected ride sound tracks.

If I Ran the Zoo ★★½

APPEAL BY AGE	PRESCHOOL ★★★★★	GRADE SCHOOL ★★★½	TEENS ★★★
YOUNG ADULTS ★★★	OVER 30 ★★★	SENIORS ★★★★	

What it is Play area. **Scope and scale** Diversion. **When to go** Anytime. **Special comments** Kids may get wet. **Authors' rating** A nice break for parents; ★★½.

DESCRIPTION AND COMMENTS An interactive play area and outdoor maze, themed to Dr. Seuss rhymes and filled with the fantastic animals and gizmos from Seuss stories.

TOURING TIPS Tour anytime. Note that much of the play area is unshaded; bring a drink and hat for the little ones.

Oh! The Stories You'll Hear! ★★★

APPEAL BY AGE	PRESCHOOL ★★★★½	GRADE SCHOOL ★★★	TEENS ★★
YOUNG ADULTS ★	OVER 30 ★★★	SENIORS ★★½	

What it is Character-filled storytelling show. **Scope and scale** Minor attraction. **When to go** Scheduled showtimes. **Special comments** Audiences stand during show. **Authors' rating** Warm and fuzzy; ★★★. Duration of show 9 minutes. **Probable waiting time Negligible**.

DESCRIPTION AND COMMENTS Featuring many of Dr. Seuss's most beloved characters (including The Lorax, The Grinch, Thing 1 and Thing 2, Sam I Am, and the Cat in the Hat), *Oh! The Stories You'll Hear!* is a fun singing and dancing show staged in an outdoor area between One Fish, Two Fish, Red Fish, Blue Fish and The Cat in the Hat Ride. After each 9-minute show, the characters separate for individual meet-and-greets and autographs.

TOURING TIPS Shows run daily, starting usually by 11:30 a.m. and continuing every hour until about 5 p.m. on a schedule published in the park map. During inclement weather, the show takes place within the Circus McGurkus Cafe Stoopendous restaurant nearby. On Sundays, they skip the show but still do the meet-and-greets on schedule.

One Fish, Two Fish, Red Fish, Blue Fish
(Universal Express) ★★★

APPEAL BY AGE	PRESCHOOL ★★★★★	GRADE SCHOOL ★★★½	TEENS ★★½
YOUNG ADULTS ★★★½	OVER 30 ★★★	SENIORS ★★★	

What it is Wet version of Dumbo the Flying Elephant. **Scope and scale** Minor attraction. **When to go** Before 10 a.m. **Special comments** Plan on getting wet. **Authors' rating** Who says you can't teach an old ride new tricks?; ★★★. **Duration of ride** 2 minutes. **Probable waiting time per 100 people ahead of you** 9 minutes. **Loading speed** Slow.

DESCRIPTION AND COMMENTS Imagine a mild spinning ride similar to Disney's Magic Carpets of Aladdin, TriceraTop Spin, and Dumbo rides, only with Seuss-style fish for ride vehicles, and you have half the story. The other half involves yet another opportunity to drown.

Guests board a fish-shaped ride vehicle mounted to an arm attached to a central axis, around which the ride vehicles spin. Guests can raise and lower their fish 15 feet in the air while traveling in circles and trying to avoid streams of water sprayed by other fish mounted to "squirt posts" around the ride's perimeter.

You can avoid most of the spray by going up or down at the right time. If you pay attention to the color of your vehicle and listen to the song played in the background, you can (eventually) figure out when to move your fish.

TOURING TIPS We don't know what it is about this theme park and water, but you'll get wetter than at a full-immersion baptism. Lines can build in the afternoon, so ride early while you'll still have time to dry off.

SPECIAL EVENTS *at* UNIVERSAL'S ISLANDS *of* ADVENTURE

ISLANDS OF ADVENTURE DOESN'T HOST NEARLY as many special events throughout the year as Universal Studios Florida, but the one it has is first-rate and included with standard admission.

GRINCHMAS *(early December–early January)*

YOU'LL FIND CHRISTMAS DECOR throughout Islands of Adventure's Port of Entry and more modest ornamentation elsewhere in the park (the decor in The Wizarding World of Harry Potter is disappointingly restrained), but the epicenter of the holiday at IOA is obviously Seuss Landing. The star, naturally, is the Grinch, the iconic icky-green grump who famously stole Christmas from the Whos, only to return it when his undersize heart finally grew.

The Grinch is normally represented in the park by a masked representation of the cartoon character, but during Grinchmas, a speaking actor wearing professional prosthetic makeup impersonates Jim Carrey's live-action film incarnation. The Grinch meets and greets guests during the days inside the All the Books You Can Read store; he takes time to interact before each photograph, usually to hilarious effect, which results in a very slow-moving line. If meeting the Grinch is a priority, make this your first stop in the morning.

In addition to greeting guests, the Grinch stars in his own **Grinchmas Who-Liday Spectacular,** a half hour musical performed six to eight times each day inside a soundstage located behind the Circus McGurkus Cafe Stoo-pendous. The show, which blends the original book and cartoon with elements from the Carrey flick and musical accompaniment arranged by Chip Davis of Mannheim Steamroller, is a must-see for Grinch fans. It features a first-rate cast (some of whom have appeared on Broadway), expansive set, and even an appearance by a live canine as the Grinch's faithful pet Max.

Showtimes are listed in the park map and typically begin between 10:45 a.m. and noon, and continue until around 6 p.m. Line up near the One Fish, Two Fish ride a minimum of 20 minutes before showtime, as performances will sell out early on busy days. You will be directed to a seat once inside, but the venue is shallow enough that even the back row has an acceptable view.

The Grinch character breakfast is held in Circus McGurkus Cafe Stoo-pendous on select mornings during December. It costs $26 for adults, $13 for kids age 9 and under. Theme park admission is required; see "Character Meals" on page 183 in Part Six for information.

UNIVERSAL'S ISLANDS *of* ADVENTURE TOURING PLANS

DECISIONS, DECISIONS

WHEN IT COMES TO TOURING IOA efficiently in a single day, you have two basic choices, and as you might expect, there are trade-offs. The Wizarding World of Harry Potter–Hogsmeade sucks up guests like a Hoover, and the 20-acre section of the park will be quickly overrun by crowds on days of moderately heavy attendance. Because of Harry Potter and the Forbidden Journey's several preshows, it takes about 25 minutes to experience, even if you don't have to wait, which compounds the challenge of creating an optimal touring plan.

If you're intent on experiencing **Harry Potter and the Forbidden Journey** first thing, be at the turnstiles waiting to be admitted at least 30 minutes before the park opens. Once you're admitted, move as swiftly as possible to The Wizarding World and then ride Forbidden Journey, followed by Flight of the Hippogriff and Dragon Challenge, in that order.

If the rides operate as designed, you're golden. You can get Hogsmeade out of the way in about an hour, and be off to other must-see attractions before the park gets crowded. Then come back to The Wizarding World late in the day to explore Hogsmeade and the shops. If, on the other hand, the ride suffers technical difficulties, you may be stuck in line a long while, during which time the crowds will have spread to other areas of IOA. By the time you exit Forbidden Journey, there will be long lines for all of the park's other popular attractions.

Unless you have Early Park Admission privileges at IOA, a much better choice (and the path we follow in our recommended touring plans) is to skip Potterville first thing. Instead, enjoy other attractions in IOA, starting at Marvel Super Hero Island. The good news is that The Wizarding World usually clears out in the afternoon and is often empty in the last hour, even on busy days. You can ride Forbidden Journey with a minimal wait if you step in the queue shortly before closing time.

ISLANDS OF ADVENTURE ONE-DAY TOURING PLAN FOR ADULTS *(page 371)*

THIS TOURING PLAN IS FOR GUESTS without park-to-park tickets and is appropriate for groups of all sizes and ages. It includes thrill rides that may induce motion sickness or get you wet. If the plan calls for you to experience an attraction that doesn't interest you, simply skip it and go to the next step. Be aware that the plan calls for some backtracking.

If you have young children in your party, customize the plan to fit their needs and take advantage of child swap at thrill rides.

ISLANDS OF ADVENTURE ONE-DAY TOURING PLAN FOR PARENTS WITH SMALL CHILDREN *(page 372)*

THIS PLAN IS FOR GUESTS WITHOUT PARK-TO-PARK tickets and eliminates all rides with a minimum height requirement greater than 40 inches. The plan includes a midday break of at least two hours back at your hotel. It's debatable whether the kids will need the nap more than you, but you'll thank us later, we promise.

ISLANDS OF ADVENTURE ONE-DAY TOURING PLAN FOR SENIORS *(page 373)*

THIS PLAN IS FOR GUESTS WITHOUT PARK-TO-PARK tickets and is specifically designed for seniors and grandparents, taking walking distances and attraction ratings from this group into account. This plan focuses on shows and family-friendly attractions and avoids thrill rides.

Also see pages 291–292 in Part Seven for our multiday and multipark touring plans.

PART NINE

UNIVERSAL ORLANDO CITYWALK

MUCH LIKE THE STORY OF UNIVERSAL ORLANDO'S theme parks, the story of its nightlife offerings is one of punches and counterpunches. Back in the 1970s and '80s, developer Bob Snow's Church Street Station attracted tourists and locals alike to downtown Orlando with the area's first themed nightclub complex. Disney took aim at Church Street throughout the 1990s with its now-demolished Pleasure Island, which slowly smothered the once-successful Station. Finally, Universal Orlando opened CityWalk with IOA in 1999 and essentially put Disney out of the nightlife business. Though downtown has bounced back a bit, and Disney is busy remaking the long-dormant Pleasure Island as part of the new Disney Springs complex, CityWalk is still the most popular spot among area visitors (and many residents) for postpark partying.

CityWalk is a shopping, dining, and entertainment venue that doubles as the entrance plaza for the Universal Studios and Islands of Adventure theme parks. Situated between the parking complex and the theme parks, CityWalk is heavily trafficked all day but truly comes alive at night. The complex is arrayed in a crescent shape around the waterway that connects Universal's two theme parks with the resort's Deluxe hotels. Along its streets, CityWalk offers a number of nightclubs to sample, and many of those entertainment and restaurant venues depend on well-known brand names. You'll find a Hard Rock Cafe and concert hall; Jimmy Buffett's Margaritaville; Emeril's Restaurant; a Bubba Gump Shrimp Co.; a branch of New Orleans's famous Pat O'Brien's club; an NBC sports bar; and a reggae club that celebrates the life and music of Bob Marley. Places that operate without big-name tie-ins include The Red Coconut Club, a lounge and nightclub; The Groove, a high-tech disco; and CityWalk's Rising Star, a karaoke club with a live backup band.

Another CityWalk distinction is that most of the clubs are also restaurants, or alternatively, several of the restaurants are also clubs.

Continued on page 332

Universal Orlando CityWalk

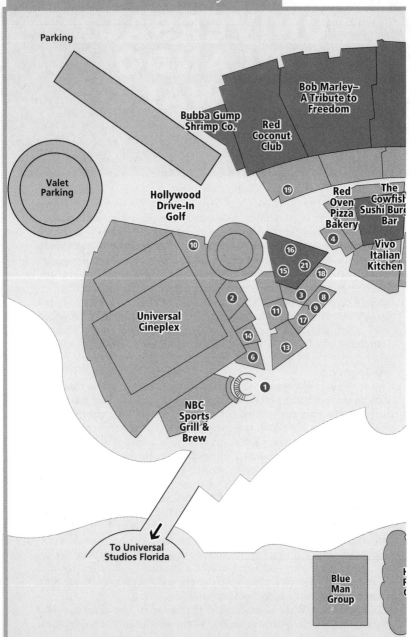

Parking

Valet Parking

Bubba Gump Shrimp Co.

Red Coconut Club

Bob Marley– A Tribute to Freedom

Hollywood Drive-In Golf

Red Oven Pizza Bakery

The Cowfish Sushi Burger Bar

Vivo Italian Kitchen

19

10

16

15 21

18

4

2

3 8

11 9

17

14

6 13

1

Universal Cineplex

NBC Sports Grill & Brew

To Universal Studios Florida

Blue Man Group

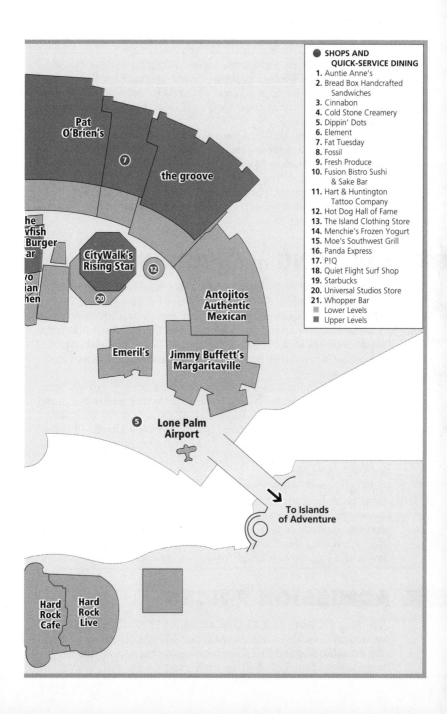

Continued from page 329

Though there's a lot of culinary variety, restaurants and nightclubs are different animals. Sight lines, room configuration, acoustics, intimacy, and atmosphere—important considerations in a nightclub—are not at all the same in a venue designed to serve meals. Though it's nice to have all that good food available, the club experience is somewhat dulled.

Red Coconut Club, The Groove, and CityWalk's Rising Star are more nightclub than restaurant, whereas Margaritaville is more restaurant than club. Bob Marley's and Pat O'Brien's are about half-and-half. The Hard Rock Cafe, Antojitos, Emeril's, Vivo, and The Cowfish are restaurants, profiled in Part Six. The venue for the Blue Man Group is strictly a performance space, though a full bar and snack food are available.

ARRIVING *and* PARKING

THE UNIVERSAL ORLANDO COMPLEX can be accessed by car from I-4 West via Exit 74B or 75B, or from I-4 East via Exit 75A or 75B. CityWalk visitors park in the same garage as Universal theme park guests. Self-parking costs $5 between 6 and 10 p.m. (free for Florida residents with ID) and is free after 10 p.m.; preferred and valet parking is also available. See Part Three for detailed driving and parking directions.

Universal Orlando on-site hotel guests can reach CityWalk using the same water taxis, buses, and walking paths that lead to the theme parks. The water taxi hub is located along the waterfront path before the bridge to USF. Guests walking from Hard Rock Hotel and Portofino Bay enter CityWalk closest to USF near Hard Rock Cafe, while guests walking from the other hotels enter CityWalk near Jimmy Buffett's Margaritaville.

As you enter CityWalk from the parking structure, you'll see a concierge kiosk beneath the escalator outside Starbucks, offering information, guide maps, restaurant menus, and dining reservations. Guest Services, the restrooms, an ATM, and First Aid are all located to your left, immediately past Cold Stone Creamery. A secondary ticket window where you can purchase Party Passes is located near The Groove.

ADMISSION PRICES

CITYWALK'S **Party Pass All-Club Access** is $12 (plus tax), which gets you into all the clubs: Margaritaville, Bob Marley, The Groove, Rising Star, Pat O'Brien's, and Red Coconut. You can pay an individual cover charge of $7 (tax included) at each club. Given that, getting the all-access pass makes the most sense if you plan to visit more than one club in an evening, though if you arrive before the cover charge kicks in (typically 9 p.m.), you can enjoy your first club for free.

Complimentary admission to the above clubs is also included with any multiday Universal theme park ticket (valid for 14 consecutive nights, starting the first time the ticket is used). Premier Annual Pass holders also get free club admission for themselves, as well as for a guest on Sunday–Thursday nights. Preferred and Premier Pass holders get 20% off additional Party Passes (up to four per night). Party Passes (free or otherwise) are only valid during regular operating hours and not during special events such as New Year's Eve.

Nightclubs not enough for you? CityWalk offers a number of combination tickets that may save you a few dollars, providing you choose carefully. The standard Party Pass can be combined with an adult ticket to any standard screening at the AMC Cineplex for $16 (including tax); you can upgrade to a 3-D or IMAX film for a $4–$6 additional fee). Because a movie ticket normally costs $11.49, getting one for about $4 is a great deal if you feel like seeing a flick.

If you're hungry, for $21 (tax and gratuity included; only sold at the CityWalk box office) the **Meal & Party** deal includes club admission with dinner at Bob Marley, Margaritaville, Pat O'Brien's, or Fusion Bistro Sushi. You get an entrée and soft drink but must order from a very limited menu. If you like Jamaican curry, fish sandwiches, spicy tuna rolls, or jambalaya, the meal deal (valued at around $13, including a 15% gratuity) can save you $10 or more on dinner, depending on what you order.

Not in the mood to go clubbing? The **Meal & Movie Deal** is $22 (tax and gratuity included) and combines—what else?—dinner at one of the above CityWalk restaurants and a movie ticket. Finally, the **Meal & Mini-Golf Deal** ($24) includes dinner and one 18-hole round of golf at the Hollywood Drive-In.

For the value obsessed, here is a breakdown of what each element in the various CityWalk deals is worth, and how much of a savings they represent:

PARTY PASS	$7.14 ($5.63 saving)
MOVIE	$8.84 ($3.40 saving)
MEAL	$13.10 ($3–$11.50 saving)
GOLF	$10.84 ($5.12 saving)

▌▌ CONTACTING CITYWALK

CONTACT CITYWALK GUEST SERVICES at ☎ 407-224-2691, or visit its website at **citywalk.com.** Keep in mind, though, that CityWalk personnel may not be up on individual club doings, so your best bet may be to contact specific clubs directly when you reach the Orlando area.

CITYWALK CLUBS

THE FOLLOWING NIGHTCLUB VENUES are mostly located along the elevated curving pathway that sits behind and above CityWalk's central plaza. At most of these venues, you must be 21 or older (passport or photo ID required) to enter after 9 p.m. Pick up a CityWalk City Guide brochure from the concierge stand or Guest Services for a monthly listing of live performances and drink specials.

Bob Marley—A Tribute to Freedom

What it is Reggae restaurant and club. Hours Daily, 4 p.m.–2 a.m. Cuisine Jamaican-influenced appetizers and main courses. Entertainment Live reggae bands and DJ in the outdoor gazebo every night. Cover $7 after 9 p.m. nightly (more for special acts).

Comments This club is a re-creation of Marley's home in Kingston, Jamaica, and contains a lot of interesting Marley memorabilia. The open-air court-yard is the center of action. Must be age 21 or older after 9 p.m. Sunday is Ladies Night, with no cover charge for women before midnight and drink specials. Island Sounds Wednesdays also features free cover for ladies all night long, and drink specials 9 p.m.–2 a.m.

CityWalk's Rising Star

What it is Karaoke club with live band and backup singers Tuesday–Saturday (Sunday–Monday, sing to recorded tracks with live backup singers). Hours Nightly, 8 p.m.–2 a.m. Cuisine Red Oven pizza delivery. Entertainment Karaoke. Cover $7 (no extra charge to sing).

Comments With live musicians backing you up, you can pretend that you've hit the big time at this opulent karaoke, which started life as CityWalk's jazz club. The good news is that, instead of a canned "tiny orchestra," Rising Star gives you a full live backing band to perform with on Tuesday–Saturday nights, and a live host and backup singers (with pre-recorded music) on Sundays and Mondays. The bad news is that the song list is rather short, with only a little more than 200 options instead of the thousands you may be used to back home. Even so, this is an extremely popular spot; be sure to put your selections in as early in the evening as possible if you want to get on stage. While waiting your turn, you can get your courage up with one of its supersweet specialty cock-tails; pizza delivery from Red Oven is available if stage fright makes you hungry. Guests 18 and older are welcome Sunday–Thursday, but the club is restricted to 21+ on Friday and Saturday.

The Groove

What it is High-tech disco. Hours Nightly, 9 p.m.–2 a.m. Cuisine No food. Entertainment DJ plays dance tunes. Sometimes there are live bands. Cover $7.

Comments Guests must be age 21 or older to enter this très chic club designed to look like an old theater in the midst of restoration. There are seven bars and several themed cubbyholes (the ultramodern Blue Room, laid-back Green Room, and brothel-like Red Room) for getting away from the thundering sound system. Dancers are barraged with strobes, lasers, and heaven knows what else. VIP reserved tables with premium bottle service is available for those with money and liver cells to burn; call ☎ 407-224-2166 to book your party. Attire is casual chic with no hats or tank tops permitted for men.

Jimmy Buffett's Margaritaville

What it is Key West–themed restaurant and club. **Hours** Daily, 11 a.m.–2 a.m. **Cuisine** Caribbean, Florida fusion, and American. **Entertainment** Live rock and island-style music. **Cover** $7 after 10 p.m.

Comments   Jimmy's is a big place with three bars that turns into a nightclub after 10 p.m. Jimmy Buffett covers are popular (no surprise) as is island music and light rock. If you eat dinner here, you'll probably want to find another vantage point when the band cranks up on the main stage around 9 p.m. There's always an acoustic guitarist strumming on the Porch of Indecision from 5 p.m. daily. If you are already inside the restaurant eating dinner before the cover charge kicks in, you won't be kicked out when the band kicks off.

Pat O'Brien's Orlando

What it is Dueling pianos sing-along club and restaurant. **Hours** Daily, 4 p.m.–2 a.m. **Cuisine** Cajun. **Entertainment** Dueling pianos and sing-alongs. **Cover** $7 after 9 p.m. for piano bar only.

Comments   A clone of the famous New Orleans club of the same name. A solo pianist starts playing a little after 5 p.m., and he or she is joined by a second starting around 9 p.m. These are some of the most talented singing musicians in town and will happily handle nearly any request you throw at them (even—gasp!—Disney tunes) as long as you write it on a generous gratuity. You can dine in the courtyard or on the terrace without paying a cover. You must be age 21 or older to hang out here after 9 p.m.

The Red Coconut Club

What it is Modern lounge and nightclub. **Hours** Monday–Saturday, 7 p.m.–2 a.m.; Sunday, 8 p.m.–2 a.m. **Cuisine** Appetizers; Red Oven pizza delivery after 10 p.m. **Entertainment** Lounging and dancing. **Cover** $7 after 9 p.m.

Comments   This nightspot is billed as a nightclub and ultra-lounge, advertising talk for "hip place to be seen." The eclectic mix of decor—part 1950s, part tiki—and three bars on two levels would make it a great later-day hangout for the Rat Pack, if Frank and Dean happened to be resurrected in Orlando. There is a dance floor, and the bar serves signature martinis and mojitos. An evening here can quickly add up, with VIP bottle service starting at $100; a daily happy hour 7–9 p.m. brings the drink and appetizer prices down to more reasonable levels. Thursday is Latin Ladies Night with DJ Leony and no cover charge for women.

▌ CITYWALK ENTERTAINMENT

BEYOND THE NIGHTCLUBS, CityWalk's attractions include an array of separately ticketed entertainment venues. None of the following attractions are included in basic Party Passes or theme park tickets.

AMC UNIVERSAL CINEPLEX 20 WITH IMAX

IF YOU WANT TO TAKE a break from "riding the movies" inside Universal's parks, and just want to watch one instead, the 20-screen AMC Universal Cineplex at CityWalk has you covered. This is one of the nicer theaters in town, with comfy high-backed rocker seats, hot foods such as chicken fingers and pizza at the snack bar (along with the usual overpriced cinema standards), and a full liquor bar. All screens have digital projection, surround sound, and stadium seating.

The Cineplex's digital IMAX theater was added by retrofitting a larger screen over an existing one; it's bigger than the screens and delivers more impact in 3-D films but isn't ginormous like the true IMAX screen at Pointe Orlando on I-Drive.

In addition to playing all the newest blockbusters, Universal's Cineplex also screens independent films, classic revivals, and cult films; The Rich Weirdoes (**richweirdoes.com**) host an audience participation performance of *The Rocky Horror Picture Show* every second and fourth Friday and Saturday of the month. Note that children under age 6 are not permitted to attend R-rated films after 6 p.m., thanks to AMC's distraction-free environment policy.

Tickets cost $11.49 for adults ($8.83 for kids ages 2–12) for showings starting after 3:55 p.m. 3-D films cost $4 extra, IMAX is $5 extra, and IMAX 3-D is $6 extra. Afternoon matinees cost $9.89 for adults, and shows starting before noon on weekends and holidays are only $6.50. Seniors age 60 and over pay $6.38 for all shows on Tuesdays, and $10.43 for evening shows the rest of the week. Students with school ID pay the kids' price on Thursdays. Preferred and Premier Annual Pass holders get $3 off admission (cannot be combined with other discounts).

Use Fandango or visit **amctheatres.com/movie-theatres/universal -cineplex-20** to see showtimes and buy tickets, or call ☎ 407-354-3374 to hear a recording of what's playing. Tickets can be retrieved from automated kiosks located to the right of the box office. You can save the $1 or $2 online service fee by joining AMC's Stubs rewards club.

BLUE MAN GROUP

NO PIECE OF ENTERTAINMENT better encapsulates the "Universal Difference" than the Blue Man Group's nightly performances at City-Walk. Cirque du Soleil's *La Nouba*—the closest equivalent at Walt Disney World—is epic, opulent, and elegant, appealing to infants and grandparents alike. Blue Man Group, in comparison, is intimate, offbeat, and occasionally ornery, with elements of avant-garde performance art that are as likely to provoke a loud "WTH?" as applause. Both are phenomenal pieces of theater in their own right, and well worth every penny. But Disney doesn't provide ponchos to patrons seated in the first four rows for protection against flying paint.

The three blue men of the Blue Man Group are just that—blue—and bald and mute. Wearing black clothing and skullcaps slathered with bright-blue grease paint, they deliver a fast-paced show that uses music (mostly percussion) and multimedia effects to make light of contemporary art and life in the information age. The Universal act is just one expression of a franchise that started with three friends in New York's East Village. Now you can catch their zany, wacky, smart stuff in New York, Las Vegas, Boston, Chicago, and Berlin, among other places. The one-hour, 45-minute Orlando production was updated and reimagined in 2012 to reflect cultural changes in the use of technology in daily life; it includes some segments similar to those seen in other cities but isn't identical.

Funny, sometimes poignant, and always compelling, Blue Man Group pounds out vital, visceral tribal rhythms on complex instruments (made of PVC pipes) that could pass for industrial intestines, and makes seemingly spontaneous eruptions of visual art rendered with marshmallows and a mysterious goo. The weekly supplies include 25.5 pounds of Cap'n Crunch, 60 Twinkies, 996 marshmallows, and 9.5 gallons of paint. If all this sounds silly, it is, but it's also strangely thought-provoking and deals with topics such as the value of modern art, the ubiquity and addictive nature of tablet devices, the way rock music moves you, and how we're all connected. (*Hint:* It's not the Internet.)

A live percussion band backs Blue Man Group with a relentless and totally engrossing industrial dance riff. The band resides in long, dark alcoves above the stage. At just the right moments, the lofts are lit to reveal a group of pulsating neon-colored skeletons.

Audience participation completes the Blue Man experience. The blue men often move into the audience to bring guests on stage. At the end of the show, giant glowing balloons drop from the rafters for the audience to bat around like beach balls. And a lot of folks can't help standing up to dance and laugh. Magicians for the creative spirit that resides in us all, Blue Man Group makes everyone a coconspirator in a joyous explosion of showmanship.

This show is decidedly different and requires an open mind to be appreciated. It also helps to be a little loose because, like it or not, everybody gets sucked into the production and leaves the theater a little bit lighter in spirit. If you don't want to be pulled onstage to become a part of the improvisation, don't sit in the first half-dozen or so rows.

The Blue Man Group Box Office (☎ 888-340-5476 or 407-BLUE-MAN [258-3626]) is open 7 a.m.–7 p.m. EST, or you can buy tickets online at **bluemanorlando.com.** Advance tickets at the Universal Orlando website run $60–$110 for adults, $30–$57 for children ages 3–9; tickets purchased at the box office cost $10 more. The show isn't recommended for kids under age 3, but they may attend without a ticket if they sit on a lap. AAA members and Preferred and Premier Annual Pass holders save 20% on up to six tickets, and students with school ID can buy two tickets for $34 on the day of the show, if any are left. You can also save a few dollars by bundling a Blue Man Group ticket with theme park admission or a meal at CityWalk. All Blue Man Group tickets include free CityWalk club admission after the show.

A $20 VIP upgrade option includes access to the Bluephoria private lounge 45 minutes before and after the show, two free drinks (alcoholic or soft), and a photo op with a Blue Man. The lounge is undersized, but the drinks alone are almost worth the upgrade, and the brief meet-and-greet is a great bonus.

The show is staged in the Sharp Aquos Theatre, which was originally the Nickelodeon soundstage. It can be accessed from CityWalk by following the path between Hard Rock Cafe and Hollywood Rip Ride Rockit, or by exiting Universal Studios Florida through the side gate near Despicable Me Minion Mayhem. Center seats in rows B, C, and D go for a premium price; we recommend center seats in rows E–L, at least nine rows back from the stage.

CITYWALK STAGE

AT VARIOUS TIMES OF THE YEAR Universal offers free concerts and DJ performances on a stage located in the plaza at CityWalk. The stage may be positioned in front of the water feature between Vivo and The Universal Studios Store, or it may be located closer to the waterline at the bottom of the amphitheater. Performances are almost exclusively at night, though the space has been used for live tapings of morning talk shows. When One Direction launched its 2014 album with a free concert here, they drew traffic-snarling crowds, but there's normally no problem getting a view. The entertainment is usually free, but on New Year's Eve and a few other occasions, the entire area is reserved for those purchasing special-event tickets.

HARD ROCK LIVE

LOCATED ACROSS THE LAGOON from most of CityWalk, adjoining the Hard Rock Cafe and separate from the Hard Rock Hotel, this theater hosts concerts, contests, and various private events. Musical acts, both nationally known and up-and-coming, as well as stand-up comedians, appear regularly. Recent shows have run the gamut from Ralphie May and Demetri Martin to Alice Cooper and Wilco. Great acoustics, comfortable seating (for up to 3,000), and good sight lines make this the best concert venue in town.

Hours vary with live shows; performances usually begin 7–9:30 p.m. Ticket price varies depending on the act, ranging from $24 to $163. There is a full liquor bar, and (depending on the event) you can order food from the restaurant's kitchen. Floor viewing is from removable chairs, or sometimes standing-room only depending on the act, while guests in the VIP balcony can get cocktail service delivered to their leather armchairs. Annual-pass holders save $5 on tickets to the Classic Albums Live series, where talented studio musicians re-create records from the 1970s through 1980s note for note.

If seeing a show here, be sure to leave plenty of time for parking and security. You'll be inspected again before entering the venue, and the line can be agonizingly slow.

For information and an events calendar, see **hardrock.com/live /locations/orlando/calendar.aspx** or call ☎ 407-351-7625. To purchase tickets for an event at Hard Rock Live, call ☎ 407-351-LIVE (5483) or visit Ticketmaster at **ticketmaster.comvenue/278539/?brand =hrorlando.** (*Warning:* Exorbitant service fees apply.)

HOLLYWOOD DRIVE-IN GOLF

SO THIS IS WHAT MONEY and imagination can do. On one edge of the Universal Orlando CityWalk entertainment complex, these 18-hole courses are awash in elaborate settings, props, and even audio. The theme is a drive-in movie showing two features: *Invaders from Planet Putt* and *The Haunting of Ghostly Greens*. Players can choose a single (18 holes) or double (36 holes) feature.

The Invaders from Planet Putt course entertains with non-frightening statues and props such as rocket ships and little green men; a pretend newspaper box shows the *Roswell [New Mexico] Register* of July 8, 1947, with the blaring headline, "UFO SIGHTINGS CONTINUE."

The Haunting of Ghostly Greens course features a giant spider, a graveyard, and a basement-lab scene. This course is particularly nice at night but may creep out younger golfers. At various holes, the sound effects are a mooing cow, a chain saw, and a ray gun (we guess, as we've never actually heard a ray gun).

The courses are quite easy, and the greens are in superb condition. We rank Hollywood Drive-In as the best mini-golf in Orlando, along with Disney's Fantasia Gardens and Congo River in Kissimmee. Note that one of the courses is fully wheelchair accessible, while the other requires navigating some stairs.

Hollywood Drive-In is located at the entrance to CityWalk, between the AMC Cineplex and the valet parking loop. As you exit the parking garages and moving sidewalks, Hollywood Drive-In Golf is on your immediate right, down one level.

The course is open daily, 9 a.m.–2 a.m. For 18 holes, it costs $15 plus tax for adults, and $13 plus tax for children ages 3–9. For 36 holes, it costs $27 plus tax for adults, and $23 plus tax for children ages 3–9. Preferred Annual Pass holders, Florida residents, military, adults age 62 and older, and AAA members all save 10% on 18 holes for up to five players; Premier Pass holders save 15%. You can purchase online in advance, saving up to 13%, but online tickets can't be used on the same day and aren't refundable if unused.

You must pay the usual parking fee to play Hollywood Drive-In, which drastically boosts the price of playing these courses if you aren't already visiting Universal Orlando.

Call ☎ 407 802-4848 for more information, or visit **hollywood driveingolf.com,** where you can purchase discounted tickets. There's also a free scorecard app for Apple and Android that you can download in preparation for your putting.

PART TEN

WET 'N WILD

WET 'N WILD WAS STARTED IN 1977 by SeaWorld creator George Millay as the world's first modern water park. It was independently owned until 1998, when it was sold to Universal Orlando; the land under and around the park was purchased by Universal in 2013. Universal markets the park under the Universal Orlando Resort banner, selling combination park tickets through its website and providing free transportation to on-site hotel guests, but the attraction isn't thematically or geographically integrated into the resort.

Universal has begun constructing the Volcano Bay water park just south of Cabana Bay Beach Resort, and (according to permit filings) will feature 13 attractions reaching up to 200 feet tall. The new water park will have a tiki theme, including a volcano. The new park is scheduled to open in 2017, and Wet 'n Wild will close December 31, 2016. What happens to it after that is anyone's guess; the land could then be used for hotels or even another park. Until that happens, Wet 'n Wild continues to operate as Orlando's fourth-most popular water park.

Disney's water parks, and to a somewhat lesser extent SeaWorld Aquatica, are distinguished more by their genius for creating an integrated adventure environment than by their slides and individual attractions. At the Disney and SeaWorld water parks, both eye and body are deluged with the strange, exotic, humorous, and beautiful. Both Disney water parks are stunningly landscaped. Parking lots and street traffic are soon far removed from the swimming areas and out of sight. Also, each park has its own story to tell, a whimsical tale that forms the background for your swimming experience. Once you've passed through the turnstile, you're enveloped in a fantasy setting that excludes the outside world.

Continued on page 344

Wet 'n Wild Orlando

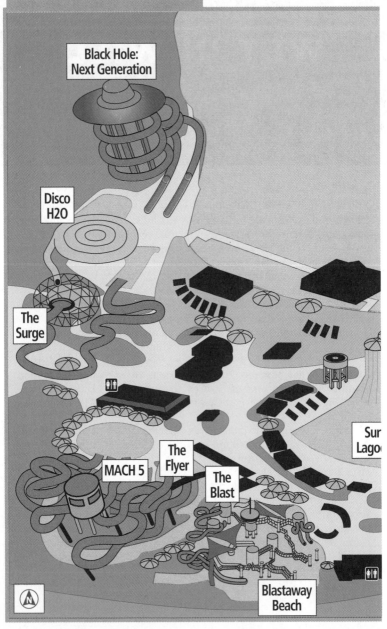

Black Hole: Next Generation

Disco H2O

The Surge

MACH 5

The Flyer

The Blast

Blastaway Beach

Sur Lago

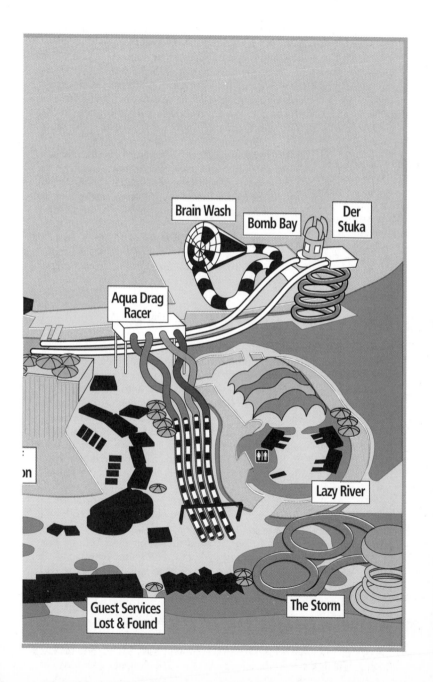

Continued from page 341

Unlike Typhoon Lagoon and Blizzard Beach, in which scenic man-made mountains and integrated themes create a colorful atmosphere, Wet 'n Wild's only themes appear to be concrete, plastic, and water. For many, however, the novelty of the theme is quickly forgotten once they hit the water, and the appreciation of being in an exotic setting gives way to enjoying specific attractions and activities. In other words, your focus narrows from the general atmosphere of the park to the next slide you want to ride. Once this occurs, the most important consideration becomes the quality and number of attractions and activities available and their accessibility relative to crowd conditions. Fortunately, the thrill, scope, and diversity of its rides make Wet 'n Wild an excellent alternative to the Disney swimming parks. Viewed from this perspective, Universal's Wet 'n Wild gives Disney more than a run for the money. Besides, contrary to what some Disney execs might believe, their water isn't any wetter.

*un**official* TIP**
Wet 'n Wild is cluttered and not very appealing to the eye, but water parks are one area where the heightened thrills of Universal's water rides may outweigh the decor of the Disney water parks.

■ GETTING *to* WET 'N WILD

WET 'N WILD IS LOCATED at the bustling intersection of International Drive and Universal Boulevard in Orlando, one block east of I-4 at exit 75A. From I-4 East, take Exit 75A and make a right onto Universal Boulevard. From I-4 West, take Exit 75A onto Kirkman Road southbound, make a right onto Carrier Drive, and then turn right onto Universal Boulevard.

Wet 'n Wild's parking lot is across the street from the park; enter from Universal Boulevard south of International Drive. Parking costs $13 for cars, $17 for RVs and trailers. Parking is ample; just be sure to hold the kids' hands when crossing the street because this is a notoriously busy intersection.

Universal and other nearby hotels provide free transportation to Wet 'n Wild via the Super Star Shuttle (see page 129 in Part Three); visit your hotel concierge for schedule information. Mears Transportation operates a shuttle to Wet 'n Wild that stops three times a day at Disney hotels. It's the same shuttle that commutes between Walt Disney World and Universal Orlando (see page 129). The park is also serviced by the Lynx bus and I-Ride Trolley.

■ ADMISSION PRICES

A SINGLE DAY ADMISSION to Wet 'n Wild costs $57 for adults ($52 for children ages 3–9) at the gate. Tickets are $10 cheaper if purchased in advance online. For an extra $5 (or free during certain online promotions), you can upgrade to a Length-of-Stay Pass valid for 14 consecutive days. Multiday Universal park-to-park tickets with Wet 'n Wild admission are available online through **universalorlando.com** and **wetnwild orlando.com,** and three-park unlimited tickets are sold through some third-party vendors (see page 35 in Part One).

Florida residents get a significant discount on single-day tickets and can buy an annual pass for the price of a regular one-day admission through the "Buy a Day, Get the Year Free" program. Universal annual-pass holders save an additional 10% on single-day tickets, or $20 off Wet 'n Wild annual passes, and get 10% off in the beach shop. Check the website for military and other seasonal discounts.

For an extra $80–$190, depending on the season, you and five friends can relax in a private cabana on the island in the middle of the Lazy River. A cooler of bottled water, towels, a lockbox, and lounge chairs are included, along with a 20% discount at the beach shop. Park admission is required and not included.

Finally, just like Universal's theme parks, Wet 'n Wild sells Express Passes to skip the lines, which can become quite lengthy. Express access starts at $20 per person and is available in both single use and unlimited varieties, with prices varying by the season. Express Passes may not be available during slower times and are not included with Universal Orlando on-site hotel stays.

OPERATING HOURS

WET 'N WILD IS OPEN 365 days a year but uses a half-dozen different operating schedules, ranging from 10 a.m. to 5 p.m. in January and February, to 9:30 a.m. to 9 p.m. in the summer. Call ☎ 800-992-9453 or 407-351-1800, or visit **wetnwildorlando.com** for up-to-date operating hours. Also check the website's maintenance schedule, as some major slides may be closed for refurbishment during colder months.

Ticket prices are similar to those of the Disney parks, but attending during the summer when the park is open late allows visitors to hit the slides in the morning, go back to their hotels for lunch and a nap, and then return for a dip at night. Disney water parks typically close by 6 or 7 p.m.

*un*official **TIP**
Wet 'n Wild's later summer hours may mean shorter lines for the slides in the evenings.

POLICIES *and* SERVICES

LOCKERS RENT FOR $6–$12 per day, plus a $3 refundable deposit. Towels rent for $4, but life vests are free. Smoking is restricted to designated areas, and there are no pet-care facilities.

"Appropriate apparel" (as judged by the lifeguards) is required, and bathing suits are required for all rides. T-shirts and water shoes may not be worn on the single-person speed slides (Bomb Bay, Der

Stuka, or The Storm), and cutoffs or shorts with metal fasteners or rivets are banned on all slides.

All the slides outside the Kids' Park have a 48-inch height requirement except for multi-passenger slides, for which the minimum height is 36 inches if an adult accompanies the short rider; the only exception to this is Aqua Drag Racer, which has a 42-inch minimum.

EATING *at* WET 'N WILD

WHEN YOU GET HUNGRY, the main food pavilions are the Wild Tiki Lounge, Bubba's Fried Chicken 'n Ribs, Riverside BBQ, Manny's Pizza, and Surf Grill, together offering such staples as burgers, pizza, and barbecue-pork sandwiches as well as more-nutritious (and nontraditional) items such as veggie burgers and tabbouleh. Wait times are long—Wild Tiki has flat-panel TVs to keep you occupied—and prices are high but not outrageous. During the busier months, Riverside BBQ offers an all-day all-you-can-eat plan with unlimited entrées, desserts, and soft drinks.

For guests whose budgets and impatience thresholds are less flexible, feel free to bring in a reasonably sized cooler or picnic basket of lunch fixings (remember, glass containers and alcoholic beverages are prohibited, but you can purchase beer inside).

WET 'N WILD ATTRACTIONS

A FLUME-TO-FLUME COMPARISON

IN STANDARD THEME PARK JARGON, the water parks refer to their various features, including slides, as attractions. Some individual attractions consist of several slides. If each slide at a specific attraction is different, we count them separately. Runoff Rapids at Blizzard Beach, for example, offers three corkscrew slides, each somewhat different. Because most guests want to experience all three, we count each individually. At the Toboggan Racers attraction (also at Blizzard Beach), there are eight identical slides, side by side. There's no reason to ride all eight, so we count the whole attraction as one slide.

Do the numbers tell the story? In the case of Wet 'n Wild, they certainly do. If you can live without the Disney and SeaWorld parks' theme setting or story line, Wet 'n Wild offers more variety than any of the other parks. Plus, from mid-June through mid-August, Wet 'n Wild is open until 9 p.m. Summer nights are more comfortable, lines for the slides often are shorter, and you don't have to worry about sunburn. Did we mention the giant toilet bowl? Wet 'n Wild has an attraction dubbed The Storm. The ride actually looks like a lot of fun, but in all honesty it strongly resembles a huge commode. Riders wash down a chute to gain speed, and then circle around a huge bowl before dropping into a pool below. This must be how that goldfish you flushed in third grade felt.

Generally speaking, during the day, you'll find Wet 'n Wild less crowded than the Disney and SeaWorld parks, which quite often sell out by about 11 a.m. Though not approaching Disney's or SeaWorld's standard for aesthetic appeal and landscaping, Wet 'n Wild is clean and attractive, with outstanding water-activity areas for younger children and some unique and interactive rides.

BODY AND MAT SLIDES

SLIDES AT WET 'N WILD INCLUDE AQUA DRAG RACER, Mach 5, Bomb Bay, Der Stuka, and The Storm. **Aqua Drag Racer,** opened in 2014, features four side-by-side slides, down which a quartet of "racers" are simultaneously dispatched face-first on foam mats. The slides start 65 feet off the ground as enclosed tubes that twist around each other, before opening up into parallel lanes for the final dash to the checkerboard finish line. The entire run is 350 feet long and takes a little more than 10 seconds to complete.

The **Mach 5** tower, located to the left of the park entrance, consists of three mat slides. The mats increase your speed and eliminate the chafing often experienced on body slides. To go even faster, try to get a newer mat with a smoother bottom. They are easily distinguishable: The new mats have white handles, while the old mats have blue ones.

unofficial **TIP**
Though ride attendants say that all three of the Mach 5 slides are equal, the center slide appears to be the zippiest route to the bottom.

Among the body slides (those without mats or rafts) are **Bomb Bay** and **Der Stuka,** twin speed flumes with pitches up to 79 degrees that descend from the top of a six-story tower. On Bomb Bay you stand on a pair of doors that open, dropping you into the chute. You have to work up the nerve to launch yourself on Der Stuka. The lack of a fully enclosed tube (such as the one on the Humunga Kowabunga speed slide at Typhoon Lagoon) adds the (perhaps justifiable) fear of falling off the 250-foot slides, but their ability to float your stomach somewhere near your teeth is a pretty unforgettable thrill.

The Storm body slide, located near Bomb Bay and Der Stuka, is a hybrid ride: half slide, half toilet bowl. The steep slide creates enough momentum to launch riders into a few laps around the bowl below before they begin slipping toward the hole in the center, eventually falling into a 6-foot-deep pool. The ride is exhilarating and disorienting; when the lifeguard at the ending pool begins hollering, just stumble toward his voice and give him a thumbs-up.

RAFT AND TUBE RIDES

THE HEADLINERS AT WET 'N WILD are the raft and tube rides, including Brain Wash, Disco H2O, The Surge, Black Hole: The Next Generation, The Flyer, and The Blast.

Wet 'n Wild Attractions

AQUA DRAG RACER 42″ • Four side-by-side 360-foot slides; race to the finish.

BLACK HOLE: THE NEXT GENERATION 48″ • A two-person tube spirals through deep space.

THE BLAST Children 36″–48″ must be accompanied by adult • A two-person tube travels down a ruptured pipeline.

BLASTAWAY BEACH None • The largest water play area in Florida, with a six-story sand castle, two pools, 15 slides, and more.

BOMB BAY 48″ • The floor falls out from underneath you before you plunge six stories.

BRAIN WASH 48″ • A four-person tube ride through a 53-foot vertical enclosed funnel.

DER STUKA 48″ • Six-story free fall.

DISCO H2O Children 36″–48″ must be accompanied by adult • A four-person tube travels through a 1970s disco club.

THE FLYER Children 36″–48″ must be accompanied by adult • A toboggan ride with a four-person raft.

LAZY RIVER Children under 48″ must wear life jacket • Your typical lazy river with waterfalls.

MACH 5 Must be able to control mat; children under 48″ must wear life jacket • Three different twisty slides.

THE STORM 42″; must be strong swimmer • Like being flushed down a toilet.

SURF LAGOON Children under 48″ must wear life jacket • 17,000-square-foot wave pool with 4-foot-high waves.

THE SURGE Children 36″–48″ must be accompanied by adult • A four-person tube ride on a 600-foot slide with lots of turns.

Brain Wash is an extreme six-story tube ride with a 53-foot vertical drop into a 65-foot funnel; tubes hold two or four riders.

Disco H2O holds up to four people in one raft, ushering them down a long tube into a 1970s-era nightclub complete with lights, music, and a disco ball. The basic design of the ride is similar to that of The Storm (a long tube into a bowl), only not as frantic and disorienting; the disco theme, coupled with the fluidity of the ride, makes it a main draw.

The Surge launches from the same tower as Disco H2O and uses the same four-person rafts. Riders spin down the open-air course, drifting high onto the walls on each banked corner. To reach the top of the walls, try to go with a full raft—as with all raft rides, the more riders squeezed in, the faster you'll all go.

Directly across from The Surge's splashdown pool is the entrance for **Black Hole: The Next Generation.** Bring a partner for this one; Black Hole requires two riders on each raft, and honestly, who wants to embark into endless murk without some company? As impressive as the ride seems from afar, the anxiety created by the gaping entrance is the most exciting part of the ride. Yes, it's dark—there is track lighting down the entire course—but besides the darkness, the ride lacks the dips and turns found on the other slides. If you're claustrophobic and scared of the dark, this isn't the ride for you; if tight spaces and inky blackness don't give you a rush, then this isn't the ride for you either.

The gentler raft rides are **The Flyer** and **The Blast.** Both launch from the same tower as the Mach 5, but their entrance is accessible through the Kids' Park. At the base of the entrance are one- and two-person rafts; these are only for The Blast, so don't carry them up to the tower to The Flyer entrance. The Flyer is a calmer, toboggan-style ride in which riders sit one behind the other; it's suitable for families with smaller children.

The Blast is a themed ride, like Disco H20, and is the wettest you can get without swimming. The theme of The Blast appears to be a broken waterworks, complete with spinning dials and broken pipes, all painted in comic book red and yellow. From mist to falling water to spraying pipes, this is the best way to cool off at Wet 'n Wild.

OTHER ATTRACTIONS

THE CENTRAL FIXTURE AT WET 'N WILD, the **Wave Pool Surf Lagoon,** is on par with Blizzard Beach's. Unlike at Typhoon Lagoon, there's no surfing in this wave pool, but you can rent tubes at the main rental stand or go bobbing with your body. The wave-making machine takes long breaks every day, so when you walk by and see waves, be sure to wade in. Another any-time-of-day option is the **Lazy River.** Unlike the Lazy River at Typhoon Lagoon, the Lazy River at Wet 'n Wild is misnamed: The circuit is short, the current fast. Don't even bother trying to walk upstream to catch a tube—it's better to swim down the river or wait patiently until one passes within reach.

Wet 'n Wild's 1-acre **Blastaway Beach,** located to your immediate left after you enter the main gate, has about a zillion things for the younger kids to do. Look for the oversize sand castle and the zany play area decorated in every color from the Crayola box. Also included are an upper and lower pool, totaling about 15,000 square feet, and more than 160 water jets, a cannon, waterfalls, and 15 slides.

APPENDIX

READERS' QUESTIONS
to the AUTHORS

FOLLOWING ARE QUESTIONS from *Unofficial Guide* readers.

QUESTION:

When you do your research, are you admitted to the parks for free? Do the Universal people know you're there?

ANSWER:

We pay the regular admission, and usually the Universal people don't know we're on-site. Similarly, both in and out of Universal Orlando, we pay for our own meals and lodging.

QUESTION:

How often is The Unofficial Guide *revised?*

ANSWER:

This is the inaugural edition of our guide to Universal Orlando. We will publish a new edition once a year.

QUESTION:

Where can I find information about what's changed at Universal Orlando in between published editions of The Unofficial Guide?

ANSWER:

We post important information online at **touringplans.com.**

QUESTION:

Do you write each new edition from scratch?

ANSWER:

Nope. For this first edition of *The Unofficial Guide to Universal Orlando,* we've built on our quarter-century of coverage about the resort. When it comes to a destination the size of Universal Orlando, it's hard enough to keep up with what's new. Moreover, we put a lot of effort into communicating the most useful information in the clearest possible language. For future editions, if an attraction or hotel has not changed, we're reluctant to tinker with its coverage for the sake of freshening the writing.

QUESTION:

How many people have you surveyed for your age-group ratings regarding the attractions?

ANSWER:

Since the first *Unofficial Guide* containing Universal coverage was published in 1992, we've interviewed or surveyed almost 47,000 Universal Orlando patrons. Even with such a large survey population, however, we continue to find that certain age groups are underrepresented. Specifically, we'd love to hear more from seniors about their experiences with coasters and other thrill rides.

READERS' COMMENTS

OUR READERS LOVE TO SHARE TIPS. An Iowa City, Iowa, couple offers this observation about being in touch with your feelings:

> We didn't build rest breaks into our plans but were willing to say, "OK, I'm just not having fun right now—we should leave the park," and go on to something else (like a water park, hotel pool, or shopping trip). This is a skill I would like to see more people develop. I can't count the number of people or families I saw who were obviously not having fun.

A Norwalk, Ohio, mom searched for happy feet:

> On the subject of footwear, support is just as important as comfort. On one trip I wore Keds—big mistake. My shins ached unbelievably before the end of the second day. From then on I was a die-hard tennis shoe girl, until I discovered FitFlops [go to **fitflop.com** for stores]. You get the support of a tennis shoe with the comfort of a flip-flop.

A woman from Mount Gretna, Pennsylvania, had some questions about theme park attire:

> There wasn't a section that addressed whether you could wear dresses on rides. Quite a few amusement parks have security straps or bars that come up between one's knees, making it very difficult and immodest to wear dresses or skirts. Many women want to wear dresses for convenience, comfort, or cultural/religious convictions. I was concerned as I was packing whether this would limit any rides I could get on. I was quite pleased that it did not.

A Columbia, Missouri, woman offers advice for wives with anxious husbands:

A smartphone is the best thing in the world for keeping your husband busy in line. As long as mine had that phone, he could check e-mail, check dinner plans, and take and send pictures of the kids to family back home. He never complained about waiting in line, ever.

All for the love of Mom, writes a woman from Haddon Heights, New Jersey:

I was traveling with my mother, who has an artificial knee, a herniated disc, and bad feet. My mantra was, "Try not to kill your mother." Without the book, I would have undoubtedly come home an orphan.

Finally, a Somerville, Alabama, woman is succinct if nothing else:

Everything, other than my husband, was perfect.

And so it goes. . . .

INDEX

Universal Studios Florida

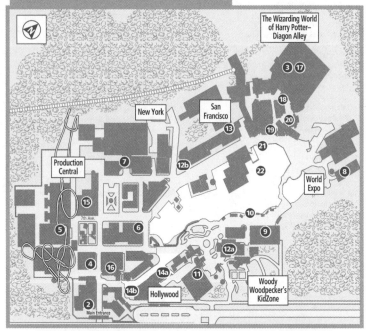

UNIVERSAL STUDIOS FLORIDA ONE-DAY TOURING PLAN FOR ADULTS

1. Buy admission in advance. Call ☎ 407-363-8000 the day before for the official opening time.

2. Arrive at USF 90–120 minutes before the official opening time if Early Park Admission is offered and you're eligible, or 30–45 minutes before opening for day guests. Pick up a park map as soon as you enter.

3. Early-entry guests should ride Harry Potter and the Escape from Gringotts if it's operating. If it's not, enjoy the rest of Diagon Alley but don't get in line.

4. Before early entry ends, hotel guests should exit Diagon Alley and ride Despicable Me Minion Mayhem. Day guests should wait in the front lot until permitted to ride Despicable Me.

5. Ride Hollywood Rip Ride Rockit.

6. Experience Transformers: The Ride 3-D.

7. Ride Revenge of the Mummy in New York.

8. Ride Men in Black Alien Attack in World Expo.

9. Ride The Simpsons Ride.

10. Ride Kang & Kodos' Twirl 'n' Hurl if 50 or fewer people are in line.

11. Ride E.T. Adventure in Woody the Woodpecker's KidZone.

12. Work in *Animal Actors on Location* (**12a**) and *Beetlejuice Graveyard Revue* (**12b**) around lunch (we recommend Fast Food Boulevard), according to the daily entertainment schedule. If you are running behind, skip *Animal Actors*.

13. Experience *Disaster!* in San Francisco.

14. See *Universal Orlando's Horror Make-Up Show* (**14a**) and *Terminator 2: 3-D* (**14b**) according to the daily entertainment schedule.

15. See *TWISTER . . . Ride It Out* in New York.

16. See *Shrek 4-D* in Production Central.

17. Ride Harry Potter and the Escape from Gringotts. If this is your first ride, take the standby queue. For re-rides, use the single-rider line. The Gringotts queue may close before the rest of the park if the posted wait time exceeds remaining operating hours by more than 60 minutes.

18. See the wand ceremony at Ollivanders and buy a wand if you wish.

19. Tour Diagon Alley. Browse the shops, explore the dark recesses of Knockturn Alley, and discover the interactive effects. If you're hungry, try the Leaky Cauldron or Florean Fortescue's Ice Cream Parlour.

20. See the *Celestina Warbeck* and *Tales of Beedle the Bard* shows.

21. Chat with the Knight Bus conductor and his shrunken head. Also look for Kreacher in the window of 12 Grimmauld Place, and listen to the receiver in the red phone booth.

22. If scheduled, see *Universal's Cinematic Spectacular* from Central Park (directly across the lagoon from Richter's), Duff Brewery, or the embankment in front of London.

Universal Studios Florida

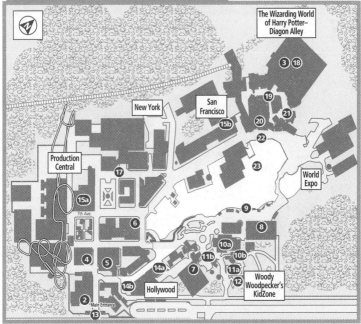

UNIVERSAL STUDIOS FLORIDA ONE-DAY TOURING PLAN FOR PARENTS WITH SMALL CHILDREN

1. Buy admission in advance. Call ☎ 407-363-8000 the day before for the official opening time.

2. Arrive at USF 90–120 minutes before the official opening time if Early Park Admission is offered and you're eligible, or 30–45 minutes before opening for day guests. Pick up a park map as soon as you enter. Rent a stroller if needed.

3. Early-entry guests should ride Harry Potter and the Escape from Gringotts from the standby queue, and use child swap or exit after the elevators. Or just enjoy the rest of Diagon Alley.

4. Before early entry ends, hotel guests should exit Diagon Alley and then ride Despicable Me Minion Mayhem. Day guests should wait in the front lot until permitted to ride Despicable Me.

5. See *Shrek 4-D* in Production Central.

6. Experience Transformers: The Ride 3-D.

7. Ride E.T. Adventure in Woody's KidZone.

8. Ride The Simpsons Ride.

9. Ride Kang & Kodos' Twirl 'n' Hurl.

10. See *Animal Actors on Location* **(10a)** and *A Day in the Park with Barney* **(10b)** according to the daily entertainment schedule. If you're hungry, get a snack on Fast Food Boulevard while waiting for the first show to start.

11. Between shows, work in Woody's Nuthouse Coaster **(11a)** and time in Fievel's Playground **(11b)**.

12. After the shows, let the kids loose at Curious George Goes to Town. Be warned: They'll get wet.

13. Take a break from the park for at least 2 hours,

depending on how late the park is open. If staying nearby, return to your room for a nap. Otherwise, take a rest at CityWalk or a resort hotel.

14. Return to the park a couple hours before Universal Superstar Parade. If your kids are brave, see *Universal Orlando's Horror Make-Up Show* **(14a)** and *Terminator 2: 3-D* **(14b)** according to the daily entertainment schedule.

15. Experience *TWISTER . . . Ride It Out* **(15a)** in New York and/or *Disaster!* **(15b)** in San Francisco between the above shows if you think your child can handle the storm and earthquake effects.

16. If your kids aren't up for any of the above, greet characters such as Shrek, SpongeBob, and the Transformers at locations shown on the park map.

17. See the late afternoon Superstar Parade from the New York area near Revenge of the Mummy.

18. Ride Harry Potter and the Escape from Gringotts from the standby queue (if you didn't earlier), and use child swap or exit after the elevators.

19. See the wand ceremony at Ollivanders.

20. Tour Diagon Alley. If you're hungry, try the Leaky Cauldron or Florean Fortescue's Ice Cream Parlour.

21. See the *Celestina Warbeck* and *Tales of Beedle the Bard* shows.

22. Chat with the Knight Bus conductor and his shrunken head. Also look for Kreacher in the window of 12 Grimmauld Place, and listen to the receiver in the red phone booth.

23. If scheduled, see *Universal's Cinematic Spectacular*.

Universal Studios Florida

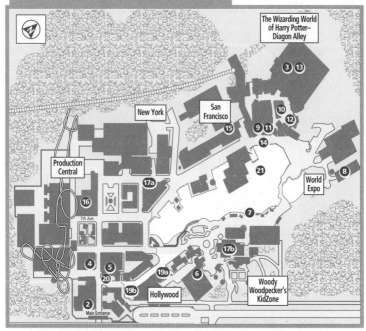

UNIVERSAL STUDIOS FLORIDA ONE-DAY TOURING PLAN FOR SENIORS

1. Buy admission in advance. Call ☎ 407-363-8000 the day before for the official opening time.

2. Arrive at USF 90–120 minutes before the official opening time if Early Park Admission is offered and you're eligible, or 30–45 minutes before opening for day guests. Get a park map as soon as you enter. Rent a wheelchair or ECV if needed.

3. Early-entry guests should ride Harry Potter and the Escape from Gringotts from the standby queue. Exit after the elevators if you don't wish to experience a mild roller coaster. Or just enjoy the rest of Diagon Alley.

4. Before early entry ends, hotel guests should exit Diagon Alley and then ride Despicable Me Minion Mayhem. Day guests should wait in the front lot until permitted to ride Despicable Me. Stationary seating is available on request.

5. See *Shrek 4-D* in Production Central. Stationary seating is available on request.

6. Ride E.T. Adventure in Woody's KidZone.

7. Ride Kang & Kodos' Twirl 'n' Hurl in World Expo if 50 or fewer people are in line.

8. Ride Men in Black Alien Attack if you can tolerate some moderate spinning.

9. By this time, you should be able to enter Diagon Alley without waiting, even on busy days. Have an early lunch at Leaky Cauldron.

10. See the wand ceremony at Ollivanders and buy a wand if you wish.

11. Tour Diagon Alley. Browse the shops, explore the dark recesses of Knockturn Alley, and discover the interactive effects. If you're still hungry, try Florean Fortescue's Ice Cream Parlour.

12. See the *Celestina Warbeck* and *Tales of Beedle the Bard* shows.

13. Experience Harry Potter and the Escape from Gringotts via the standby queue (if you didn't earlier), and exit after the elevators if you don't wish to experience a mild roller coaster.

14. Chat with the Knight Bus conductor and his shrunken head. Also look for Kreacher in the window of 12 Grimmauld Place, and listen to the receiver in the red phone booth.

15. Experience *Disaster!* in San Francisco. Opt out of the subway finale to avoid being shaken.

16. Experience *TWISTER . . . Ride It Out* in New York. Stationary viewing is available on request.

17. See *The Blues Brothers Show* (**17a**) and *Animal Actors on Location* (**17b**) according to the daily entertainment schedule. If time is short, skip *Animal Actors*.

18. Have an early dinner inside the park at Fast Food Boulevard, Finnegan's, or Lombard's.

19. After dinner, see *Universal Orlando's Horror Make-Up Show* (**19a**) and *Terminator 2: 3-D* (**19b**) according to the daily entertainment schedule. Stationary seating is available at *Terminator* on request.

20. Explore *Lucy—A Tribute* in Hollywood.

21. If scheduled, see *Universal's Cinematic Spectacular* from Central Park (directly across the lagoon from Richter's), Duff Brewery, or the embankment in front of London.

Universal's Islands of Adventure

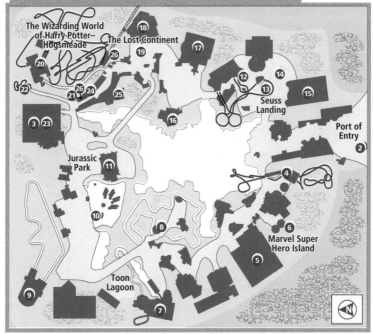

UNIVERSAL'S ISLANDS OF ADVENTURE ONE-DAY TOURING PLAN FOR ADULTS

1. Buy admission in advance. Call ☎ 407-363-8000 the day before for the official opening time.

2. Arrive at IOA 75–90 minutes before the official opening time if Early Park Admission is offered and you're eligible, or 30–45 minutes before opening for day guests. Get a park map as soon as you enter.

3. Early-entry guests should ride Harry Potter and the Forbidden Journey. Ride Flight of the Hippogriff and Dragon Challenge as well if you have time.

4. Exit Hogsmeade before early entry ends, and head to Marvel Super Hero Island to ride The Incredible Hulk Coaster. Guests without early entry should begin here.

5. Ride The Amazing Adventures of Spider-Man.

6. Backtrack to ride Doctor Doom's Fearfall.

7. Continue clockwise and ride Dudley Do-Right's Ripsaw Falls in Toon Lagoon.

8. Ride Popeye & Bluto's Bilge-Rat Barges.

9. Take the Jurassic Park River Adventure.

10. Explore Camp Jurassic.

11. Check out the exhibits in the Jurassic Park Discovery Center.

12. Ride the High in the Sky Seuss Trolley Train Ride! in Seuss Landing.

13. Ride the Caro-Seuss-el.

14. Ride One Fish, Two Fish, Red Fish, Blue Fish.

15. Ride The Cat in the Hat.

16. Return to Lost Continent and eat lunch at Mythos.

17. Experience *Poseidon's Fury*.

18. See the next scheduled performance of *The Eighth Voyage of Sindbad Stunt Show*.

19. Chat with the Mystic Fountain before or after the *Sindbad* show.

20. Enter The Wizarding World of Harry Potter–Hogsmeade, and ride Dragon Challenge, or walk through the queue to see the Triwizard Tournament artifacts.

21. See the *Frog Choir* or *Triwizard Spirit Rally* perform on the small stage outside Hogwarts.

22. Ride Flight of the Hippogriff.

23. Ride Harry Potter and the Forbidden Journey. If the wait is more than 30 minutes, request a castle tour to experience the queue, and then use the single-rider line.

24. See the wand ceremony at Ollivanders and buy a wand if you wish.

25. Have dinner at Three Broomsticks.

26. After dinner, see the stage show you didn't see earlier. Pose for a picture with the Hogwarts Express conductor, and explore the shops and interactive windows around Hogsmeade. Sample (or at least smell) some sweets at Honeydukes.

27. Revisit any favorite attractions, or remain in Hogsmeade until closing, enjoying the atmosphere.

Universal's Islands of Adventure

UNIVERSAL'S ISLANDS OF ADVENTURE ONE-DAY TOURING PLAN FOR PARENTS WITH SMALL CHILDREN

1. Buy admission in advance. Call ☎ 407-363-8000 the day before for the official opening time.

2. Arrive at IOA 75–90 minutes before the official opening time if Early Park Admission is offered and you're eligible, or 30–45 minutes before opening for day guests. Get a park map as soon as you enter. Rent a stroller if needed.

3. Ride Flight of the Hippogriff **(3a)**, see the wand ceremony at Ollivanders **(3b)**, and ask for a castle tour at Harry Potter and the Forbidden Journey **(3c)**.

4. Exit Hogsmeade before early entry ends, and head to Marvel Super Hero Island to ride The Amazing Adventures of Spider-Man. Guests without early entry should start at this step.

5. Backtrack to ride Storm Force Accelatron.

6. Continue clockwise around the park through Toon Lagoon to Jurassic Park. Ride Pteranodon Flyers if your child is 36–56 inches tall.

7. After the ride, let the kids play in Camp Jurassic for about 20 minutes.

8. Return to Toon Lagoon. Explore Me Ship, The Olive.

9. Take a break from the park for at least 2 hours, depending on how late the park is open. If staying nearby, return to your room for a nap. Otherwise, take a rest at CityWalk or a resort hotel.

10. Return to the park. Check for the next scheduled showtime of Oh! The Stories You'll Hear! in Seuss Landing.

11. Explore If I Ran the Zoo while waiting for the show.

12. Ride The Cat in the Hat.

13. Ride One Fish, Two Fish, Red Fish, Blue Fish.

14. Ride the Caro-Seuss-el.

15. Ride the High in the Sky Seuss Trolley Train Ride.

16. See the next scheduled performance of The Eighth Voyage of Sindbad Stunt Show.

17. Chat with the Mystic Fountain before or after Sindbad.

18. Experience Poseidon's Fury in The Lost Continent.

19. Cross the bridge to Jurassic Park and see the exhibits in the Jurassic Park Discovery Center.

20. Enter The Wizarding World of Harry Potter– Hogsmeade, and ride Flight of the Hippogriff (if you didn't ride earlier).

21. See the Frog Choir or Triwizard Spirit Rally perform on the small stage outside Hogwarts.

22. Request a castle tour of Harry Potter and the Forbidden Journey.

23. See the wand ceremony at Ollivanders and buy a wand if you wish.

24. Have dinner at Three Broomsticks.

25. After dinner, see the stage show you didn't see earlier. Pose for a picture with the Hogwarts Express conductor, and explore the shops and interactive windows around Hogsmeade. Sample (or at least smell) some sweets at Honeydukes.

26. Revisit any favorite attractions, or remain in Hogsmeade until closing, enjoying the atmosphere.

Universal's Islands of Adventure

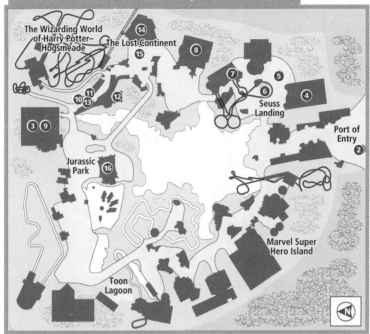

The Wizarding World
of Harry Potter–
Hogsmeade

The Lost Continent

Seuss Landing

Port of Entry

Jurassic Park

Marvel Super Hero Island

Toon Lagoon

UNIVERSAL'S ISLANDS OF ADVENTURE ONE-DAY TOURING PLAN FOR SENIORS

1. Buy admission in advance. Call ☎ 407-363-8000 the day before for the official opening time.

2. Arrive at IOA 75–90 minutes before the official opening time if Early Park Admission is offered and you're eligible, or 30–45 minutes before opening for day guests. Get a park map as soon as you enter. Rent a wheelchair or ECV if needed.

3. Explore the shops of Hogsmeade. Ask for a castle tour at Harry Potter and the Forbidden Journey.

4. Exit Hogsmeade before early entry ends, and head to Seuss Landing to ride The Cat in the Hat. Guests without early entry should start at this step.

5. Ride One Fish, Two Fish, Red Fish, Blue Fish.

6. Ride the Caro-Seuss-el.

7. Ride the High in the Sky Seuss Trolley Train Ride.

8. Experience *Poseidon's Fury* in The Lost Continent.

9. Enter Hogsmeade and request a castle tour of Harry Potter and the Forbidden Journey (if you didn't earlier).

10. See the *Frog Choir* or *Triwizard Spirit Rally* perform on the small stage outside Hogwarts.

11. See the wand ceremony at Ollivanders (if the line is short) and buy a wand if you wish.

12. Have lunch at Three Broomsticks.

13. After lunch, see the stage show you didn't see earlier. Pose for a picture with the Hogwarts Express conductor, and explore the shops and interactive windows around Hogsmeade. Make sure you sample (or at least smell) some sweets at Honeydukes.

14. See the next scheduled performance of *The Eighth Voyage of Sindbad Stunt Show*.

15. Chat with the Mystic Fountain before or after the *Sindbad* show.

16. Cross the bridge to Jurassic Park and see the exhibits in the Jurassic Park Discovery Center.

17. Walk counterclockwise around the park, paying attention to the quiet paths along the waterfront in each island.

18. Revisit any favorite attractions, or remain in Hogsmeade until closing, enjoying the atmosphere. Or exit the park for an early dinner in CityWalk.

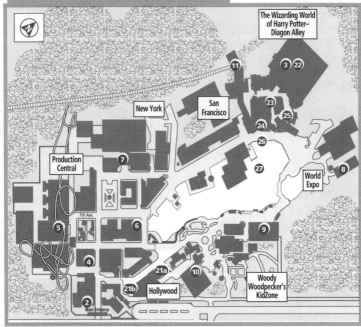

Universal Studios Florida

The Wizarding World
of Harry Potter–
Diagon Alley

New York

San
Francisco

Production
Central

7th Ave.

World
Expo

Hollywood

Woody
Woodpecker's
KidZone

Main Entrance

UNIVERSAL ORLANDO HIGHLIGHTS ONE–DAY/TWO-PARK TOURING PLAN

(Assumes: 1-Day Park-to-Park Ticket)

1. Buy your admission in advance; call ☎ 407-363-8000 the day before your visit for the official opening time.

2. Arrive at Universal Studios Florida 90–120 minutes before the official opening time if Early Park Admission is offered and you're eligible, or 30–45 minutes before opening for day guests. Line up at the shortest open turnstile, and pick up a park map as soon as you enter. **Alternative:** If only Islands of Adventure is open for Early Park Admission and you're eligible, arrive at IOA's turnstiles 75–90 minutes before the official opening time. Ride Harry Potter and the Forbidden Journey. Ride Flight of the Hippogriff and Dragon Challenge as well if you have time. Take the Hogwarts Express to King's Cross Station before USF officially opens for the day, and continue at the next step.

3. Early-entry guests will be led directly to Diagon Alley. Ride Harry Potter and the Escape from Gringotts if it is operating. If Gringotts is not operating, enjoy the rest of Diagon Alley but don't get in line.

4. Before early entry ends, hotel guests should exit Diagon Alley and return to the front of the park to ride Despicable Me Minion Mayhem. Day guests should wait in the front lot until permitted to ride Despicable Me.

5. Ride Hollywood Rip Ride Rockit.

6. Experience Transformers: The Ride 3-D in Production Central.

7. Ride Revenge of the Mummy in New York.

8. Walk through San Francisco and past the London waterfront to ride Men in Black Alien Attack in World Expo.

9. Ride The Simpsons Ride.

10. Ride E.T. Adventure in Woody Woodpecker's KidZone.

11. Ride the Hogwarts Express from King's Cross Station to Islands of Adventure. Have your Park-to-Park ticket ready.

(Continued on next page)

Universal's Islands of Adventure

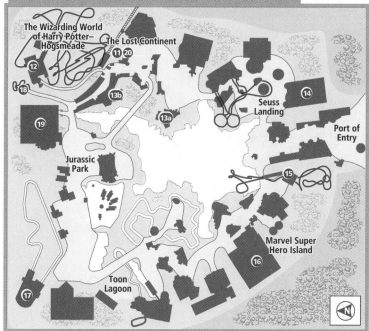

The Wizarding World of Harry Potter–Hogsmeade

The Lost Continent

Seuss Landing

Port of Entry

Jurassic Park

Marvel Super Hero Island

Toon Lagoon

UNIVERSAL ORLANDO HIGHLIGHTS ONE-DAY/TWO-PARK TOURING PLAN
(Continued from previous page)

12. Ride Dragon Challenge in The Wizarding World of Harry Potter–Hogsmeade.

13. Eat lunch at Mythos in Lost Continent (**13a**) or Three Broomsticks in Hogsmeade (**13b**).

14. Ride The Cat in the Hat in Seuss Landing.

15. Ride The Incredible Hulk Coaster on Marvel Super Hero Island.

16. Ride The Amazing Adventures of Spider-Man.

17. Continue clockwise through Toon Lagoon, and take the Jurassic Park River Adventure.

18. Enter Hogsmeade, and ride Flight of the Hippogriff if the wait isn't too long.

19. Ride Harry Potter and the Forbidden Journey. If the wait is more than 30 minutes, request a castle tour to experience the queue, and then use the single-rider line.

20. Return to USF via Hogwarts Express, or walk back to the other park if the posted wait exceeds 20 minutes.

See map on previous page for the following steps.

21. See the next showing of *Universal Orlando's Horror Make-Up Show* (**21a**) upon returning to USF. If the remaining *Horror Make-Up* show-times aren't convenient, substitute with *Terminator 2: 3-D* (**21b**).

22. Ride Harry Potter and the Escape from Gringotts. If this is your first ride, take the standby queue. For re-rides, use the single-rider line. The Gringotts queue may close before the rest of the park if the posted wait time exceeds remaining operating hours by more than 60 minutes.

23. See the wand ceremony at Ollivanders and buy a wand if you wish.

24. Tour Diagon Alley. Browse the shops, explore the dark recesses of Knockturn Alley, and discover the interactive effects. If you're hungry, try the Leaky Cauldron or Florean Fortescue's Ice Cream Parlour.

25. See the *Celestina Warbeck* and *Tales of Beedle the Bard* shows.

26. On your way out of Diagon Alley, chat with the Knight Bus conductor and his shrunken head. Also look for Kreacher in the window of 12 Grimmauld Place, and listen to the receiver in the red phone booth.

27. If scheduled, watch *Universal's Cinematic Spectacular* from Central Park (directly across the lagoon from Richter's), Duff Brewery, or the embankment in front of London.

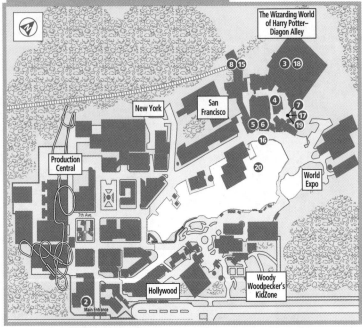

Universal Studios Florida

WIZARDING WORLD ONE-DAY/TWO-PARK TOURING PLAN

(Assumes: 1-Day Park-to-Park Ticket. Excludes: All non-Potter attractions.)

1. Buy your admission in advance; call ☎ 407-363-8000 the day before your visit for the official opening time.

2. Arrive at USF 90–120 minutes before the official opening time if Early Park Admission is offered and you're eligible, or 30–45 minutes before opening for day guests. Get a park map as soon as you enter. **Alternative:** If only IOA is open for Early Park Admission and you're eligible, arrive at IOA's turn-stiles 75–90 minutes before the official opening time. Ride Harry Potter and the Forbidden Journey. Ride Flight of the Hippogriff and Dragon Challenge as well if you have time. Take the Hogwarts Express to King's Cross Station before USF officially opens for the day, and continue at the next step.

3. Early-entry guests should ride Harry Potter and the Escape from Gringotts if it is operating. If Gringotts is not operating, enjoy the rest of Diagon Alley but don't get in line.

4. See the wand ceremony at Ollivanders and buy a wand if you wish. Gringotts may have a long line by the time the park officially opens if Early Park Admission was offered, so day guests should begin with Ollivanders if the posted wait time for Gringotts is more than 30 minutes.

5. Tour Diagon Alley. Browse the shops, explore the dark recesses of Knockturn Alley, and discover the interactive effects.

6. Have breakfast at the Leaky Cauldron or Florean Fortescue's Ice Cream Parlour (hey, you're on vacation!).

7. See one of the two *Tales of Beedle the Bard* shows.

8. Exit Diagon Alley and ride the Hogwarts Express from King's Cross Station to Islands of Adventure. Have your Park-to-Park ticket ready.

(Continued on next page)

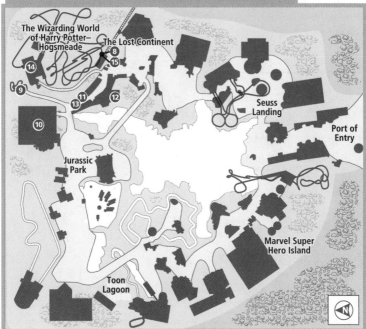

Universal's Islands of Adventure

WIZARDING WORLD ONE-DAY/TWO-PARK TOURING PLAN

(Assumes: 1-Day Park-to-Park Ticket. Excludes: All non-Potter attractions.)

(Continued from previous page)

9. Enter Hogsmeade and ride Flight of the Hippogriff.

10. Ride Harry Potter and the Forbidden Journey. If the wait is more than 30 minutes, request a castle tour to experience the queue, and then use the single-rider line.

11. See the *Frog Choir* or *Triwizard Spirit Rally* perform on the small stage outside Hogwarts.

12. Have lunch at Three Broomsticks.

13. After lunch, see the stage show you didn't see earlier. Pose for a picture with the Hogwarts Express conductor, and explore the shops and interactive windows around Hogsmeade. Make sure you sample (or at least smell) some sweets at Honeydukes.

14. Ride Dragon Challenge, or walk through the queue to see the Triwizard Tournament artifacts.

15. Return to USF via Hogwarts Express, or walk back to the other park if the posted wait exceeds 20 minutes.

See map on previous page for the following steps.

16. Chat with the Knight Bus conductor and his shrunken head. Also look for Kreacher in the window of 12 Grimmauld Place, and listen to the receiver in the red phone booth.

17. Reenter Diagon Alley and catch the *Tales of Beedle the Bard* show that you didn't see earlier.

18. Ride Harry Potter and the Escape from Gringotts. If this is your first ride, take the standby queue. For re-rides, use the single-rider line. The Gringotts queue may close before the rest of the park if the posted wait time exceeds remaining operating hours by more than 60 minutes.

19. See the *Celestina Warbeck* show.

20. Stay in Diagon Alley until closing time, enjoying the atmosphere. The fireworks of *Universal's Cinematic Spectacular* look fantastic over the Gringotts dragon.

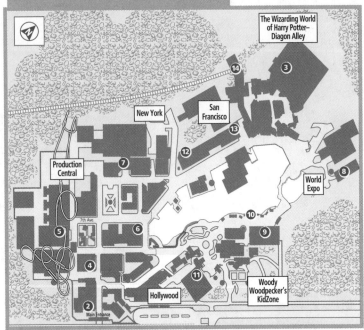

Universal Studios Florida

UNIVERSAL ORLANDO COMPREHENSIVE TWO-DAY/TWO-PARK TOURING PLAN: DAY ONE

(Assumes: Multiday Park-to-Park Ticket)

1. Buy your admission in advance; call ☎ 407-363-8000 the day before your visit for the official opening time.

2. Arrive at USF 90–120 minutes before the official opening time if Early Park Admission is offered and you're eligible, or 30–45 minutes before opening for day guests. Get a park map as soon as you enter.

3. Early-entry guests should ride Harry Potter and the Escape from Gringotts if it is operating. If Gringotts is not operating, enjoy the rest of Diagon Alley but do not get in line.

4. Before early entry ends, hotel guests should exit Diagon Alley and ride Despicable Me Minion Mayhem. Day guests should wait in the front lot until permitted to ride Despicable Me.

5. Ride Hollywood Rip Ride Rockit.

6. Experience Transformers: The Ride 3-D in Production Central.

7. Ride Revenge of the Mummy in New York.

8. Walk through San Francisco and past the London waterfront to ride Men in Black Alien Attack in World Expo.

9. Ride The Simpsons Ride.

10. Ride Kang & Kodos' Twirl 'n' Hurl if 50 or fewer people are in line.

11. Ride E.T. Adventure in Woody Woodpecker's KidZone.

12. Work in *Beetlejuice Graveyard Revue* around lunch (we recommend Fast Food Boulevard), according to the daily entertainment schedule.

13. Experience *Disaster!* in San Francisco.

14. Ride the Hogwarts Express from King's Cross Station to Islands of Adventure. Have your Park-to-Park ticket ready.

(Continued on next page)

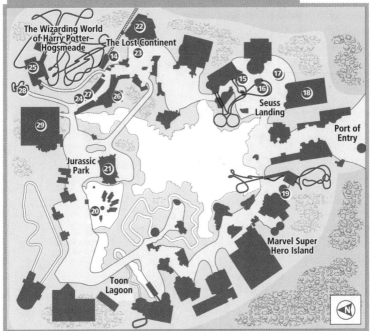

Universal's Islands of Adventure

UNIVERSAL ORLANDO COMPREHENSIVE TWO-DAY/TWO-PARK TOURING PLAN: DAY ONE

(Assumes: Multiday Park-to-Park Ticket)
(Continued from previous page)

15. Ride the High in the Sky Seuss Trolley Train Ride in Seuss Landing.

16. Ride the Caro-Seuss-el.

17. Ride One Fish, Two Fish, Red Fish, Blue Fish.

18. Ride The Cat in the Hat.

19. Cross through Port of Entry to Marvel Super Hero Island and ride Storm Force Accelatron.

20. Walk through Toon Lagoon to Jurassic Park and explore Camp Jurassic.

21. Check out the exhibits in the Jurassic Park Discovery Center.

22. See the next scheduled performance of *The Eighth Voyage of Sindbad Stunt Show*.

23. Chat with the Mystic Fountain before or after *Sindbad*.

24. Enter Hogsmeade, and see the *Frog Choir* or *Triwizard Spirit Rally* perform on the small stage outside Hogwarts.

25. Ride Dragon Challenge, or walk through the queue to see the Triwizard Tournament artifacts.

26. Have dinner at Three Broomsticks.

27. After dinner, see the stage show you didn't see earlier. Pose for a picture with the Hogwarts Express conductor and explore the shops and interactive windows around Hogsmeade. Make sure you sample (or at least smell) some sweets at Honeydukes.

28. Ride Flight of the Hippogriff.

29. Ride Harry Potter and the Forbidden Journey. If the wait is more than 30 minutes, request a castle tour to experience the queue, and then use the single-rider line.

30. Remain in Hogsmeade until closing, enjoying the atmosphere.

(Day Two is on next page.)

Universal's Islands of Adventure

The Wizarding World
of Harry Potter–
Hogsmeade — The Lost Continent

Seuss
Landing

Port of
Entry

Jurassic
Park

Marvel Super
Hero Island

Toon
Lagoon

UNIVERSAL ORLANDO COMPREHENSIVE TWO–DAY/TWO–PARK TOURING PLAN: DAY TWO

(Assumes: Multiday Park-to-Park Ticket)
(Day One is on previous pages.)

1. Buy your admission in advance; call ☎ 407-363-8000 the day before your visit for the official opening time.

2. Arrive at IOA 90–120 minutes before the official opening time if Early Park Admission is offered and you're eligible, or 30–45 minutes before opening for day guests. Get a park map as soon as you enter.

3. Early-entry guests should ride Harry Potter and the Forbidden Journey. Ride Flight of the Hippogriff and Dragon Challenge as well if you have time.

4. Exit Hogsmeade before early entry ends, and head to Marvel Super Hero Island to ride The Incredible Hulk Coaster. Guests without early entry should start at this step.

5. See The Amazing Adventures of Spider-Man.

6. Backtrack to ride Doctor Doom's Fearfall.

7. Continue clockwise around the park and ride Dudley Do-Right's Ripsaw Falls in Toon Lagoon.

8. Ride Popeye & Bluto's Bilge-Rat Barges.

9. Take the Jurassic Park River Adventure.

10. Ride Harry Potter and the Forbidden Journey if you didn't ride earlier. If the wait is more than 30 minutes, request a castle tour to experience the queue, and then use the single-rider line.

11. Ride the side of Dragon Challenge that you didn't experience yesterday.

12. Experience *Poseidon's Fury* in The Lost Continent.

13. Eat lunch at Mythos in Lost Continent (**13a**) or Three Broomsticks in Hogsmeade (**13b**).

14. After lunch, take the Hogwarts Express from Hogsmeade Station to Universal Studios Florida, or walk back to the other park if the posted wait exceeds 20 minutes. Have your Park-to-Park ticket ready.

(Continued on next page)

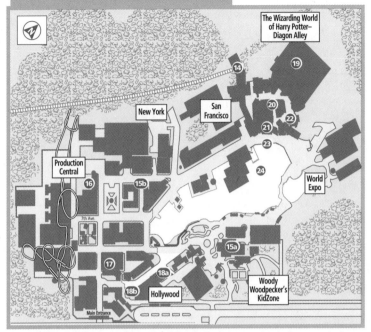

Universal Studios Florida

UNIVERSAL ORLANDO COMPREHENSIVE TWO-DAY/TWO-PARK TOURING PLAN:
DAY TWO

(Assumes: Multiday Park-to-Park Ticket)
(Continued from previous page)

15. Work in *Animal Actors on Location* **(15a)** and *The Blues Brothers Show* **(15b)** according to the daily entertainment schedule. If time is short, skip *Animal Actors.*

16. See *TWISTER . . . Ride It Out* in New York.

17. See *Shrek 4-D* in Production Central.

18. See *Universal Orlando's Horror Make-Up Show* **(18a)** and *Terminator 2: 3-D* **(18b)** according to the daily entertainment schedule.

19. By this time, you should be able to enter Diagon Alley without waiting, even on busy days. Ride Harry Potter and the Escape from Gringotts. If this is your first ride, take the standby queue. For re-rides, use the single-rider line. The Gringotts queue may close before the rest of the park if the posted wait time exceeds remaining operating hours by more than 60 minutes.

20. See the wand ceremony at Ollivanders and buy a wand if you wish.

21. Tour Diagon Alley. Browse the shops, explore the dark recesses of Knockturn Alley, and discover the interactive effects. If you're hungry, try the Leaky Cauldron or Florean Fortescue's Ice Cream Parlour.

22. See the *Celestina Warbeck* and *Tales of Beedle the Bard* shows.

23. On your way out of Diagon Alley, chat with the Knight Bus conductor and his shrunken head. Also look for Kreacher in the window of 12 Grimmauld Place, and listen to the receiver in the red phone booth.

24. If scheduled, watch *Universal's Cinematic Spectacular* from Central Park (directly across the lagoon from Richter's), Duff Brewery, or the embankment in front of London.